SITTING IT OUT

Books by David Westheimer

SUMMER ON THE WATER
THE MAGIC FALLACY
WATCHING OUT FOR DULIE
THIS TIME NEXT YEAR
VON RYAN'S EXPRESS
MY SWEET CHARLIE
SONG OF THE YOUNG SENTRY
LIGHTER THAN A FEATHER
OVER THE EDGE
GOING PUBLIC
THE OLMEC HEAD
THE AVILA GOLD
VON RYAN'S RETURN
RIDER ON THE WIND

Sitting It Out
A World War II POW Memoir

David Westheimer

Rice University Press
Houston, Texas

Requests for permission to reproduce
material from this work should be
addressed to:
Rice University Press
P.O. Box 1892
Houston, Texas 77251

Library of Congress Cataloging-in-
Publication Data
Westheimer, David.
    Sitting it out / David Westheimer.
        p.   cm.
    ISBN 0-89263-315-8 : $24.95
    1. Westheimer, David.   2. World
War, 1939–1945—Prisoners and
prisons, Italian.   3. World War,
1939–1945—Prisoners and prisons,
German.   4. World War, 1939–
1945—Personal narratives,
American.   5. Authors, American—
20th century—Biography.   I. Title.
D805.I8W47   1992
940.54'7243—dc20   92-50058
                              CIP

IN MEMORIAM

Sgt. Norman George (*Killed in Action*)
Lt. Kent Leader (*Killed in Action*)
Sgt. Frank Spindler (*Killed in Action*)

Padre Stanley Brach
George Radovanovic

Contents

CONTENTS

David Westheimer tells me that, when he was a student in my Creative Writing class at Rice University more than fifty years ago, the very first example of student writing that I read aloud to the class was a story of his. I read it (David says) as a fine example of how the other students ought *not* to write!

All I can say here about this little episode is that David has learned a powerful lot in the last fifty years—or else that I myself had a powerful lot to learn back in those old days. I prefer to believe the former. David, however, remains politely noncommittal on the subject.

In any case, since then David has enjoyed a career as a successful journalist, a novelist whose books have been translated into many languages, a sensitive playwright, and a scriptwriter.

His present book, *Sitting It Out*, is unlike anything else he ever wrote. As an extensive and minutely detailed account of life in Italian and German prisoner-of-war camps during World War II, this book is unique. Though it is true that a few short, generalized, and often impersonal books about life in World War II prison camps have appeared, none of them can be even remotely compared with this book of intimate recollections by an American aviator shot down and captured in the earlier years of the War.

First, the book is as suspenseful as a detective story. The suspense is ready-made and built-in: the reader hangs on through thronging details and episodes because he or she knows that a satisfactory ending (Allied victory and release of American prisoners) is inevitable.

Second, even though the book is long and its subject is what could be considered the dull and static life of prison, it moves along at a fast clip. The book's fluid progression depends on the changes constantly occurring in the author's anything-but-static life in "the bag": frequent moving from one site to another, personnel constantly changing as more prisoners are captured or moved out, changes in the guards, unpredictable daily living conditions. It seems surprising that a book about two years and four months of prison life would not be an awful drag. But the reader will discover few pages in this book that make one want to skip ahead.

Finally, the writing style fits its subject perfectly: unpretentious; flowing; direct and simple, even bare; obviously honest, sincere, factual. If I were teaching that old Creative Writing class today, I would suggest that my students read some pages of this new book of David Westheimer to find out how they *ought* to write!

Aside from its literary distinction, this book is also informative. Were I a historian of World War II, I don't see how I could ignore its value as a reference source. The author tells me that his own source for this book was a manuscript, nearly 200,000 words long, that he wrote over a period of a few weeks immediately after he was discharged from the armed services after the War. He wanted to have on record the facts (names, places, moves, conversations, orders, incidents, and the like, however small) of his imprisonment before time erased them from his mind or dimmed them.

For me, the book is also a source of useful information that has nothing to do with prison camps. Since the American prisoners of war featured here were confined deep inside Italy and Germany, these prisoners, even in their confinement, had better insights into the minds of wartime Italians and Germans than most other Americans did. Scattered occasionally throughout this book, such insights reveal that ordinary Italians and Germans were not *monsters*. Generally, they were as kind, helpful, and compassionate as their superiors would allow them to be. And this brings up a question that nobody seems ever to try to answer: Why do good and decent people (in Italy, Germany, Great Britain, America, or anywhere else) allow themselves to become killing monsters just because the people in charge tell them to? *Sitting It Out* encourages some basic speculations about that question.

The story of the Red Cross and personal parcels sent from America and Great Britain to their prisoners is fascinating. These packages, containing food, cigarettes, toilet articles, reading matter, clothing, and other goodies, came through Switzerland and wartime Germany with an astounding efficiency and regularity that could not have been achieved without full German cooperation at many levels. The German authorities at the prison camps, with only occasional lapses, delivered these packages promptly and intact to the prisoners, even though they knew that the packages sometimes gave the prisoners varieties of food and amenities that the guards seldom enjoyed in their straitened economy and war-poor nation—canned meat, sweets, dried fruits, and cigars. And the prisoners had all these blessings because of the efficiency and honor of their German hosts. It is touching.

I don't know whether the author intended it, but throughout this book I get the impression that Italians and Americans and Germans and Americans would have fraternized with one another if given half an opportunity. They *liked* one another.

> Had he and I but met
> By some old ancient inn,
> We should have set us down to wet
> Right many a nipperkin! . . .
>
> Yes; quaint and curious war is
> You shoot a fellow down
> You'd treat if met where any bar is,
> Or help to half a crown.
> —Thomas Hardy

However intriguing we find David Westheimer's book, I hope that he never has an opportunity to write another like it. His memoir is the fruit of an unspeakable tragedy that happened because a few people in power disregarded the humanity of untold millions. When human beings begin to see each other, and themselves as well, not as Italians, Germans, Americans; not as Muslims, Christians, Jews; not as black, white, or yellow; not even as capitalists, communists, nationalists—but as human beings first, there will be no more prisoners of war, but rather an end to the tragedies, tears, and conflicts that human beings still believe they must wage against their own kind.

GEORGE WILLIAMS

"One could not help feeling that this . . . would seem to an observer worse than it was."

Lester Atwell, *Private*

SITTING IT OUT
Route Map

- - - - Air
·········· Train
——— Foot

0   100   200 Miles
0   100   200 Kilometers

NETH.

BEL.

FRANCE

Berlin•

Muskau
Spremberg•   •Sagan
                      Stalag Luft 3

                    •Breslau

POLAND

G E R M A N Y

•Prague

SLOVAKIA

Munich• •Moosburg
          Stalag VII A
          April 29, 1945

•Vienna

Innsbruck
Brenner Pass

SWITZ.

•Bolzano

Milan•   I   •Venice

Bologna•

HUNGARY

•Budapest

R O M A N I A

Florence•

T
A
L
Y

A d r i a t i c

Poggio
Mirteto

Pescara
Chieti P.G. 21

Rome•

Sulmona

S e a

Y U G O S L A V I A

B U L G A R I A

Naples
        X
Salerno

Tyrrhenian

Sea

A L B A N I A

Ionian

Sea

GREECE

•Palermo

©David Westheimer, 1991

M e d i t e r r a n e a n   S e a

ALGERIA

TUNISIA

L I B Y A

L I B Y A
        Tobruk•
        L.G. 139
        December 11, 1942

A Dubious Honor

WE ALMOST DIDN'T make the mission.

We'd flown out to Landing Ground 139 from our field at Kabrit on the Suez Canal. LG 139 was a tent-and-messkit kind of field. We were to stage through it—top off fuel tanks and bomb up—for an attack on the harbor at Naples. But our nosewheel went flat and our plane, *Natchez to Mobile, Memphis to St. Jo,* was scrubbed from the mission. (We'd taken the name of our plane from the destination of a bus that kept crashing through the Yokums' cabin in the comic strip, "Li'l Abner.") Then some efficient type back in Cairo got a replacement sent out in time for us to be rescheduled.

We took off the morning of December 11, 1942. Sixteen hundred miles to the west, the Allies had launched Operation Torch against North Africa less than five weeks earlier. Eighteen desert-pink B-24 Liberator bombers. A sizeable force for that time and place. We crossed the coastline west of Tobruk on a northwest heading for Naples. Naples was eight hundred miles away, five or six hours flying time, depending on the winds aloft. We flew low over the Mediterranean in four elements of three. We were in the third element.

We flew one hundred feet above the water, keeping our circle of visibility from the surface tight. We'd remain at that altitude for several hours, until it was time to begin the slow climb to bombing altitude. There was another dividend to flying low. Navigators could read the surface winds from the face of the sea. Wind speed from the number and nature of whitecaps, direction from the way they broke. At extremely low altitude, surface winds were the ones affecting us.

Knowing the wind was vital. Crosswinds blew you off course. Tail winds increased ground speed, head winds decreased it. Without knowing the wind we couldn't predict when we'd reach a target, or even find our way to it.

Navigator was not a comfortable position in a B-24. Navigators didn't have chairs. When we weren't standing, we sat on our fold-down plotting table. It had a metal ridge across the front to keep our navigating paraphernalia from sliding off in turbulent weather and it dug in. After a long mission you could always identify a navigator by pulling down his flight coveralls and checking the red creases across his butt.

We started our climb to bombing altitude well off the boot of Italy and fell into trail—one element after the other. From 18,000 feet the green of Italy looked inviting after all the desert we'd seen on earlier missions. A nice place to visit after the war. It was our crew's first raid on Italy and the Group's second.

Mount Vesuvius was up ahead and to the right, blowing smoke. A navigator couldn't ask for a better checkpoint. Almost there. We tightened formation. Up ahead, the first element dropped its bombs and headed out to sea. The sky at our altitude was peppered with flak from shore batteries and warships in the harbor. We'd seen worse over the Italian cruisers at Navarino Bay in Greece. Lt. Russ Gardinier, the bombardier, bent over his bombsight doing what bombardiers did. Then, without warning, our element leader banked hard left, well short of the target. The last we saw of his plane, it was heading for the first element, now on a course for home.

Our plane and the other wingman closed formation and continued the bombing run. There was a towering fire at the target, probably a gas storage tank. We dropped our load and continued out to sea. I gave Lt. Larry Kennedy, the pilot, the course for home. And then we were jumped by Macchi 202s, Italy's firstline fighters. They'd picked on our two-plane element instead of the three-plane elements, which had greater firepower.

The two B-24s fought a running battle with the persistent fighters. One in particular kept boring in close. Fire from the twin .50 caliber guns in our top and tail turrets and the two .50s in the waist shook the plane. Gardinier and I manned the three flexible .50s in the nose. I never got off a burst. The Macchis were in and out too quickly for me. Gardinier was busy, though. He loved to shoot those .50s. We heard a lot of cussing over the interphone. Gunners did that a lot. Then a cry of pain. Kennedy called Gardinier and told him that Sgt. Armando Risso, waist gunner and assistant aerial engineer, had been hit. One of the bombardier's jobs was to tend to the wounded. Once he'd dropped his bombs, his regular job was finished.

Gardinier got the first-aid kit and crawled back through the tunnel under the flight deck. I gave up trying to track the fighters with the .50s and tried to follow our erratic course so I'd have some idea where we were when the fighters broke off and we headed for home. It would be dark before we got there and we'd be on our own, navigating by the stars.

We took hits in number 3 engine, the one next to the fuselage on the right side. Oil and smoke streamed from it. The engine quit but the propeller kept spinning. Faster and faster. Windmilling it was called. I could hear Kennedy on the interphone, cussing and shouting orders to Lt. Kent Leader, the copilot. He couldn't feather the prop. Feathering the prop was turning it edge on into the airstream so it would stop windmilling. Sgt. Al Barnes, the radio operator–top turret gunner, called over the interphone.

"Sir, I'm running out of ammo."

At just that moment the engine froze up, all the oil having leaked out, stopping the windmilling prop dead. That tore number 3 right out of the wing. It fell into number 4, knocking it out of the wing, too. I looked out the Plexiglas window into two gaping holes where the engines had been. Nothing left but metal straps and dangling wires and cables. Ugliest sight I'd ever seen. Scariest, too. And the landing gear was down, having dropped when the hydraulic system went out.

So Kennedy said, "Don't worry about it, Barnsie. We're running out of engines."

By now, the other B-24s and all the fighters but one had left us. It kept coming, flashing in from one side, diving below us and climbing to hit us from the other. Capt. Joe Kilgore from Texas, leader of one of the other elements, saw our plight and left his formation to help. He kept placing his plane between ours and the attacking fighter, dropping below us with the fighter and reappearing at our altitude on the other side when the fighter tried another pass. Gardinier came crawling back.

"Charlie's hit, too," he said.

That was Capt. Charles Jennette, our squadron adjutant, who'd come along for the ride when Flapjack, our aerial engineer, came down with a cold. Gardinier took off his flying boots and calmly put on his GI shoes, lacing them to the top and tying neat bows. We were losing altitude steadily. It was obvious we'd never make it back to the desert over hundreds of miles of Mediterranean. I started figuring an alternate course to Malta, the nearest friendly territory. I gave that up when Kennedy called us to the

4   flight deck. He said he couldn't maintain altitude and was going to try to land on the beach. He didn't want to bail out because we were over water and had wounded aboard. I was relieved. I didn't like the idea of jumping out of an airplane. Back in preflight there'd been a rumor we'd all have to jump before getting our commissions. Our tactical officer reassured us. "You don't practice what you have to do right the first time."

By now the last fighter, and with it Kilgore, had left. We were all alone off an unfriendly coast, gear down, two engines gone and wounded aboard. We had no idea what to expect from the Italians. We'd been briefed on what to do if we came down in the desert. We had maps of Libya and Egypt printed on parachute silk and little compasses that looked like uniform buttons. We even had "goolie chits," printed in Arabic, to give to Arabs who might stumble upon us. The chits offered rewards for delivering downed Allied airmen to friendly forces, more than the Germans offered for turning us over to them. They were called goolie chits because, the British told us, the Arabs called testicles "goolies" and sometimes instead of turning downed airmen over to the Germans, if there were no rewards promised, they gave them to their women, who performed primitive surgery.

But for Italy, nothing.

Gardinier and I crawled through the tunnel and onto the flight deck. Kennedy and Leader were fighting the controls to keep the plane straight and level. Barnes was at his radio trying to raise Malta to report our situation and Sgt. Norman George, the assistant radio operator and the youngest among us, was just standing around, as scared as I was. Gardinier went off toward the back of the plane. At the coastline Kennedy started looking for a beach wide enough and long enough for him to set our wounded bird down. There wasn't one.

Gardinier came back dragging Risso. Risso was broad and powerfully built, a lot heavier than Gardinier. How Gardinier had gotten him over the narrow bomb bay catwalk I couldn't imagine. Kennedy said we'd have to ditch. Gardinier took off the overhead escape hatch, took hold of one of Risso's legs and told me to take hold of the other. We held him with his head out of the hatch while Kennedy and Leader struggled to give us a controlled landing. It wasn't easy. They couldn't reduce speed, as for a normal landing, because with the two engines gone the plane might have dropped like a stone.

Kennedy came in nose-up to let the tail touch down first and cut our speed as it dragged through the water. Slowed us down just as hoped. Then the landing gear hit the water. It was like hitting a wall. The plane snapped in half at the bulkhead, plunging the nose into the sea. Water surged into the flight deck from the shattered nose. It hit me in the chest and drove me backward. I'd have fallen if it hadn't been for my grip on Risso's leg. I don't know if it hurt him or not. Gardinier had shot him up with morphine from the first-aid kit earlier. (Forty-odd years later, years in which I hadn't seen or heard from Risso, a friend of his came up to me at a Bomb Group reunion and told me Risso had asked him to thank me for saving his life if he ran into me. I told him Risso had Gardinier to thank. I was just glad he hadn't been nursing a grudge against me for jerking on his leg.)

Gardinier told me to help him shove Risso out of the escape hatch, then stood back to let me scramble out before he did. We went out ahead of the others because we were already there.

The surface was littered. The big auxiliary fuel tank had broken free of the bomb bay and was floating beside the broken-off nosewheel. The very nosewheel that had been flown out to us from Egypt over five hundred miles of desert just in time to see us on our way to Naples. It bobbed serenely amid bits and pieces of the plane and my maps and charts from the nose. I should have destroyed the chart thumbtacked to my worktable with our route on it before I left for the flight deck. Maybe nobody would know.

I didn't know how many of us were in the water when the front part of the plane slid under. The rear part had sunk quickly. My Mae West didn't inflate. Gardinier, who'd pulled the cord on both his and Risso's life vests was floating next to him. I paddled over to them and, close to whimpering, asked Gardinier if I could hang on to him. Instead of answering, he took off his Mae West and thrust it at me, treading water and holding lightly to Risso. Two rowboats came out to pick us up. The Italians had to haul me into one of them without any help at all from me. I was too tired. Fright must be exhausting. The first thing I saw when I was fished out of the water was a basket full of anchovies staring at me with cold, accusing eyes. But I didn't smell them. I smelled sweat and strong tobacco. Gardinier, Risso and Sgt. Matt Brazil, one of the waist gunners, were in my boat, along with two sweating fishermen at the oars and a *carabiniere* (it was only later I learned he was a policeman and that's what they were called; I'd thought

6 he was a soldier) who hadn't even bothered to unsling his little carbine and point it at us. Not much like the movies I'd seen with fast boats coming out with Nazis on their decks with machine pistols, ready and eager to spray any airman reluctant to be picked up. It was kind of embarrassing.

But looking at it another way, we weren't captured, we were rescued. We were the first American bomber shot down attacking Italy and maybe the first ever shot down by Italian fighters.

To paraphrase Mark Twain, given a choice, we probably would have declined the honor.

It was the *Natchez to Mobile, Memphis to St. Jo's* twenty-eighth mission and my twenty-ninth. I'd flown two missions with another pilot and my crew had flown one with another navigator when I was grounded with a cold. We'd spent one week less than five months getting from Morrison Field in West Palm Beach, Florida, to the bosom of the Mediterranean south of Salerno.

We were members of the 344th Squadron of the 98th Bombardment Group (Heavy). The 98th flew its own planes overseas, taking with them key ground personnel, spare parts and all the personal gear of the crew. We flew the southern route—Trinidad; Belem and Natal, Brazil; Accra, Gold Coast (now Ghana), and Khartoum, Sudan—to our first combat base, Ramat David, Palestine. More than mere adventure. Mystery, too. We traveled under secret orders, not knowing our final destination or even our stopover destinations except from point to point. We were briefed only one stage at a time. Heady stuff for a twenty-five-year-old who'd never been farther from Houston, Texas, than New Orleans before joining the Army Air Corps in 1941.

The 344th departed Morrison the night of July 18, 1942, the first squadron to go. Its commanding officer was Maj. John R. "Killer" Kane who, as a colonel and commanding officer of the 98th, was later to win the Medal of Honor on the low-level attack on the oilfields at Ploesti.

Seven members of the crew who flew the southern route together were aboard the *Natchez to Mobile, Memphis to St. Jo* on its last mission. Pilot Larry Kennedy, copilot Kent Leader, navigator David Westheimer, bombardier Russel Gardinier, waist gunner-assistant aerial engineer Armando Risso, radio operator–top turret gunner Albert Barnes and tail gunner Staff Sgt. Frank Spindler. Technical Sgt. John Plavchack, Jr., "Flapjack," the aerial engineer who made all our missions but the last, was also a member of the southern route crew.

We were a week getting from West Palm Beach to Ramat David, more than two and a half days of which were aloft. Flying navigator across oceans and continents in a B-24 may not be as comfortable as flying first class in a jetliner, but for sightseeing you couldn't beat it. The navigator had as good a view all around from the nose as the pilot did from the flight deck. Even better, when you looked out through the Plexiglas astrodome (that's what we shot the stars from). The Bahamas, Hispaniola, Trinidad, the vast smear of brown ocean where the Amazon discharged into the South Atlantic, the rain forests of Brazil, the great stretch of starlit ocean from Natal to Accra, the utter blackness of African jungle at night lit only by remote pinpricks of fires far below, the Nubian Desert, empty during the nine and a half hours from Khartoum to Ramat David except for a solitary caravan, the Suez Canal, the Sinai, and the fields of Zionist farmers, green patches in the parched browns and yellows of unclaimed desert.

It was a different story on the ground. The only time I managed any sightseeing at all was in Belem and Khartoum, the two stops where I was able to get to town. In Trinidad, Natal and Accra I'd been too tired or too busy to go to town. I had to practice with my octant of choice, a particularly tricky instrument for celestial navigation. The only free time I had in Accra I played poker with some Australian, South African and New Zealand fliers as transient as I was. They played unfamiliar variations of the game using a wide variety of currency—U.S., British, Brazilian and Palestinian.

I had to sit on my hard-edged worktable or stand during the eleven-hour night crossing of the South Atlantic. Sometimes I fell asleep standing, waking only when my legs relaxed and my knees buckled. With nothing to guide us but the stars, I kept busy shooting them and plotting fixes. It was crowded up there in the nose with Gardinier and me, our B-4 bags and some spare parts. It got worse when one of our passengers came crawling out of the tunnel. He was a big guy and had to squeeze through it. He said Kennedy had sent him down to trim up the load. We knew better. It was to make more room on the flight deck. The passenger fell asleep on the floor, taking up most of it. I stepped on him a few times shooting stars but never on purpose.

The longest leg was over the heart of Africa. Fourteen and a half hours from Accra to Khartoum. Nearly all of it by night, with nothing below but blackness pierced from time to time by lonely jungle fires and nothing above but overcast. With no stars to shoot, we flew blind. A no-wind course, which meant if there were crosswinds we could end up anywhere. One of our planes strayed and went down in the jungle, to be found months later with all aboard dead, including the group flight surgeon. The crosswinds, if there were any, must have canceled themselves out over the long haul because we reached Khartoum almost on time and almost on course. It helped my reputation as navigator to have a crackerjack radio operator like Al Barnes on board to tune in to a radio compass, a device that points you to where you're going if your destination has a transmitter.

We landed at Ramat David, our destination, July 25. The runways were pinkish concrete explaining, for the first time, the color of our planes. It had been a Royal Air Force (RAF) Hurricane fighter station and the ground personnel, except for the few we'd flown in with us (our ground echelon arrived later, by ship), were British, as were the rations. British cooks and British rations.

The airfield was just across the road from the kibbutz of Ramat David, twenty miles southeast of Haifa. On the other side of the airfield lay the settlement of Nahalal, unique because it was perfectly circular. Its one-story cement block homes were arranged on the outside of its circular road, with their outbuildings and fields ranged behind them. After we found our way around, members of our crew would go to a "private table" in the home of a German-Jewish refugee couple for fresh milk, eggs, chips and tomatoes.

At Ramat David we lived in tents on what had only recently been a barley field. The stubble was still there. Our first and shortest bombing mission, six hours, was on August 1. Some vehicle repair shops at Mersa Matruh, in the desert. We were briefed by the RAF at Kabrit, on the Suez Canal. I never learned if we hit anything at Mersa Matruh. The longest mission was to Tripoli, fourteen hours, forty-five minutes. On one of our three Tripoli missions, we were homing in on a local radio station, listening to but not enjoying Arab music, when we ran into a solid weather front and had to turn back. The scariest mission was a night raid on Tobruk. We got caught and held in the searchlights there. It was so bright in the nose I could see every hair on my arm. They were all standing. We knew that the converging beams gave the flak guns a fix on our altitude. Kennedy racked the plane over a lot of sky and finally wrenched us out of the lights. We were supposed to make nine runs on the target, dropping a single bomb each run. (We learned later that the mission was a diversion to cover a landing by a British commando team intent on killing or capturing General Rommel. It failed.) We were on the second run when the lights caught us. On the third run we dropped the rest of our load and lit out for home.

My second scariest experience was on the ground. I was on my way to a briefing and ran into Killer Kane. He growled (he was like a bear when annoyed, which was often), "Westheimer, where's your forty-five?" We always wore sidearms on missions. I reached for my belt, where the holstered pistol was supposed to be, and it wasn't there. "I forgot it, Sir," I said. "Lieutenant," the Killer said, "some of these days you're gonna wish you had it." And I said the first thing that popped into my head. "Sir, I wished I'd had it when you asked me where it was." The Killer never cracked a smile.

And I never left that .45 behind again on a mission until months later. On purpose. In the nose of *Natchez to Mobile, Memphis to St. Jo* on December 11. If I'd been picked up wearing it, the Italians might have thought I meant them harm. Anyway, I never could hit the side of a barn with a pistol.

Our missions were mostly against shipping, either in harbors at Tobruk, Benghazi, Suda Bay in Crete and Navarino Bay in Greece or in convoys on the Med. There wasn't an hour in the twenty-four we didn't operate. All-day missions, all-night missions, missions that took off at night and landed by day, missions that took off by day and landed at night.

On one that landed at night I was flying with another crew, replacing its temporarily grounded regular navigator. It was a convoy strike. We always got a little lost on such missions. We'd fly out to the spot where Intelligence said we'd find the convoy and then do a square search looking for it. By the time we found it, if we did, dropped our bombs, and headed back, night usually fell hours before we got home. Having done something called "dead reckoning" during the approach and square search, with no wind information to make it reasonably precise, we got our position from three-star fixes. They were only dependable within ten miles or so. That wasn't good enough because we couldn't head toward Haifa when approaching the Palestine coast. If we approached Haifa, they'd set off air raid alarms, which would upset everybody, especially the Killer. So we'd need a land checkpoint before crossing the coast. This particular night the coast was blanketed by an undercast. I got on the Lydda radio. Ramat David didn't have radio facilities at the time. Lydda (now Lod) was the airfield at Tel Aviv, fifty miles or so from Ramat David. We homed into Lydda on the radio compass and headed for it. The field was blacked out, of course. They only turned on runway lights when you identified yourself. The radio compass needle kept pointing at the field while the pilot circled it. I gave him the heading for Ramat David and our ETA (estimated time of arrival). After flying until our ETA plus fifteen minutes and seeing only the unfamiliar shapes of mountains in the darkness below, I told the pilot I was lost and we'd have to return to Lydda. Which we did, following the radio compass. We landed. It wasn't Lydda. It was Ramat David. The next day Group sent up a plane to see how an aircraft could home in on Ramat David on the Lydda frequency. It couldn't. We never did find out how we managed it. Our Lady of Loreto, maybe, the patron saint of aviators. I'm Jewish but maybe the pilot was Catholic.

Later in the month two of the 98th's four squadrons began operating from St. Jean, Killer Kane commanding, on the Mediterranean coast just across the road from the ancient walled city of Acre. We shared the base with the British but had our own rations and cooks. There were other amenities as well. Cinderblock quarters instead of tents, indoor showers with hot water, a movie across the road. We'd seen *Intermezzo* at Ramat David kibbutz. It had French, Hebrew and Arabic subtitles, the French at the bottom and the other two vertically on either side. It was shown in the barnyard. The bales of fresh hay we sat on did a lot to hide the smell.

The St. Jean movie, a RAF operation, changed shows every week. The RAF audience stampeded out of the theater the moment the film ended to avoid having to stand during the obligatory playing of "God Save the King." Not that they had anything against King George. They just didn't like standing at attention.

After the 98th moved from Palestine to Kabrit we had a movie theater on the base. Kabrit was as much an improvement over St. Jean as St. Jean was over Ramat David. At St. Jean we were four to a room, all the crew's officers sharing. We slept on cots. At Kabrit there were only two to a room, with real beds. Kent Leader, the copilot, and I shared. We'd been on a three-day pass together back in Palestine. The usual destination was Jerusalem but we'd heard there was more action in Beirut. That's where we went.

It was true about the action. There was no rationing in Lebanon and the atmosphere was French. In Beirut we saw our first brioche, our first croissant and our first bidet. We had a room at the St. Georges Hotel overlooking the Med. The St. Georges is gone now, like so many of the good things in Beirut. The Mimosa Club is probably long gone, too. A British officer took us there. It provided entertainment for Allied officers. We spent one night in Beirut, another in Aley, a mountain resort town on the road to Damascus, and a night in Damascus, hitchhiking all the way. A Lebanese businessman who gave us a hitch in his hired taxi on the way to Aley told us we were both handsome Americans but to a Lebanese, Leader was more beautiful than a girl.

Leader was a quiet type, with a twinkle. He was a pipe smoker and a reader, dipping in two or three books at a time. Among other things, he'd been a forest ranger in Idaho. Or maybe it was Utah. One of those states so far from Texas it didn't matter.

We took another three-day pass together from Kabrit, this one with Kennedy, to Cairo. We had our pictures taken on camels with the Sphinx and two pyramids in the background. We had rooms at Shepheard's Hotel, which is even longer gone than the St. Georges. Maybe we were just bad luck for hotels. While we were on pass, the 98th had made its first raid on Italy. We got back just in time to make the second, the one where Leader was killed.

Very Rich Americans

IN OUR ROWBOAT, BRAZIL'S wounds were the worst. A deep, ragged tear inside his thigh and gashes on the back of both ankles. We'd played tennis once at Kabrit, wearing GI shoes because we had no sneakers. It'd be a while before he'd play tennis again, if ever.

Both of Risso's legs were riddled with small holes. His wounds weren't as shocking as Brazil's but they would do. I'd never seen wounded men before. The worst thing that had ever happened to anyone on our crew had been a hangover.

Gardinier and I had only scratches. Not Purple Heart quality. I didn't know how I'd got them.

The Italians had laid Brazil and Risso out on the bottom of the rowboat. Risso pulled himself to a sitting position on the plank seat. He was strong. He asked where Kennedy was. He was the first to inquire about the others. I was ashamed. Not about being unwounded or being alive but because I hadn't been thinking of anyone but myself. Gardinier told him Kennedy was okay. He'd seen Barnes pull him out of the flooded escape hatch. They were in another rowboat. Brazil was staring at the gash in his thigh. Gardinier told him not to look at it. Brazil grinned.

"Naw," he said. "It's pretty."

Gardinier began swearing. Broken bones, internal injuries, I thought. He held up his left arm. The one that was broken?

"It's supposed to be waterproof!" he raged. "It cost me fifteen pounds in Cairo!"

The Movado wristwatch he'd bought on our three-day pass had stopped. I wore two wristwatches. Navigators did. A personal watch with local time on one wrist and a GI watch on the other set to Greenwich Mean Time, navigation time. The GI watch had stopped but the personal one I'd bought in Haifa was still ticking. The only good thing that had happened that day.

As the Italians pulled for shore, I got out my wallet and went through it. We'd been ordered not to take anything on missions that might prove useful to the enemy. My Short-Snorter—an Egyptian pound note signed by other flyers and meant to be a memento of my travels; a swatch of the blue brocade shot with silver threads I'd bought six yards of in Damascus; and my Army Air Forces pass. Was there anything here of use to enemy intelligence? While I was pondering, one of the fishermen motioned me to throw it overboard. So I did. It floated but the carabiniere either didn't see it or pretended not to. For enemies, these guys weren't so bad.

The two rowboats scraped up on the beach one after the other. A small welcoming party of poorly dressed women, old men, and one wide-eyed boy gaped at us. The fishermen and the carabinieri lifted Brazil and Risso out of the boat. Gardinier and I followed them to a small building overlooking the Mediterranean. It was December, late afternoon, and my flight coveralls were soaked but I didn't feel cold. Just tired, and bewildered.

Kennedy, Jennette and Barnes came in with another carabiniere. Jennette had a neat hole through an ankle, in one side and out the other. Kennedy was in shock. He kept shaking his head and saying, "It's awful, it's awful."

Wounded though he was and in pain, Jennette demonstrated that an adjutant serving as a gunner was still an adjutant.

"Let's see," he said briskly. "Everybody here? Where's Kent? Jesus Christ!"

Frankie Spindler, the tail gunner, and Norman George, the assistant radio operator, hadn't made it, either. It hadn't really hit me yet that they were dead and I'd never see them again. But I didn't feel guilty about being alive.

The carabinieri had stretched Risso and Brazil on the stone floor and wrapped them in blankets. Risso called out to Kennedy. Kennedy went to him. He knelt by Risso and Risso wrapped him in his thick arms. There were tears in Risso's eyes.

"You're all right, Lieutenant, you're all right."

It helped. Kennedy was pretty much himself again. He asked Risso if he was badly wounded. Risso lied and said he wasn't. Brazil said nothing. The grin was frozen on his face now. He was in shock. We all were, more or less, except maybe Gardinier and Jennette.

The three of us were sitting in front of a small fire watching a bubbling black kettle dangling over it. I wondered if the Italian attitude toward Jews was anything like the Germans'. We hadn't been briefed on that and I didn't think so but why take chances? My dogtags had "H" stamped on them for "Hebrew." I surreptitiously took them off the chain around my neck and threw them into the fire. Kennedy came back and sat with us. He told us that when the plane snapped in half the armor plate behind Leader's seat tore loose and smashed him into the instrument panel.

By the time Kennedy unbuckled his safety belt and struggled out of his seat the flight deck was under water. The last thing he remembered was feeling the glass tubing of the fuel gauge at the back of the flight deck and realizing he'd overshot the escape hatch. He'd started gulping water to get it over with. And the next thing he knew he was on the beach.

Jennette didn't know how he'd gotten out of the plane. He'd been in the rear section and had taken his position with his back against the bulkhead, braced for ditching. The plane hit, he was thrown around, and the next thing he knew he was paddling in the sea. No one knew exactly how Spindler and George had died. Jennette said Spindler had been against the bulkhead, too. He'd probably been caught in the break-up. George had been standing at my right elbow, near the top turret. The turret may have torn loose on impact and crushed him.

The carabinieri hovered around us anxiously, helping the wounded as best they could. They motioned for us to take off our cold, wet clothing. One of them found a sodden pack of cigarettes in Kennedy's shirt pocket. The others gathered around admiring it. My contribution to their joy was a waterproof package of D-ration chocolate. Before we hit the water I'd taken it out of my parachute kit and stuffed it into my coveralls. One of the carabinieri took the cigarettes out of the pack and put them by the fire. The carabinieri were all laughing and shouting. It couldn't have been just the American cigarettes. They probably didn't have a lot of exciting things happen at their little post.

Two of them pulled out their own packs of cigarettes and offered them around. At the time we didn't realize how generous that was. Gardinier, Barnes and I, nonsmokers all, turned them down. Kennedy took one hungrily, glared at us, accepted a light, and took a deep drag. It wracked him and he coughed. I thought the smoke had done him harm. Then he took another drag and said, "Why in God's name didn't you take them cigarettes?"

(Kennedy was a college graduate with teaching credentials but was careless with his grammar. He'd been a salesman in civilian life and talked the way his customers did.)

"We don't smoke," Gardinier said.

"Well, I do," Kennedy said. By the fire, the carabinieri were lighting up Chesterfields. "Look at them guys go after my cigarettes. The last thing I did before we hit was grab 'em off the ledge and put 'em in my shirt pocket. I thought we were gonna' float."

A carabiniere bumped Risso's wounded leg straightening his blanket. Risso swore explosively in Italian. The carabinieri surrounded him quickly, enchanted.

"Italiano, Italiano!" they shouted.

Risso raised himself on an elbow and swore at them, in English.

"No!" he cried. "Americano!"

That delighted them, too. They offered Risso and the rest of us something out of a bottle. It was strong and stomach-warming. A carabiniere broke spaghetti into the black kettle bubbling over the fire. They dished it out in little earthen bowls. They offered to share their dinner with us but none of us could eat.

A burly carabiniere offered cigarettes around. Kennedy looked at us fixedly and everybody took one, nonsmokers included. As if our bladders were on the same frequency, suddenly everyone had to pee. The carabinieri took us all out to a smelly little courtyard, helping the wounded. I dropped my dogtag chain in a dark corner.

Back inside, a dried-up, sour-faced little civilian in an old black suit was waiting. He tended to our wounded. Roughly, as if he didn't mind hurting them. Wounds had cooled. Risso and Jennette groaned quietly through gritted teeth. Brazil didn't make a sound.

The big fellow who'd cooked the spaghetti looked at me grinning and took up a boxing stance. He pointed at me and said, "Max Schmeling." He laughed and shadow-boxed. I wasn't big and muscled like the German boxer, but I had his eyebrows and cheek muscles. The Italian looked sort of like Schmeling himself. Somehow he conveyed to me he'd been a light heavyweight fighter before the war. He mentioned Primo Carnera. I said I knew all about Primo. I mentioned the name of another Italian fighter who'd made a name for himself in the U.S. One of the lighter weights. Handsome. He'd married an American heiress and quit the ring. My new friend liked that a lot. He asked where I was from, Risso interpreting. Name, rank and serial number only was the drill, but I couldn't resist saying, "Texas." He and his friends thought that was great. They cocked thumb and forefinger at me like a pistol and said, "Tom Mix."

A car stopped outside and a tiny man in a drab blue uniform hurried in. He spoke with the one in the black suit. They waved their arms a lot and shouted. The man in the black suit turned to Jennette. Jennette, a captain, was the ranking officer among us. Black suit took out a little, worn dictionary, put on some bent-framed glasses, and with many pauses to look up words, he informed Jennette we were to be taken to a nearby military post.

Our clothes hadn't dried yet. The carabinieri scared up a thin blanket for each of us and shook hands goodbye. We piled into a sort of station wagon with a well-groomed Italian officer sitting behind the driver. Two of our wounded had seats and the other was on the floor. We immediately sank into our own thoughts. I felt guilty not thinking more about Leader but what was uppermost in my mind was how the news of my capture would affect my mother. How long would it take her to find out? What lay ahead for our bunch?

The station wagon bumped along a tortuous mountain road. The December air was icy, not like Egypt. Everyone was shivering. Teeth chattered. The road circled and climbed. It got colder. The Italian officer turned to Gardinier, who was sitting next to him, and asked carefully, "Why does a country so rich make war on a country so poor?"

Gardinier muttered, "I don't know," without turning his head.

The officer looked hurt.

At last we stopped at a huddle of buildings. The wounded were taken to a long, low structure on one side of the road and the rest of us to a large, dark building on the other. A soldier on an inside stair saw us coming and called out. A frowzy woman stuck her head out of a door to gape at us.

The officer whose feelings Gardinier had hurt escorted us to a large room furnished with desks, benches and chairs. Training posters on the walls: what to do in case of strafing, how to identify Allied soldiers' rank and branch of service, like that. A lot of soldiers sitting or standing around talking and gesturing—I was getting used to the combination—ignoring the two officers among them. A tough-looking gray-haired officer came in and everyone shut up and came to attention. An officer told us to salute the *colonnello*. So we did. He inspected us silently. He grunted and left. I guess we failed the inspection.

A tiny Italian soldier—there were a lot of those in the enemy forces we'd seen so far—came in with a stack of Italian uniforms. We traded our blankets for cotton breeches, shirts, blouses and socks. An officer, not the one from the station wagon, asked us in broken English "Why does a country so rich make war on a country so poor?"

Kennedy turned out an empty pocket of his new pants.

"Ah, yes," he said. "Very rich Americans."

It got laughs, even from the officer who'd asked. So far the Italians we'd encountered had been friendly, though kind of raunchy, except the officers. They'd all been impressed by my two watches. I gave my issue hack watch to the little fellow who'd brought us the uniforms. I had no use for it. The seawater had killed it. The others yelled at him and he gave it back.

We were led out to a waiting truck. Risso, Jennette and Brazil were already stretched out in the truckbed, shivering. I sat on the tailgate and shivered with them. Just before the truck started off, a slim soldier with deep, sad eyes took off his overcoat and handed it up to me. Startled, I mumbled thanks. He shook my hand.

It was a hard ride. The truck had no springs. Jennette moaned and cursed as the shattered bones in his leg grated with every jolt.

"Go slower, you dirty bastards!" he cried.

None of the Italians understood. I knocked on the back of the cab and shouted, "Largo! Largo!" I figured that meant "slow" in Italian. Largo movements in symphonies were kind of slow. It didn't work.

Brazil groaned for the first time. He said, "Lieutenant, tell that guy to quit pushing my leg."

A guard perched on the sideboard had slid down and was pressing against Brazil. I gestured for him to give Brazil some room and he moved away. But then he'd fall asleep and slump against Brazil again.

To occupy myself I watched the late night stars to know what direction we were going. In a plane that was called "follow the pilot." I kept Kennedy informed. Long habit. Maybe we'd get a chance to jump off the truck and I might be able to figure out where we were and get back to the coast. Fat chance. I wasn't jumping off unless Kennedy told me to.

From time to time I'd yell, "Largo, largo," at the driver or wake the guard and ask him to move off Brazil's leg. I was cold. And wretched. It helped some to talk with Kennedy. About what was going to happen to us, mostly.

Another army post. Those of us who could walk were led up some stairs and given woolen uniforms in exchange for the cotton ones. An interpreter told us the colonnello wanted to see us and that we must stand at attention and salute him. It didn't seem like a whole lot to ask. We were forlorn and anxious to oblige. The colonel could have been the twin of the one at the last post. Small, gray, abrupt. While we stood at attention the interpreter went along our line pointing, "Tenente, tenente, tenente, sergente." Disdain crept into his voice at "sergente." It didn't seem to bother Barnes.

The colonel gave us the searching look we were starting to expect from colonnellos, grunted the matching grunt, and dismissed us.

Back in the truck, Risso, Jennette and Brazil were exactly as we'd left them. The truck took us to a railway station, deserted except for a sentry and a dapper lieutenant with three soldiers not much bigger than the little rifles slung over their shoulders. The driver of the truck turned us over to the officer, took my borrowed overcoat, and left. I'd wondered how the compassionate soldier was going to get it back.

Kennedy, Barnes and I faced Gardinier, a guard and the dapper lieutenant in an unheated compartment. The lieutenant wore polished ski boots, short wool socks over neat army stockings, sleek gray gabardine breeches and blouse and a rakish cap. His face was thin, handsome and insolent. He smoked constantly without offering the pack around.

He studied us silently for a while. When he finally started to speak, Kennedy nudged me.

The lieutenant said, "Why does a country so rich make war on a country so poor?" Only he said it in French. Gardinier and I understood him (I just barely; my Rice Institute French was vestigial). Kennedy and Barnes guessed.

Gardinier told him in English we hadn't started the war. The lieutenant demanded to know why we had come so far just to kill innocent people. Gardinier said it was because they wouldn't come to us. Kennedy asked if he could check on our wounded in the next compartment. The guard escorted him.

Kennedy returned bleak with rage. Risso, Jennette and Brazil were half-conscious from cold and pain. The compartment window was wide open and they had no blankets. Kennedy complained bitterly to the lieutenant. The lieutenant listened, bored, and said indolently, "C'est la guerre." Kennedy took everyone's blouse and went to spread them over our wounded in the other compartment.

Daybreak. Cold. Stiff legs knee to knee across the narrow aisle. Outside, the landscape was wintry. Drooping olive trees and black stumps of grapevines. Dead brown earth. We were ravenous.

The train stopped in a bustling station. Well-dressed civilians were curious about us but not hostile. For our wounded, lying on stretchers on the platform, they showed sympathy. Kennedy, Barnes, Gardinier and I squatted by the stretchers trying awkwardly to say comforting things. It wasn't easy to squat on stiff, sore legs. An ambulance arrived to take Risso, Jennette and Brazil away. We all shook hands and said we'd be waiting for them when they got out of the hospital. Risso and Brazil looked bad. We wondered if they'd make it. (I never saw either of them again but long after the war Barnes visited Risso, still hampered by his old wounds. We heard that Brazil had survived the war, too.)

The callous officer and the two guards stayed with us. We eyed the young women on the platform, some of them blondes. We hadn't expected blondes in Italy. Several of them eyed us back. You could see Kennedy would have dearly loved to begin a lasting friendship. He had a knack for forming lasting friendships with young women wherever we might be.

Kennedy's prospects evaporated when a police van picked us up. It had benches along each wall. We could stretch our legs out. Plenty of room for Leader, if he'd been there. It was the first time I'd thought about him in hours, my closest friend on the crew. We couldn't see much through the heavy gratings on the back doors of the van, but we knew we were in a good-sized city (Salerno, we were to learn).

The van stopped. The doors opened. We were led into an imposing stone building where a lot of officers looked busy. Our escorts sat us down in a large antechamber. We'd been twenty-four hours without food and sleep and were giddy.

Kennedy was the first to be led into an adjoining room for interrogation. A soldier followed him with a bunch of rolled charts under his arm. They look alarmingly like mine. Gardinier, Barnes and I agreed we'd give only name, rank and serial number. No matter what.

I went in last. It was a large room with big windows overlooking a quay and the Mediterranean. If it had been in a hotel, they'd have charged extra for that view. Three officers were waiting for me: a small, shrewd colonel, a slick-haired officer bent over a notebook and a jolly one, standing. The colonel asked the questions, the slick-haired officer wrote down my answers, seldom looking up, and the jolly one interpreted. He stood where he could see the colonel's face and mine.

My navigation chart was spread out on the colonel's desk. Oh, shit! I'd destroyed my "flimsy," the onionskin sheet with the colors of the day and locations of emergency landing fields, but I'd expected the chart to go down with the plane. I took some comfort from the fact I hadn't started our course from Landing Ground 139 but at the point where we crossed the Libyan coast.

The colonel asked my name, rank and organization. I gave my name and rank. As to my organization, I said, "I don't know." And said the same when asked where we'd flown from, the range, speed and armament of our plane, and the name of my Group commander. The colonel got madder and madder with every "I don't know." He shouted at the interpreter, who seemed to find it all terribly funny.

The interpreter said, "The colonnello says do not say 'I don't know.' Do you take us for children? If you do not wish to tell, say so, but do not say, 'I don't know.'"

"Where do you come from?" the colonel demanded again.

"The United States."

The colonel's face got redder. The jolly one was having a hell of a time not laughing.

He said, "He means where did you base your attack from?"

"I don't . . ." I stopped myself before the colonel exploded. "I am ordered not to tell."

The colonel shot me a hard look and his tone became threatening. The jolly one lost control and laughed as he translated.

"The colonel says do you know what the Japanese do to their prisoners when they refuse to talk?"

I was beginning to enjoy myself. I got careless and let it slip that I was the navigator. I also told the colonel there were ten men in the crew, because I wanted it known that three men were missing.

The most persistent questions were about Jennette. Did we expect them to believe a captain, the ranking man on the plane, had merely come along for the ride? Admit it. We were going to drop him to commit sabotage. Or was he taking pictures of important future targets? I didn't tell the colonel Jennette was our squadron adjutant.

The colonel grew more tolerant. Maybe he'd gotten information from me without my knowing it. He took a newspaper clipping from his desk and passed it me. The jolly one said it was found in Risso's wallet.

The clipping had a photo of our Group commander, Col. Hugo P. Rush, and a brief account of one of our shipping strikes. The colonel asked if I knew Colonnello Rush and I said I did.

"So," the colonel said, "he is your commanding officer."

"No."

"But you say you know him."

I pointed at the picture of Mussolini over the colonel's desk and said, "I know him and he's not my commanding officer."

The colonel smiled. The jolly one laughed out loud. The slick-haired officer stayed bent over his notebook. The colonel said something that made the jolly one laugh harder.

"The colonnello says, 'He is now,'" the jolly one said.

I saluted the colonel when he dismissed me. In the U.S. Army Air Force you didn't salute without your hat on, but I didn't have a hat. And maybe it was different in the Italian army.

We compared notes when we reassembled on benches in a different room. We'd all been asked pretty much the same questions and denied saying anything significant. Gardinier wanted to know if anyone had told them he was the bombardier. We all said we hadn't. The colonel had asked Kennedy, "Why does a country so rich make war on a country so poor?"

Until now we'd been docile, but hunger made us bold. We raised such a fuss our guard found an officer who knew some English. We demanded to be fed. We were quickly brought two small apples, a brownbread bun, and an undersized wedge of cheese per man. We wolfed down everything, including the apple cores, but not the cheese rinds. We kept them. Before Kennedy put his away he held it up for all to see and said, "Very rich Americans."

After a while they took us back to the paddy wagon. A crowd of ragged civilians, nothing like the natty ones at the train station and mostly old folks and children, quickly gathered around us. Cheering us. Acting as if they wanted to touch us. We hadn't expected so warm a welcome. We were the enemy. Guards forced a path though the throng. Our admirers weren't cheering. They were hissing. Some of them spat at us. We were glad to reach the safety of the paddy wagon.

At the police station we were turned over to a plump carabiniere officer who wasn't much friendlier than the mob. One of our guards went down the line pointing, "Tenente, tenente, tenente, sergente," with that deprecating change in tone at "sergente." I grinned at Barnes. The plump officer gave an order and Barnes was hustled off by himself. The rest of us were taken to a suite of offices and left with two portly, middle-aged carabinieri. Friendly types. They sent down for soup all around. One of them held out a pack of cigarettes. Kennedy kept his eyes on us until we'd all taken one.

It was night by the time they brought Barnes back to join us. He'd been kept in a big, dark room all by himself. He'd had a bowl of soup, too. He said he'd been worried. And lonesome.

They moved us out in an old school bus. Just the few of us and all those seats. It wasn't too cold in the bus and the seats had padding. Pretty comfortable, compared with the train and the paddy wagon. The officer escorting us asked me in French, "Why does a country so rich make war on a country so poor?" I'd worked out and memorized an answer to that.

I said, "To keep what we have," in a mixture of French and English.

He shrugged and sat back in his seat. The road was good and there wasn't much traffic but we stopped often at roadblocks. Sometimes pillboxes, other times only movable barbed-wire barricades. We saw Mount Vesuvius in the distance, its twin craters glowing red in the night. Could it have been only the day before yesterday we flew by it on the way to bomb Naples harbor?

It was still night when we reached a military airfield outside

Naples. We heard planes taking off and landing after we were locked in a small room with a guard. There was one chair in the room, which the guard took, a table, and a little electric heater that didn't do much good. I got out my cheese rind from Salerno and gnawed on it. Kennedy grinned. I said, "Very rich American," and the four of us broke down laughing. Scared hell out of the guard. He thought we were pretty hard characters, I guess. All bigger than he was, with drawn, grimy, unshaven faces.

We took turns sleeping on the table, if restless squirming was sleeping. Early in the morning a skinny civilian with a Fascist emblem in his lapel joined us. He talked a lot, looking up words in a pocket English dictionary. We said we were hungry. The best he could arrange was some coffee substitute. It was vile but hot and sweet. He gave us Red Cross forms to fill out explaining, "so your people would know as quickly as possible you are safe." The printed cards had lines for name, rank, serial number, home address, name of next of kin and military unit. We didn't fill in the military unit space, of course, but after a discussion we gave our home addresses and names of our next of kin. We wanted our folks to know we were alive.

Later in the morning three Italian officers came to see us: a florid-faced, beefy man in tailored gabardine flying coveralls and two stocky, clear-eyed fliers. The beefy man said he was an aerial observer. His English was flawless. He introduced the other two as pilots who'd been in the formation that attacked us. They both spoke English pretty well. The beefy man said one of them was the pilot who'd shot us down. We didn't congratulate him but we all shook hands. We told them we'd had three dead and three wounded. They were sympathetic. The beefy man looked like a German to me. All of us disliked him instinctively, not because he looked German but because he was unctuous.

The pilot who was supposed to have shot us down said he'd done it with a burst of only nine bullets. We nodded politely but didn't believe him. The beefy observer said he had a brother who taught at Harvard. Probably in a concentration camp by now. He didn't believe us when we said his brother was probably still teaching at Harvard and that we didn't have concentration camps in America. We knew a little about Japanese relocation camps in the U.S. but certainly did not equate them with German concentration camps. He changed the subject. They'd shot down five of our planes on the Naples raid, he said. I already disliked him and this really pissed me off. I started arguing with him. He gave me all his attention. Kennedy shut me up before I said anything useful. Seeing I'd cooled off, the observer lapsed back into his oily, affable manner. Kennedy told him we were hungry and hadn't slept for two days. He promised to have food brought in and assured us we'd soon have beds somewhere.

We shook hands again when they left. It seemed the natural thing to do. They bore us no grudge, nor we them. We were all fliers. The civilian led us outside. An enormous plane roared overhead. We counted six engines in its massive wings. Our first sight of the German Me 323, "Der Gigant."

The civilian took us to see a colonel. We came to attention and saluted. By now we'd learned the drill. He gave us "At ease," through the civilian and his pocket dictionary. The civilian was sweating. He knew he was a lousy interpreter. The colonel asked all the usual questions and we gave the usual answer, "We are ordered not to tell." He did not press us.

He took a photograph of a fighter plane from his desk and held it so all of us could see it. Pointing at it, he asked a series of questions. The interpreter said he was asking where we were hit, at what altitude and at what airspeed. Kennedy told him to ask the pilot who'd shot us down. The colonel, who'd been so courteous and correct, turned icy. He dismissed us abruptly. We couldn't understand the change.

On the way back to our room, the interpreter told us what had angered the colonel. Kennedy telling him to ask the pilot who'd shot us down. The beefy observer had lied to us about who had done it. Barnes had shot down the pilot who'd actually downed us. He was a captain and a leading Italian ace, and had just died of his wounds in a hospital. The colonel had been asking where his plane had been hit, not ours. We'd have apologized if we could.

When visitors to the office next to our detention room dropped in to view us, our guard went down the line with the familiar, "Tenente, tenente, tenente, sergente," and the deprecatory tone at the end. Barnes said, "I'm getting an inferiority complex."

A German noncom came in and asked if anyone spoke German. When no one answered, I said I did, a little. He had three British airmen captured after a raid the night before. He wanted to turn them over to me. Unkempt and unshaven though I was, he thought I was an Italian soldier.

I said I would accept his prisoners. He handed me a paper to sign. I was doing so when a real Italian caught on and snatched the paper out of my hand. He berated the German, who shrugged and left. I ran to the door before he drove away and tried to speak with the British airmen in his vehicle. But they thought I was Italian, too, and wouldn't respond.

Lunchtime. For us it was dinner and breakfast time as well. In came lunch from the Italian officers' mess. At least the German-looking observer hadn't lied about that. It beat the food from our own mess back at Kabrit. Served on spotless china with heavy silverware. Macaroni in spicy red sauce, sliced roast beef, potatoes with onions, greens. Walnuts and tangerines for dessert. Kennedy said, "We're in the wrong air force."

After lunch they took us to the Naples railway station. We passed a funeral procession on the way. The officer escorting us said it was for a civilian killed in our bombing raid. He was disappointed when we didn't apologize.

We boarded a sleek, modern train. Ours was a first-class car divided into luxury compartments. We had to squeeze our way through prosperous-looking standees packed in the aisle. Our escorting officer, a dapper second lieutenant with a hairline mustache, evicted several civilians from the compartment to make room for us. They left with surprising good grace.

The standees stared at us through the glass of the compartment. The guard posted there kept busy answering their questions about us. The train hadn't started yet when a woman began screaming hysterically, "Alarum! Alarum!" The guard quieted her. We remained calm. We figured the station was a safe distance from the harbor, the likely target of any air raid.

The train pulled out with a rush. Quietly, quickly, smoothly. It was fast. It beat any American train I'd ever seen. Maybe we weren't first in everything after all.

There were three civilians in our compartment. A heavy-lidded, somnolent old man with a Fascist party rosette in his lapel, a young man and a plump, plain girl who'd been crying. She spoke to our escort in Italian, then asked us if we spoke French. She knew a little German and English, too. In a combination of languages she told us she was a cousin of the Italian pilot we'd shot down. She was returning to her home in Rome from the hospital where he'd died. (Had we been deliberately placed in her compartment?) She wasn't bitter. War was a bad thing, she said. Everyone would be happy when it was over. We told her about Leader and the others. She was genuinely sympathetic.

It was dark when we got to Rome. We said goodbye to her and were led to a dispensary near the depot. An orderly put iodine on our scratches. We all had them on the backs of our hands and didn't know how we got them. I noticed a deep scratch on my ankle for the first time. All of us were discovering new aches and bruises, especially Kennedy. His thighs and lower abdominal muscles were giving him trouble. He thought it was because of the pressure he'd exerted on the rudder pedals to keep the *Natchez to Mobile, Memphis to St. Jo* from falling out of the sky when our starboard engines ripped out of the wing. But it had saved his life. He was braced for the impact when we hit the water. He said we'd been doing 155 miles an hour.

After being taken two at a time, under guard, to a dark, smelly public lavatory across the street, we were installed in a bare, dusty office above the dispensary. We asked the officer in charge for something to eat. He said he had not been ordered to get us anything and let it go at that. There were three tables in the office, on which we took turns sleeping. The officer got us up before dawn and put us on a train. It was still dark when we detrained at a lonely station and climbed into a beat-up old bus.

The bus creaked and swayed between walled lanes, over rutty roads. It was frigid inside. It stopped at last before a forbidding gate. The driver honked. The gates swung open. We were herded along dark stone corridors and up cold stairs. I thought uneasily of a book I'd read, Jan Valtin's *Out of the Night*. It was about dark stone corridors. And prisoners. And torture.

Sleeping with a Sergeant

IN AN OFFICE A GAUNT-FACED Italian officer sitting behind a desk said gravely that military discipline was observed in this prison. He was *maresciallo* and when we came into his office we must stand at attention and salute. We learned later that a maresciallo was a warrant officer and all of us except Barnes outranked him. He asked us the usual questions and we gave the usual answers. A guard who'd accompanied us from Rome went down the line. "Tenente, tenente, tenente, sergente." Barnes and I were too tired to smile.

Kennedy and Gardinier were assigned to a room. Before putting Barnes and me together the maresciallo asked if I objected to sharing quarters with a sergente.

The room was a pleasant surprise. Two real beds with sheets and thick blankets, a desk, two chairs. The dark gray wool blankets had "RA" and an insignia on them. We learned they were Reggia Aeronautica, Italian air force, blankets. It was still dark. We climbed into our beds and slept immediately.

Knocking on the door woke us. Morning. Beady eyes peered at us from a spyhole in the door. A voice shouted in Italian. We figured it meant "Get up!" and we did. The guard showed the way to a foul latrine at the end of the hall. We washed ourselves at a tap in the latrine. Back in our room, a squatty, muscular man in fatigues burst in shouting, "Acqua caldo!" I thought it meant "cold water" but it was hot. My first Italian lesson. He gave us tin plates, cups and spoons and filled the cups with hot water from a steaming pail, all the while laughing and talking. We smiled at him and called him every dirty name we knew. He laughed harder and kept up his chatter. He was probably cursing us, too. We all enjoyed it. The next guard wasn't any fun at all. Large, surly. He gave us a safety razor with one blade, a molting shaving brush and a sliver of soap. He indicated we were to shave and make our beds. We nicknamed him "Dogface."

Later in the morning we were interrogated, one at a time. First by an Italian colonel asking the usual questions, then by a German colonel with a different approach. He didn't seem much interested in our operations. He was more interested in the larger issues: morale, production, politics. He was a handsome man, distinguished-looking. He was informal. Almost casual. But he wanted to put me on the defensive and did, asking if I knew American troops had shot German prisoners in North Africa. And if I knew that the British had chained Italian prisoners in Egypt. I was about to hotly deny that, saying I'd seen prison camps on the Nile Delta and they looked clean and comfortable. That would have told him we were based in Egypt, something the Italians had been particularly keen on learning. They'd mentioned England, Malta, North Africa and Libya but never Egypt. I was grateful to the fisherman who'd motioned me to throw my wallet into the water. The colonel said he'd been an executive with an importing firm in America before the war. I told him I'd been a journalist. I knew I'd blundered when his interest quickened, but it died when I said my beat had been music and the theater. (My colleagues on the *Houston Post* hadn't thought it much of a beat, either, except for the free show tickets.) Did I know what I was fighting for? I said to preserve what we had. He laughed. Surely I didn't think Germany had any designs on my country. To the contrary. Europe wanted Germany's protection and the United States was the aggressor. I was tempted to argue but didn't. It wasn't just that I feared I might let valuable information slip. I also didn't want him to learn how dumb I was politically. He was egging me on and he was a lot smarter than I. He soon realized I wasn't worth any more of his time and dismissed me with a handshake. I saluted him before leaving. I wanted him to know I still considered myself a soldier.

Barnes was waiting outside. His interrogation was a short one. Our captors had the strange notion that while lieutenants might know something worthwhile, mere sergeants didn't. (I learned after the war that at Dulag Luft, Germany's premier interrogation center, they got more information out of officers than sergeants, but only because officers were more easily conned into talking.)

After interrogation we were summoned to the maresciallo's office. We saluted meekly. He radiated benevolence. He had a Red Cross parcel for us. First one we'd ever seen, or even heard about. It was a Canadian parcel. We tore it open. What abundance! Hard biscuits, pork roll, corned beef, sugar, tea, chocolate, powdered milk, canned butter, jam, salmon, sardines and dried fruit.

We could take items to our room but the parcel had to remain in his office. Prisoners sometimes tried to escape, he explained gravely, when they had a supply of food to take along. And, he warned, the parcel had to last us ten days. We had to sign a receipt for it. He was very businesslike. Barnes and I chose jam, butter, corned beef, tea, chocolate, sugar and milk.

The maresciallo had a shelf of books in English and told us we could each borrow one. I took *Ivanhoe.* I'd never gotten around to reading it when I had better things to do with my time.

A tall, handsome soldier with wavy chestnut hair stood by while we were selecting our treasures. The maresciallo told us the soldier spoke no English but understood French and German. We could speak with him in either of those languages if we wished. At interrogations we had denied knowledge of either so I didn't take advantage of the offer. Before we left we were allowed to "buy" paper and pencil and told we could write home. As prisoners of war (POWs) we were entitled to the equivalent pay of our rank in the Italian army. Nine hundred and fifty lire a month for first lieutenants, which we were, and far less than our U.S. pay. We had no idea how Italian first lieutenants got along on it.

Back in our room, Canadian biscuits—round, hard, large as a man's palm—smeared with butter and jam. What joy! After a long debate we decided to put off opening the corned beef. We could hear Kennedy and Gardinier moving around next door. They must have gotten their parcel, too. We opened our window and started singing "The Prisoner's Song." "Oh, if I had the wings of an angel, over these prison walls I would fly." Kennedy and Gardinier opened their window and joined in. We had a pretty good quartet going until a guard banged on our door and shouted, "Silencio." We shut up. We were good prisoners.

Our window overlooked a partially walled yard with trees and gravel walks. It sloped down on two sides to a long green valley. To the left was a garage-like building and the gate we'd entered. Just below us was a long, narrow open pavilion with a hardpacked dirt floor.

We inspected our room carefully for the first time, looking for hidden microphones. We found only one suspect opening.

Enough to make us agree to speak of military matters as little as possible and, when we did, for one of us to keep whistling while the other spoke.

The house rules were posted on a wall in English and Italian. We were in an air force quarantine hospital, it stated, and would be well-treated as long as we complied with regulations. Which included making beds promptly, not sitting on them during daylight hours, avoiding loud singing and talking, not communicating with prisoners in neighboring rooms, not speaking to soldiers outside the room, keeping clean and well-shaved and maintaining discipline. Plus a warning that sentries were posted around the area and on the roof with instructions to fire without warning at prisoners attempting to escape.

Barnes and I spent the morning composing our letters home. I gave my mother the usual reassurances, not all of them factual. "I have to exercise a lot to keep from getting fat." "The scenery where I am is very beautiful but of course I am not able to do any sightseeing." Plus a list of my friends to be notified. I bragged on the Red Cross and said they'd answer all her questions and if Uncle Sam was still paying me to give the Red Cross $10 a month. Barnes wrote a similar letter to his wife, Shirley. (I was to meet her in October, 1945, in Miami Beach, where Barnes and I were sent for something called rehabilitation and orientation. We went to dinner and for dessert we all had our first Baked Alaska. He repaid me for that dinner in 1986 at a 98th Bomb Group reunion in San Antonio. I was long married by then. He and Shirley took my wife, Dody, and me to lunch at a Mexican restaurant.)

At noon the merry little guard we nicknamed "Laughing Boy" would bring in our lunch. Almost always it was a bowl of soup, a dab of greens, a morsel of cheese and a slice of bread for each of us. Another guard, an older man with a tired, kindly face, often came in and told us the Italian names for what we were eating. We got pretty much the same at night. We developed a routine with Laughing Boy. After he gave us our ration we'd just stand there holding out our utensils and looking at him wistfully. Often as not, he'd laugh and give us extra. Mornings we got nasty coffee substitute, which we drank for the warmth. Twice a day the "acqua caldo" man visited—we nicknamed him "Monkey Man." We made tea with the hot water. Our teabag was a scrap of cloth from my ragged underpants. With a pinch of powdered milk and sugar from our parcel the tea wasn't bad.

Barnes and I got along well as roommates. We'd been friendly enough before, but officers and crewmen lived separately and didn't see each other as much on the ground as in the air. Now, though, we learned all there was to know about each other. And liked what we learned. Barnes was generous, accommodating and utterly guileless.

Sometimes to entertain me, and himself, while speaking of Shirley, he'd hug his pillow and say, "She loves me." I asked him if it were okay if I dreamed about her, too, and he said I could.

We covered every topic we could think of. God, capital punishment, women (I did; he'd only talk about Shirley), food, our prospects, the war, money, family, education, ambitions, hopes, desires and philosophy. Sometimes we'd talk far into the night and a guard would bang on the door and order us to shut up.

We talked about our Red Cross parcel, too. And thought about it a lot. We were always hungry and our little store of milk, corned beef, jam, biscuits and powdered milk tempted the hell out of us. We'd get through a whole day agreeing not to touch it. Then we'd go to bed for the night and lie there awake. And I'd say, "Al, how'd you like to eat a biscuit and jam?"

He always said, "I will if you will."

We learned our prison had once been a monastery and was just outside the town of Poggio Mirteto. The second night we were there I dreamed about Leader. He came sideways through the door with his back to me. I recognized him by his round head, thick neck and powerful torso. He put his elbows on the windowsill and rested his chin on his hands. God, I was glad to see him.

"How'd you get here?" I cried.

He didn't answer. I thought it must be raining outside because he was dripping wet.

I said, "You must be tired. Take my bed."

Then, in the dream, Barnes woke up and said, "No, take mine, Lieutenant. I'm only a sergente and I can sleep on the floor."

Leader shook his head. I woke up. It was a while before I understood it was only a dream.

Nights, after we stopped talking and before falling asleep, we'd listen to the sentry pacing on the roof. We'd snuggle in our blankets and feel sorry for him. Mornings, we'd look out the window a lot. We'd watch the guards play *bocce*, a bowling game, in the dirt-floored pavilion just below.

Nights were frigid and days weren't a whole lot warmer except for the few hours a day when the sun shone in our window. My feet got red and swollen and hurt. I'd never seen a chilblain before but I guessed that's what I had. Seven of them. It was hard to get my shoes on so I left them off a lot despite the cold.

One morning we saw two RAF types walking in the yard from our post at the window. One of them wore a dress blouse, with shirt and tie. The other was in blue battle dress and winter flying boots. I'd have given a month's pay, if I were still being paid, for those boots.

Monkey Man was watching the bowling game. When he saw us looking out the window he started doing acrobatic tricks on the iron piping of the pavilion. We applauded. The RAF types didn't look our way. After a while we heard the door to Kennedy and Gardinier's room open, and footsteps in the hall. Before long, Kennedy and Gardinier appeared in the yard. We waved from our window and they waved back until their guard made them quit.

We got our walk that afternoon. Despite my sore feet it was marvelous being out of doors and in the sun. Our guard saw me limping and with signs asked me if something was wrong. I said no. They might make me go back inside. The RAF types were in another part of the yard. We tried to get their attention but they didn't respond. We'd forgotten we were in Italian uniforms.

That night we heard them talking in the next room. We tried talking to them through the wall but they wouldn't answer until Barnes and I started singing "Sixpence."

"I've got sixpence, jolly, jolly sixpence,
I've got sixpence, to last me all my life."

They joined in. That's when I learned they'd taught us the wrong words at preflight. We'd sung, "I've got no pence to lend and no pence to spend and no pence to send home to my wife." The RAF types sang, "I've got fuck all to lend and fuck all to spend and fuck all to send home to my wife." We adapted handily to their version.

"Sixpence" sweetly rendered, one of the Englishmen sang "There Was an Old Lady from Wheeling," with some terrific obscene lyrics, finishing with "That was a cute little rhyme, sing us another one, do." So Barnes and I did. After that, they believed we were what we claimed to be and we talked.

They were members of a Stirling bomber crew shot down

over Turin. Everyone had gotten out but the skipper (that's what they called their pilot), who'd kept the plane flying straight and level while his crew bailed out. We'd have talked all night if a guard hadn't banged on our doors ordering us to be quiet.

We visited the maresciallo's office regularly to select food items from our parcel and change our books. On occasion a guard we learned to call "Changadabook" would come to our room to exchange books for us. We called him Changadabook because "Changa da book" is what he always said. During our Poggio Mirteto retreat I read a book of Aldous Huxley essays that gave me a lasting dislike for him. Kennedy and I both read two "American" novels by British authors. One a western and the other about a cocaine-sniffing, drug-dealing gangster. We entertained each other quoting the unintentionally hilarious dialogue.

When there wasn't a bocce game going on below us and no guards in the yard, we'd talk with Kennedy and Gardinier window to window. Our chief topic was where we were going from Poggio Mirteto. We'd learned the average stay there was only a couple of weeks. After that prisoners went to a regular POW camp. We hoped we wouldn't be sent to Germany. The war was still raging in Tunisia, but we figured Italy would be invaded and out of the war before Germany, however long that might be. Barnes was worried that he might be sent to a different camp from us because he was an enlisted man. Whenever we spoke with the maresciallo, Kennedy, Gardinier and I always requested that Barnes be sent to the same camp we were.

We were desperate for news of the war. Occasionally a guard would have a newspaper and we'd try to sneak glances at it even through we knew no Italian. We wrote off our guards' version of the news as propaganda.

One morning I woke up with my armpits itching. I hadn't had a bath in more than a week but that wasn't it. I was infested with crab lice. Dogface looked in the spyhole and saw me picking them off. That afternoon Barnes was moved out of the room, my armpits were shaved (with a dull razor), and I was dusted with some sort of powder.

The four days I spent alone were intolerable. I imagined they'd used the lice as a subterfuge to get Barnes out of the room so they could break me down. At several interrogations they'd asked us our religion. Since the others told theirs I felt I had to say something. I said I was a Freethinker but probably wasn't too convincing explaining what that was. What if they'd found the dogtags with "H" on them I'd thrown in the fire at the carabinieri post south of Salerno? Maybe they were going to send me to Germany. Whenever I tried to talk with Kennedy a guard stopped me. I wasn't even allowed to walk in the yard. Instead, I was taken to the enclosed cobbled courtyard where we'd come in the first night. It was sunless. After a few minutes of angry pacing I said I wanted to go back inside. First time I'd ever asserted myself at Poggio Mirteto. Unlike the British. They sang and yelled as often and as loud as they pleased, and when they were hungry they'd shout, "Bring us something to eat, you wop bastards." Got away with it, too, as far as I knew.

The second day of my solitary confinement the tall soldier with the chestnut hair, the one who spoke French and German but no English, came to visit me. He was terribly ill at ease and wouldn't look me in the eye. It was several moments before he spoke. Fluent English with only a trace of an accent.

He asked me if I was Jewish. I'd never obeyed any of the dietary laws or, after adulthood, gone to services even on high holidays except to please my mother but somehow I couldn't and wouldn't deny my heritage. I said I was.

He said in a rush, as if desperate to get it over with, "The German colonel who spoke with you wanted you sent to Germany, but we will not let him take you if you will tell us all the dates (he meant data) on your aircraft."

I was frightened, but I was angry, too. I said, "You know I can't do that."

He was so relieved. He gave me a sheepish, apologetic look and left immediately. Naturally my paranoia blossomed. It wasn't until I was considered cured and Barnes brought back to the room that I got over it. Barnes was as relieved to be back as I was to have him. He'd been alone, too, and nearly as paranoid. But it hadn't been all bad. He'd been put in a sunny, comparatively warm room and one day he'd had a wash in his tin basin using his handkerchief as a washrag. He'd let the sun dry him. He was proud of his cleanliness. He pretended my smell offended him. It probably did.

Eventually we four Americans were the only prisoners left in the Poggio Mirteto quarantine camp. Because we were the first Americans shot down over Italy they may not have known what to do with us. Things got better once we were the only guests.

Barnes and I were allowed to visit Kennedy and Gardinier in their room and to speak with them when we took our walks. We got a little more food, too.

Kennedy was an impatient man when not in the air. Aloft, he was not only patient but cautious and thorough, which were some of the reasons he was such a good pilot. But on the ground he couldn't stand empty time. He filled a lot of it playing cards. Not just poker, to which I was partial myself, but also hearts and casino. When he saw a pack of greasy playing cards in the maresciallo's office, he asked if he could buy them. The maresciallo sold him the cards, entering the transaction in a ledger he kept meticulously.

Kennedy, at twenty-six the oldest officer in the crew, made Gardinier, the youngest at twenty-two, play casino a lot more than Gardinier wanted to. The first time we were allowed to visit them in their room, Kennedy was very pleased with himself and Gardinier looked glum. It was because Kennedy always won.

Kennedy chain-smoked the harsh Italian cigarettes he charged to his lire account. They were rationed, but Barnes, Gardinier and I all dutifully bought our ration to turn over to him. Barnes's cigarettes were debited to our officer accounts. Italian sergentes couldn't afford cigarettes. Guards sometimes came into his room just to marvel because they always found him smoking, even in bed after lights out. He'd toss his butts against the wall by the door. Mornings, the guards competed to get there first.

Kennedy asked us why we called the guards to take us to the latrine at night. "When it's dark, we just take a leak out the window."

Gardinier brightened. "Yeah," he said. "The other night I almost got a sentry."

Now that we were pampered guests we walked in the yard more often. On one of the walks, the chestnut-haired soldier joined Barnes and me. At first we were wary of him because we'd heard through the grapevine he'd been planted as an Australian with a British flier. And had gotten away with the deception until he called a condom a "preservative." Now, as best Barnes and I could tell, he had no interest whatsoever in military matters, but he was intensely interested in ordinary life in America and eager to learn anything we knew about important hotels. He knew the names of most great American hotels. He said before the war he'd worked in luxury hotels throughout Europe and spoke fluent

English, German, French, Spanish and Italian. Did all Americans really have electric iceboxes, radios and automobiles, and how much money did a man have to earn to buy them? And how much did an experienced hotel man earn at a leading hotel? Obviously he wanted the war to end as much as we did, and his postwar plans were to emigrate to the U.S. and work in a hotel.

My friendship with Kennedy went back to our combat crew training days in Florida. When crew positions were assigned he'd drawn another navigator but asked for me. Before regular crews were formed I'd been his navigator on an antisub patrol over the Gulf of Mexico when he had to make his first landing with depth charges aboard, at night and in a rainstorm. Those things draw men together. Maybe not as close as being shot down together. But close enough.

Being POWs together drew bonds even closer. As pilot, Kennedy had always been in charge, but now I regarded him as leader, the one to look to for advice and instruction. He was a curious mixture of cynic and optimist, of worrier and joker. One moment he could worry about whether he'd ever get paid for the car he'd left behind and his father had sold to Kennedy's brother, and the next he'd describe, his blue eyes merry, his immediate postwar plans. They included a hundred dance band records, a hotel room, a bottle of bourbon, and a blonde-haired woman.

He led us daily in marathon games of hearts and casino. He was unbeatable at casino. We'd talk about escape during cards but without conviction. It was just too damn cold and hungry out there and we didn't know the country. We'd wait until we got to our permanent camp.

When Barnes and I went to get the tea from our second Red Cross parcel it wasn't there. The maresciallo paled and said the theft was a serious thing that placed every man in the prison under suspicion. He said it was the first time a prisoner in his care had ever lost anything. If the Red Cross learned of our loss they might stop sending parcels. He promised a rigid search and severe punishment for the culprit, if discovered. He gave us some tangerines by way of apology. The kind-faced guard later informed us there'd been a thorough search of the guards' quarters and they'd all been lectured and warned. Dogface, Changadabook and Monkey Man scowled at us for several days afterward. The tea was never found. We wondered if we'd taken it on an earlier visit and forgotten. We agreed not to mention that possibility to the maresciallo.

Christmas Eve. Mixed emotions. Happy to be alive but miserable about where we were. The maresciallo let us buy a bottle of vino on condition we share it equally. He'd let four Englishmen buy a bottle, and one of them had drunk it all and become very troublesome. Moved by holiday spirit, he increased rations for the day and added tangerines and boiled chestnuts.

We spent Christmas Eve over cards and nostalgia. What were our friends and families doing right now? Did they know yet what had happened to us? We'd been assured the Red Cross cards we'd filled out in Naples would be forwarded quickly by the Vatican and that Radio Rome had already broadcast our names as POWs in Italy. Mail to us, we knew, would have been returned stamped "Missing in Action." We didn't admit it to each other but we didn't mind that at all. It made us feel tragic and heroic. We knew damn well we weren't heroes, except for Gardinier, and Kennedy had done a heroic job of ditching, but we wondered if maybe we'd get a medal as a sort of consolation for being shot down. We'd had a lot of missions (we later learned we'd been awarded Distinguished Flying Crosses and Air Medals for them), and Barnes had shot down an Italian ace. And we reminisced about our last mission, with harsh words for our element leader, who'd turned short of the target and left us hanging out to dry. And where would we be this time next year?

New Year's Eve. Vino again. And as I was coming out of the latrine, a happy, singing, drunken guard stopped me. He shook my hand and pulled out a wallet bulging with snapshots of young women (fully clothed) for me to look at. They weren't too pretty but I said, "Bella ragazza." I'd been washing out my bowl and had it in my hand. He bellied up closer and tilted his canteen over it, slopping a rivulet of hot red wine into it. He staggered off still singing.

Our guards sang a lot, sometimes what sounded like ballads, other times operatic arias. They all seemed to fancy themselves potential opera stars and sang arias as if on stage.

A few days after New Year's the maresciallo told us we were soon to be transferred to another camp. All except Barnes. We hated that. We appealed to the maresciallo to let him come with us. He said he could do nothing. The orders came from Rome. We were officers and must go to an officers' camp. But there were some enlisted men at our camp and he'd try to get Barnes sent there later.

The maresciallo let Barnes come to his office with us when

we signed out. He brought his ledger with his lists of our expenditures. He wanted us to sign it but not before he went over each man's account meticulously to make sure we understood and approved of every deduction. We found we'd been charged for part of our bread, having received more than the official ration, and for some extras for Barnes and a couple of other American sergeants we hadn't even known were there. He was a fair and decent man.

The maresciallo gave us travel rations—a bun and a piece of cheese. The officer who was to escort us struck up a conversation in English. He said since the capture of the Ukraine there'd been plenty of food in Italy. Gardinier said, "In that case, how about some more bread and a bigger piece of cheese?" The escorting officer and the maresciallo joined in our laughter.

Before releasing us to our escorting officer, the maresciallo took care of one last piece of business. He gave us a receipt for the unpaid balance of our pay. We wanted to leave it for Barnes but it wasn't allowed. We hated leaving Barnes but were chipper about going to a regular camp.

The maresciallo came to the railroad station with us. It was as if he hated parting with us. We were the only ones on the platform. The train was a while coming and Kennedy made us hunker down on the platform and play casino. The maresciallo found that amusing. When the train came he shook our hands and asked us not to forget him.

We were led off the train in Rome and kept in the same office where we'd spent a night earlier. Kennedy had us playing hearts the rest of the day and, when nightfall found us still there, switched us to casino. He played cards at a furious pace—shuffle, deal, snap 'em down, pick 'em up—and if you hesitated, he urged you on.

We had the standard night ride. Long, cold and uncomfortable. It was still dark when we reached our destination, rainy and bleak. The escorting officer went off and left us in a small, chilly military office with our guards.

A soldier dozed at a desk. Our guards stretched out on benches and fell asleep. We were too cold and uncomfortable to do the same. Kennedy nudged Gardinier and nodded toward the guard sleeping nearest the door.

"Watch him," he said. "He's playing possum. He's gonna try to escape. Don't let him get out the door."

The escorting officer came back to us at first light. We were

on a paved street a couple of hundred yards from a high wall over
which we could see the tops of long buildings. The officer was
feeling frisky and suggested we run instead of walk. He'd obviously spent a better night than we had. He started running. Our
feet hurt and we were tired, stiff and hungry but not about to let
him show us up. So we ran after him. The guards lagged behind.
They had nothing to prove.

Chieti Soup

OUR ESCORT KNOCKED ON massive double gates set into the wall. After a display of documents the gates opened and we had our first view of our new home. Beyond an inner barbed-wire fence hundreds of POWs milled furiously up and down a paved street between two rows of one-story masonry barracks. On our side of the fence, grass and trees. On their side, bare earth. Hard-packed and looking like stone. As we were being led to a building on our side of the fence, prisoners spotted us and began rushing to the wire.

We were hustled into the building, and taken to a cramped room with two men and a stove in it. One of the men was in Italian uniform, the other in British battle dress. The Italian said in colloquial American English that he was an American like us but had been caught in Italy by the war while on a visit and given a choice of a concentration camp or the Italian army. So here he was a sergente in the wrong army. He said living conditions were good in the camp. The one in British uniform was a POW, a Jewish Palestinian. I was relieved to see a Jew there and looking so well. He said he'd been captured in the battle for Crete.

The inevitable small colonel came in to inspect us. He spoke harshly to the guards who'd brought us and without warning began screaming and waving his arms. The guards cowered, and we did too, a little. After a final high-pitched barrage he stamped out of the room on little well-shod feet. The sergente who said he was American like us said the commandante was upset because our Italian uniforms hadn't been marked to identify us as prisoners of war.

We undressed, and our clothing and bodies were searched for escape material and lice. Guards gave us blankets to wrap up in and went off with the uniforms. Kennedy laid out a game of solitaire on the floor by the stove. When our guards weren't watching he stuffed more coal in the fire.

When our uniforms came back they'd been marked inexpertly with white paint. Runny stripes around the sleeves and legs, circles on the knees, P.G. (for Prigioniero di Guerra, prisoner of war) on the left breast and, in a circle on the back of the tunic, another P.G. The sergente led us back outside.

Prisoners massed at the wire in hundreds at our approach. "Yank or British?" they shouted.

"Americans," we yelled back.

The sergente opened the gate and let us in. We were engulfed in a shouting, bizarrely dressed mob. Flying suits, blankets, strange combinations of battle dress and desert khakis. Even a man in kilts. There were more questions about us and the progress of the war than we could answer.

A voice pierced the babble. "Jesus Christ! Russ. Welcome to P.G. 21."

"Bob!" Gardinier yelled back. "You old son of a bitch! What are you doing here?"

He shook hands with a skinny kid with a shock of wiry black hair and introduced him to us. Bob Adams, an underclassman of his at basic flight training. Gardinier had washed out of pilot training.

The sergente led us through the mob toward a low stone and plaster one-story building, one of several in a row along the center road. There was another row just like it across the street. We answered what questions we didn't think might be useful to the Italians as we moved though the press. The mob fell away at the door. Adams was among the few who went in with us.

Inside were more shouting, jostling men and unpainted wooden two-decker bunks, plain board tables and slab-sided stools. Yet it seemed as empty as it was crowded. Was it because of the high ceiling, the tile floor—the *permanence* of the place— and the plainness of its furnishings? There were six large living bays, each divided by the corridor down the middle of the building. We were to live in the last bay.

An American lieutenant colonel with short, graying hair and steel-rimmed GI glasses took us in charge. He was dressed in khakis and had a blanket draped around his shoulders because the bay wasn't heated. Army Lieutenant Colonel Max Gooler, the Senior American Officer (SAO) at P.G. 21. He was upset by the condition of our uniforms. He told us not to answer any more questions until we'd been officially interrogated by the camp's senior officers and received further instructions. This while surrounded by our new roommates and spectators from the next bay. Another crowd looked on through a big window at the side of the bay. We were delighted to be there but bewildered by the confusion.

Another of our new roommates introduced himself. A plump, bland man with sad eyes. Larry Allen he said. Associated Press (AP) war correspondent. He nodded toward a bulletin board bearing the familiar Associated Press logo. We thought it a whimsy of his until we learned he really was an AP war correspondent, captured at Tobruk when the British warship he was on sank. The Italians claimed he didn't have civilian status because he'd been with the British navy. He said, okay then, he was an admiral, but the Italians assigned him the rank of second lieutenant.

A tiny, thin prisoner with wild eyes pushed his way to the front of the crowd outside the window and asked me if it were true Tripoli had fallen. He wore a desert shirt and shorts and held a faded blanket around his shoulders. I told him the last I'd heard we were pushing toward Benghazi, forgetting what I'd just been told by Colonel Gooler. He asked where I'd been captured. He seemed so desperate for news I hated not to tell him. But I told him I couldn't. He smiled and said, "Good show."

Colonel Gooler wanted to know if we'd had breakfast. When we said we hadn't, he rounded up bread, butter and jam. We didn't realize at the time what largesse that was. Kennedy threw his cigarette butt on the floor. Colonel Gooler picked it up and gave it back to him.

"These things are precious," he said.

Kennedy assured him he had plenty more where that came from and offered him one. It was a struggle, but Colonel Gooler turned him down. Kennedy insisted. Colonel Gooler took one, reluctantly. Kennedy offered the pack around. No takers.

"Don't do that any more," Colonel Gooler ordered.

He said people in here didn't offer or accept cigarettes. They were too scarce.

After our bread and jam we were assigned bunks. Colonel Gooler had to turn the whole room out to find the headboards and bedboards that had been rustled. Our roommates fitted in the boards and fetched grass-filled palliasses and pillows. Two very tiny Italians in blue coveralls brought in our bedding, two coarse narrow blankets and a canvaslike sheet.

Beds made, Colonel Gooler conducted us to one of the

smaller rooms at the front of our building for interrogation. He, the Senior British Officer, (SBO, a full colonel and the camp's ranking officer), and a sharp British major questioned us closely about the war in general, ourselves and our unit in particular, and everything that had happened since our capture. They wanted to know, among other things, if our wounded had been cared for and if any of our personal belongings had been confiscated. That done, they questioned us just as closely about the home front. Movies, plays, books, the latest scandals, everything going on outside the wall. They were starved for news of any kind.

We were in Campo Concentramento Prigionieri di Guerra 21, east of Rome, twelve kilometers from Pescara, on the Adriatic, and overlooked by the village of Chieti. There were eight double bungalows, as our buildings were called, including the guard barracks, the prison office, a hospital, our mess halls and cookhouse, all inside a brick wall which ranged from ten to fourteen feet high. There were sentry boxes at each corner of the wall and in the middle of the two long sides. The prisoners were divided into two sections, or *settori*, on either side of the road. We were in Settore II, to the left facing the gate. The Italian officer in charge of Settore II was a small, elderly major. We liked him. He always had a smile and a friendly greeting for us. When our hosts issued an order, we were to salute all Italian officers of equivalent or superior rank. The major was the only one we saluted cheerfully. We evaded saluting the others as much as possible.

Our barracks was next to the guards' barracks, with a double barbed-wire fence between them. There were about thirty men in all the bays but ours, the American bay. The open court between the wings of the U-shaped bungalow was bare dirt with a well and a pump tower in it. Beyond our bay, at the back of the wing, was the latrine on one side and washroom on the other. Each side of the room had a long board table, and each prisoner had a heavy wooden stool. The small light bulbs high up in ceiling at both sides of the bay were turned on and off from a central switch in the Italian compound.

There were fourteen men in the American bay when we arrived. Two Canadians, an American who'd taken British nationality, two Americans who'd driven ambulances with the Free French in Syria and Libya, American members of the Royal Air Force and Royal Canadian Air Force, an army doctor, a Catholic chaplain and a handful of other American officers.

After interrogation we were issued special British Red Cross Christmas parcels. Full of goodies, including a raisin cake in a tin box. It was the first week in January, and our roommates had already devoured their Christmas parcels. They slavered at ours but wouldn't accept handouts when we offered. It was the last time we ever offered to give away food. Besides the parcels, we got a week's Red Cross cigarette ration, forty British Players. Our new friends stressed they were very valuable for trading. I gave Kennedy half of mine and kept the rest to trade. He said they were the last cigarettes he'd ever take from me.

At one o'clock someone yelled, "Grub up!" and we joined a stampede for the back door. Our companions carried Red Cross parcel boxes that clanked and rattled with their contents.

We were assigned to specific seats at long tables and issued knife, fork and spoon. At each place there was a brown bun, a wizened apple and a handful of dried figs and almonds. British Other Ranks (ORs, enlisted men) brought large, chipped bowls of soup from a washroom converted to a serving room. A British officer at the end of our table ladled out scrupulously equal portions to each of us. Cauliflower leaves, pumpkin and plenty of water. As a newcomer, I was given a little extra. We got that pumpkin soup regularly. We called it "Chieti soup." I never learned to love it but I never turned any down.

I took a bite of bread with my soup. The British officer who'd ladled out the soup stopped me. It was my bread ration for the day. The practice was to have half for breakfast, when our hosts served no food, and the other half with tea. Tea? I would learn.

The bay after lunch was as busy as an anthill. Everyone doing something. Scrubbing one of the board tables, fetching bread to pile on it. Rissoles, someone said. Whatever that was. Each man had contributed half a bun (we learned to call them loaves, not buns), an onion from a previous issue and half a cheese issue. They wouldn't let us contribute.

A powerfully built, blond Royal Canadian Air Force (RCAF) fighter pilot was in charge of the operation. Claude Weaver, from Oklahoma. Only nineteen, he'd already had twelve victories when shot down six months earlier.

His assistants crumbled the insides of the bread and grated the crusts on homemade graters and diced onions into bits. When they'd done that, Weaver waved them aside, pushed his sleeves up, added a little olive oil and water to the mass on the table and

began kneading it with his bare hands. From time to time he'd **45**
shout "pepper," or call for curry powder, or salt, or mustard, or
more water. When he'd mixed it all to his satisfaction, he molded
the lot into thirty-four cakes, two for each man in the room. They
were stacked on a headboard and carried off to the cookhouse to be
fried. Weaver explained that twice a week we could have food
cooked to order, one morning and one afternoon. This was our
bungalow's afternoon.

One of our roommates, a second lieutenant in the British
army they called "the Admiral" (I never learned why), introduced
himself and immediately gave me a role in a sketch he'd written
with another roommate, Peter Glenn, from Clarksdale, Mississippi, an American Field Service ambulance driver. Admiral was
short, swarthy and saturnine, dressed in blue woolen battle dress
jacket, khaki desert shorts and broken desert boots. He said he
was from Chicago but didn't sound like it. Although he had no
accent, it didn't sound as if English were his mother tongue. He
didn't look American, either, but neither did a lot of other Americans. He claimed to have been in the Mexican army (but didn't
know what frijoles were), to have been a loyalist major in the
Spanish Civil War in command of all tank forces, and to have been
the last man to surrender at Tobruk. I learned later there was no
one in P.G. 21 who'd known him at Tobruk. It made him suspect.
He was a lot of fun, though.

He knew some French, German and Italian, the words and
music to any song, popular or classical, that you requested, and he
never failed to identify any tune whistled or played for him and, if
there were lyrics, sang them in the language in which they'd been
written. He knew any number of blackouts and skits and was a
better than fair comedian. He knew as many dirty songs as any
British officer in P.G. 21—the British outshone Americans at
that—and could dance an acceptable soft-shoe. He was also suspected by some of being light-fingered with other people's sugar
and the occasional cigarette, but no one ever caught him in the act.

There was a commotion in the front room. Someone shouted,
"Tea up!" which resulted in a mad scramble everywhere for tin
cups and prisoners running for the front door. One of our roommates grabbed two tin buckets with rope handles and ran after
them. While he was gone, another roommate brought the rissoles,
now lovely, toasty brown, from the cookhouse. The man who'd
run out came back with his buckets full of hot tea. Roommates lent

us cups made from tin cans. We had rissoles and tea. Delicious. We were going to like P.G. 21.

The bugler played taps at nine-thirty. It sounded a lot like our own. I hadn't heard taps played since preflight training at Maxwell Field. It had a nice melancholy sound. A welcome sound. All through the camp prisoners got ready for bed. In our bay we lay in our bunks talking until lights out at ten-thirty. When some prisoners kept on talking, there were shouts of "Pipe down!" and "Knock it off!" But talk continued until Colonel Gooler climbed out of his bunk and ordered silence.

I couldn't fall asleep. Too much excitement for one day. I got my Christmas raisin cake out of my parcel box, cut a slice, buttered it and munched in the darkness. Bliss.

We quickly fell into the routine of camp life, as if we'd been there forever. Without knowing how much forever still lay ahead. Up around eight to wash up. The water came on about fifteen minutes later and was shut off again shortly before morning roll call at nine. During the coldest weather roll call was inside. The water sometimes went on again for a few minutes after roll call. It wasn't potable. Drinking water for the hundreds of us in P.G. 21 came from outdoor water taps.

Breakfast was about nine-thirty. Late for the military, but it did make the day seem shorter. We ate in. Our hosts provided a hot beverage. Tea one morning, so-called coffee the next. A selected roommate fetched ours from the mess hall, where it was served out of a huge kettle called a dixie. Some rooms went to the mess hall for breakfast. On coffee mornings the brew was on the kitchen tables in bowls. On tea mornings it was served out of the dixies because with tea on the tables, some prisoners would sneak in early and take more than their fair share. The coffee was too nasty to steal. Except on cooking mornings, the normal breakfast was half the loaf sliced thin, with a film of margarine and jam, issue cheese or fish paste.

Lunch about one. Usually what we'd had our first day, Chieti soup. More rarely, rice. Pretty tasteless stuff. We seasoned it with pepper or curry powder from Red Cross parcels. With the soup and daily loaf there'd be a scattering of dried figs, apples, tangerines, oranges or almonds. The cheese and fish paste issue came twice a week.

Around six, supper. Chieti soup again, but once in a while grayish macaroni sauced with canned tomatoes held out of our parcels for the cookhouse. Twice a week thin soup touched with M and V (tinned meat and vegetable stew also held out from parcels) and sometimes an onion or two, a dab of antipasto or a few dates.

Tea around four, and at eight a hot beverage—coffee, tea or Di-Maltina, an Italian drink like Ovaltine—and once in a while a thick, white drink from a British "comforts parcel." It was a brew meant for invalids and tasted like it. The hot brews, except for the invalid drink, weren't nourishing but they were warming.

Sustenance four times a day and all we thought about was food. Well, girls, too, and maybe home. But mostly food. Doc Henry Wynsen, who bunked with Father Stanley Brach, our resident chaplain, claimed our diet was more healthful than we'd had on the outside. No rich foods, sweets or alcohol. We didn't like hearing that, but he was probably right because our only roommate who showed signs of malnutrition was Larry Allen, the AP man. He wouldn't eat pumpkin soup and traded his sugar for cigarettes.

Nights were restless. My bunk was on the aisle. All night long a parade of men from other rooms passed it on the way to the latrine. And that was just part of the stir. I grew accustomed to it all even if sometimes a Kipling title suggested itself: "The City of Dreadful Night." First, lights out, then a diminishing babble of chatter. In the top bunk across from mine, Marty Lawler, an army captain, wound himself in his blankets, grunting and puffing, his bunk creaking loudly. Allen, usually the first to fall asleep, had nightmares and snorted, groaned and sighed in his sleep. One night he called out, "Mama." Don Waful, an army officer and trombone player, muttered and hummed hot licks in his sleep. From everywhere, coughing and tossing. The creak of a bunk, a groping for shoes, labored breathing as they were pulled on, footsteps hurrying toward the latrine, the bang of the door between it and our bay, the returning footsteps more leisurely, shoes dropping to the floor, again the creaking bunk. Even into the early morning hours the bay was ever alive with gasps, snorts, groans, footsteps, sighs and muttering. And from outside the tread of sentries, their creaking gunslings and muffled conversations when the guard changed. And now and then, a late-night bed-check with whispering in Italian and flashlights playing over bunks. Just before dawn, church bells. First only one, then others joining until we seemed surrounded by churches. (In the spring nightingales joined the chorus, singing the night away in an apple

48   tree outside the wall. Enchanting, but I'd rather have heard mockingbirds.) Some nights there were air raid sirens in the distance (we called them "angels singing") and perhaps the beat of an aircraft. Once an Italian plane started to land in the camp, taking the perimeter lights for runway lights. We could hear the increasing roar of his engine as he let down. When we saw the glow from his identification flares we hit the floor. The sentries turned on their searchlights and warned him off.

Despite the distractions I slept fairly well once I'd nodded off, but unless I was thoroughly tired there'd first be a procession of night thoughts. Implausible escapes. Visions of girls who'd been kind to me and girls who hadn't and imagined girls, the imagined girls sometimes Italian and mingled with the implausible escapes. More often than girls I'd think of food. Crowded shelves in grocery stores, my mother's crab gumbo, James Coney Islands (chili dogs), hamburgers, steaks at Kelley's, spare ribs and hot links, shrimp and crab in all their variations at the San Jacinto Inn ("It cost two dollars," I'd tell slavering fellow prisoners, "but it was worth it.") Banana cream pie at Brooks One's A Meal. Shrimps Arnaud at the Pickwick in Montgomery, Alabama. The meals I'd had on pass in Beirut and Cairo, even the second-rate ones in Haifa. When Kennedy went to eat with me, which was only when he had absolutely nothing better to do, he never even looked at a menu. He's just ask the waiter if they had pork chops. Now he'd sometimes say to me ruefully, "I wish I'd done like you when I had the chance." I guess his mother never told him, as mine did when I went off to be a soldier, to be thrifty but never try to save on food.

The latrine, the goal of so much night traffic, was continental. No seats, just a hole between two raised tiles the right distance apart for efficient squatting. After use, you filled a kitchen-size tomato paste can from a sawed-off cask and slopped the water between the raised tiles. The cask was heavy and unwieldy and took a while to fill with water carried from the washroom taps. Once when there was only a puddle in the bottom too shallow to scoop up in the tomato can, Connie the weightlifter picked the cask up in his mighty arms and emptied it into the hole.

The bungalows, with their tile floors and masonry construction, were like refrigerators. On sub-freezing nights we sat in our bunks or on our stools with our legs drawn up to avoid the tile floor. (During the Korean war when I was at the Pentagon we lived in Falls Church, Virginia, in a house with floor heating. Whenever I stepped out of bed onto that floor I thought about P.G. 21 in winter.) We got a stove in February. We suspected the Protecting Power, a Swiss representative of the International Red Cross who made periodic inspections of our camp, had something to do with getting it. It wasn't much of a stove. Squarish, made of tiles so thick you could sit on top with a fire going full blast inside it and not scorch your ass. If we'd had fuel to keep it properly stoked, the tiles might have radiated some warmth, but the weekly allowance was miserly. My bunk was only four feet from the stove and I never got a calorie's benefit. The stove wasn't entirely useless. Patches of the top got hot enough to toast bread and heat brew water. We made up a roster and put Arthur "Honeybear" Bryant in charge to see everyone got his fair turn on the stove.

We walked a lot for exercise and to kill time. Around the perimeter or up and down the street, even on rainy days. The English wouldn't miss their constitutionals. Some of them marched double time at attention. All that movement made the ferment that had so fascinated us when we first saw into the camp the day we arrived.

There was one English officer who couldn't walk in a straight line. Small, slim, with an operational mustache. He'd been blown up by a land mine in Palestine and it had done something to his sense of balance. He'd drift off to port when he walked and have to make corrections to starboard, getting to where he was going in a series of tacks, like a sailboat. He'd laugh as he did it so we felt free to laugh, too. There was little enough impromptu entertainment to be had.

When we first came to P.G. 21 we were allowed to walk the full perimeter, which included the sidewalk along the wire separating the Italian settore from ours. But after Peter Glenn tried to escape there our hosts blocked it off with barbed wire and painted a line on the street we weren't allowed to cross about thirty feet inside our settore. They also painted the room windows overlooking the fence bright blue so we couldn't see what our guards were doing. We kept scratching "V-Domani" (Victory Tomorrow) in the paint until Colonel Gooler made us quit. He was as fond of "Ite-baiting" as any of us if it made trouble for our hosts, but he was campaigning to have the paint removed. Instead, they covered the window with a white pigment we couldn't scratch through.

The walkable perimeter was narrowed by a nine-meter strip inside the wall, marked by a low, one-rail wooden barrier, the "guard rail." Signs painted on the wall and hung on the guard rail said, "Passage and Demurrage No Allowed." We assumed we'd be shot at if we stepped over the guard rail. When spring came, the only grass in the prisoners' settori grew between the guard rail and the wall. It would have been nice to walk in it barefoot but not worth being shot for.

The warning was more specific than Passage and Demurrage No Allowed just inside the back door of the bungalows. It promised that anyone exiting the back door after dark would be fired on without warning. We didn't believe the guards could hit anything at a distance, but none of us ever tested their marksmanship.

The wall blocked the view of our immediate surroundings except for a few roofs and treetops. The top of an apple tree showed over the wall just behind our bungalow. (When spring came and the nightingales sang in it, it blossomed with rare beauty.)

The countryside was visible in the distance over the wall. To the south, mountains, snow-covered now, said to be the site of a fashionable ski resort. To the east, more hills and, barely visible to the north, toward Pescara, still more. The choice view was to the west. On a hill sloping down to the wall sat the village of Chieti, a smear of buildings against the sky, girt with winter-grayed fields and olive groves. With warmer weather there would be work animals and people in the fields. During air raid alerts civilians would run down into the olive groves for safety. Sometimes girls stood just below Chieti and looked down into our camp, too far away to tell if they were pretty. We liked to think they were. We wondered if they stood there just to tantalize us and we fantasized about them.

A little trolley came along regularly below the crest of Chieti's hill. It looked like the Toonerville trolley in the American comic strip, and that's what we called it. We all intended to ride it when the war was won and we were released. (It didn't happen. It was 1965 before I managed to visit Chieti and by then the trolley line was no more. I did have a good lunch in Chieti, much grown, and I looked down into what had once been P.G. 21 just as I'd once looked up at the village from inside. I hadn't recognized the camp at first. I'd been driven there from Rome in a car provided by Dear Films, which was cooperating with Twentieth Century-Fox in making a movie based on *Von Ryan's Express*, a novel suggested by my P.G. 21 experiences. They'd given me an interpreter and a photographer as well as a car and driver. In a sentry box at the gate was a spit-and-polish soldier who wouldn't let me in until the interpreter got him to phone inside and explain my mission. The forbidding doors were gone from the entrance, replaced by one you could see through into grounds with trees, shrubs, flowers and lawns. It had become an Italian army technical school. My old bay had been subdivided into airy classrooms with white plastered walls. The commandant had himself been a prisoner of the Germans in World War II after Italy's exit. I gave him a copy of *Von Ryan* in Italian and showed him a photograph of the P.G. 21 messing staff taken in front of a paneled wooden door in 1943, with me swarthy in British battle dress at the upper right. He gathered some of his own officers and had my photographer shoot us in exactly the same poses, the commandant himself front and center, as our quartermaster had been in the original. And me swarthy as before, only now in a silk Brioni suit I'd just had made in Rome. The two photos hang together in the room where I work.)

Padre Brach was our spiritual leader, though he didn't push it, and most of us didn't feel or act as if we would benefit from one. He was from New Jersey, regular army, having signed up soon after the seminary. We all thought he was a Jesuit. (I didn't learn differently until 1984 although I'd corresponded occasionally with him for years. I'd started writing for the *Houston Post* and one of the first columns I did was about him. In the course of it I mentioned he was a Jesuit. Padre Brach had a parish in San Antonio then and someone sent him the column. He phoned the paper and left his number. I was living in Los Angeles but happened to be in Houston. I called him. He had liked the column but said he wasn't a Jesuit. He said maybe we all thought so because he was always spouting off. He'd resigned his commission in the Fifties and had been working with the poor in Laredo, Texas, before getting his San Antonio parish. "I'd never had a parish before," he said. "I didn't even know how to run a bingo.") Even in uniform he looked like a priest. Tall, gaunt, gentle but resolute. The Italians often gave him a hard time. What was he, a Catholic priest, doing in the army of Godless America? He was absolutely fearless. A prisoner from his unit said Padre Brach had been at an advanced position helping tend wounded when Stukas dive-bombed the area. Everybody mobile hit the dirt except Padre Brach. With the bombs still falling, he walked calmly among the stretchers. "Look," he said, reassuring them, "don't you think I'd be on the ground if I thought any bombs might land here?" He never requested the repatriation to which he was entitled, but he did request a transfer. To a Japanese POW camp, where he thought he could serve God and his fellow prisoners better.

He was forbearing. We all swore a lot, and obscenities came as naturally as breathing. (It was "fuck all" for none or nothing, "fuck off" for beat it, and "you fuckin' A" for you're absolutely right.) We sang wonderfully disgusting songs we learned from the British: "The Good Ship Venus" ("Her figurehead was a whore in bed and her mast was a rampant penis") and "Cats on the Rooftops" ("Cats on the rooftops, cats on the tiles, cats with the syphilis and cats with the piles") were a couple of them. Padre Brach took me aside once and said, "David, I think you're a very good boy but do you have to sing those awful songs?"

I took him on sometimes, on subjects like the double standard for men and women, but I always lost. We all argued, and lost, with Padre Brach at one time or another. When you had a resident priest, you made the most of it.

Padre and Doc Wynsen had been captured together when they strayed into enemy territory while on a burial party. Doc kept his bristly hair short. His teeth stuck out a little and he wore glasses. He had a sense of humor, dry and deadpan. He claimed he was an obstetrician in civilian life, but we didn't know whether to believe him or not. He joked a lot. He claimed he was carving a chess set. He'd done only one piece, which he carried in his pocket and enjoyed displaying. A penis. "The king," he'd say. "The queen will be different."

"Oh, You Lucky People"

IT HAD NOW BEEN ALMOST A month since I'd had a bath. There was a hot shower room on the end of the cookhouse opposite the theater but it was kept locked. I'd have to use the facilities in the communal washroom. The washroom had a bare tile floor as cold as the floors everywhere else and a water tap set waist high in a tile wall.

At seven in the morning I lay shivering in my bunk, full of dread. Half an hour later came a shout from the washroom. "Water on." I draped myself in my sheet and tried to tiptoe over the frigid tiles to the washroom. I joined the line of scrawny men waiting their turn at the gushing tap. I had to sit on the floor to get under it. The icy water was breath-stopping. I'd heard downed airmen couldn't survive more than five minutes in the North Sea in operations out of England. Not here, either. My butt felt frozen to the floor. My chilblains throbbed. I had to rotate my body to present every inch to the water. If the enemy were doing this to me, I'd be telling them whatever they wanted to know. Then to my feet to get my soap from the ledge where I'd left it and rejoin the line. Soaping up as the line moved forward. Under the tap again. There are some things which do not come easier with repetition. This was one of them.

I wrapped myself in the sheet and raced back to my bunk, drying myself as I ran. We had no towels. My roommates applauded. Numbness turned to glow. I'd never felt as clean before and I was damn proud of myself. I had every right to be. (Since liberation I haven't taken showers if I can help it. Just a long soak in a hot tub.)

Later, I steeled myself to take a bath every week or ten days. In between I'd bathe at a gooseneck tap in the washroom from a basin, using a soapy rag. There were several such taps over troughs along the walls and a trough in the center of the washroom.

When we came to P.G. 21 clothes were scarce. Most of the prisoners were British officers taken in desert khakis that summer at the fall of Tobruk. Mostly shorts and short-sleeved shirts. Their captors hadn't added to their wardrobe, so they wore blankets, one like a skirt and the other draped over the shoulders or, with a slit in it, poncho-style. Jock, a Scot I got to know (we called all Scots "Jock"), a tailor in civilian life, had made himself a proper kilt. He said he wore nothing under it, and if you tried to lift it to look you'd be on your back without knowing how you got there. He claimed it was warmer than trousers. Jock told me haggis (actually a Scottish "delicacy" made of sheep heart, liver and lungs boiled with oatmeal in a sheep's stomach) was a bird that could only be bagged with a shotgun with a crooked ("crew-kid" he pronounced it) barrel that would shoot around corners. I carved a grotesque bird that I named Rosebud and gave it to him. He dyed it black with ink and said it was a night-flying haggis. He kept it in his bunk and offered it breadcrumbs.

With our woolen Italian uniforms, Kennedy, Gardinier and I were better off than most, though Kennedy called them clown suits. Colonel Gooler was incensed by what the commandante had done to them. He was frequently incensed by the commandante.

On the Protecting Power's first visit after our arrival, Colonel Gooler had us hang around wherever he went. The Italian sergente who told us he was really American the day we arrived saw what was going on and left the prisoner compound. Within a few minutes we were summoned to a storeroom and given our pick of new Italian uniforms. They even let us try them on for size. We purposely got them too large. Blouses down to our thighs, pants past our shoetops. Warmer that way.

My wardrobe wasn't extensive but it was adequate. Blouse, pants, shirt, cotton drawers, white Italian socks (thick, hard), my thin GI socks and rubber-soled GI shoes. The shoes were sturdy and damp-proof, but the soles were no insulation from the cold floors. Kennedy and Gardinier got chilblains, too.

Kennedy's thighs and stomach muscles continued to bother him. He thought maybe he'd done himself permanent harm fighting the rudder controls. Doc Wynsen examined him and said not. He'd be okay once it got warm.

We'd gotten our first weekly Red Cross parcel the Saturday after we came. Two men to a parcel. Kennedy and I shared one. Gardinier shared with an Englishman in the next room. The parcels were usually British. Occasionally we had a Scottish parcel issue and more rarely, Canadian, like those we'd had at Poggio Mirteto. Most prisoners preferred Canadian parcels, with their pound can of Klim (powdered milk), a pound each of bully (corned beef) and pork luncheon meat, a big chocolate bar, butter instead of margarine and other things not as available in England. We'd try for a Scottish parcel instead of British when there was a choice. Scottish parcels had a can of compressed oats, which you could get a hell of a trade out of a Scot for, and either cocoa or a can of four dried eggs. British parcels had more variety but, like the British home front, suffered from restrictions. The meat roll was mostly cereal, the condensed milk didn't go half as far as a can of powdered milk, and there was margarine instead of butter (one kind had a paper liner and always tasted rancid), and a little can of turkey, ham or lobster paste that didn't taste like turkey, ham or lobster. But a British parcel might surprise you with pudding, canned bacon (there had been canned bacon at Ramat David; the British cooks' idea of preparing it was putting the can on the stove and letting it warm), pancake flour, pepper, curry powder or mustard. The canned fish varied, too. Sardines, pilchards or herring.

Some of the American prisoners had received American parcels at one time or another. They agreed American parcels weren't very good. The tobacco issue was separate. A choice of forty Players cigarettes or half a four-ounce tin of Players tobacco a week. Later, when we went on full parcels and got American and New Zealand parcels as well as British, we found American parcels were better than they'd been rumored to be but had their drawbacks. Margarine instead of butter, evaporated instead of powdered milk, which didn't go far and soured quickly in hot weather, and a package of orange drink powder nobody wanted. For Vitamin C, Doc Wynsen said. But he didn't like it, either. We'd never heard of the brand names of the chocolate and some canned goods. Maybe they were fobbing cheap goods off on us because we were prisoners. Except for a few like Padre Brach, Doc Wynsen and Alan Stuyvesant, an American Field Service ambulance driver, we were pretty paranoid. Nobody except the International Red Cross and the YMCA and the Vatican cared enough or did enough for us. Where was our mail? Where were our personal parcels?

There were American cigarettes and pipe tobacco as well as

food in the American parcels. The Americans liked that but were angered, too, because, like the canned goods, the cigarettes were brands they'd never heard of.

New Zealand parcels were a treat. Canned creamery butter, outstanding jams, canned bacon and rabbit—some of the Americans had never eaten rabbit before; I'd always liked it but never had it canned—thick, sweet coffee essence, a box of dried peas and British army-ration chocolate in flat tins highly prized for cigarette cases. Some artistic types punched beautiful nailhole designs in their cases.

British prisoners also got personal parcels, but the U.S. wasn't organized for it that early in the war. Because he had connections in Washington, Stuyvesant was the first American to receive personal parcels. His parcels came packed in sturdy plywood boxes and no corned beef or pilchards for him. Canned boned chicken, ham, tongue and his own private blend of pipe tobacco. He shared everything with his roommates except the tobacco. As far as I know, he was the only prisoner in P.G 21 who ever shared a parcel. Of all of us there except Padre Brach, he seemed least oppressed by being a prisoner.

Kennedy and I allowed ourselves only dabs of our Red Cross food at a time. We always had a collection of open cans with remnants in them. We'd carry them with us to the mess hall in cardboard Red Cross boxes with our tin cups and eating utensils, as did everyone else. Hence, the clanking and rattling we'd heard on the way to the mess hall our first day at P.G. 21.

We got four ruled letter forms and three ruled postcards a month. We weren't allowed to write between the lines. My first letter home was mostly a list of things I wanted sent. Large bath towel, sweets, cigarettes for trading, books, ruled notebooks, fountain pen, pencils, socks, woolen underwear, woolen army uniform, khaki uniform, food items. My early letters were full of such lists.

Soon after our arrival at P.G. 21 the British, who liked to keep busy, started up a "university." I signed up for French and German, ancient, modern, medieval, English, and military history, literature, political economics and philosophy. I'd majored in chemistry at Rice and now, with so much spare time, I'd be able to round out my education.

One course I attended wasn't posted on the bulletin board. Sabotage. How to put locomotives out of commission without explosives, how to set up roadblocks from available materials, how to string decapitating wires, how to derail trains, how to shut down dynamos and power plants, and how to destroy aircraft on the ground. Kennedy and I were among those chosen to attend. The instructors always posted lookouts and when a guard approached switched to innocent subjects.

Stuyvesant taught French—he'd been educated in France. Among my other instructors was a skinny, very tall second lieutenant who'd been a full professor at the University of Calcutta and who wore a skirt and shawl of blankets and began each lecture, "It is now exactly nine o'clock and I will begin."

Back at Rice, in my freshman year I'd dropped engineering drawing after a few weeks because I never got the hang of anything connected with engineering drawing. Then, I made excuses to my mother; now I shed one course after another and never mentioned it to her. I was soon down to French and military history. I'd had a year of freshman French at Rice as a senior and made the poorest grades of my college career in it but I liked learning from Stuyvesant and I liked the smell of his pipe tobacco. He had a few grammars from somewhere that we passed from hand to hand. I still have a little notebook I made for his class. The cover is a piece of cardboard from a Red Cross parcel box, lettered PRISONERS' PARCELS, BRITISH RED CROSS & ORDER OF ST. JOHN, and the pages of folded ruled paper are handstitched into it. In the notebook are just a few pages of French vocabulary, a list in very tiny printing of everything left in my room when I was shot down.

A British major, a London stockbroker in civilian life, taught military history. His memory was prodigious. Without notes or books he lectured in meticulous detail on military figures from Alexander of Macedon to Wavell of England and analyzed their major battles. It was said he'd helped General Wavell with the strategy that routed Marshal Graziani's vastly superior forces in the 1940 Western Desert campaign.

It was hard for me to concentrate on studies but reading was different. A book could take you out of the camp. The problem was that of the few books in P.G. 21, all were privately owned. Where they'd got the books I wasn't sure, except for a British pilot with two. He'd had them along when he was shot down. He flew out of Malta. "I'd intended attending the cinema after the do," he said, "and thought I'd drop the books off at the library on the way." Instead he got shot down. He arrived at P.G. 21 dressed for the cinema in tunic, necktie, nicely creased trousers, and well-blacked boots and with the two books intact.

Men who owned books tended to trade reads and what books were available to nonowners had long waiting lists, so I became an owner, trading fifty cigarettes to Peter Glenn for *Dombey and Son.*

Cigarettes were our currency. Fifty for a can of bully beef or Klim, fifteen for a can of sardines, ten for two ounces of sugar. I didn't buy *Dombey* because I was partial to Dickens. I'd only read him when I had to in school. I bought *Dombey* because it was the only book on the market. (In London in 1965 I ran across a purportedly first edition of *Dombey and Son* at Dickens' Old Curiosity Shop on Portsmouth Street. Nine pounds, nine shillings. I bought it, of course, completing a circle. I was in London on the proceeds of *Von Ryan's Express.*) Glenn sold it only because he needed cigarettes to buy chocolate bars and tinned cheese for an escape ration. He was selling off everything he couldn't take with him when he slipped through the wire.

I dived into *Dombey and Son.* I sat in my bunk submerged, coming up for air reluctantly at mealtime. When I'd finished it I urged Kennedy to read it. I intended to charge rental in cigarettes but not to Kennedy, if he read it quickly. He had to read it so we could discuss it, as in the past we'd discussed our favorite comic strip, "Li'l Abner," and most-quoted author, Damon Runyon. Kennedy stayed up all night reading.

We'd been in the camp only about a month when the Red Cross sent in a shipment of British uniforms. Since Kennedy, Gardinier and I had only Italian uniforms, we got the full British issue, battle dress jacket and trousers, wool underwear, sweater, socks, cap, greatcoat. We kept our GI shoes. They were still in good shape and more comfortable than the stiff, heavy British boots. We had to turn in our Italian uniforms. The Escape Committee, a secret organization that reviewed escape plans and helped when it could, asked us to hold out one complete uniform. We managed that by turning in all our Italian clothing but one uniform in a single bundle. The Italians didn't bother to count.

When we were first equipped with Italian uniforms we'd been given three blankets instead of two because we had no greatcoats. We had greatcoats now but the Italians were careless with their inventory and let us keep the extra blanket. We may have slept warmer than anyone else in P.G. 21.

When I was a child in Houston, I went to the show every

Saturday. It was the same at P.G. 21. Our second night at P.G. 21, we'd gone to the theater. It was at one end of the cookhouse. The stage was built on mess tables. The sets were fashioned from newspapers and Red Cross boxes. We brought our own stools. The play was called "Dear Aunt Isabel," about an escape from a German prison camp. We liked it and the idea of it. Those of our hosts in attendance liked it too, but not the idea of it.

Every Saturday there was a variety show or band concert in the cookhouse theater, two a day, so everyone got in. I was on stage myself in the show the Admiral had cast me in on my arrival. Admiral, by the way, tagged me with the nickname "Little Caesar" almost from day one. He said I looked like Edward G. Robinson in the movie of that name. Thereafter, except to Kennedy and Gardinier, I was Caesar. I played a Chicago gangster (not selected for my accent) in a skit for something called the All-American Variety Show. I was teamed with Harold "Mouse" Rideout, a sleepy-eyed American pilot called "Mouse" because of his wispy mustache and furtive air. He was a P-40 pilot. He never saw the plane that shot him down and only learned the details when a pilot came into camp who'd seen it happen. His light blue eyes were rarely fully open. He seldom took them off the ground when he walked. He was small and deceptively fragile-looking but was actually strong and agile. Four of us once tried to wrestle him to the floor to shave off his pitiful golden cat's-whiskers mustache. He squirmed and twisted until we all ended on the floor with Mouse still standing. He never gave a direct answer to any question. What day was it? "Why do you want to know?" He worshipped Claude Weaver and followed him around, Weaver striding around the yard, his handsome blond head held arrogantly, Mouse at his heels, eyes on the ground, hands in pockets. Weaver led him into reckless actions he might never have taken on his own.

In the show, Mouse played a fallen woman I was trying to shake down for my boss, played by the Admiral. Mouse and I rehearsed interminably. Show time. He jumped a cue, I jumped one, and we left out most of our lines. No one in the audience seemed to care, or know. P.G. 21 audiences weren't hard to please.

Stuyvesant played a hillbilly in the sketch, with a large, ragged brood. Casting against type. Stuyvesant (care of the Knickerbocker Club, New York City) was of venerable and distinguished Dutch-American lineage, a brawny, kind, blue-eyed man

60   with a full, reddish-brown beard and a pipe always in his mouth, sometimes with tobacco in it. He hadn't waited for America to enter the war. He'd been a champion boxer in college and was powerfully built but couldn't get into a combat unit because of his age (he must have been in his late thirties or early forties), flat feet and a ruptured eardrum. So he donated an ambulance to the American Field Service and organized a unit which he took to France at his own expense. After France fell, he went to Syria and later to the Western Desert, where he was taken prisoner. His brother, who'd served with him, had been wounded and invalided home. Stuyvesant hated Fascism but bore no personal grudges, even against the commandante and the capitano, the camp adjutant whom we hated. He'd spent much of his childhood in France and his salad days sharing a Paris apartment with his brother. He sometimes entertained us with stories of the smart international set, but as a cynical observer. By birth and education he was in the circle but didn't consider himself a part of it. When we first met, I'd taken a walk with him on the camp street. He asked me what business I was in as a civilian. I told him and asked what business he was in. "My own," he said. I thought he was telling me to mind my own business until he explained he managed some of the family properties. (Stuyvesant was later repatriated. Despite his age and disabilities he talked his way into the military and parachuted into France, where he served fearlessly with the Resistance. After the war, he died in a bizarre fall down the steps of an ocean liner.)

Stuyvesant wasn't our only roommate of distinguished Dutch-American lineage. Joseph Frelinghuysen, a tall captain from New Jersey, was the son of a former U.S. senator and the fifth in a line of military officers reaching back to the Revolutionary War. (He never mentioned the latter to me; I learned of it some decades later from a newspaper interview with him.)

For concerts we had a jazz band, a string ensemble, an accordion band, a Dixieland combo and an understrength symphony orchestra. Some of the instruments were bought from the Italians, the rest provided by the Red Cross, the YMCA and the Vatican. (The Vatican also sent us art materials. The Christmas before our arrival the Vatican had sent other gifts, including valuable stamp albums. At Easter it sent us extra message blanks to mail home. To us, the Vatican had no connection with the enemy.) Tony Baines, a London Symphony bassoonist, led the symphony orchestra. In the latter months of our stay Dick Perry, an American, took it over. He was a P-38 pilot who'd been a composer and conductor for Disney Films in Hollywood. Tom Holt, we called him "Tim" after the actor, was another American who made music for us. A big man with a barrel chest. At first sight he seemed fierce but he was actually kind of prim. The war had interrupted his studies for opera. Instead of singing tenor on stage, he'd become a U.S. Army ranger. He sang with the orchestra and in recital. Arias, "Ave Maria," "Danny Boy," "Smilin' Through." He was a marvelous whistler, too. Whole symphonies. On his stool, making up his top bunk, he'd imagine he was on a podium and get carried away. He'd conduct a phantom orchestra with all the appropriate gestures, whistling passages or hissing through his teeth for the string section. (In 1984 I went to Las Vegas to a reunion of ex-prisoners of Oflag 64, the German camp to which the army officers from P.G. 21 were sent, to see him, Padre Brach, Waful the trombonist, Honeybear and other friends from the Italian days. I asked him if he still conducted the symphony orchestra before he went to bed. Don Waful cried to his wife and Holt's, "See! See! You didn't believe he did that!")

The band had some sheet music, but many of its arrangements were written out by hand, from memory or copied from records. A Scot, Tommy Sampson, the cornet player, was the bandleader. He had lip if not lung and we worshipped him. The baritone sax was Tony Baines, the London Symphony bassoonist. He held his horn in his mouth like a pipe. Nowadays he'd be called laid-back. He made faces when he played, calculated to make us laugh. They did.

The dance band played popular favorites like "Georgia on My Mind," and "Mood Indigo," tunes from original camp musicals, German *lieder*, and, as new men arrived to hum them, the latest hits from home. "White Christmas," "Cow Cow Boogie." Our favorite tunes were "I'll Be Seeing You" and "We'll Meet Again." Lumpy throat stuff. Eventually, with the arrival of a red-headed pilot named Max, who played sax and sang scat, and Vince Shank, a B-17 bombardier who'd been a professional trumpet player, we had a pretty good ensemble.

Though monotony ruled day and night, the British did much to temper it with a variety of entertainments. Some of the plays were originals. Tony Maxton-Graham, husband of Jan Struther, author of *Mrs. Miniver*, wrote an unusually good comedy. Non-

62   originals included *The Merchant of Venice*, *H.M.S. Pinafore*, *The Admirable Crichton* and *Androcles and the Lion*. I had a minor role in a Cole Porter musical. An American reporter with only ad lib lines.

All-male casts, of course, even for a bang-up performance of *The Women*. It got a lot of unwanted laughs when a leading lady swung around and presented an enormous sweep of broad, powerful back in her evening gown. There was bit of a casting problem with *Of Mice and Men*, as well. The physically well-cast Lennie was a Yorkshireman named Bill with an accent you had to be British to truly understand. He was an internationally famous cricket player before the war. George, played by a bushy-haired double first from Oxford who taught in the camp university, had an upper-class British accent. It didn't fit George too well but it was understandable. Bill was good, though, when you got used to his accent. So was the double first, who also did passable water colors, played in the band, and recited humorous doggerel in variety shows. The plays ran as long as there was an audience for them. Italian officers often attended, either because they were as starved for entertainment as we were or to keep tabs on us. Though several of them spoke fair English, British humor usually baffled them.

The British officers were generally polished performers. The public school types had been doing amateur theatricals from childhood through university and some of them had continued to do them after that. A couple of the officers did what our British friends said were fine imitations of music hall stars. One of them introduced us to the style of Max Miller, bounding out of the wings dressed in a flashy suit made of cheesecloth and scraps and shouting, "Oh, you lucky people!" Our Max Miller favorite was "I tickle me lady's fancy with the end of me old cigar." The other, in drag, did a famous comedienne whose signature song was, "My old man said to follow the van, but don't dilly dally on the way." And there was an officer who busker-clogged, another who did Buster Keaton with a dash of Harpo Marx, and a champion boxer from the Indian army who did Cockney bits.

The British worked in drag without embarrassment. They'd been doing it in all-boys' schools for generations. An officer in a Sikh regiment (Sikhs were notably brave and their British officers had to be the same, we were told) made an alluring tall, willowy blonde. He let his hair grow long for his roles and on demand could move and gesture fetchingly. Not so with one of our other drag regulars. He was too broad-shouldered and narrow-hipped to dare turn his back on the audience. (Windell "Dell" Myers, an American pilot from Tyler, Texas, made a gorgeous blonde but was only persuaded to attempt it once. He was so embarrassed he could hardly get through the performance.)

The major who taught military history had a small collection of records and a player. I discovered that early in my stay. I was taking a walk and heard music coming from the front of a bungalow. I climbed onto a ledge and looked in. The major and several of his friends were in a close circle around the record player listening intently to Carmen Miranda. The major doted on her. He'd been one of our interrogators the day we came in and after penetrating questions about military matters had been eager for news of her. He invited me in. I climbed in the window and joined the circle. When he'd played the rest of his records he repeated those I'd missed. When I learned later how scarce records and phonograph needles were at P.G. 21, I realized what a favor he'd done me.

One day there was a furious clamor in the yard. Ten or fifteen officers in American uniform were ushered through the gate. Kennedy, Gardinier and I became part of the same kind of pushing, shouting crowd that had first greeted us. We learned they'd been captured about the same time we were but had been interned in a particularly dirty camp instead of the quarantine camp at Poggio Mirteto. They were mostly artillery officers whose guns had been overrun in Tunisia. There were some infantry, tank and flying officers, too.

Two of the airmen were in poor shape. Dell Myers and his navigator, William "Mike" Mikolasy. Particularly Dell. His shirt was stiff and black with dried blood from a wound in his neck covered with a filthy bandage. Both men were crawling with lice and badly bitten. They'd been confined in infested quarters and hadn't had a bath or changed clothes in more than a month. Dell was sent off to the hospital at once. Mike took a bath under a washroom tap while his clothes were fumigated. He emerged clean but deathly pale.

The next American arrived alone. A B-24 navigator from New Jersey named Ted Schoonmaker. He had a hard time getting his story out. His voice faltered and he groped for words. He'd spent two weeks at Poggio Mirteto, as we had, but still hadn't gotten over the trauma of being shot down. He was the only one of his ten-man crew to survive and had seen one of his friends fall past, his chute streaming above him like a Roman candle.

He was from the 376th Bomb Group, a B-24 outfit stationed at Lydda, near Tel Aviv. He said he'd been on the mission where we'd bought it and that our plane was seen to have ditched offshore, with fishermen pulling toward the wreckage in rowboats. And also, that three days after the raid, Radio Rome broadcast our names as prisoners of war. Comforting to learn.

I gave him bread with jam and butter, as our roommates had done for us on arrival. I was an old hand now. He had plenty of Italian cigarettes and, as Kennedy had done, offered them around. No takers, naturally. He couldn't understand that.

The night after Schoonmaker arrived the lights went off soon after dark, signifying the approach of Allied aircraft. We didn't hear any and the lights came on again. Guards rushed in for a surprise roll call. The lights went out again while they were trying to count. When they came on again, Dogass Newman, Mouse Rideout and Claude Weaver were in their bunks, red-faced and panting. Roll call. The count got to Peter Glenn.

Peter Glenn, P.C.T. Glenn, from Clarksdale, Mississippi. A practicing romantic who was always trying to escape as much for the thrill of it as to get back to the outside world. Just graduated from Dartmouth, he volunteered for the American Field Service because one of his favorite instructors had served with the AFS in World War I. He wore a floppy Australian hat with the side turned up and a muffler tossed carelessly across his shoulder. He'd read classic Greek dramas in the original and knew Dante's *Divine Comedy* in both Italian and English.

A voice said, "Here." But it wasn't Glenn's. It belonged to Dell, who was supposed to be in the hospital. The guards left and returned with a hospital orderly, who recognized Dell. While they were still counting the rest of us, guards brought in Nobby Sproule, one of our roommates who'd been in the hospital with a prison sore. He'd slipped out of the hospital to answer roll call for a missing British officer.

Nobby. Noble Sproule. Gun-crazy, baby-faced, slim and powerful. Except for his unruly blond hair, he was what we called "regimental." Heavy boots spit-shined, pants always washed and pressed (under his palliasse) with the crease sewn in. His first personal parcel had a button-polishing kit in it and he used it regularly. Born in upper New York State, he'd grown up in Canada. He'd become an officer in the British army and had taken British citizenship to do so. Captured in the Western Desert. Those who knew him there said he was recklessly fearless. His favorite diversion was night patrol behind German lines to bring back prisoners or kill. He'd done commando raids in Syria against the Vichy French.

He and Dell were taken back to the hospital to await transfer to the cooler—solitary confinement. Nobby took it in stride but Dell was bewildered. He'd been hustled to the hospital as soon as he arrived and didn't know any of us, even Glenn, whose place he'd taken. And now he wasn't going to meet anyone for another thirty days.

Glenn and his friend Toby, the officer Nobby substituted for, had gotten past the fence but had been captured in the Italian compound. The guards had been almost as glad to get Glenn's escape ration chocolate bars, Red Cross cheese and Red Cross biscuits as they were to get Glenn himself.

It was a rough night for Schoonmaker. Still shaky from his disastrous final mission, he wondered what kind of place he'd landed in. We tried to convince him that sort of thing didn't happen every night.

Next morning at roll call—the British called it "parade"—we all agreed to shout "cooler" when Glenn's name was called. So, when his name was called, I did. I was the only one. The capitano gave me one of his lingering inspections. Tall, slim, with a pointed black beard and a neat mustache, he was dressed as usual in impeccable gabardines and polished riding boots. (Sometimes he wore ski boots instead.) He lounged gracefully with a little tilt from the waist, regarding me through his monocle, elbow on hip, left glove in his gloved right hand. Sometimes, but not today, the hand also held the leash of a German shepherd puppy. (We managed to lure the puppy into our room once when the capitano was in the guard compound and painted a large V for victory on its back.) The capitano looked every bit the perfect villain in a Hollywood movie. We suspected he cultivated the image deliberately.

Whether it was a façade or not, we actively disliked him even more than we disliked the commandante and the sergente who claimed to be one of us. Although the commandante was the ultimate authority at P.G. 21, it was the capitano who enforced his many petty regulations and he seemed to enjoy doing it. He was rumored to be a count. His English had only a slight, and to us sinister, accent.

We saw considerably less of the commandante than of the capitano, who presided at roll calls and who might pop in unexpectedly any time. But sometimes we'd hear the commandante shriek at his own troops as he had at us the day of our arrival.

We saw a lot of the sergente, too. He often visited with Americans, pretending secret sympathies. We thought him a spy and sneak, trying to make points with both sides. He loved America, he said, and planned to return after the war.

Now, shrinking under the capitano's gaze, I was afraid I'd soon be joining Glenn, Toby and Dell in the cooler, but my embarrassment was enough to gratify him. He let it pass.

Everything considered, it was one of my better days at P.G. 21. During the night before, between blackouts, I'd made a pudding for Kennedy and me. Soaked prunes, raisins, bread, grated biscuits and orange peel, almonds and a touch of Klim, sugar and jam. Now I cut up onions and meat roll. It was a cooking day and Kennedy and I were having the meat roll and pudding for tea.

And it was payday. And we got our first hot shower.

First lieutenants drew a hundred lire twice a month in camp money. The rest of our Italian pay went into a daily messing fee and a reserve fund kept by our hosts. Some of that was apparently like a clean-up deposit for renters. If an escape team broke through a floor to start a tunnel, for example, when it was discovered the cost of repairs was deducted from the reserve fund. Where the rest went we never learned.

We used the camp money to buy things from the room canteen, which stocked, not necessarily all at the same time, toothpaste, razor blades and the like, imitation leather wallets, pens, paper, ink and Italian sweets that weren't very sweet but were very expensive—some sort of toffee, imitation chocolate, dried fig bars, a fluffy white nougat. The sweets were scarce and we bought them by roster. Sometimes when a man's name came up he was too deep in the hole to pay, as happened to me on occasion. My money usually went for paper, pen, ink and poker debts. Dennis Newman, Fort Worth, Texas, ran the canteen. He was a Wimpy (Wellington) bomber pilot in the RCAF and was shot down twice before it finally took. We called him Dogass but the name didn't fit him. Black, wavy hair, neat black mustache. He was always twisting the ends and claimed to own a couple of bawdy houses in Buffalo, New York, but we didn't believe him. Too much the gentleman. He admired Aldous Huxley's writing, which I'd learned to dislike at Poggio Mirteto, finding Huxley a terrible snob. We had long arguments about it. Dogass was good at figures and kept the canteen accounts. He spent most of his waking hours trying to reconcile his books and dunning the roommates who owed the most.

You could get a haircut for one camp lira at a barber shop of sorts in the washroom of the mess hall on the other side of the cookhouse from ours. The two OR barbers were expert. I never learned if they'd been professionals before the war or had gotten good with practice. There were no hot towels for a P.G. 21 shave, nor hot water. But we were used to that. I got haircuts but seldom bought a shave. Cheaper to do it myself with blades no duller and water no colder than the barber shop's. Haircuts were by appointment but you could get a shave just by showing up early in the morning before roll call. The few times I bought shaves there were always four Scots in another room in the mess hall practicing Scottish dancing to the skirl of several bagpipes. More than worth the price of the shave. There was another room with a piano in it. Every morning the same British officer was at it practicing "Liebestraum," making the same mistakes and starting over again. He never got any better.

I was in the hole to the canteen for months. Paydays, my camp money went into my account instead of my pocket except for ten lire diverted to a fund for second lieutenants. They got no camp money because their allowance didn't even cover the reserve fund our hosts held out for damages to Italian property. But this payday, which was also shower day, I had money coming.

The showers were on the opposite end of the cookhouse from the theater. It was cold that day. We stood in line outside, wearing only shoes and greatcoats. We'd all brought our stools to sit on while dressing and our sheets to use for towels. When the group ahead of us came out looking clean and smug, my group rushed in and spread out among the white shower stalls. Pristine. We left our shoes, greatcoats and sheets on our stools. A guard turned on the hot water. Heaven. Five minutes to soap up, rinse off and luxuriate. The guard turned on the cold water. We were all out of the stalls by the time the cold water hit the floor. Dry, dress, out. Next group, please.

We were told we'd have regular showers from then on, but they lied. We'd gotten the showers to impress the Protecting Power, who was due in any day.

Learning the Trade

IN FEBRUARY *Il Popolo Di Roma,* one of the papers allowed in camp, ran a photograph of a B-24 it claimed had been captured intact in Sicily. Blonde Bomber II. We knew Blonde Bomber was a 98th Bomb Group plane but couldn't remember who the pilot was. We fretted over that until one day about three weeks later a British friend hurried into the room and told me four American airmen had just arrived at P.G. 21 and were at the mess hall being fed. I ran to the mess hall and found "Dapper" Dan Story from the 343rd Bomb Squadron; his bombardier, Ed Griffin; navigator, Jerry Perlman; and copilot, Jim Giblin, whom I didn't know. (We called Dan "Dapper" because he wasn't.) I cried, "Dapper, what the hell are you doing here?" (Why did we always greet newcomers we knew with that?)

He looked at me uncertainly, then at the orderly who'd brought them their Chieti soup.

"Is it all right for me to act like I know you?"

When I told him it was, he said he'd hoped to run into Kennedy and the rest of us but was afraid if he acknowledged he knew us it might reveal something to the enemy. His plane had been badly shot up on a Naples raid. After coming off the target, Perlman had been unable to keep track of their position because of Dapper's violent and prolonged evasive action. Alone in the dark, crippled, with an undercast hiding all below and an overcast obscuring the stars Perlman needed to get a position, their only hope was to try for Malta, the nearest friendly territory. The radio operator tuned in to the Malta beam and Perlman homed in on it. A tip of land appeared through a hole in the undercast. Dapper circled. The radio compass needle kept pointing to the tip of land. Malta, confirmed. From the ground a green-green flare, indicating they were cleared to land. Dapper brought the badly damaged plane in safely. Did a hell of a job, Griffin said.

Dapper crawled out first. He'd landed on Malta before. Now he didn't recognize anything. Dark shapes scurried in the darkness at the edge of the strip. He called out to them, asking where he was.

"Sicilia, Sicilia!" was the answer.

"At first I didn't know what the hell was going on," Dapper said. "Then it hit me they were talking Italian."

He scrambled back in the plane and told the crew. The radio operator punched a button that blew up the I.F.F. (Identification, Friend or Foe) device and Griffin emptied his .45 into the bombsight. They were trying to smash the gas gauge before setting the plane on fire when the enemy closed in, firing as they came. They thought Griffin's shots had been at them. The crew never got a chance to destroy the aircraft.

Dapper was downcast about that, and about being lured into landing in enemy territory. He figured he was in deep trouble back at Group. It continued to trouble him even after he learned that experienced British pilots who flew off Malta had been tricked in bad weather by the false Malta signal beamed from the Sicilian airfield. Eventually he learned that all was known, and forgiven, back at base. And that he'd become something of a legend. His plane, patched up and flown by the enemy, was sometimes seen birddogging elements of the 98th on bombing missions. They called the plane *Story's Ghost.*

Story told us that Killer Kane had become commanding officer of the whole group and that some of our friends were finishing up their missions and going home. It didn't cheer us up a whole lot. And we'd all been awarded Distinguished Flying Crosses and Air Medals for combat hours (one hundred for Air Medal, two hundred for DFC) in a ceremony in the Western Desert. Others were decorated at the same ceremony but, Dapper said, a hush fell when our names were called and the Group adjutant whispered to the visiting general making the awards that we were POWs. That we did like.

Dapper was first assigned to an all-British room. An outgoing Texan from Corsicana, he never really adjusted to English reserve, and everyone was happier when Colonel Gooler managed to get him reassigned to our room.

Not long after Dapper Dan joined us instruction started in judo and silent killing, taught by British commandos and American rangers. My Scottish friend Jock was one of the instructors. I didn't take the course but Schoonmaker did. He'd gotten over the trauma of being the only man on his crew to survive but still spoke with frequent pauses. Seems it was natural with him and had nothing to do with trauma. (When he visited us in Houston shortly after the end of the war my wife kept trying to finish his sentences for him; she's an impatient woman.)

Barnes arrived, finally. We hadn't expected him. He wasn't allowed to bunk with us. He went to the OR quarters across the way. A staff sergeant, he turned out to be the camp's ranking noncom and so was put in charge of the enlisted staff, which didn't sit well with some of the British ORs who'd had a lot more time in the bag than he did. After our first joyful reunion he came to our room frequently to visit.

As an enlisted man, Barnes got the working bread ration, almost triple ours. We didn't work and were on garrison rations. We didn't even make our own beds or sweep our own rooms. It was a British camp and operated the British way, and the British way was for officers to have orderlies.

Barnes and the ORs didn't get some of the extras that officers received, fruit, for example. It was because the extras weren't part of the regular ration and had to be purchased on the Italian market. The black market, it was rumored. Q, as we called our camp quartermaster, a British captain who'd been a German POW in World War I (the British called it "the 14-18 War"), often distributed some of our extras among the ORs. He'd been one himself in the other war.

Generous as always, Barnes sometimes offered Kennedy and me some of his bread. (Gardinier had made close friends in another room and wasn't around much.) He wouldn't take other food or camp money for it so at first we seldom accepted.

Barnes and I visited frequently and I made many friends among the ORs, most of whom never came to the officers' barracks except sometimes to work. Americans thought it odd to maintain so rigid a military caste system when we were all in the same sorry plight. However, it was a British camp and we didn't openly flaunt the rules.

Barnes never ate his full ration of bread, so finally when he insisted I take a loaf or two back for Kennedy and myself I'd accept. In return, though he resisted, we'd buy him things at our room canteen or force camp lire on him to make purchases at the OR canteen. Other Ranks worked hard and their quarters were more crowded than ours but those who'd been at OR camps said they were treated better here than in the exclusively enlisted camps. As a rule they seemed content with the British caste system, but there were two who resented it fiercely. One was an American sergeant from Oklahoma who'd been a minor league pitcher and who owned a good-sized ranch. A scowl seldom left his face when he made up bunks in our bay. I didn't blame him. There were officers among us he wouldn't have hired to work for him in civilian life. The other was an always meticulously groomed British sergeant with what Americans called an Oxford accent. He spent what time he could with American officers who didn't consider ORs socially inferior.

Our hosts were much stricter with Other Ranks than with officers. Four of them were sent to the cooler for laughing during roll call. The Senior British Officer got them out before they'd served their whole sentence.

But being an OR had an advantage: close contact with Italian enlisted men. Things like tea and soap weren't worth much within the camp but were highly prized outside. The Other Ranks got them at bargain rates and traded them to their guards. Neither Other Ranks nor officers were supposed to trade with the Italians but ORs ignored the rules. On the whole, they were better at making do than officers. I learned a lot from them.

Books trickled into the camp from the Red Cross and YMCA and from British personal parcels. The prisoner staff started a library in one of the small front rooms across the road from our bungalow. There weren't enough books on the shelves for general circulation so the library had a priority system. Contribute two books, you got an A card and went first. One, a B card and went second. No card got the leavings, and very slim pickings they were. I contributed *Dombey and Son* and got a B card. After that I read a lot.

P.G. 21 had a well-developed barter system. The economy was based on cigarettes. We didn't trade cigarettes as much as we did food items but the price system was based on value in cigarettes. Prices were usually stable but subject to change when a new lot of parcels brought scarce items. When Scottish parcels were distributed, for example, tinned oats went down.

I developed trading fever. Though trading never came naturally to me, I became indefatigable at it. I was always open to a deal, and some of them took long-range planning, but parcel day was the most active time. A typical parcel day's trades: an OR loaf for half a British meat roll, two Canadian and six English biscuits (the English biscuits were smaller); the biscuits for half a tin of bacon; a British meat roll for a half-pound tin of margarine; half a can of evaporated milk for a bottle of Italian ketchup (offered by an OR who refused to reveal its source). The ketchup was a gamble. It was such a novelty I expected to unload it at a huge profit. I did get some nice offers but in the end Kennedy and I had it ourselves. My major trade of the day was a painfully-amassed cocoa tin of sugar for six OR loaves.

I took my tea straight to save sugar, worth ten cigarettes for two ounces and popular with the ORs. They brewed the officers' tea and therefore always had more tea than the officers. You could get several OR loaves, which were bigger than ours, for a tall cocoa tin of sugar. Barnes helped with those trades.

And I haunted the bulletin boards in the front of every bungalow studying swap notices. It was like the commodities market, sort of. Kennedy wouldn't trade. I had to do it for both of us. (After the war I was never in the market, ever. But Kennedy was active in the market and real estate, too. Made a killing in commodities one year and was killed bigger the next. So he switched to mutual funds.) I drove hard bargains, except with Kennedy and Barnes, and got a bad reputation. Not as bad as Weaver, though.

On parcel days he ranged the camp like a timber wolf, looking for victims. He had no shame. The more lopsided the bargain, the better he liked it. He was a super trader. (When Italy got out of the war he and Mouse escaped together. Weaver returned to combat and was killed on a RAF fighter sweep over France.) He traded Colonel Gooler two tins of British sugar (four ounces) for a tin of English biscuits. He went off and within the hour returned with two bags of Canadian sugar (eight ounces) for the English biscuits. And gloated.

Weaver was Colonel Gooler's cross. He was wild and reckless and always getting in trouble. On sleety nights he'd go to the window and call out to the freezing guards walking the wire outside our bungalow. "Dormi bene, sentinello." "Sleep well, sentry." Sometimes he, Mouse and Dogass saved their dried figs and after lights out pelted everyone with them. One night after Colonel Gooler had banned such food-throwing, Jack "Jake" Otten, a Canadian pilot shot down on the first torpedo run ever made by a

Wimpy, started things by hitting Weaver with an apple core. Weaver responded with a barrage of dried figs.

Colonel Gooler rose from his bunk in all his wrath, strode to Weaver's bunk, and ordered him to cease fire. Weaver said someone else had started it. A grave mistake. Colonel Gooler gave him the most artistic eating out I'd ever heard. A great surprise to all. As a captain in the Regular Army, he'd commanded high school ROTC units and Civilian Concentration Corps camps. He was more scoutmaster than Senior American Officer and treated us more like a troop of Boy Scouts than a roomful of restless, rowdy, dirty men. He had a genuine scoutmaster's understanding of unruly youngsters. Paternal, sort of, especially with Weaver. Until now we hadn't an inkling he was such an expert at racking a man back.

We knew about his temper, though. Once when he had a cold he organized some cough medicine from the dispensary. It was a scarce item, like all medications at P.G. 21. He'd taken only two doses when he dropped the bottle on the tile floor. He turned white, then red, stamped his foot a little but didn't yell. To the dispensary again for another bottle. This one he dropped taking his first dose. He stomped. He swore. We hid our faces in our pillows to stifle our laughter. Kennedy and three others were playing bridge a few feet from Colonel Gooler's bunk, with nothing to hide behind. Kennedy was the first to break. He jumped up and ran to the latrine. The other three bridge players weren't far behind. We could hear them hooting with laughter in the echoing latrine. After a while Colonel Gooler simmered down and apologized to us.

When warm weather came the Italians let enough parcels in to give us our proper ration, one per man per week. Food prices went down and my trading fever abated. I gave good deals. My reputation improved retroactively. Most of those I'd dealt with now thought I'd been a fair trader all along.

I didn't do nearly as well at poker as I did on the commodities market. I'd usually won in our daily sessions on the porch at St. Jean before the Group moved to Egypt. No longer. Maybe it was the kind of games we played in P.G. 21. Twistertit, a deadly high-low game. A game called Blood. We had no chips or markers, so we recorded all transactions. We bet large sums, much more than we had, or ever would. Admiral kept the books. We paid off by a complicated system he devised based on the amount lost by the second biggest loser. Somehow Admiral never had a losing day at the poker table.

Sometimes we played all night. The only light was in the washroom so we moved the table in there. The guards reported that. The capitano was sure we were only doing it to cover up tunneling operations and made us stop playing after lights out.

Kennedy wasn't interested in poker. He got into bridge. He'd never played before, but he had great card sense and quickly got good at it. He made me learn bridge so I could be his partner. I didn't have card sense. He dropped me and partnered with Willie, an American bomber pilot with the RAF. Willie had hoboed around a while before going to college and getting a degree in geology. Intelligent, well-educated, shrewd. He was hard and bitter and a pugnacious troublemaker sometimes, but he could be a good friend, and he was to Kennedy and me. He escaped after Italy capitulated. (After the war, when I was back at the *Houston Post*, Willie phoned me at the paper. He was in town on business. Could my wife and I join him for dinner? She couldn't so there was just the two of us. He had a few drinks and began staring belligerently at a party of men at a nearby table. Luckily for them and me, they ignored the challenge.)

The bridge players kept the same long hours as the poker players. We overdid everything because we had so much time on our hands. When an activity cloyed, we turned to something else. But there was no escaping time.

Westry, a British officer I'd come to know when I was an active trader, helped me find a new outlet. Woodcarving. He was good at it. Working with bits of razor blades, he'd made a beautiful pocket chessboard, complete with case and pieces. I'd done a little woodcarving myself. I'd gotten into it while waiting late at night for Hubert Roussel, my boss on the *Houston Post*, to tell me I could go home. In those days zinc engravings were mounted on beechwood blocks for printing photos in the paper. Beech was excellent for whittling and I spent some productive hours with my pocketknife. And while at St. Jean I'd bought a block of olive wood in Haifa, carved a buxom reclining woman, and polished it and rubbed it down with bombsight oil until it glistened. I named it "Wishful Thinking." I still have it.

Westry showed me how to secure shards of razor blades into handles of bent tin. With these and my table knife, well-sharpened on cement, I did some carvings of my own. I gave them to friends.

Gardinier developed a knack of his own, and a more useful one than mine. He became one of our leading tinsmiths. He invented a cup handle with self-locking seams made out of folded cocoa tins that everyone wanted. He made handles for Kennedy, Barnes and me. When the demand for Gardinier handles overwhelmed him, he made patterns so his friends could make their own. The only flaw in his design was that the handles were made to fit butter tins, which held less than the standard cup made from a British biscuit tin. For normal use I preferred a cup with a wooden handle fastened to a biscuit tin with twisted wire. I carved my handle into a slender nude, which was widely admired. With frequent use the cups became encrusted with a heavy brown deposit. When the deposit got thick enough to taste we changed our handles to other tins.

Westry told me I couldn't pronounce Houston or even my own name. Houston shouldn't be pronounced Euston, as in Euston Station, but should be pronounced Howston. And Westheimer, that should be Weemer. As Cholmondoly is Chumley. He always called me Weemer. He said the difference between the Americans and the English was that Americans thought they were the best and Englishmen knew they were. And he told me since I'd been a journalist I should visit a certified novelist in another room in our bungalow. Victor Canning. I went to Canning's room and introduced myself. As a fellow writer, sort of. A newspaperman. Canning was unimpressed and made no effort to conceal it. (In 1948 my first novel, *Summer on the Water*, shared space with his tenth, *Panther's Moon*, in the Literary Guild publication *Wings*.)

We came to prefer British slang to our own, just as we preferred their dirty songs. More colorful and inventive. "Bumpf" for toilet paper. To "have had it," to have run out of luck or be done for. To "have bought it," to be killed. We retained our own "buy the farm," to crash and die. "In the bag," to be in prison camp. "Push the tit," press the gun-trigger. "Duff," pudding but "duff gen" was misinformation. "Scoff," eat or food. "Bash," eat the whole thing. "Piece of piss," like "piece of cake," something easy. Some slang was Indian army. "Pukka gen," authentic information. "Give a shuftee," have a look (ours was "run a reccy"). "Dhobi," wash clothes. And from Egypt, "buckshee" (same as New Orleans' lagniappe).

I had recurring dreams. Not about women. We all had sexual

dreams but more rarely than would be expected of young men deprived of women. Despite considerable sexual tension, cold, hunger, uncertainty, and perhaps subconscious fears shaped our dreams. My most common dream was finding myself on leave from P.G. 21 for the weekend and shopping in a big grocery store in Houston. The shelves were filled with the things I most wanted. I scrambled to buy as much as I could before my time was up, but I always had to get back to camp without having bought a thing. Other times I'd be in a soda fountain with an elaborate sundae before me from which I never managed to take a bite.

Or I'd dream I was back home, not knowing if I'd escaped or been liberated. But home. And no one made anything of it. My friends and even my mother acted as if I'd never been gone, greeting me with only a casual "Hello." Sometimes my mother would scold me for something minor when she answered the door.

Or Kennedy and I would be back at Kabrit, having escaped (I never dreamed of the actual escape), and Killer Kane would order us out on a mission after one day of rest. I'd protest that I'd forgotten my navigation and Kennedy's flying was rusty. Sometimes we were flying again and our plane crashed but never as it actually had happened.

I dreamed about Leader. Always the same. He'd come into our room and I'd tell him I thought he was dead. He'd laugh and say he'd gotten away but they'd finally captured him.

Kennedy may have had similar dreams but the only one he bothered telling me about was that he was in a hotel in Kansas City, so vividly real that when he woke and felt the wooden post of his bunk he wanted to cry.

At P.G. 21 I started smoking. I hadn't smoked a cigarette since I was twelve, showing off. At thirteen or so I'd smoked a cigar and been fearfully sick. I hadn't smoked a cigar again until Cairo, when I saw a selection at Shepheard's Hotel and had an urge. I asked Kennedy to pick a good one for me. It was only after I paid for it that I realized it cost sixty cents, U.S. Big money. In Houston you could buy dinner for that. It wasn't bad, for a cigar. I thanked Kennedy for his choice. He said he didn't know anything about cigars. He never smoked them himself. He'd picked it because it was the most expensive.

Italian cigars were different. They were thin, crooked and dry. We sometimes got them as part of our Italian tobacco ration, which was more usually cigarettes. I would smoke a cigar when I was cold, hungry and dejected, which was fairly often during the winter. I'd light up and join the throng taking the air out on the street. About halfway through I'd get sick. Really sick. I'd sweat and want to throw up. I'd run to my bunk, and for a while, fighting nausea, I'd forget cold and hunger. It was an acceptable trade-off. (Years later, back in Houston, a friend of mine named Jim Lattanza offered me one of the imported Italian cigars he favored. I said Italian cigars made me sick. He said this one wouldn't. Two puffs and I was ill and back at P.G. 21 in memory.)

The room canteen got in a small stock of pipes, and after finally settling my account with Dogass I bought two for souvenirs. They sat idle in the Red Cross box where I stored my worldly possessions until we began getting an occasional American Red Cross parcel issue. Among the contents was a package of George Washington pipe tobacco. I tried to trade mine but there was no market. So I began smoking it myself. At first I got almost as ill as I had with the poisonous Italian cigars. I persevered. There were few pleasures available in P.G 21 and I wanted to take advantage of any I could even if I hated it.

After a while I could smoke without problems if I did it out of doors and on the move. Eventually I could smoke indoors, sitting.

One day Mouse, the room's messing representative, forgot to tell us to bring our knives to the mess hall to cut up onions. We did that when there was to be fried onions on the menu the next day. Apparently Mouse had fouled up the detail before because Colonel Gooler fired him on the spot. And gave me the job. I'd been trading Colonel Gooler cigarettes for sugar at an honest rate and he appreciated it.

There were duties involved, but there were perks, too. I took my meals with the rest of the messing staff in the mess hall washroom–serving room, took my turn on the roster helping the orderlies set up tables and serve up brews, issued the Italian sugar ration to my roommates, and gave them mess hall gen.

With Frelinghuysen's and Allen's help with the translation, I posted daily menus on our bulletin board:

"Dejeuner—Potage a la Chieti (pumpkin soup), Corbeille de Fruit (an apple or an orange), Pan (the loaf), Fromage (the sliver of cheese). Pranzo—Minestra con Carne (the M & V stew), Frutta (dried figs)."

On my orderly officer days for afternoon tea my only duty was to see that the orderlies brought the big dixies from the cookhouse. For evening brew I went to the cookhouse with three volunteers from the bay to pick it up. It took four of us to carry a dixie. Two handles stuck up from the top of a dixie across from each other. In the cookhouse, a winch and pulley lifted dixies by the handles but for outside transport we used a long, stout pole stuck through them. Two men at each end. It was about two hundred yards from the cookhouse to our bungalow, the last in the row. Quite a haul for men as out of shape as we were except for the few like Frelinghuysen, who exercised vigorously. And he was too tall to be a good carrying partner.

At the bungalow I'd stick my head in the door and bellow, "Brew up!" The occupants spilled out and formed double lines to the dixie, where the previous day's orderly officer and I ladled out the brew. There were always a handful of men hanging around while the last room was being served. They were real tea addicts, waiting to see if there'd be any left in the bottom of the dixie. There usually was. And when they'd had their seconds, if there was still tea left I'd stick my head in the door and shout, "Buckshee!"

Another orderly officer duty was seeing that meals were brought to the mess hall. The cookhouse wasn't equipped to cook anything but soup for all the prisoners at once. Our mess usually had a somewhat different menu from the one across the street. We might be having fried onions and the other mess not. I had to insure we got the fried onions and not them.

I'd meet our mess orderlies at the cookhouse and, checking with Derek, the officer who ran it, see that we had the proper ration. Soup was heavier than tea and the British orderlies generally smaller than the officers (not true with American officers and enlisted men). It was a struggle for some of the orderlies even though the mess hall was just across from the cookhouse. Sometimes, though rarely, an orderly would stumble and spill soup. Short rations that day. In the serving room I'd help dish it out, following a list. So many sixes, so many sevens (the number of men at a table).

I'd also divide the regular jam issue. It came in big blocks. Frank, the head orderly, a blond Welsh youth, did most of the work. His father had served with Q, our quartermaster, in World War I and Q took a paternal interest in him. We'd slice the blocks after evening mess for distribution the next day. The issue had to come out even. I liked Frank to do the dividing because he was able to do that with usually a dab left over. Which he gave to me. He helped in another way, too. When I couldn't understand the dialect of some of the other orderlies, he translated for me. He once showed me a photo of his family. His father, a stony faced Welshman; his extraordinarily plump mother; and his two round-faced sisters.

Q divided the sugar ration, half an ounce per day per man, issued weekly by room. Sugar was too precious to be trusted to less-experienced hands. Q was an intimidating sort—burly, florid-faced, black popping eyes, bristling mustache, rough-talking—but fair and even entertaining. The messing officers gathered in the mess hall to watch him measure the rations. Q always managed to get a little buckshee sugar from the camp quartermaster. If there was enough extra to notice, he'd add it to a room's ration according to a roster he kept. If it was skimpy he'd divide the surplus among the messing officers. A fairly innocent racket which our roommates suspected but were never able to prove. Even though we took our meals separately from the other prisoners, we never got any more of anything else than they did. Well, there sometimes was a puddle of soup left in the bottom of a dixie. But hardly what you could call seconds.

Eating in the serving room was pleasanter than in the communal mess. Less noise, less hurry. And occasionally that leftover soup. Chieti soup didn't really satisfy hunger, but it gave the stomach a welcome tight feeling.

Most of us looked well-nourished but it may have been bloat from the liquid diet because we were always hungry. Hidden hunger for fats and sweets, maybe. But psychological hunger, too. When you didn't have a cupboard or a refrigerator to go to for whatever you wanted whenever you wanted it, you thought about food a lot.

Everything considered, the cookhouse did a superb job of feeding the prisoners. All cooked food was prepared there and the cookhouse also distributed the uncooked rations. The only utensils were the dixies. The iron crane that raised and lowered them from the enormous, roaring, woodburning stove was fixed to the stove. Another iron crane, on casters, moved the dixies around. Everything and everyone around the stove were black with soot. The dixies, the stove, the chains of the cranes, the floor, the cooks.

Derek, the kitchen officer, had been a prosperous caterer in civilian life ("civvy street," the British called it). He ran the kitchen like a well-ordered business. When we started getting more food and greater variety, especially in the Red Cross issue, he provided increasingly elaborate meals. And he was inventive.

Unable to make the macaroni ration palatable, he ground it into flour and made pancakes and puddings. Instead of using the occasional meat issue in soups, he took to boiling it whole and serving it as boiled beef. It was gristly and tough but prized. Meat-starved though I was, I couldn't eat it. I had, and still have, a puerile aversion to gristle and fat.

He gave us feasts—they were feasts to us, anyhow—when he managed to get hold of bulk Red Cross oatmeal or dried eggs. He posted his menus in the cookhouse window a week in advance so we always knew when oatmeal, pancakes, powdered eggs or pudding were coming up. Men thought about little else the whole week and sometimes rose from sick beds rather than miss one of Derek's specials.

Some of the prisoners themselves became pretty fair hands at cookery. We did the preparation, not the actual cooking. But preparation was all. What care we lavished on our ingredients. Soaking Canadian biscuits in just enough water in the bottom of a Klim tin just long enough so they would absorb just enough liquid to be doughy but not soggy. Fried in olive oil at the cookhouse on our cooking day they became pancakes, to be eaten with margarine and jam. A Canadian biscuit recipe of my own: cheese soufflé. Time-consuming but not tedious. With us, the longer a task took the better. Take one Canadian biscuit, two if you are cooking for a friend as well, grate on a tall cocoa tin punched with holes from the inside, add grated stale bread and cheese, salt and pepper to taste. Boil until gummy.

Soon after we came to P.G. 21 Allen put me to work writing a column of home news for his AP board. "America at War." Irony intended. I got my news from letters and incoming prisoners. I was allowed to attend interrogations, and after the military part was done I questioned the newcomers about the really important things back home. Hollywood, Broadway, sports. What was the latest on Errol Flynn and which movie queens were doing what with whom?

Then I did a dumb thing. I wrote what I thought was a funny character sketch of Allen and passed it around. Among other things I joked about his appearance, "a plump, unhappy captive with mournful brown eyes," his plaintive tone when he spoke of his many wrongs, how he wore everything to bed except his shoes, how he fed his raging cigarette habit with contributions from worshipping "journalism students," and how, when you did something nice for him, he'd put his arm around your shoulder and say, "I'll put your name in the paper for that. Three hundred and fifty million people read what I write. You'll be famous." I guess I was pretty heavy-handed. He complained to Colonel Gooler and threatened to punch me in the nose. I knew I'd really hurt his feelings because Allen was not the sort to punch people in the nose. I apologized and, to my relief, we were friends again.

Allen had the gift of languages. He picked up Italian from newspapers and the radio. He hadn't a typewriter, almost no paper, very little ink, a scratchy Italian dip-pen and no place to work, but he got out the news. His paper was the wrappers of Red Cross parcels and cigarette packages and any other odd bits he could beg or buy. The kitchen boiled up his rice ration into paste. For a news board he used the side of an old crate. His news sources were the Italian papers, incoming prisoners, the loud-speaker and, in the last few months before the capitulation, the Italian radio. He changed the board as often as the news warranted, sometimes several times a day.

His AP service had competition from a British group, CNA, for Central News Agency. Prisoners who couldn't get close to his board because of the crowds sometimes read the English version of the news. Allen delighted in scooping the CNA and did so regularly. His staffers snatched copy dripping from his pen and raced to the bulletin board while his competitors were writing their leads. He editorialized through two female cartoon characters, "Silly Sally" and "Sophisticated Sue." When the commandante banned all news not literal translations from the Fascist newspapers, we knew Allen's barbs had struck home.

He received mail from the U.S., Switzerland, Spain and Portugal. The letters were addressed to Mr., Commander, Lieutenant, War Correspondent and even Rear Admiral. The Italians were just as confused about his status as his correspondents because of his capture while on a vessel of the British fleet. They finally assigned him the rank and pay of a lieutenant. He was the most unmilitary figure in camp. He wore his shirttail outside his pants and smoked while at attention. He never obeyed Italian regulations if it interfered with his newsgathering.

He started a journalism class and from it selected a staff of translators, newswriters and feature men. We joked he'd started the class to scrounge cigarettes from his students (his habit was worse than Kennedy's), but we knew it was only a joke. He liked news even better than nicotine. (When the Germans took over his custody from the Italians he was repatriated. He went back to being an AP correspondent, and he lectured on the circuit about his wartime experiences, including his time at P.G. 21. And in whatever city he visited, he never failed to contact the next of kin of his P.G. 21 roommates.)

One night after lights out the whole room for some reason fell into a swamp of miserable nostalgia. "Do you remember apple pies?" "Do you remember shacking up with a blonde?" "Do you remember leaving bread on the table?" "Do you remember being clean and taking hot showers whenever you felt like it?" "Do you remember having all you want to eat?" From bunk to bunk across the room. On and on. Doc Wynsen grew weary of it.

He raised himself up (we could hear his bunk creaking in the darkness) and said, "Do you remember toilets that flush?" Silence, followed by laughter and the quiet Doc wanted.

Doc Wynsen probably could have been repatriated but chose to look after us. There were Italian doctors available to us but we believed them incompetent and certainly uncooperative. Doc made the most of what little equipment and medication were available. Fortunately for us, his medical knowledge was wide-ranging and his skills honed. And he always had a puckish grin on his face. Even mornings.

Not so Jake Otten, tall, pale-eyed, a Wimpy gunner, wearing sergeant's stripes when shot down but with his commission as pilot officer in the works. Before P.G. 21 he'd spent time in an OR camp but was transferred when his commission came through channels. Due officer's pay for the months he'd drawn OR pay as a POW, he was by virtue of his back pay the wealthiest man in our room in lire. A little dour, he was nevertheless good-natured and easygoing. Except when he first woke up in the morning. I had only to say, "Good morning, Jake," to the nose and pale eye sticking out of the covers for him to be sore at me all day. And if I touched him, he'd curse me. He was Nobby Sproule's bunkmate.

They had a close OR friend in the cookhouse who was always bringing them food. Kennedy and I didn't envy them as much as others in our bay did. We had Barnes.

Looking To Get Out

MORE AMERICANS ARRIVED. More than would fit into our room, the "American room." We spread out into the next room, displacing British officers. They didn't like it much. One room was like another and none of us had more property than could be carried easily in one trip, but we all had prison inertia. Any move, except to freedom, was a bad one.

Among the last arrivals assigned to our bay was a fighter pilot named Zubaric, so small I wondered how he'd passed the minimum height standards for pilot training. And in contrast to Bill Wendt, a hulking American in the RAF who "wore a Spit" (Spitfire fighter), he flew a P-38 Lightning, the Army Air Forces' only twin-engine, twin-fuselage fighter plane. He'd been awaiting court-martial back at his unit when he was shot down over Sardinia. An ace, he'd been given a thirty-day leave at a North African rest camp but instead had hitchhiked home to Chicago, intending to keep a low profile and get back to the rest camp with no one being the wiser. But his proud mother couldn't resist calling the newspapers. He got major coverage as a returned war hero. When he got back to the rest camp, a few days AWOL, he was arrested and released to his unit while the charges were reviewed. That didn't keep him from flying missions. Apprehended while evading capture, he mistook an Italian soldier's "come here" hand signal for "go away," kept walking, and was shot in the leg. The Italians who'd found his crashed plane were unfamiliar with the twin-fuselage design and asked him how many men were in the crew. "Two," Zubaric said.

"They're probably still looking for the other guy," he told us.

By spring so many Americans came in that they were put wherever there was an empty bunk. It broke up the well-knit American contingent where everybody knew everybody else.

Jennette came in April, unexpectedly, after a long hospital stay. He arrived at a time of high morale, with Eisenhower and Montgomery linking up in Tunisia and a sense of victory in the air. Jennette had always been slight, but now he was down to under one hundred pounds, with a limp even though his wound had healed. Neither of us was usually very demonstrative, but we hugged. He was deliriously happy to be back with us again. When I went with him to draw a British uniform to replace his Italian one, he couldn't stop grinning at me and punching me in the ribs, saying, "You old joker, you."

He said the pilot we'd shot down had died in the same hospital where he, Risso and Brazil were taken. An Italian doctor came and shook his bed, aggravating the pain in his broken leg, grating, "Our capitano dies and you live!" Risso, he said, had been good company, always brave and cheerful. But he hadn't gotten along with Brazil. Most of our enlisted men hadn't liked Jennette too much. He'd never been friendly with any of them. (He had helped Barnes out of a tight spot with the Killer once, though, and Barnes still speaks highly of him.)

Eventually every American POW in Italy except for high-ranking officers, those in hospitals, and a few strays in other camps was confined at P.G. 21. Something more than two hundred.

One day our hosts sent a little fire truck in to pump out a well where a stolen Italian uniform was believed to be hidden. We sprinkled broken glass in its path, cut the pump hose in two places, and stole the tools three times (we kept being caught). Those caught in the act went to the cooler. The rest of us were only confined to our bungalows until the fire truck left. The commandante usually obeyed the Geneva Convention decree against mass punishment. And they never did find the Italian uniform.

Spirits rose with the temperature. No more chilblains and frigid bungalows. We were doing better at the mess hall, too. Canned mussels (I'd never eaten a mussel before), antipasto (mustardy mixed vegetables), anchovies, fruit—fresh figs, watermelon, cherries, grapes, oranges, nespoli (I was the only one at my table who'd ever seen one; I'd never eaten one, though. In Houston they grew on ornamental trees and we called them Japanese plums. Rightfully they were medlars.) Years later in Milan, I asked the waiter in our hotel if they had ness-pole-e, putting the accent on the wrong syllable. But he knew what I meant and brought us some, delighted that a tourist knew about them. Every cherry had a little worm at its center. We stopped cutting them open to remove it and pretended that *this* cherry had no worm.

My favored dessert was a thick paste of sugar and Klim poured over a tin dish of peeled figs. (In Houston in the 1950s, we had a fig tree in our back yard. My wife would peel them, lay them in a crust of crushed graham crackers, and top them with stiff whipped cream. Her way was better.)

I found another food source and for a while it was mine alone. Green sprouts from rotting onions, a delicacy Kennedy and I enjoyed regularly until our roommates learned my secret and joined the hunt.

Our Italian rations included a small vino issue. In Italy wine had as much place on the table as salt or bread. And our hosts may have made money on it. We received two small glasses a week, usually sour and full of a dark red sediment. More rarely it was what an English tablemate told me was marsala and even more rarely a watery vermouth. A lot of us found the usual issue undrinkable. Others endured the taste for the effect and bought unwanted wine rations for food or cigarettes, sometimes enough to get drunk, resulting usually in retching and almost always in a thunderous hangover.

Willie usually managed a toot every week. Once Kennedy joined him. When they ran out of vino, they'd had enough to crave more and not to care where they got it. They ranged the camp hunting vino. They looked in our mess hall and saw a vino issue ready for distribution. They crawled in a window and took it, outside the walls a drunken prank but inside a major crime. Theft in a place where everyone had so little ranked just below murder and collaboration with the enemy.

P.G. 21 was in an uproar. It was only when Kennedy woke up the next morning, nursing the inevitable hangover, that he realized what he'd done. Kennedy, one of the most scrupulously honest men ever, was horrified. He wanted to report himself to Colonel Gooler but was persuaded the consequences were too awful to contemplate. Court martial after liberation, maybe.

Because it had been vino taken and not food or clothing, the senior officers didn't conduct a very serious investigation and it blew over. Despite that, it preyed on Kennedy's mind for weeks and he never drank more than his own ration of vino again.

It was a different matter when a bread thief was caught. We "sent him to Coventry," meaning the silent treatment. We acted as if he weren't there. The SBO demanded that he be transferred to another camp. Our hosts complied.

Allen and Frelinghuysen liked their vino but never more than they could handle. When Allen had a few his voice took on a slightly higher pitch and his stories got funnier. He'd do a Mussolini imitation in Italian, supplying the crowd's "Duce! Duce! Duce!" or sing "Deep in the Heart of Texas" in Italian. Frelinghuysen might get a little red in the face but that was it. Eventually he started his own winery when Stuyvesant gave him one of the plywood boxes his personal parcels came in. He soaked it until it was watertight and put in water, raisins, prunes, cut-up fig bars, orange drink powder and anything else he thought might ferment or contribute flavor. On vino days he'd add his ration to the mixture. Of an evening he'd dip out a cup. It was always working—you could see the bubbles—but it never seemed to affect his health. He remained in much better physical condition than most, which served him well when he escaped.

Escape activities, which went on constantly, picked up with warmer weather. Tunneling, forging passes, making Italian and German uniforms, tailing the guards and recording their routine, assembling escape rations. Escape rations were toughest. Things we had the greatest craving for—milk, margarine, chocolate, biscuits, sugar, raisins—were mixed together into a paste, packed in cocoa tins, and baked secretly in the cookouts, smeared on top with margarine to keep out moisture and hidden away or kept in plain sight with a half-inch layer of jam on top for camouflage.

There were usually several tunnels going at the same time. Two of them eventually got beyond the wall but not far enough to be opened safely. You didn't open a tunnel until the escape attempt. I was never on a tunneling detail but often served as a lookout. Once I gave an outdoor lecture to a gathering of attentive British officers as cover for a bold, daylight operation. The Italians had been pretty successful finding tunnels in the obvious, hidden-from-view places. The Escape Committee approved a plan to start a tunnel in the front courtyard of the bungalow across from mine. The tunnelers started at a site not visible from the guardboxes on the walls but in plain view of patrolling guards. They began it at night and kept digging in darkness until it was deep enough to conceal a digger. Then they dug days. To cover it, they advertised a course of outdoor lectures on bulletin boards throughout the camp. Every day a different group of British officers would assemble to hear the talks. They brought stools and blankets and listened raptly for an hour or so. One blanket covered the tunnel's camouflaged cap. My lecture topic was "American Meals I Have Eaten." Lookouts signaled when guards approached, and the man on the blanket knocked to warn the digger to stop.

Once at dusk, when I was returning from the mess hall, a man rose out of the solid cement in front of me. I thought I was hallucinating. It was only when he climbed the rest of the way out that I saw it was a tunnel entrance. (I used that scene in a TV pilot I wrote for NBC in 1964 for an Italian POW series that never got a sponsor.) I looked away quickly, hoping no guard had seen my startled face.

When a tunnel entrance was found between two bunks in another bay, we had to move all our bunks end to end along the walls. Before we'd had them parallel, giving us a little semi-privacy between bunks.

The most elaborate tunnel began under the cookhouse steps. It was equipped with lanterns and a ventilator made out of cans by Gardinier. It was discovered by accident. A guard taking his ease on a slope overlooking the camp had a direct view through a window of a shift crawling into the tunnel. The tunnelers were taken to the cooler and fined heavily for destroying Italian government property.

Hiding dirt from a tunnel was a major problem. Usually it was strewn around the courtyards from Red Cross boxes when the guards weren't looking. It had to be carefully scattered and scuffed around so it wouldn't look fresh. We grew onions in it, too, the scattered shoots peeping out of the dirt in boxes five feet long, two wide and two deep.

Our hosts were more efficient at stopping escape attempts than finding tunnels. We didn't have a successful escape from P.G. 21 the whole time I was there. Some prisoners got as far as the wall in the Italian settore but never got over it. The wall is what made escaping so unlikely. It was under constant observation on all sides and impossible to scale quickly. There was talk of throwing ladders against all four walls simultaneously and staging a mass break but the plan was vetoed by the Escape Committee. To my relief. One hopeful submitted a plan to pole vault over the wall. The applicant being in poor physical condition, there being no pole available, and the lowest available wall being twelve feet high and two wide, the Escape Committee turned him down.

Our hosts were always looking for tunnel activities and contraband—escape rations, maps, forged passes. Tiny soldiers in baggy blue coveralls often walked through the bungalows tapping floors and walls with long screwdrivers. We called them snoopers and usually stopped whatever we were doing to watch them at their work. It embarrassed them, especially when they had to get down on the floor on their stomachs to poke under a bunk. When our hosts were really serious they'd search the prisoners, too, while the snoopers were in the bungalows. We'd file out the door one by one, empty-handed, and be searched. Inside the empty bungalows the little fellows would prowl at their leisure, tapping floors without an audience, going through our bags and boxes, and probing pillows and palliasses with long needles. They hardly ever found anything we didn't want them to, so sometimes they'd take innocuous things like notebooks and paper just to show the capitano they were on the ball.

We got really persistent searches after escape attempts. Those always threw our hosts into terrible flaps. Searches and roll calls came one after the other.

A rumor ran through the camp that on the next search the Italians would confiscate gold rings and watches in retaliation for alleged similar acts against Italian POWs by the British. I hid my Rice 1937 ring in a can of margarine. I treasured it even though it was only ten-carat gold. I kept it hidden for months, adding margarine when the level in the can got low. Our hosts never did confiscate rings or watches from our room, but they took Nobby Sproule's wedding band. He happened to be in the cooler at the time. When he refused to give it up, a guard detail came into his cell and took it from him at bayonet point.

Weaver probably had the most cooler time of any American, although Glenn and Toby were such escape artists our hosts moved them into the OR barracks for a while, made them report regularly throughout the day, and posted a guard outside their room nights. On one escape attempt Weaver got a beating as well as cooler time. He'd shaved off his mustache and cut his hair short in German military style. Wearing some borrowed clothing that might pass for a German uniform from a distance and carrying a forged pass I'd signed for him using my own last name (the only one I could write in German script), he crawled under the wire next to our bungalow one foggy night while I was at a play. The guards, as the British put it, got the wind up as they always did in fog. They kept shouting back and forth and played the searchlights constantly on walls and guard rails. During the first act, we were electrified by the sound of a shot. Then a lot of yelling and two more shots. We wondered if it were Weaver they were shooting at or if it were only the usual nervous reaction of our hosts to blanketing fog. They shot at shadows a lot on foggy nights. It was a wonder they never hit a fellow guard, which we all devoutly wished they would.

Next morning Weaver was absent at roll call. Maybe he'd escaped. We knew he hadn't been shot or we'd have heard it. On reflection we realized he must only be in the cooler because our hosts didn't seem terribly surprised when he didn't answer. Harris, the cooler orderly, later told us that Weaver had gotten tangled in the wire and been caught by a guard who began cursing him and beating him with his rifle butt. Several other guards joined in the fun. They all knew Weaver by sight and hated him because of his taunting. An Italian Red Cross captain had stopped them. He told them Weaver's escape attempt was only a boyish prank, but privately he told Weaver he was lucky not to have been shot. There'd been so many escape attempts the commandante was putting a lot of pressure on the guards.

In the afternoon the capitano made the rounds of the posts on the walls and had each sentry in turn fire his rifle into the air. It was intended to frighten us. Instead, we were entertained by it. We followed the capitano from post to post in growing numbers. By the time he got to the post on the corner wall near the mess hall he'd drawn a crowd. The sentry was flustered by all the attention. He tried to fire with the bolt open. When he'd corrected that, the rifle misfired. The sentry was horribly rattled. The capitano was livid. On the third try, the rifle discharged. We cheered. The sentry gave us a sheepish grin.

Weaver did manage to get out of P.G. 21 on another try but only to another camp when a number of prisoners, mostly British but with a few Americans including Allen, were transferred to a camp farther north. Although P.G. 21 was reputedly the worst officers' camp in Italy, most of those to be reassigned objected bitterly. They preferred staying with their friends. Weaver, who wasn't scheduled to go, had no trouble persuading an Englishman to let him assume the Englishman's identity. Weaver's plan was to jump off the train taking them to the new camp. He shaved his mustache again—it had grown back out since his previous attempt—and marched out with the transferees. He had a duffel bag over his shoulder, shielding his face from the capitano, who was keeping a sharp eye at the gate. Weaver didn't jump off the train. An English officer beat him to it and was shot dead. Security got even tighter. Even Weaver didn't like those odds.

Our hosts knew there had been several assumed identities among the transferees. Late one night the capitano staged a surprise roll call with a large detail of guards in attendance. We were rousted out of bed and, as was customary for indoor roll calls, assembled on one side of the bay. Each man answered when his name was called and went to the other side of the bay under the capitano's scrutiny. The Englishman Weaver had replaced ran to our room when the Italians first entered our bungalow. When Weaver's name was called he answered to it and crossed to the other side. The capitano studied him, obviously aware he wasn't Weaver. But with his usual sense of melodrama he did the roll call all over again to heighten the suspense. And again. The third time the Englishman answered to Weaver's name the capitano stroked his black beard and said, "Hmmm. I think I know you. You are not Claude Weaver. Come here. Ah, yes. I remember you."

He fondled his beard in silence for a long moment, his eyes never leaving the false Weaver. Then, with quiet menace, "Come with me. I think we will take a little ride together." But all he did was walk him to the cooler.

Weeks later Weaver and all the other Americans in the transferred group returned. There'd been a mistake. All Americans were supposed to be confined in P.G. 21. They weren't happy to be back. When they entered the other camp its commandant greeted them with, "Welcome, gentlemen." None of our hosts had ever called us gentlemen. Then the commandant accompanied them to the mess hall, where a hot meal was waiting, and chatted with them as they ate. He assured them he would do all in his power to lighten the burden of captivity. There was no wall. Only barbed-wire fences. The camp was in a town, and the prisoners could watch local activities through the wire. Views which included girls. Prisoners sent their laundry out to a convent across the street. The sisters did it beautifully for a pittance.

They'd lived in rooms instead of bays, only a few men to each room. Real beds, with mattresses and springs. An officers' bar with vermouth, vino and beer. A well-stocked canteen with quality Italian and British merchandise. The British goods were from personal parcels. British POWs there got them more regularly than those in P.G. 21. Most wonderful of all, as Allen described it on his AP board on his return with the others, they had toilets from which came "a roaring, gushing torrent of crystal clear water."

We were all in on one "escape" that gave us more long-running entertainment than anything in the theater. A British major learned that he was scheduled for transfer. He didn't want to leave his friends at P.G. 21 and hid in a tunnel when the guards came for him. He was reported missing. Consternation. Roll calls, searches. He hid in his tunnel during all of them. Even surprise searches were of no avail because they were never really surprising. Our hosts always unintentionally announced "surprise" searches by throwing a cordon of guards around the bungalows. The moment the guards came through our gate, warnings spread over the camp, giving everyone time to stop doing anything they shouldn't be. The Italians finally accepted as fact that he'd escaped and reported it to Rome and announced at roll call that the major had been shot resisting capture near Rome and let that be a lesson to all would-be escapers. It was six weeks before they caught the major. The sergente recognized him as he was coming out of the theater after a teatime concert.

When it was warm enough, we started sunbathing. At first we had to prop our bedboard racks against our stools for windbreakers against the chilly breeze. We went outside with our palliasses after roll call and lolled about all day. When it got hot enough to do without the windbreakers, Colonel Gooler decreed P.T. (physical training) for all. Frelinghuysen and a barrel-chested American named Connie were our trainers. (Frelinghuysen never lost his passion for fitness. He's run marathons, and in 1976 he coauthored a book, *Keep Your Heart Running*, with Dr. Paul Kiell.)

The grass stuffing of our palliasses had twisted into hard knots over the winter. Out in the sun, we took the palliasses apart and untwisted the knots. An all-day job but we had nothing better to do.

When we tired of sunbathing, we'd sit on the bungalow

steps or on the packed dirt of the yard philosophizing and arguing. We argued a lot, at length and in detail. We had the time for it. After we finished picking the bones of a subject, we generally forgot about it and went on to another. Except once. I'd struck up a friendship with Dapper Dan's copilot, Jim Giblin. He hadn't known anyone in the camp well, even his own crewmates, because they'd been captured on his first mission. He'd stayed hungry into the warm months when we were on full parcels and most of us finally felt that we were getting enough to eat. With full parcels and my trading activities I often had more bread than I needed and I'd occasionally give him some. You can't have a bond much stronger than that in a POW camp. So we were sitting in the yard by a scrawny shrub talking about books. He thought only nonfiction worth reading, and I insisted you could learn more about life from good fiction. He thought that pretty unreasonable but suffered it. We were buddies after all. Then we pondered the weighty question of how best to judge our fellow prisoners. Giblin said a man's true nature emerged in captivity and how he behaved in the bag was how he truly was. I disputed that. A POW camp was not a man's natural environment, and you shouldn't judge him in it any more than you'd judge a fish out of water. Giblin told me coldly if that's what I believed, although he'd thought highly of me in the past, he'd now lost all respect for me. I thought he was joking but he wasn't. We were never as close again. (Until about forty years later, when he was a U.S. Customs agent in Laredo, and I a writer in Los Angeles, we got to corresponding. He didn't remember a thing about that fateful argument. In 1985, at a 98th Bomb Group reunion in San Antonio, I was having lunch with Joe Kilgore—the pilot who'd come to our rescue when we were shot down—Dapper Dan Story, Al Barnes and my wife and theirs, and Padre Brach. Kilgore asked us if we'd known a man named Jim Giblin in the Italian prison camp. I said I had and we'd been close friends. And Dapper Dan said he knew Giblin, too, but not very well even though Giblin had been his copilot for Giblin's only mission. Kilgore said the reason he'd asked was that Giblin's daughter, a lawyer, was working for his law firm in Austin. After the reunion I visited her there. I told her about the famous falling out. She promised to give her father my regards next time she saw him. Kilgore, by the way, was awarded the silver star for helping us and is a retired major general and former U.S. Congressman.)

Along with the warmer weather we got movies. We were

assessed a few lire weekly for the privilege, a stiff rental for scratched films and an old projector. Our hosts showed the movies in the courtyard of the bungalow across the street from ours, by back projection because of air raid regulations, onto a cheesecloth screen. All right-handers became lefties and when there were subtitles they were backward, and pretty dim. Wetting down the screen helped a little. For some reason medical science has never been able to explain to my satisfaction, I got nearsighted in my good eye and more nearsighted in my bad eye after a few months in the bag. (Slightly less than normal vision in my left eye had kept me from applying for pilot training; navigators didn't have to be perfect.) I usually couldn't tell one actor from another. The movies were either Italian or dubbed in Italian. Unless someone was shot, kissed or hit in the face with a custard pie I was seldom sure what was happening onscreen. One of the British officers was an eye doctor. He got me some horn-rimmed glasses from the Italians, and I began getting more out of the films.

It was frustrating to watch English-language films dubbed in Italian when we could otherwise have understood them perfectly well, but hearing Laurel and Hardy arguing in Italian or a London bobby saying, "Grazie," was fun. Among our movies were *Thunder Over Mexico*, with Warner Baxter (nee "Robin Hood of El Dorado"), a 1936 Hollywood tribute to the Mexican bandit-hero, Joaquin Murietta; a German number starring Max Schmeling, and a Hungarian historical movie notable for its scene with a sloe-eyed beauty bathing nude in a lovely garden pool. Fortunately I had my spectacles by then. (The theme song for *Thunder Over Mexico* was "La Golondrina," often called the goodbye song. It became and remains my favorite Spanish song.)

Allen, Frelinghuysen and others who spoke Italian would explain the action between reels. Once when Frelinghuysen was doing that the capitano asked who he was. Stupidly, I told him. Curses from the British, who knew the capitano wanted to identify Italian-speakers among us. I slunk around for days.

We took our stools to the movies, as we did to the theater, and once the picture began we were stuck for the duration because movies ended after curfew. Guards were posted around the area to see that no one strayed from the courtyard, primed, for all I knew, to shoot without warning. (Poetic justice. In my movie-reviewing days at the *Houston Post* before the war I'd leave a boring movie early and say bad things about it in the paper.)

We were as much interested in the progress of the war as we were in food and home. We lapped up the news Allen translated from Italian newspapers (the commandante cut them off briefly between visits by the Protecting Power) and Radio Roma. We had speakers in our compound now, but the controls were in the settore office. We got news we trusted more than either from new prisoners.

One April day in 1943 Glenn and I were on our way to a matinee performance of *The Merchant of Venice* when the sergente rushed up to Glenn and told him he and Stuyvesant were being repatriated. I was deeply stirred but Glenn seemed to take it calmly. When I asked him if he wanted to call off going to the play he said, "Of course not." He sat through the entire performance. In his shoes I couldn't have done it. As it was, I couldn't get really interested in what was happening onstage for thinking about Glenn going home. Or was it more because I found Shakespeare boring?

When he left P.G. 21, he gave away everything except his chocolate and cigarettes. He intended trading them for food on the outside, not expecting our hosts to be too solicitous of his needs. He gave me his complete works of Shakespeare and promised to write to me when he got home. Which he did, from London, even before going home. I got his letter in August. (Some years after the war we met for lunch at the Shamrock Hotel in Houston. He said that after repatriation he'd joined the military and been stationed in India on the staff of General Auchinleck. He was currently employed by a United Nations organization. He had his paycheck with him. When he attempted to cash it at the hotel the cashier had never heard of the organization, and I had to vouch for him before he could get his money. It was the least I could do for a man who'd given me the complete works of William Shakespeare.)

April 11 was my twenty-sixth birthday. I celebrated it with Derek, who was assistant quartermaster as well as OC (officer in charge) of the cookhouse, whose birthday was the same. We had two major repasts, the first at noon in our mess and the second at teatime in his room. Cake, puddings, and rarest of the rare, coffee. Someone in a nearby bungalow had acquired a canary from God knows where, and it must have known what was going on because it sang to us all afternoon. Afterward Derek's roommates threw us in the water trough. Being British, they let us take off our major clothing first.

A Hike in the Sun

WE WERE ALLOWED A PAROLE walk about the middle of the month. The countryside was ravishing to men who'd seen expanses of green only from a distance. Fruit trees in blossom, olive groves, burgeoning fields. I wore my mild weather wardrobe, much of it acquired in trade—Italian socks, American shoes, Australian shorts, English shirt, South African jacket. I'd tried to trade for a Scottish tam but no Scot would part with his. We were supposed to be on parole, meaning we promised not to try to escape on the walks, but we were surrounded by guards anyway. We went in groups lined up four abreast in military fashion, dressed in our best. We marched smartly out the gate, giving the commandante, who saw us off, a crisp, "Eyes right!" The column made a proper military right turn onto the paved highway, marching at a fast clip. We had to stay in step to keep from treading on the heels of the rank ahead. We assumed it was the commandante's idea to do it that way, that Rome had ordered walks and he wanted to make them as joyless as possible.

The guards, as usual, were small and short-legged. They had to hustle to keep up with us. From time to time Kennedy would nudge me, nod toward one of the panting guards, and say, "Watch him. He's gonna make a break for it."

It was more a hike than a walk but it was invigorating to have a view not obstructed by a wall and to see houses, civilians, a sweep of open land. If only we might have stopped, broken ranks and stretched out on the grass a while. But we turned around and marched back the way we'd come.

We had a spring fair about that time—hula "girls," pitch-penny stalls, fortune tellers, clowns, races, sideshows and rube spectators. The commandante relaxed enough to allow a spumoni man inside. He sold us tiny dabs of ice cream for camp lire, which he exchanged for the real thing in the settore office. I never got to taste it. The line was too long. I wasted my money trying to rope a pair of socks on a ring-pitch board. I also contributed to the afternoon's entertainment. Billed as "Little Caesar, the World's Strongest Man," I wore longjohns stuffed with newspapers where muscles belonged. I did a simulated weightlifting act with imaginary weights. Got a few smiles from the Americans but it convulsed the British.

We were allowed to plant a garden with seeds from the International Red Cross. We dug the garden in the only open space available, the northeast corner, by the cookhouse. The pump tower occupied the northwest corner. It was brick, by far the tallest structure within the walls, and decorated with the Fascist emblem, the fasces, a bundle of rods around an ax, the ancient Roman symbol of authority. Two undersized softball diamonds and two nonregulation basketball courts took up the rest of our space.

Each bungalow had its own plot in the garden. Those wanting to work in it took turns digging and cultivating and shared the yield. We collected picks and shovels from the storehouse mornings and returned them at the end of the day. Our hosts kept a close eye on us. The only digging with their tools was to be in the garden. The ground was compacted and devilishly hard to break but working in the garden was a way of killing time. And we did share a few radishes, tomatoes and lettuces.

One day our settore major watched us toiling and asked why we were working so hard. We probably wouldn't be there long enough to enjoy the fruits of our labor, he said, confirming our own views about the progress of the war. He, and we, would be proven wrong, of course.

Sports flourished with warmer weather. Boxing, badminton (with homemade paddles and shuttlecocks), basketball, volleyball (the Other Ranks had a variation using only heads and feet to get the ball over the net), softball and cricket. The British loved basketball but disregarded the rules about fouling. With them it became a rough and dangerous game. They were appalled by our manners at the first softball game they witnessed. We hissed and jeered and cursed the umpire and called him a thief. They were accustomed to watching in silence, greeting outstanding play with polite handclaps. And afterward giving a restrained and organized "hip, hip, hurrah" for the losing side. Their news service, CNA, published a scathing attack on American sports barbarism and several British officers wrote measured but angry protests to the AP, just as if it were the *London Times*. It wasn't long, however, before the British were screaming, "Kill the umpire!" along with the rest of us. They retained their own style, though, urging on a British batter facing an American pitcher with, "See here, Ronald, he isn't going to eat you alive!"

Sometimes I sparred with Jennette. I outweighed him by forty-five pounds and he had that gimpy leg, but I couldn't lay a glove on him. He was incredibly fast and shifty and had boxed in college. He pulled his punches or he'd have cut me to tatters. Gardinier and I sparred some, too. We were pretty evenly matched. We'd usually lose our tempers when hit and go at it until Jennette stepped in and separated us. No hard feelings afterward, though.

Among the spring arrivals was a captain who quickly became the most disliked man among us. A doctor. He was captured with half a battalion of other Americans in Tunisia after a sudden thrust by German forces. He was taken with all his personal luggage, which he brought to P.G. 21 with him—changes of uniform, socks, underwear. He shared with no one nor did anyone expect him to. He was loud and, perhaps deliberately, obnoxious. He'd give detailed descriptions of women patients he'd examined and make crude sexual jokes about wives and girlfriends of his roommates. I often wondered what Padre Brach thought of him.

He was Sicilian-born and loved to stir our juices by defending everything Italian that we criticized or complained about, including our hated commandante and capitano. It showed a lot of gall, but it took guts, too, under the circumstances. He was the only Italian-American I ever ran across in the bag who had a kind word for our captors. If anything, Italian-Americans were more rigidly anti-Fascist than other Americans. As with our crewmate Risso, they were often singled out for especially harsh interrogation by the Italians. One sergeant arrived at P.G. 21 dazed and shaken. He said he'd been slapped, cursed, called a traitor, threatened with death, and beaten with the flat of a dagger by a colonel during interrogation.

Later in April men came in who'd been shot down on my birthday. They were from our squadron, the 344th, but we didn't know any of them. They were replacements. The men we'd flown with had finished their missions and gone back to the U.S. Kennedy, Gardinier, Barnes and I sulked for a couple of days. We'd have been the first crew to go home. We weren't as cordial to the replacements as we should have been. Oldtimers tended to be patronizing to new prisoners anyhow.

We learned of the fall of Tunisia from Radio Roma. Even those of us who knew no Italian understood the Axis had suffered a great defeat because the general who made the announcement sounded on the verge of tears. We cheered and waved at the capitano looking on from the Italian side of the wire.

Regardless of what we learned from newspapers and the radio, we fed on rumors. About mail, parcels, the war. As early as February we heard that Pantelleria had fallen (it didn't happen until June) and that thirty-nine American paratroopers, that exact number, had been captured at Naples. We eagerly awaited their arrival at P.G. 21 but they never came. No matter how farfetched a rumor might be, we seldom dismissed one out of hand. Not a good one.

About that time the British thought ORs were becoming too friendly with officers, and the SBO decreed they were not to visit officer bungalows except in line of duty and then only through the back entrance. We assumed the rule did not apply to Americans, but when Barnes came to the room to play cards with Kennedy and me, a captain said, "You know better than that, Al." A senior captain, he'd become our room commander when Colonel Gooler was moved into a front room to join three other lieutenant colonels who'd come in together. It took a moment for his meaning to sink in. Barnes was hurt and embarrassed, Kennedy and I angered even though we knew the man was only following regulations and didn't much like having to do it. Kennedy was a captain, too, now. His promotion had been in the works when we were shot down and had gone through. He told Barnes not to go but Barnes didn't want to make trouble and left. Kennedy took his grievance to Colonel Gooler and next day the order was rescinded for American enlisted men. That this did not sit well with the British was of no great concern to us. Those of us from aircrews never learned to adopt the British relationship between officers and Other Ranks. When American enlisted men arrived at P.G. 21 in sufficient numbers and they replaced ORs as room orderlies, we were all, officers and enlisted men alike, embarrassed when they'd come in to make our beds and sweep our floors. We soon got over it, agreeing it was better to be an orderly in an officers' camp than to endure harsher conditions in an enlisted men's camp. The only sergeant who didn't agree was the Oklahoma rancher who never smiled until I got to know him well enough to joke with him about his involuntary servitude.

We saw more of our guards than we did of our own enlisted men. We watched them all the time and not just to log their routines. We watched them washing their clothes, digging in their gardens, or just taking the sun. They never stripped to their shorts as we did. Prudish or fearful of sunburn? We never learned which. They'd get self-conscious under our steady, silent gaze. Some of them couldn't stand it all and would retreat back into their barracks.

Like the guards at Poggio Mirteto, they loved to sing. On Sunday afternoons they'd have songfests in their barracks, sometimes attended by women whose comings and goings we watched avidly. Once the singing went on for two days, with a musical director and accordion and guitar accompaniment. Allen said they were celebrating the anniversary of the founding of the Fascist blackshirt militia, which didn't prevent us from enjoying it.

I got a guitar of my own. When the band got a new one, I bought the old one. My Poggio Mirteto pay had finally been credited to my account and I was flush. I'd always wanted to play the guitar and now I had the time to learn. The band guitar player gave me a few lessons and I practiced in the unused shower room, where real musicians did. I got as far as scales and picking out "Old Black Joe" and not a note further. I had absolutely no aptitude for the instrument. It wasn't a complete waste. There was a South African officer named Tweedy who could play any tune you asked and many you'd never heard of—dirty songs, Boer songs, Zulu chants, American cowboy songs. He didn't have a guitar of his own so he'd come to our room to play mine. My favorite was a cowboy song I'd never heard before, "I Had To Say Goodbye to Mona," Mona being the cowboy's faithful steed he'd had to shoot when she broke her leg. I liked the way Tweedy sang "boo-lets" for bullets.

Despite our improved circumstances, one of the men in our bay began to fail. Devere Thompson, Tommie, a Ranger captured in Tunisia after a disastrously bungled landing in a failed surprise attack on Bizerte. He began losing weight and couldn't stand without swaying. He got too weak to get out of bed. He wouldn't write home because his shaky handwriting would worry his family, and he wouldn't let me write for him because that would also alarm them. Over Tommie's protests, Doc Wynsen sent him to the camp hospital. The diagnosis was anemia and delayed shock. I visited him regularly. He needed extra rations, which the hospital could not supply, so I'd take his parcel items that had to be cooked and trade them for bread and other bulk food. I made him a pudding once. (I kept that a secret. If anyone learned I'd given food away, it might damage my credibility as a trader.) My roommates gave me cigarettes for him and Dogass Newman sent canteen items. I had to climb in a window to visit him. The hospital had been put off limits to visitors, with guards to enforce it, ever since Nobby and Dell slipped out of their beds to substitute for missing men at roll call. Tommie's condition worsened. He was sent out of the camp to a real hospital. We never expected to see him again but we did, weeks later. He came back cured.

Ross Greening, one of the lieutenant colonels in Colonel Gooler's room, did portraits with pastels sent by the Vatican. He'd do a portrait for anyone who asked. He had a long waiting list. He didn't smoke but two of his roommates did. Colonel Gooler, of course, and one of the new lieutenant colonels, Sam Agee. They charged all comers ten cigarettes a portrait, which they divided between them. He did a highly idealized portrait of me that made me look like Smilin' Jack, a dashing, handsome comic strip character. Maybe it was my mustache. I grew a variety of them during my stay at P.G. 21, none of the luxuriant type the British called "operational." I was clean-shaven about half the time but eventually arrived home with a neat brush type. I thought it gave me a certain air. (My wife-to-be said it was cute. After our marriage she made me shave it off.)

Colonel Agee's addiction to cigarettes was as bad as Colonel Gooler's. During tobacco shortages they'd scavenge for butts right alongside second lieutenants. They started getting up two hours before roll call to beat their juniors to the hunting grounds. They joked about placing the richest butt areas off limits to all below field grade but didn't. In a POW camp, that would be carrying RHIP (rank has its privileges) too far. Like their subordinates, they stored their butts in New Zealand chocolate tins and rolled the tobacco into cigarettes in toilet paper. Toilet paper was almost as scarce as cigarettes (I still have a packet I carried up Italy, across Austria, deep into Germany, and back to France; it was one treasure I wouldn't discard). We tore up newspapers for bumpf and were partial to pieces with pictures of King Victor

Emanuel or Mussolini on them. Those of us who tried to read our toilet paper during latrine visits learned a few words of Italian.

Learning Colonel Agee was a West Pointer, I asked him if he knew Captain James Luper, another West Pointer, class of 1938, and the only officer I'd ever seen tougher than Killer Kane. Luper was Commandant of Cadets at preflight at Maxwell Field. He'd been a first lieutenant when my class arrived but made captain shortly thereafter. He was lean and mean, dark, granite-jawed, with piercing, intimidating eyes. We were all terrified of him. Rumors were that he'd been captain of the boxing team, had accumulated more gigs (demerits) at West Point than any cadet since Ulysses S. Grant, and had courted and married the commandant's daughter. Colonel Agee said yes, he'd known Luper. And remembered him well. He'd been Agee's underclassman. Luper hadn't been captain of the boxing team but he'd been on it. Agee didn't know how many gigs Grant had but Luper'd had plenty. And he seemed to recall that Luper had, indeed, married the commandant's daughter.

A vogue for South America swept the Americans. We thought it would be a good place to go after the war. (Later it was Alaska. Anywhere but here.) We read all we could on South America and wrote home for books on the subject. Kennedy began studying Spanish. I'd made a half-hearted attempt to learn Italian but gave up quickly, even more quickly than I'd given up learning French. The Italians who needed to communicate with us spoke English and we didn't try to speak with those who didn't. If we tried we might have learned some Italian from newspapers and the radio, but even though time hung heavily on us we lacked the initiative for serious study. What Italian we did pick up was what we heard often from our guards or what appeared regularly in the news. "Nostri valorosi truppi" for "our valorous troops." "Il barbarosi nemici" for "the barbarous enemy." From our guards, "doppo" (later) or "domani" (tomorrow), their answers whatever the question. We learned their gestures readily. They used their hands a lot. Palm up, wagging, was a threat, the same as drawing a finger across the throat. Holding up the right hand with little finger and forefinger extended and grasping the right forearm with the left hand said something evil about your mother and your sister.

Kennedy stuck with his Spanish. Sometimes he'd study six hours a day, usually with Willie. At first he didn't have a text and copied vocabularies out of other people's books and memorized them. After he got a grammar of his own things went faster. Then the fortunes of war brought him a patient, willing and capable instructor, Lieutenant Alexander Alvarado, a B-17 pilot from San Antonio. He came in with Zeak Buckner, a B-17 bombardier from Dallas. Alvarado's accent was pure Texan, but he was equally comfortable in Spanish. He'd spoken Spanish at home but in school kids were fined a penny if they used a Spanish word. He was massive, slab of a chest, big hands. We called him "Little Alvie." He was dark and Indian-handsome, quiet and slow-talking, with gentle brown eyes. (In the seventies I modeled a major character in a novel on him, Tomas Alvarado, "El Azteca," in *The Olmec Head.*)

Buckner, paunchy with a rubbery face and a W.C. Fields nose, despite his appearance was bright and sensitive. And waggish. He'd sneak up on you and chuck you under the chin, crying, "I got your sugar," which might have gotten him a punch outside the walls but in P.G. 21 was considered good sport. And when Alvarado would prod or tickle him in his bunk he'd mutter, "I don't feel a thing. I'm asleep. Sleep, sleep, sleep." (I played his games with my children when they were little. They loved them.) Once when he was really napping, face down, I swatted him on his abundant behind just for the hell of it. To my great surprise he turned over slowly, grinned and said, "Why, hello, Caesar." I'd expected him to jump up and retaliate. I asked him why he wasn't sore at me. He said, "Young man, I am a very well-bred person."

During my South America phase I'd written home for a Spanish grammar, a history of the Americas and, to acquire a little culture in my spare time, a book on music appreciation. In addition to food and tobacco parcels from home we were allowed five pounds of books every three months. When I finally got a book parcel it contained the Spanish grammar and the history of the Americas but not the book on music appreciation listed in the contents. I had no idea why it was confiscated. My books, like all those arriving in personal parcels, had been stripped of their hard covers, which might conceal contraband.

The library, which had grown considerably, accepted books without covers, books in any condition, in fact. There were officers who knew how to rebind and repair. Thanks to their efforts, I read *Nicholas Nickleby, The Old Curiosity Shop, Return of the Native, Henry Esmond,* Joinville's *Chronicles of the Crusades, A*

Mind That Found Itself (as far as I know the first insider account of life in a mental institution) and G.U. Ellis's *There Goes the Queen*, a novel for some reason particularly affecting to someone in a POW camp. When not improving my mind with serious works, I read every detective novel I could get my hands on.

The fall of Tunis and Bizerte in May 1943 got all our hopes up. Italy must be next on the list. And mail arrived from the States. Most of us spent more time fretting about mail than pondering escape. I rationed my letter forms, writing most often to my mother and to my friends by a roster I kept. My most anxious moments came at mail calls. I sweated them out from the moment the sacks were brought through the gate and taken to the sorting room. There was always someone who'd peek in the window and pass the word about how much was there. Our room got very little mail at first. Most of us hadn't been in the bag long enough. Dogass had already received two letters when we arrived at P.G. 21, one from a girl who'd heard his name in a list of local war heroes on a Buffalo radio broadcast and another forwarded from a motor-boating companion who didn't even know he'd been shot down. Stuyvesant, Allen, the Admiral and Glenn got some mail, too. Allen's letters came from the AP and the U.S. Department of State, both of which were trying to get him reclassified as a noncombatant so he could be exchanged. Those letters ended when the Protecting Power came to our room and told him they'd failed.

My ordeal finally ended. Two letters for me, five for Gardinier, seven for Kennedy. Oh, joy to the world! My letters obviously were not the first mailed to me. The mail was like that. Older letters came in the same bag with more recent ones. We figured the Italians let POW mail accumulate in Rome until someone felt like shipping it out, and then not necessarily in the order of arrival. Barnes got no mail. Our hosts were even less solicitous of enlisted men than of officers.

During mail call I couldn't breathe listening for my name. When it wasn't called I'd be almost physically ill with disappointment. And when it was, let Heaven and Nature sing. (I thought that after liberation I'd be freed of sweating out the mail, but soon after returning home I set out to be a freelance writer, sending stories to magazines and waiting in hope and dread for the mailman.)

British POWs generally did better than Americans. Their

letters didn't have as far to go. They got their personal parcels pretty regularly, as well. Clothing, cigarettes, books. One unfortunate British officer got his first parcel only after being in the bag eight months. It arrived in the summer, its only contents an army greatcoat. And he already had one.

Their cigarettes came a thousand at a time, not often enough to spell abundance. Despite cigarettes' value for trading, the British were generous with them to their American allies. It wasn't uncommon for a British officer to slip into our room, hand Colonel Gooler a hundred or so for distribution, and slip out again furtively, as if afraid of being thanked. As far as I know, only one American cigarette parcel arrived at P.G. 21. It was sent to a British officer by a friend in the U.S. In our room Nobby and Otten got Canadian cigarettes. With the cigarettes and their friend in the cookhouse they lived well.

When a cigarette parcel came in, the recipient picked his cigarettes up loose in a Red Cross box brought along for the purpose. Our hosts emptied them out of their packages looking for concealed messages or maps. I thought it just another way for the commandante to harass us, but after the war I learned contraband really was slipped into POW camps in cigarette packages.

By the end of June 1943 I'd received eleven letters, most of them from family. One letter told of getting a War Department telegram reporting me missing in action, followed after a lapse of more than a week by a telegram reporting me a prisoner of war. (The missing-in-action telegram and my medals are framed in my older son's library, as are my wife's first husband's killed-in-action telegram and more impressive medals.) Another letter said that Leader's family would like to hear from his crew. Kennedy and I both wrote his parents. My letter described our leave together in Lebanon and Syria and ended, "I know he was calm and that his coolness played a large part in saving the lives of his seven crew members who escaped. I know that the end was quick, clean and painless and that he met it without fear. I know you can be proud of your boy."

IN JUNE WE BEGAN SENSING the war against Italy was approaching its climax. The islands of Pantelleria and Lampedusa surrendered, the first Italian soil to fall to the Allies. New prisoners brought news that in North Africa vehicles were being waterproofed. It could only mean preparations for an amphibious assault. But where? We dogged the radio and watched our hosts for signs of anything unusual.

The answer came in July. Sicily. Spirits soared and we talked of nothing else. We knew resistance was collapsing when prisoners began arriving at P.G. 21 only a few days after being captured, some without even being interrogated. When a pilot came in shot down only the day before, still smeared with oil, soot and dried blood, we felt as if the war raged just beyond our walls. We began keeping careful records of the sounds of transport on the road outside the camp, hoping it might be useful to the pursuing Allies.

Warmer weather and overcrowding brought parasites and our hosts fumigated the bungalows. We carried out all foodstuffs early in the morning and spent the day outside. Workmen put gas cartridges in the bungalows and sealed doors and windows. Late in the afternoon, after we assembled upwind from the bungalows, the seals were broken. A rumor swept the camp that when one door was opened a lively, healthy cat strolled out.

Summer brought a water shortage. Only a trickle flowed from the two taps in our courtyard. It took ten minutes to fill a one-liter vino bottle. The orderly for the day had to stand in line up to five hours to fill the bay's water bucket. But summer brought a treat we couldn't have expected from the commandante: swims in the nearby Pescara River.

The swimming party lines up in our compound, has a head count, and marches into the Italian compound to pick up our guards. Outside, unlike our walks, we are allowed to set our own pace. Despite the armed guards on either side, we have a sense of freedom and unbounded space. A hundred yards or so down the Pescara highway we turn off onto a dirt road. Over railroad tracks, past a small bridge with a guard posted on it. Now a dusty lane, an orchard, a building or two, and then another lane, just as dusty but tree-shaded. Miserable stone houses on either side, all with gardens, some with tobacco leaves drying on frames. A few civilians, all ragged, most wearing black mourning armbands. A blonde girl, maybe fourteen, with a beautiful, dirty face. And large breasts, the focus of our two-hundred hungry eyes. Undisturbed, she continues on her way with downcast eyes. Beyond the houses, open green fields. Grain growing in one of them, a tent in the middle of it. What was the tent for? In another field, a farmer cultivating his rows behind bullocks. Big, slow, lumbering beasts. What we have on meat days? I never tire of the view here. Hills in every direction in the distance, green as home.

Past the fields, a well-kept farmhouse set back from the road, and then two squalid houses side by side. Dirty dogs and dirty children playing together in dirt yards. Retreating toward the houses as we approach. The children look undernourished, the boys wearing only shirts not long enough to cover their nakedness. Urinating unselfconsciously into the dust at their feet as we pass. The lane narrows. Dust stirred by our boots hangs in the air. Wild raspberries grow on either side. We snatch them as we pass, ignoring the sting of thorns. We suck off the dust, spit it out and eat. Another turn, and another. And then, down a slope, the river. Sparkling blue in the sun.

It must once have changed course because the skeleton of a barge sits in a sandy depression nearby and the barn behind a weathered two-story house hangs over a ledge, as if it had once backed up to the river. Down river, willows. Up river, sycamores. Our hosts have pitched a screen of tarpaulins for us to undress behind so women in the house can't see. We don't care if they can. We feel no connection with anyone who is not a prisoner. Even when we leave the camp we bring our wall with us. The stretch where we are permitted to swim has been roped off. Maybe fifty feet of river for the hundred of us. Although we have given our parole (word of honor we would not attempt to escape), guards are posted on both banks and around our clothing. The water is shallow, deep enough to swim in, barely, in one small stretch in the center. But cool and refreshing. Children steal through the tall meadow grass to watch. The guards shout and chase them away. They run just far enough to stop being a threat to the guards' peace of mind and swim naked in the river. (Just as I did as a boy in Brays Bayou in Houston.)

Some of us go downstream under the suspicious eyes of guards to wash with the soap we've brought along. Time's up. We climb out and dry off on whatever bits of cloth we've brought along and pull our uniforms over our wet undershorts. The road back is hot and dusty. We arrive back in camp dirtier and sweatier than when we left.

The swims were by roster. After the novelty wore off many officers passed up their turns because of the confined area at the river and the hot, dusty walk back. And that POW inertia which made so many of us distrust changes in routine. I was able to go to the river as often as I wished. Swimming had always been my favorite recreation, most of all in rivers and bayous. Sometimes an hour out and back. I could swim only a few strokes in the Pescara River, but it was the nearest thing to freedom. The swims stopped before the end of July, but when the water shortage eased we luxuriated under the washroom tap until someone rigged up a jam bucket punched with holes under the pump in our courtyard and we took evening showers there.

July 19 American planes bombed Rome. A stray hit the Basilica di San Lorenzo. Response in the Italian newspapers was frenzied. A crime against civilization, the most barbaric act in history. Though the only bomb-damage pictures they ran were of San Lorenzo, they said it was just one of many sacred places hit. The commandante called in Padre Brach and demanded to know what he thought of his precious Americans now. Padre Brach said the basilica had undoubtedly been hit by accident but if the destruction of churches occurred in an action that would save lives by ending the war sooner, God condoned it. The commandante was furious. He revoked Padre Brach's noncombatant privileges, including extra letter forms, and stopped letting him leave the camp to attend mass at a local church.

The Italian press responded to the bombing of Rome with outrage. British and American air forces were the targets of their most virulent propaganda. Sometimes the British were the chief villains. They were the ones who bombed indiscriminately while the Americans hit only military targets. Then the roles would be switched. The papers claimed Liberator bombers came down and strafed civilians after dropping their bombs and that the Allies were dropping booby-trapped fountain pens, dolls, lipsticks and pencils to kill the innocent. They ran photos of purported booby traps and infant victims with mutilated limbs. It was through a newspaper article we learned how feared our B-24s were. The article went to great lengths explaining how it was possible to shoot one down despite its heavy armament. We pointed out to the B-17 types among us that the Italians didn't seem to respect Flying Fortresses as much as they did Liberators.

President Roosevelt and Americans in general were frequent propaganda targets. When Roosevelt declared an "I Am an American" day, the Italian newspapers said it was better called "Io Sono uno Bastardo," "I Am a Bastard," day because Americans were a mongrel race. They attacked America for its treatment of Negroes but, on the other hand, ran a photograph of Paul Robeson and a white Desdemona to illustrate racial mixing in our degenerate society. Usually crude, their propaganda specialists could sometimes be clever. They used a photo of an American submarine being launched sideways to demonstrate that Americans were so inefficient their ships often capsized on launching.

One night in the final week of July our guards were up late in their barracks, shouting and cheering, and next morning we were told a very important announcement was to be made in the afternoon. After which, we were ordered, there were to be no violent demonstrations. The camp seethed. What could they tell us that was so important? An Allied landing on the mainland? Was Italy quitting? Allen, who had a war correspondent's knack of sniffing out things, told me in private. Mussolini had been forced to resign.

We lined up in the street in ranks. When the announcement came we went wild. Disobeying the SBO, we broke ranks, yelling and singing. Across the wire, the guards waved and called to us, flashing V for Victory hand signals. Joy on both sides of the wire. Only the commandante and the capitano were glum.

The celebration continued the rest of the day and into the night after lights out in our bay, venting lots of bottled up emotion. Pebbles started rattling around our beds. It took us a few moments to realize the sentry outside our window was throwing them. We yelled at him to cut it out. He told us in Italian to shut up and go to sleep. We kept celebrating. Willie shouted "Bastardo!" out the window. Bang! Loud, startling. The patter of falling plaster on the floor. The sentry had fired into our ceiling. Talk about chastening. Abrupt silence broken only by the sound of heavy breathing. No more singing, no more talking, even whispers, the rest of the night. In the morning we learned from the marks on our ceiling that the sentries were using bullets that split into four pieces. We figured it was not that they wanted to mutilate us but that they couldn't shoot straight and needed the advantage of scattershot.

It wasn't the first time a sentry had let off a round with bad intentions in our camp. One had shot an OR who came out of his bungalow for a breath of fresh air after curfew, and another fired into the front of our barracks at a shadow he thought had moved. And our Italian-American doctor almost drew himself a round. When the situation got desperate for Italy he started taunting our guards by shouting out train calls in his fluent Italian. (In English translation, "All aboard for Chicago, St. Louis and New York. All the way.") One day when he did it at roll call it so infuriated a guard that the guard aimed at him. The doctor scrambled behind the formation before the guard could pull the trigger. An Italian officer intervened and we all breathed easier. The affair did wonders for the doctor's popularity among us.

The public address system in our compound was used for Radio Roma broadcasts and announcements from the Italian set-tore. Curfew was nine-thirty P.M., after which we had to be inside. Radio Roma began signing off nightly at ten with "Lili Marlene," "theme song" of the Afrika Korps. All of us, British and Americans alike, found it strangely compelling. Our senior officers prevailed on our hosts to move curfew to ten-fifteen so we could listen outside. We sat on the steps in the velvet Italian night, with the bungalows' blue blackout lights shining dimly on both sides of the road, listening to the sad, passionate song sung by an unknown singer with a disturbing voice. A German chorus sang in the background and each verse ended with a poignant trumpet call. (After the war I bought two copies of the recording pressed from the original master. I learned the singer was Lale Andersen and the correct title, "Lied Eines Jungen Wachpostens," "Song of a Young Sentry." When I wrote a novel in 1967 based on my POW experiences I called it *Song of the Young Sentry*. I have only one scratchy copy of the recording left. I wore the other out.)

Despite the wondrous events outside the walls I turned a little sullen. No mail. But when at last I got some letters after seven weeks without, I recovered smartly. Scenting freedom, I grew restless and started going to the mess hall days to write short stories, all of which were misplaced in my later travels.

In August I got a spate of mail. Friends, family, the one from Peter Glenn, colleagues on the paper (one of them, Morris Frank, a legendary Houston columnist and much-sought-after master of ceremonies, wrote, "When you get back to the paper and start giving out those movie passes, remember I'm the one who wrote to you when you were in prison"). Several from young women who said they'd been in touch with my mother about me. (I hadn't been serious about any of them and wrote my mother asking her not to give any of them encouragement.) And a letter with photos in it showing a good deal more female than any of us had seen in months from a beautiful red-haired dancer I'd written about in my nightclub column in the *Houston Post*. I posted the barest on our bulletin board. Prisoners from all over the camp lined up to admire it.

And in August I got my first personal parcel, badly crushed and minus a few small items, but it was one of the first to arrive from America and I was delighted with it. Gardinier got one, too, but Kennedy, Barnes and Jennette didn't. Jennette was especially bitter. He hadn't received any mail, either. Maybe it had all been sent to the hospital where he'd spent so much time.

My parcel had chocolate, dried peas, dried soups, bouillon cubes and other concentrated foods in it. Even some chewing gum. A lot of the concentrated food went into my escape ration. I was in an escape team with Colonel Gooler and Dogass.

Colonel Gooler wanted me because I spoke a little German. He gave me a paper pattern and the materials to make an Afrika Korps cap. We would be traveling away from roads, heading for the Vatican, and anyone who saw me from a distance was supposed to think I was a German soldier. My stitches looked machine-done. It was a splendid cap. I never got to use it. The tunnel we were to escape out of was discovered. I had mixed feelings about that. I wanted out but I wasn't crazy about walking the hills with only a German cap between me and recapture. That cap would have made a great souvenir but I misplaced it somewhere along my circuitous route home.

Air activity increased as the war grew closer to Italy. We saw German Ju 88s, Stuka dive bombers and transports, including the giant six-engine type we'd seen at the Naples airport, and three-engine Italian craft we couldn't identify. We seldom saw an Axis fighter plane. There was an Italian air force primary training field north of our camp. We'd watch the trainers flying in our area hoping one might crash. Kennedy and I were inside one day when an artillery officer from our room dashed in and announced glee-fully that there'd been a midair collision with only one parachute seen to open. We cheered. (I guess you had to be there not to consider that monstrous.)

Messina fell August 17, ending the campaign for Sicily. Then, nothing. We'd hoped with Mussolini gone and the Fascist party dissolved Italy would have quickly retired from the fray and, after Sicily, there would be an immediate pursuit of the fleeing Germans across the Strait of Messina onto the mainland. But the Allied forces just sat there. We took it personally. Didn't they know how we had suffered and how long we'd awaited their arrival?

Early in September the Allies made the attack on Italy for which we'd been restlessly waiting, but across the Strait of Mes-sina, at Salerno near the toe of the boot, not to the north of P.G. 21, where a wedge across Italy would guarantee our liberation. But at least we had visual evidence of the war now, Allied planes on the way to daylight raids, once a major formation glinting in the distance, and much closer, B-24s bombing Pescara on the Adriatic. We couldn't hear the bombs, perhaps because of inter-vening hills, but we saw the billowing smoke. One formation flew toward the camp and a single plane let down a few hundred feet to make a pass directly over us. They knew we were here! Jubila-tion. Alvarado was strangely silent during the pass. He'd been bombed and didn't trust bombers. Even our own. We ribbed him unmercifully. We were to learn.

At the peak of this breathless period when we expected the war to end for us any day, the commandante entered the camp during parade and, with the capitano, approached the SBO. After a whispered conference the SBO told us gravely he was going to the headquarters building to make an important announcement over the public address system. He left with the two Italian officers, ceremoniously it seemed to us. A terrible silence fell over the ranks. What could it be but the announcement Italy had fallen? It seemed hours before his voice boomed over the speak-ers.

"Officers and Other Ranks of P.G. 21." Pregnant pause.

"Officers and Other Ranks of P.G. 21." Another pause. My stomach clenched. In our hundreds we stopped breathing.

"Orders have been received from Supreme Headquarters at Rome" . . . This is it. This is _it_! " . . . that during air alerts all POWs must return to their barracks until the all clear."

A collective sigh rose like a giant sob from among us. Dismissed, we filed back to our bungalows disconsolate. A fighter pilot we called Piccolo because he was so tiny threw himself on his bunk and said, "I just lost a hundred years off my life." He spoke for all of us.

The Allies began making two and three raids daily. It meant we spent much of our time indoors. We felt an uneasiness that we hadn't when we'd been free to roam outside. Alvarado's fault, maybe.

German troops began streaming past the open front gates, the first some of us had ever seen except from the air. We sat watching all day long except when alerts drove us inside. We monitored the radio fulltime and listened to every sound from the Italian compound. The guards grew more friendly, as if sharing our vigil.

Five days after the Allied attack on the Italian mainland a courier roared up to the gate on a motorcycle, faceless in helmet and goggles. He was admitted at once. Carrying a dispatch case, he disappeared into the headquarters building. What could it mean, we asked each other and our guards. They knew no more than we. It must mean a major Allied breakthrough, we thought. Maybe our liberators were racing toward P.G. 21 even now.

We were sitting quietly in our bay about nine that night when one of our roommates ran in, white-faced. He tried to speak but couldn't. Outside, a wave of sound, men cheering at the top of their lungs. "It's over!" our roommate gasped.

No one moved or spoke. And then we all sprang up cheering, shaking hands, slapping backs. But only for moments. An unaccountable silence fell over the camp except for sporadic shouts from the OR barracks. We were told the next day that an OR and an officer had suffered mental breakdowns.

Next morning Allen packed everything he owned and went to the gate demanding safe conduct to Rome to cover the capitulation for the Associated Press. The guard refused. Allen demanded. The commandante himself came to the gate and told Allen he was responsible for the safety of all of us until the Allies relieved him. It was dangerous outside and he couldn't risk anything happening to Allen. From that moment Allen was a frightened and bitter man. He said it was only a matter of days before the Germans would take over the camp. There were those who agreed with him and wanted to leave immediately but most of us thought him overly pessimistic. Especially when the SBO assured us there was no danger of a German takeover. The commandante had told him the Germans were evacuating pell mell to the Po River, well north of our camp, with no designs on POWs.

Padre Brach held a thanksgiving service in the mess hall for all Americans in P.G. 21. He read from the Bible awkwardly, as if unaccustomed to serving a large congregation. Maybe it was because he'd joined the army so soon out of the seminary. His brief sermon was heartfelt but clumsy. Somehow I couldn't think of him as a priest but only as my friend, Padre B., up there blundering through a service with more earnestness than eloquence. I guess his goodness was eloquence enough.

We expected great changes at once, but the SBO ordered us to continue as usual until we received specific instructions otherwise. Allen obtained a translation of the Armistice terms. One of the first conditions called for the return of all prisoners of war to their own forces, which was the only condition that mattered a whole lot to us.

No one got much sleep. Kennedy and I sat up most of the night talking about home. Solemnly. The prospect of freedom was more sobering than intoxicating.

The Italians continued to run the camp, holding roll calls and distributing our rations. We chafed under that but the SBO refused to take over. He said they were responsible for our safety until our own forces liberated us. His second in command, a hardbitten Australian lieutenant colonel, refused to accept that. One morning he declined to turn out for the Italian-controlled parade.

The capitano sent a detail of guards to fetch him. He sent them away with a message for the capitano. He wouldn't leave his room until all Italians were withdrawn from our compound and we were allowed to conduct our own roll call. The SBO went to his quarters to reason with him. You can't reason with an Australian who's made his mind up, especially when he's right. And the ones I'd encountered weren't great respecters of rank to begin with. The Italians compromised. They were still allowed to be present at roll call, but unarmed. The commandante entered our compound only when informed his presence was requested at roll call. The capitano conveniently went on leave, taking his dog with him. Shortly before the capitano vanished, the commandante launched one of his celebrated hysterical tirades against some hapless guard. We gathered at the fence in strength to enjoy it. At the height of the commandante's display, the capitano drew his side-arm and held it aloft dramatically, as if to quell any thought of mutiny among his troops. We applauded, of course.

There was much talk of deposing the SBO and replacing him with the Australian lieutenant colonel, but we were still subject to military discipline and there was no one in the camp with enough rank to challenge the SBO. (None of us had read Herman Wouk's *The Caine Mutiny*. It was yet to be written.)

Our guards were as happy as we over the capitulation and inclined to be friendly now that the capitano was gone and the commandante powerless. They stood by, enjoying the spectacle, when we tore down the fences between our compound and theirs. They traded with us enthusiastically. What we prized most were knapsacks and canteens for our anticipated departure. With them it was soap, coffee and tea. We were surprised none of them wanted to trade for food. We'd thought everyone in Italy was going hungry. I got a flat, cloth-covered Italian army canteen for one bar of soap and a capacious army knapsack for two. Weaver traded for a rifle but the SBO made him return it.

Colonel Gooler would have liked taking us out of the camp to hide in the hills until friendly forces arrived but, although P.G. 21 was technically an American camp, the British greatly outnumbered us and he was outranked by the SBO and he didn't challenge the SBO's authority.

Anxious time. We sat on our porch steps all day long watching the gate, waiting for our liberators. Would they come on foot or in tanks, or would they drop from the sky in parachutes? How long would it take them to move us out? German transport streamed past steadily, heading north. Abandoning southern Italy, no doubt.

Inexplicably, the SBO seemed to have no direct contact with Allied forces and relied on the commandante for information. The commandante told him the countryside was in turmoil and it would be unwise for any of us to venture outside the camp. An entire division of crack Italian Alpine troops was on the way to guard us against seizure by the Germans. We didn't have a whole lot of faith in their ability to do that, but since the Germans were in headlong flight and didn't have the transport to move us they'd never be put to the test. A force of *Alpini* actually did arrive and took up positions in the guardboxes wearing their little hats with a feather in them. They were friendly but military, unlike our guards.

The Italian doctors and hospital orderlies put on white smocks and came and went a lot in front of the camp gate so that P.G. 21 would appear to be a hospital to passersby, not a prisoner of war camp. A German patrol halted outside the gates one morning and a lieutenant detached himself from it and conferred with the commandante. That disturbed us. But he didn't stay long and left with his patrol. The commandante told the SBO he'd told the German officer P.G. 21 was a mental hospital. We thought it appropriate.

The appearance of the German patrol spooked our guards. When darkness set in they propped a ladder against the wall in their compound and lined up to leave. An Italian officer came out and ordered them back to their barracks. They paid no heed. He stood a while in indecision and then went off. The Alpini in the guardbox made no effort to stop them. In fact, he helped some of them lift their heavy packs to the top of the wall. A crowd of us gathered to watch them desert. They invited us to join them. We declined the offer, laughing. Next day a guard motioned to me from within the Italian compound. I thought he was drunk but he was only frightened stiff. He managed to convey that he was leaving that night and wanted me to go with him. He lived to the south and knew the territory. He'd guide me to the Allied lines and in return I was to vouch for him once we were in Allied hands. I turned him down politely, amused. (I hope he got home safely. It was a hell of a long time before I did.)

Every night more guards decamped. Soon there were only a handful left in the camp. Maybe they felt safer among us than outside among German troops.

A few days after the first German patrol another and larger one appeared at the gate under the command of a major. The commandante led the major and the major's aide on a tour of the camp. We made ourselves as scarce as possible, filled with foreboding.

The SBO said to have no fear. The commandante had told him the major had only wanted to see if we posed a threat to the

German withdrawal and had accepted the commandante's assurance that we did not. And in turn the commandante had been assured by the major that the Germans wouldn't bother us if we didn't bother them. And anyhow, we thought, they didn't have the transport.

Now we waited impatiently but without great anxiety until one day at noon when the broadcast from Radio Roma switched from Italian to German. The Nazis had taken over the station and were exhorting their Italian comrades to reject a capitulation foisted on them by their false leaders. We doubted the Italians would be persuaded in great numbers but were frightened all the same. It didn't sound as if the Germans were in disorderly retreat.

Weaver and Mouse had already gone over the wall. When we heard German on Radio Roma, Kennedy and I decided it was time for us to leave. We went to our bay and, joined by Willie, packed to leave. Kennedy and Willie went to Colonel Gooler's room to get official permission, believing now that the situation had changed so drastically he would no longer accept the SBO's authority. He told them if we left he'd see we were court-martialed for disobeying orders when we all got back to the States. He still believed the Germans had no bad intentions as long as we remained orderly and that our leaving would jeopardize those who stayed on.

So we unpacked and sourly watched the rest of the guards leave and those several of our companions undeterred by any threat of court-martial. The only Italians left among us were the commandante and a handful of officers.

The SBO set us to guarding ourselves. We had a guard duty roster much like the one I'd endured at preflight at Maxwell Field. We mounted guard twenty-four hours a day to stop any more of us from going over the wall. Arnold Feast, a sardonic Canadian pilot in our bay, stepped outside our bungalow, swept the compound with a long, thoughtful gaze, and announced, "I want to remember this. This is the first time I ever saw two-thousand cunts together at one time." He was wrong, sort of. There weren't that many of us.

A Rude Awakening

TWO NIGHTS LATER WE WENT to bed and awakened to find German paratroopers armed with machine pistols occupying the sentry boxes on the walls. We broke into the Red Cross parcel storehouse and took what food we could carry and started destroying what we couldn't. Germans inside the camp saw what was going on and put a stop to it.

We tried to believe the soldiers were there only to see that we didn't try to interfere with the German withdrawal. They didn't have the transport to take us with them. We found it reassuring when they told us they only expected to be there two or three days. They were well-disciplined and friendly and didn't regard us with the mixture of fear and arrogance many of our Italian guards had displayed. And they didn't look like our idea of Nazis. More like a bunch of Americans.

We stood in groups below their posts and chatted with them, those of us who knew a little German interpreting. All very friendly. When we asked what they thought of the Italians and they replied, "The same as you do," we laughed together. They told us what their various combat decorations were for and we told them our "there I wuz" stories (the circumstances of our capture). Hey, we wouldn't be sorry to see them go but they weren't such bad guys after all.

Two days passed quietly. We expected our Germans to be gone any day. The SBO rescinded his order against escaping, leaving us stunned and outraged. He'd waited until crack German troops were on the walls to decide the commandante had been misleading him and the Nazis intended moving us. None of us tried to go over the wall. We weren't desperate enough to go up against German paratroopers and their machine pistols.

Another day or two. Nothing changed. Maybe the paratroopers would rejoin their retreating comrades and we'd be left to our own devices. The lights went out early one night. Probably another power failure. They came back on before dawn. One of our lieutenant colonels came in and told us bluntly we were to be ready to move in half an hour.

First, numb silence. Then helpless cursing, many of us near to tears. Dully I burned my letters from home and put into a pile the things I thought might be burdensome to carry. My pastel portrait because it would smear, the complete Shakespeare Glenn had given me. My food was already stowed in a plywood box Stuyvesant had given me. I filled my Italian canteen with water and put everything else I owned into my big Italian knapsack.

Barnes came to our bay while it was still dark. We discussed our situation soberly. Kennedy and I assured him the Germans didn't have enough transport to get us out of the country. Even if they could scrape up a few trucks, they'd only have enough to take field-grade officers. In any event, it was unlikely they'd bother with enlisted men. (Tenente, tenente, tenente, sergente.)

They had the transport, all right. Our bungalow was among the first lot to go. We lined up in the road, waiting to load onto the trucks they couldn't spare to move prisoners of war. The Germans didn't bother to take roll. Jake Otten and several others had gone into hiding in a tunnel almost ready for breakout and wouldn't be missed.

Those not leaving in the first contingent crowded around us to say goodbye. The commandante hovered close to the German officer in charge to assist in the loading. We'd have killed him cheerfully. And the SBO stood in the street with a fatuous smile on his face, telling us goodbye and that he would join us after the camp was evacuated. We could have killed him even more cheerfully.

We were packed into rickety trucks. We assumed from that we hadn't far to go. Two paratroopers set up a light machine gun and fired long bursts into the railroad embankment. It got our attention. We listened and believed when a German officer warned us in English not to attempt escape.

There were only two guards to a truck, one in the cab with the driver and one with the prisoners. Our guard held his machine pistol carelessly. It would have been a simple matter to disarm him. We didn't even consider it, not with the motorcycles mounting machine guns that constantly patrolled the convoy. And we were still gripped by that prison camp inertia. Except for the

occasional Claude Weaver or Peter Glenn, we just weren't geared
to act quickly and fearlessly. No doubt if one of us had made the
move to overpower our guard the rest of us would have joined
him. And if we'd been moved after dark probably many of us
would have jumped off the truck.

We bumped along, passing through dirty little Abruzzi villages. Their inhabitants came out of their houses to watch our
convoy rumble over cobblestone streets. In my scraps of German
I asked our guard where we were going. He didn't know the name
or why we were going there, but it was another camp a few
kilometers to the south. South. My truckload was encouraged by
the thought. Maybe the Germans were dumping us to be picked
up by our own troops where there wasn't any chance of us roaming around behind their lines. We still clung to the notion they
were in headlong retreat and hadn't the transport to get their own
troops out, much less prisoners of war.

The dusty drive ended at a crowded cluster of long, low
stone and stucco barracks. The camp lay in a green valley sloping
up to hills in three directions and on the fourth facing a steep
mountain. Clots of Other Ranks watched us dismount and line up
to be counted on the dusty road. The buildings were older and
meaner than those at P.G. 21. The latrines stank. We sweated in
the sun. The ORs told us we were near Sulmona. Most of them had
broken out of the camp after Italy capitulated but had been
quickly recaptured and had no more idea what lay in store than we
did.

We waited. Someone cried, "Get these men in out of the hot
sun," which is what soldiers always said when forced to wait,
even at night in a driving rain. Our new hosts took their own good
time. At last we were marched to our barracks.

Squalor. Brick and plaster lay in huge heaps. The camp had
been divided into dark, narrow compounds by thick walls. After
the capitulation the prisoners had knocked them down. The one-
story, one-room barracks had a single entrance reached by broken
brick steps. Only a hint of sunlight filtered through tiny, dirt-
encrusted windows. The floor was littered with dirt and rubble.
Grimy folding iron camp beds lay piled in disorderly heaps. We'd
thought we had it bad at P.G. 21. Despair hung over us like a pall.

One of our senior officers came in and took command. He set
us to work policing up and drawing cots and bedding. There were
so many of us assigned to the barracks we quickly had it almost

clean. Even with our cots in solid rows against the walls, leaving no open space except an aisle down the center, our new home looked almost livable. We felt much better.

Kennedy and I were separated. The Germans were rigidly rank-conscious and quartered captains and above in a compound where the barracks had separate rooms. Schoonmaker, Buckner, Alvarado and I formed our own tight little group to bunk together and share our food and troubles.

As soon as I was settled in, I went to visit Kennedy. His compound fronted on the wire. He'd been put with an Australian who'd been the camp's officer. Apparently OR camps always had at least one Allied officer in charge. He served as liaison between the prisoners and the Italians and did what he could to see the Italians held to the Geneva Convention rules dictating the treatment of prisoners of war. Kennedy's roommate told us living conditions had been miserable in the camp. The men lived in filth on short rations. Crowded into narrow compounds, they had for recreation only infrequent soccer games in a ten-foot-deep excavation on the west side of the camp. After the capitulation they'd run wild, tearing down walls, ransacking the parcel warehouse, and demolishing the barbed-wire fences. They'd fought off Italian civilians who'd converged on the camp to loot the Red Cross stores. They waited for liberation, as we had, but not for as long. After only a few days most of them took to the hills. Very few made it. The camp was in a bowl surrounded by steep hills, and a man could walk for days before getting out of sight of it. And there was no water.

Immediately after the capitulation announcement a group of ORs had gone to a nearby prison and released a large number of political prisoners, saboteurs and paratroopers. Most of them were in bad shape from torture and deprivation. Mostly Yugoslavs but a handful of British and Americans as well.

The Australian had been one of a party scaling the mountain east of the camp. It took them six hours. After a few days of living off the country, eating a sheep they'd killed, they'd gone back to the camp to get enough food and water for the long walk south to Allied lines. The Germans had come before they got out again. Some of their Italian guards had stayed on and resisted the takeover.

Though the camp wasn't heavily guarded now, and many of the rear echelon troops doing the duty were not Germans but

Poles, the Australian was not optimistic about escape. The terrain was too forbidding and there wasn't any water. And he believed, as we still hoped, the Germans were evacuating southern Italy and couldn't spare the transport to take us with them. Kennedy was in no shape to make a break anyhow. His inner thighs were so raw and irritated from a fungus infection that walking was painful. Just wearing trousers was a torment.

I went out to check the wire with a couple of Americans who thought it might be worth a try despite the Australian's gloomy appraisal. The wire was in pretty bad shape. In some places there was only a single fence instead of the usual two with concertina wire between them. The wires had tin cans containing pebbles tied to them. The guards were widely spaced and nonchalant. I spoke with one of them who said he was a Pole. (I spoke confidently with Germans now. One of my first acts on reaching the new camp was to shave my mustache. I thought it might make me look Jewish to them.) His German wasn't a whole lot better than mine so we got along famously. His morale was a lot higher than mine. When I asked him what he thought about the fall of Tunisia and Italy's capitulation, he said they were only temporary setbacks.

He said the Germans would soon sweep the Allies out of Italy and retake North Africa. I laughed at him when he said the Allies weren't making any progress at all against German resistance. Nazi propaganda. I knew Jerry was on the run.

I toyed with the idea of escape but didn't find the thought compelling. Why risk being shot going through the wire, or if not, wandering around for a few miserable days before being recaptured and losing everything I'd acquired in nine hard months when it was entirely possible if I just sat tight liberation would come to me?

Nevertheless, I joined one of the roving bands checking out the wire that evening. The guards were friendly. And careless. Maybe it was worth a try after all. I went to see Kennedy. Outside the barracks, the camp was in ferment. Laughter, loud conversation. A friend joined us, euphoric. "It's a circus out there," he said. "They're crawling out in droves and the Germans just catch 'em and send 'em back in. I've been out twice myself."

Kennedy thought maybe we should make a nervous gesture. That's what we called making an unplanned and unprepared-for escape attempt. But we both knew he was in no shape for a long walk. And why bother when the guards kept catching people on the other side of the wire? The guards were laughing at us now, but who knew when they might get fed up and start shooting?

When I got back to my barracks a friend asked me for my canteen. He was making a break for it. I started to refuse. I might want that canteen for my own escape. Anyway, he'd just get caught and the Germans would confiscate the canteen. I admitted to myself I wasn't leaving, not before Kennedy and I could go out together, and gave him the canteen.

With so much going outside, I couldn't resist joining the action. I started walking the wire again. The Germans had grown warier and wouldn't let us get close to the fences. Restless, I went back to Kennedy's room. We were discussing our chances of escaping when his itch got better when Willie came in and asked us to go through the wire with him. We said we were waiting for Kennedy to get well. He left. (The next time I saw him was in Houston when he called me at the *Post* and we went to dinner.)

We heard whispers and furtive movements in the wire near Kennedy's window. A voice shouted in German. Feet scurried. A rifle cracked. Someone moaned, "Oh, Jesus." We ran to the door. Shapes were stealing back to gather around a figure on the ground. Some senior officers came out and ordered everyone to leave. The Germans sent in a medic. The man on the ground, a Canadian, had been shot in the hip. There were no more escape attempts that night. The guards might be friendly, careless and inexperienced in their jobs, but they could shoot straight.

In the morning we learned that droves of prisoners had escaped in the night. Most of them had quickly been recaptured but more than we'd expected were still at large, including two friends who'd invited me to leave with them. That night or some other, big Joe Frelinghuysen slipped through the wire with another artillery captain named Dick Rossbach. (While assigned to the Pentagon after being called back to active duty during the Korean War, I was on the Washington–New York train when it made a stop in Baltimore. I was looking out the window when a voice from the aisle behind me asked if the seat next to me was taken. I turned to say it wasn't and looked up into the eyes of Joe Frelinghuysen. I hadn't seen him since Sulmona. In 1990 Sunflower University Press published Frelinghuysen's account of his escape and other wartime experiences, *Passages to Freedom*.)

Although at first the Germans had merely sent men back

into the camp, toward the last they put them in the cooler, unguarded and with no names taken. Just before dawn those in the
cooler broke out and sneaked back to their barracks.

Though a man had been shot, escape still seemed much
easier than at P.G. 21. Maybe Kennedy and I would try that night
if he felt up to it. Alvarado went with me on a serious reccy. On the
west side of the compound by the sunken soccer field a low building extended all the way to the fence. A good place to cross but
within the view of a German with a machine gun in a guard tower.
Too risky. On the other side of the soccer field there was tall grass
just outside the fence. That's where we'd leave that night. Before
we could try, the Germans declared a curfew. No movement out of
the barracks area after dark.

The Germans appointed a quartermaster staff among us and
began issuing rations. They were more liberal than the Italians
had been. The bread ration was double what we'd had at P.G. 21.
We hoped it was because they didn't expect to be holding us long
and saw no need to skimp. We found it was because they never
paid for anything. An OR who'd been taken with the Germans on
a bread detail told us how they did it. They drove to a bakery in
trucks and requisitioned the baker's entire inventory. They gave
him a chit showing what they'd taken and said the Americans
would pay him when they arrived. The baker protested. The
Germans took their machine pistols off safety and he was persuaded.

I had some vegetable bouillon cubes from a personal parcel
in my food box. One morning I drew hot water for Kennedy and
me and took him a brew made with them. Jack, an American I'd
known only slightly at P.G. 21, asked me for some cubes. Reluctantly. You didn't ask for a man's food. But he was weak from
dysentery and couldn't keep solid food down. I thought he had a
lot of gall to ask but gave him a few cubes. I didn't try to hide my
feelings. I knew he must consider me a real snot. It wasn't the
first time he'd seen my hard side. He'd been behind me in line at
the room canteen when I bought some notepaper for myself and a
pair of suspenders for Barnes. It's what he'd wanted. He asked to
buy one or the other from me but I refused. Rudely. He'd stepped
far outside the bounds of POW etiquette. He was as grateful for
the cubes as if I'd given them cheerfully. I liked him from that
moment. Here was a man who wouldn't let prison life make him
any less a decent human being. (I visited him briefly in Seattle, his

home town, in 1948. He remembered me giving him the bouillon cubes but not that I'd done so ungraciously. Even said I hadn't.)

Our senior officers had a concealed radio and listened to BBC broadcasts. Allen, who roamed the camp like a prophet of doom whose prophecy had come true, gave us news bulletins from the broadcasts several times a day. The Allies were at Foggia, less than fifty miles to the south, advancing rapidly. We were sure they'd overrun Sulmona before we could be moved. And every day new rumors of Allied landings to the north of us swept the camp.

The ORs were the last to arrive from P.G. 21, Barnes among them. He told us the men who'd hidden in the tunnel hadn't been discovered and had probably broken out. The area had been swarming with Germans when the ORs left.

The Germans were more organized now and began holding roll calls to learn how many of us they had. Maybe they did intend moving us. Every roll call our senior officers had a number of prisoners hide out so the Germans could never get an accurate count. We were warned against hiding out on our own because they wanted the Germans to get the same count every day.

Kennedy, Buckner, Alvie, Ed Griffin (Dapper Dan's bombardier) and I decided to dig a hole under our barracks to hide in and wait for friendly forces if the Germans evacuated the camp. We broke a hole in the stone foundation of our barracks and began digging. Kennedy wasn't much help digging because his thighs were still raw. He became the lookout. Alvie and I did most of the digging. Griffin made a camouflaged cover for the opening. He and Buckner got rid of the dirt.

Digging was hard work. Alvie, big and strong, was a taskmaster. We'd get covered with dirt in the hole and have to shower in the stone washhouse near our barracks before every roll call. The water was icy. We hated it. It was quickly obvious we'd never have a hole big enough for the five of us to hide in up to a week. At best maybe one or two. We decided to draw lots. We never did. The Germans found the hole. They didn't try to learn who'd done the digging.

We all wanted places to hide out. Gardinier and some friends found a promising nest in the attic of Kennedy's barracks. Kennedy and I asked if we could share it. Gardinier said there wasn't enough room. The attic was infested with ants, lice, bedbugs and spiders. After a night there, Gardinier and his friends had to abandon their plan.

I'd need water if I escaped. The ORs had left a lot of clothing behind when they took off after the capitulation, and it lay in heaps throughout the camp. I found a wool sock for a cover and an old web belt for a carrying strap. I also found wool British army scarves for Kennedy and me among the discards. There was a dump by the soccer field. I scavenged a wine bottle and a butter tin there. The cork had been pushed down into the bottle. I doubled a string, let it down into the bottle, looped it around the cork and drew it out easily. I thought that was pretty clever of me. The top of the butter tin had been cleanly removed. With a little force, the wine bottle fitted into it nicely. I made a snug cover for the bottle from the wool sock and sewed the web belt to it.

Though it was now October and well into autumn, we slept warm. Kennedy had found bundles of Red Cross blankets three times as large as the Italian issue and twice as thick.

The Germans allowed Padre Brach to wander in and out of the camp at will. He seemed able to do more with the Germans than our senior officers although the Germans thought much more of the SBO than we did. They'd complimented him on our spirit because of all the escape attempts and on our high morale. Padre Brach rustled up a habit from somewhere and went to mass in a nearby church every day. He'd grown a beard and could pass for an Italian priest if he'd wanted, but he chose to remain with us. One afternoon when we were joking around he grabbed me suddenly in horseplay and just as quickly pulled away. "What if some of the Italians would see me?" he said. "They'd be horrified. They take their priests seriously. If not their religion."

With the camp bursting at the seams, we were reshuffled to another barracks in the same compound across from a barracks full of Serbs captured in Yugoslavia. Chetniks. We figured the Germans would shoot them when the time came but they didn't seem worried. Their leader was a little old man with a huge beard. They cut their bread ration into thin slices and dried them in the sun for emergency rations.

A pale youth who limped from a bullet wound wanted Alvie and me to hide out with him in the Yugoslav barracks and make our way to Yugoslavia together. We turned him down. We didn't want to be shot with the Serbs.

Jack, pretty much recovered from his dysentery, went to live with some Syrian prisoners, figuring the Germans didn't prize them enough to take them along. We all wanted places to hide even though the BBC was reporting rapid Allied advances, and we hoped the Germans wouldn't have time to round up enough transport to move us all. A hope we clung to, to the bitter end.

Kennedy had gotten better, too, and was able to walk around the camp with me every day. On one walk we saw prisoners throwing sticks into the branches of a tree. It was an almond tree. We found a few nuts on the ground. First almonds either of us had ever eaten fresh off a tree.

Among the more recent prisoners were several from our Bomb Group with leather flying jackets bearing the Group "Force for Freedom" insignia. We hadn't even known our Group had an insignia. To occupy myself, I copied one using needles, a thimble and colored thread I'd found in the camp litter and embroidered first lieutenant bars on my battle dress epaulets.

Our days and nights alternated between despair and optimism. Optimism ended when it was announced the Germans had managed to assemble a few freight cars and some of us would be moving out. The Americans were going first. We were the smaller group. We drew cards to see who would fill the first quota. The drawing was packed with drama because we believed the longer we could stay in Sulmona the better our chance of liberation. I drew a nine of hearts. I just missed being in the first group, but I was an alternate. If someone with a lower card went missing, I'd have to take his place. The unlucky ones prepared to leave. I stood by, filled with dread, which was warranted. Several of those selected had made good hiding places and were allowed by the Escape Committee to go under cover. I complained bitterly and prepared feverishly to hide in the hole Alvie and I had dug even though the Germans knew about it.

A last-minute reprieve. Colonel Gooler declared the selection process had been unfair and insisted the movement not be carried out. He must have convinced the Germans, because a group of British prisoners who hadn't been in camp long enough to get established in their barracks shipped out in our stead.

In the morning one of our majors came in and told us one of the British officers had made a break for it at the station and been killed. Jock Short, a Scottish commando. The SAO would like as many of us as possible to attend the funeral services. Most of us did. We shaved, made our rumpled uniforms as presentable as we could, and those who had them put on ties. It was drizzling and the ground was muddy. Griffin was wearing a German camouflage raincape he'd traded for or stolen. He said he'd heard that when Jock saw he couldn't get away he'd run back to a boxcar and hidden among the other prisoners. When a German officer came looking for him with pistol drawn, Jock had put his hands up. And the German had shot him in the face.

There must have been five hundred of us on the muddy road by the soccer field. There were others besides Griffin with the camouflage raincapes. The rest of us huddled in British great-coats, with here and there someone in an American field jacket. Most of us were bareheaded. We stood silently, heads bowed against the rain. The coffin was down by the gate with Padre Brach, the SBO, Colonel Gooler, six pallbearers and Vince, the P.G. 21 band's trumpet player. He had a trumpet. I wondered if he'd brought it with him from P.G. 21. German guards looked on outside the wire. The SBO asked Vince if he knew the British equivalent of our "Taps" and Vince said he did. The SBO asked about British reveille. (He pronounced it "reevelly.") Vince didn't. The SBO said to use the American.

Padre Brach said a brief service, his voice low, calm, solemn. Priestly. The coffin at his feet was of unpainted boards. The Germans had covered it with a military flag. Padre Brach finished his prayer, and Vince played the British "Taps." It brought us all to attention. We lifted our heads for the first time. The least we could do for Short was give him a proper military sendoff. The rain beat into our faces, mingling with tears. The tears weren't all for Short. The last mournful notes died away and we relaxed, ready to trudge back to our barracks. The staccato notes of "Reveille" startled us back to attention. So brisk, so lively, so unexpected, even if the SBO had asked Vince about it. I thought of a bird flying up into sunlight. A meadowlark. (When I was a boy I'd shot three of them in a row off the top strand of a barbed-wire fence. I'd never shoot another.) Maybe the bugle call's promise of renewed life was for all of us. For a moment, at least, spirits rose. I wanted to cheer.

The pallbearers bent quickly and lifted the coffin to their shoulders. The Germans, who'd all been standing at attention, sprang to open the gate. They came to attention again and, as the coffin passed to be loaded onto a waiting truck, saluted smartly. Only one gave the Nazi version. And none said, "Heil Hitler."

The SBO shouted, "Dismissed!"

We right-faced before breaking ranks, the British way. The

guards slammed and locked the gate. The truck with Short's coffin bounced off down the road. We walked back toward the barracks in small, disconsolate groups.

That afternoon a German clerk brought a box of currency into the barracks and emptied stacks of bills, some coins and a few watches onto a rough pine table. They'd been confiscated from prisoners and kept in prison offices at P.G. 21 and Sulmona. Those with receipts were allowed first pick. Kennedy's watch had been confiscated some time ago but wasn't among those on the table. He did get back twenty American dollars he'd had in his wallet when we were shot down. Most of the currency went unclaimed. We were told to help ourselves.

We looked without great interest at the little stacks of American, British, Palestinian, Egyptian, Moroccan and Tunisian bills, wishing they were sugar or chocolate bars. We started dividing it for lack of anything better to do. No one grabbed. I took an American one-dollar bill and a five, two Egyptian pound notes and a few coins for souvenirs.

The Serbs had lots of Italian lire and came around offering to trade it for British and American currency. We suspected their Italian money might be counterfeit, and even if it weren't, before long it probably wouldn't be worth much. But we traded for it. We could use Italian money if we escaped. The Serbs were looking farther ahead than that. They wanted hard currency for after the war.

That night Griffin and a friend tried to escape through the wire despite what had happened to Short. They were caught but their only punishment was the cooler. Griffin told me later that he'd almost backed out of going when Padre Brach, learning of his plans, had shaken his hand and wished him luck.

The rain stopped and the next day we ate out in the open, as we usually did. Our rations were issued from large cans. We lined up with Red Cross tins, Italian messkits and whatever else we could scare up. The German soup was better and thicker than Chieti soup. Lots of potatoes, a rarity at P.G. 21. There, finding a piece in the soup was like finding a gold nugget. Anyone finding more than one piece was suspected of picking through the service bowl. There were also potatoes boiled in their skins. We ate skins and all. We got bread and tomatoes, as well, and sometimes oranges or onions.

The Germans got serious about getting an exact head count.

We were herded into the soccer pit for a roll call and held there all day while guards scoured the barracks for hidden prisoners. We'd been warned they'd toss grenades into any attic where they heard suspicious sounds.

On an order from the German commander, guards deployed all around us on the rim of the pit. They were armed with rifles, machine pistols, light machine guns and grenades. And alert. It made us nervous. Just what were their intentions? Kennedy muttered, "Let's keep in the middle." And we did.

False alarm. The only casualty was a prisoner who got a bloody head from a rock accidentally dislodged from the rim. It was hot in the sun, though, and we were all parched by the time we were dismissed.

The Germans found some of the men hiding out, but missed a number, including Gardinier and a friend of his who'd hidden in a pile of discarded bunks.

The day after roll call we got our moving orders. Until that moment we'd continued to hope something, anything, would prevent the Germans from taking us away. First, that we'd be overrun by friendly forces. When that hadn't happened, that there'd be a landing to the north. When that didn't happen, that there'd be at least a temporary delay. A bombing raid on the Sulmona depot, or one closing the Brenner Pass. A BBC report had claimed the latter had actually happened. If it were true, the Germans couldn't get us through the Alps.

I'd found a length of half-inch iron rod in the dump and now I hid it in my blanket roll. I'd learned to squirrel away anything that might some day be useful. I was pretty well equipped for a POW. Complete winter uniform, including greatcoat, other clothing scrounged from the Sulmona rag pile, emergency rations accumulated at P.G. 21, part of a Red Cross parcel, and the big Italian blanket Kennedy had given me. Quite a load. I felt lucky to have the knapsack.

We marched out to the road where trucks waited. Before loading on, we were given two Red Cross parcels each. The Germans had cleaned out the Red Cross storehouse. I got a standard British parcel and a British comforts parcel, the kind with nourishing beverage powders and an extra tin of condensed milk. I tied them together with rope from the pack-rat collection in my knapsack. I was a moving mountain in layers of clothing topped by my greatcoat, bulging knapsack, blanket roll over one shoulder and water bottle slung over the other, and carrying two Red Cross parcels.

Kennedy, Alvarado, Buckner, Schoonmaker and I had agreed to stick together. There was no more room in the truck after the four others climbed aboard, but I was allowed to sit in the cab with the driver. A nice break for me. The driver's raincape lay unwatched between us on the seat. I wondered if I could get away with stealing it, decided I couldn't, and didn't. Just before the truck pulled out an American major was sent to join our load. Since he outranked me, the Germans put him with the driver in my place. They wouldn't allow two prisoners in the cab. I managed to squeeze in among the men in the back, burdens and all.

Sulmona station was just down the slope from the camp, hidden from view by trees. ORs who'd been prisoners in the camp said they'd had a grandstand seat for American bombing raids on it and could even see falling bombs. We formed a long line snaking to a desk behind which sat a German officer. We gave him name, rank and serial number. A German noncom entered the information in a ledger. It took a while.

There were bomb craters all around the station, and a near miss in front had blown in a wall and exposed the building's foundation. Despite the considerable damage to the building, the tracks had been kept in repair. A long string of the boxcars the Germans didn't have stood waiting on them. The Germans let us visit the latrine but wouldn't let us trade cigarettes for food with a handful of Italian civilians who were looking on. Some of the Italians smiled at us. Others stared, stone-faced.

WE WERE HERDED INTO THE boxcars, thirty men in each. These boxcars were smaller than American ones. It was a tight squeeze with our packs, blankets and Red Cross parcels. The Germans let us keep our door open and visit the latrine freely. We'd seen a formation of B-25 bombers over the station only a few days earlier and a pair of P-38 fighters making a reconnaissance run, but we didn't fear being attacked. If anything, we hoped for a raid on the station so we could make a break for it in the confusion. Not Alvarado, who'd survived a bombing. Visibly nervous, he kept his fears to himself. He didn't want to alarm the rest of us.

A big chunk of concrete had been left in our boxcar. One of the prisoners wanted to throw it out to make more room, but Kennedy and I stopped him. It might come in handy if we got a chance to break through the door. That and my iron rod.

We studied the sliding door. It locked from the outside. I put a small piece of wood against the jamb at the end of the door track to keep the door from closing all the way. It was close on to dusk when the train pulled out. The guards found the piece of wood when they came to shut the door. The door slammed shut. We were locked in.

We were crowded together among our bundles. Elbowing some room, I got the iron rod out of my blanket roll. We waited until the train got rolling before using it. Any noise we made wouldn't be noticed then. Some of the cars were wood but ours, unfortunately, was a modern steel one. It had two windowlike ventilators about two feet long and a foot high almost six feet above the floor, one on each side. They were covered with heavy steel net welded into place. We set to work on one of them with my iron rod. The rod bent without budging the metal netting. A huge prisoner with bulging muscles from weightlifting tried smashing through the net with our chunk of concrete. It made a terrible noise but brought no response from outside. After a while we realized it wouldn't work. He slammed the chunk against the sides of the car and the door. Nothing. Just deafening noise. I tried the door with the iron rod and bent the rod out of shape again. We gave up.

I'd stowed my pack and blanket roll against the side wall and had just enough room to lean back against them but not to stretch out my legs. We'd piled into the car any which way. Now we tried to arrange ourselves and our possessions to create more space. Each end of the car insisted the other half had fewer men. We counted fifteen men into each end and piled what baggage we wouldn't be needing right away between the groups. We stacked the rest against the walls, except for everything flat and soft. That stayed on the floor. Some of the prisoners had bought cardboard suitcases at P.G. 21. Most of them had burst early in the crush. The crowding was aggravated by a few men who'd managed to stretch out and now refused to sit up. They stayed up late, talking and making jokes. There wasn't much we could do about it.

The Germans had set a big can by the door for a toilet. When a man had to use it, he took a couple of friends with him to hold him steady against the swaying of the speeding train. The men with diarrhea had a particularly difficult time.

The train slackened speed only at stations. Kennedy and I talked it over. If we managed to get the door open we'd only be able to jump as the train slowed to approach a station or before it picked up speed leaving. I curled up on my blanket roll next to Kennedy, conforming my body to its loop. Hands and feet over me, under me, in my back, my crotch, my face, but I dozed off and on. I'd get cramped in a contorted position, wake, and try for another, jostling all around me and suffering curses and complaints. I was a member of the same chorus when anyone near me changed position.

When the train slowed we heard spasmodic firing. After a while the train came to a full stop. Our door slid open and Doc Wynsen and another man were thrust into our car. We objected strenuously but the guard closed the door behind them without a reply. Doc said he and the other man were the only ones who hadn't escaped from the car next to ours. It was one of the old wooden ones, with uncovered ventilators. Doc Wynsen hadn't jumped because he thought it his duty to remain with us, and the other man had been too weak from dysentery to make the effort.

Wynsen said there were guards sitting on the top of the cars in the cold. The shots we'd heard were the guards firing at prisoners jumping out of boxcars all along the train, sometimes so many the train would stop and guards would chase out to round them up. Some got away. Those that didn't were merely crowded into steel cars like ours. Many of those not caught near the tracks were eventually recaptured in the hills. Several made it all the way home. And a few simply vanished, never to be heard from again.

The train sped through the night, stopping infrequently at stations or to let the guards chase down prisoners. At first light we took turns standing on piled baggage to look out the ventilators. We had no idea where we were or where we were going. The occasional road sign told us nothing. We didn't recognize any of the town names. The terrain was hilly, with factories and stretches of cultivated farmland. There were tank barricades on the roads. Around noon the train stopped and guards distributed big rounds of Italian hardtack and small cans of Italian corned beef.

When our toilet can filled up, we'd bang on the door at stops and a guard would open up and let us empty it. When he knew the train would be standing long enough he let us out to squat in fields close to the tracks. If he didn't know how long we'd be there he kept us inside. It wasn't much of a problem except for the men with diarrhea, but with the cold we all had to pee a lot. With strong friends to help us hit the toilet can we managed.

What we lacked most, other than room to move around, was water. Alvie and I were among the few who had containers, I with my water bottle and Alvie with a Chianti bottle in a wicker cover. We filled them at stops whenever the guard let us. We became pretty popular with our thirsty companions. We worked at the door and the ventilator grills fruitlessly throughout the day, cursing the bad luck that had given us a steel car instead of a wooden one.

The second night was like the first, memorably uncomfortable. (It probably would have been more endurable had I known the train ride would be the heart of *Von Ryan's Express*, the only one of my fifteen novels to become a bestseller.) The next day when the train pulled into a station, we knew where we were for the first time. Firenze. Florence. The civilians in the station were mostly well dressed, even prosperous-looking, but when we began throwing the unappetizing Italian hardtack out the door just to get rid of it many of them hurried to pick it up. The German

134 guards wouldn't let them get close to us or let us speak with them. We were told we'd be there a while and were allowed out of the boxcars to stretch our legs and fill our water bottles. The guards wouldn't let us go all the way to the water taps but were good enough to fill our bottles for us.

During the long ride in cramped quarters some of our body functions had been hibernating. Now, more relaxed, nature called us. We were too many for the station's toilets, and anyway we wouldn't have been permitted to pass among the civilians. German guards led us to the side of our train away from the platform. We let down our pants and squatted in an almost militarily precise row. I was just thinking what a sight all our bare behinds shining in the breeze must be to civilians looking under our boxcars when a passenger train pulled into the station and came to halt just opposite us. Italian civilians stared out at us. We stared back, unabashed. We thought it kind of funny. So did our guards.

When we returned to our boxcar, we learned we were without senior officers. They'd been put in day coaches instead of boxcars and, carelessly guarded, had escaped, Colonel Gooler among them. We were bitter about that. He'd gone along with the SBO in holding us at P.G. 21, and we figured the least he could do was stick with us and look after our interests.

Padre Brach filled the breach. He strode up and down the platform asking how we were and listening to our grievances. It was probably because of him we'd been allowed to leave our boxcars for water and bodily functions. By nature patient and soft-spoken, he was adaptable. The Germans respected authority and he assumed it. He was stern with them. He browbeat them. They loved it. It didn't matter that his German was halting. During a brief conversation on the platform he told me the only way to handle Germans was to yell at them. (He was to be the inspiration for Father Costanzo in *Von Ryan's Express*.)

Aboard again, still heading north. It got colder. We were almost grateful for the crowding in our boxcar. Body heat kept us warm. Earlier, there'd always been a wait to look out the window. Now most of the prisoners tired of it. Kennedy, Honeybear Bryant and I had all the time we wanted. Our view of northern Italy was a rectangle crisscrossed by steel webbing.

The train stopped briefly in Bologna. Someone in our boxcar figured out a way to wire the door latch so it could be opened from within. While we did our squats behind the boxcars, two of our group sneaked back to our car and fastened the wire to the latch. When our guard slid the door shut it made the usual sound, but once we were under way a tug on the wire worked the latch. After a discussion about who would go first, we agreed a bomber pilot named Houston from Virginia would do it. (He'd made only four missions but three of them were memorable—the low-level attack on the Ploesti oilfields, the first Vienna raid, and the bombing of Rome.) I, Kennedy, Buckner and Alvarado would follow in order. Though we believed we were too far north to evade capture for long, the thought of a day or two of freedom made risking the jump worthwhile even if it meant leaving behind all the painfully accumulated kit we'd need for the hard German winter when recaptured. We were experienced POWs now and didn't expect severe reprisals if caught.

After much talk, we agreed our best way of getting back south to our own lines was with the help of friendly Italian civilians. Or perhaps just hiding out with an Italian family until friendly forces came to us. Preferably an Italian family with nubile daughters.

We waited until dark to crack the door. I put on my battle dress jacket over my sweater, my greatcoat over the jacket. I did my scarf ascot fashion around my neck and pulled on my gloves. Finally, I arranged my blanket roll and water bottle strap in such a way they wouldn't strangle me when I rolled. And waited, sweating in my wool cocoon from body heat and fear.

When the train slowed, we slid the door open and Houston got ready to jump. The train stopped completely and we heard guards coming on an inspection tour. We slid the door shut and waited breathlessly. The door passed inspection. It happened repeatedly, train slowing, Houston preparing to jump, train stopping, guards checking boxcars. Finally, after a stop and start, Houston jumped. A shot followed immediately. We didn't know if it were Houston who'd been fired on or someone escaping from another boxcar. Jumping suddenly got less attractive. We slid the door shut. I took off my blanket roll and water bottle, slipped off my gloves and put them in my greatcoat pocket, took off my greatcoat, folded it over my blanket roll and sat down. Kennedy, Buckner and Alvarado joined me.

At the next stop the guards came on their inspection. One of them tried our door and found it unlocked. He called out angrily to his fellows.

"Was ist los?" I demanded from the safety of massed bodies.

He threw the door open violently and shined his flashlight into the boxcar. We all feigned sleep.

"Was ist los?" he said with heavy sarcasm, and swore at us with great feeling.

We giggled like schoolboys, which made him angrier. He swore some more and banged the door locked. It didn't matter. We had no stomach for jumping and being shot out of the air. We'd already been through that.

Next day we saw distant snow-capped mountains from our window. The terrain had changed. The mountains were higher than those we'd left behind. The fields were lusher. We crossed more streams. It was getting colder. We knew we were approaching the Alps.

The train stopped at a station with a crowd of Italian men and women on the platform wearing Red Cross armbands, among them pretty girls. The civilians gave out oranges and grapes to hands reaching out from open boxcar doors. They showed surprise when prisoners spoke to them in English but kept on passing out fruit. (Padre Brach told us later that they were there to cheer up loads of Italian prisoners of the Germans.) From the window I concentrated on a girl and called out, "Veramente una bella ragazza." "Truly a beautiful girl." (I hadn't learned much Italian in my nine months but enough to say the right thing at the right time.) Others in the boxcar took up the call, making the Italians on the platform smile. They were as kind as if we'd been their own.

We weren't allowed to leave the boxcars here, but at the next stop the guards let us out to stretch. Griffin wandered off in the direction of the latrine and we never saw him again. (I didn't, anyhow, until about thirty-six years later at a 98th Bomb Group reunion. He was by then a practicing dentist in Atlanta, Georgia. After rough times he'd crossed the Pyrenees mountains into Spain accompanied by a guide and an escaping tank officer named Dan Coffee, who'd been in the same dormitory I was in at Rice Institute in 1937.)

A broad river rolled just ahead of the train. We were told the next stop was Bolzano, at the entrance to the Brenner Pass. Once through the pass we'd be out of Italy and even more firmly in German hands. We abandoned all thought of escaping from the train. Only a quick end to the war could save us now. We did find small comfort in a theory that the German takeover of P.G. 21

breached the Geneva Convention and the Allies would bring pressure on them through the German prisoners the Allies held and force them to give us back.

The train crept along the trestle over the river and stopped in the Bolzano marshaling yard across from a just-arrived German hospital train. We sat. In the distance an air raid siren. Other sirens took up the alarm, more and more of them, closer and closer. The hospital train gathered steam and chuffed away slowly. Running feet. Flak guns thundering close by. We hit the floor of our car, layered. Someone under me, Honeybear on top of me. I thought of the burned-out freight cars I'd seen at the stations in Sulmona and Florence. I tried to burrow under the man beneath me. Honeybear tried to get under us both. The throbbing roar of high-flying aircraft approaching. The flak intensified. Shrapnel pattered on the roof. Then, bombs falling. They didn't whistle or shriek as in the movies. They roared and clattered like an immense load of gravel rushing down a tin chute. This wasn't the movies. A deafening noise. Terrifying. Exploding bombs rocked the boxcar, the explosions no louder than the sound the bombs made falling. Outside, pounding feet, voices yelling in English, scattered rifle shots. A prisoner pulled himself up to a window, hysterical. He saw someone he knew and screamed again and again, "Canadian, open the door! Canadian, open the door!" His panic embarrassed me. What would the Germans think of us? I was as frightened as he was, stomach knotted, lungs contracted, but I couldn't have screamed even if I'd wanted. It was tough enough just breathing.

One man in all the fleeing mob was brave enough to help us, Tweedy, the South African who played the guitar and sang American cowboy songs. He was running by on the side opposite our door when he heard the screaming. He had to climb over the coupling to get to us. There was a lull in the action. The first wave of bombers left. As Tweedy fumbled at our door the next wave began dropping its bombs. There was seething anger in my terror. Had I endured so much only to die after all, killed by our own planes? I was sure I had only minutes to live and wished I'd been killed like Leader when *Natchez to Mobile* broke up instead of coming all the way to the Brenner Pass to buy it. In my head I kept repeating, "What a dirty son-of-a-bitching deal!"

The door slid open. Tweedy ran off without waiting for thanks. The first man to get to the open door gathered himself to leap. A shot cracked and he drew back. We screamed at him, "Jump, jump!" He did. We tumbled out after him. The guard who fired had taken cover himself and there were no more shots. Panic-stricken, instead of climbing over the coupling and running toward the relative safety of the city, we raced across the marshaling yard, the target of the bombers. And the bombs kept falling, each one sounding as if it were coming straight at us. My terror was controlled now. I wasn't locked in a boxcar blind to what was going on around me. I pounded across the yard, leaping tracks, scrambling under freight cars. Kennedy was right behind me.

A high wooden fence loomed ahead of us. Prisoners were scaling it. They dropped back to the ground. The other side was walled in. Buckner and Alvarado caught up with us. A paved street and buildings were to our left. We ran that way. The bombs had stopped falling, and we were no longer too frightened to consider this a chance to escape. We hurried along the street. There were empty fields on one side. No place to hide. We ran around a building on the corner. Into a dead end. Back to the street. We saw for the first time it curved back toward the railway station. Near us a cluster of prisoners were drinking wine in front of a shabby building. We ran inside and found ourselves in an unlit wine cellar. It was crowded with prisoners and Italian civilians drinking wine in quiet harmony. A British OR handed us cups of wine. I took a sip but was afraid to drink more. I knew my heaving stomach would reject it. Kennedy and I worked our way to the back of the cellar. We asked the proprietor if there was a rear exit. He said there wasn't. We didn't know if he were lying or not, but we left and followed the curving road. It passed under the railroad tracks. We left it to run through a weed-grown lot and scramble over a ditch to a roundhouse in the yards.

Two Italian youths in natty knickers, ski boots and tailored jackets were watching us. Kennedy called to them in Spanish. They answered in Spanish. We joined them. They were curious but unafraid. Kennedy asked how far it was to Switzerland. Fifty or sixty kilometers of difficult, mountainous terrain, they said. Kennedy asked if there were some place we could hide or get civilian clothes. They said no. They'd like to help but it was too dangerous. The Germans would shoot them if they got caught. They didn't think anyone else would dare help us, either. Their pessimism made us wonder if there was any use trying to get away. An old man came out of the roundhouse and gave us a bag of apples. It was hot and I was wearing British woolen longjohns. I'd taken off my shirt. We all took an apple and I tied off the rest in a shirt-sleeve.

Kennedy said if they couldn't hide us, could they at least tell us where to find some pretty girls. They laughed and slapped him on the back for thinking of girls at a time like this. While we were talking, a young German soldier approached within a few yards and stood watching us. Shyly. We sensed he was waiting for us to start heading back for the boxcars but was hesitant about ordering us to do so. He had a rifle but obviously was not eager to shoot anyone. So we ignored him and kept on talking to the Italians. Finally he mustered the courage to come up to us and ask us to return to the train. The Italians left immediately. We followed the young soldier back toward the boxcars. Some British ORs from our train had already built little fires beside their boxcars and were brewing tea. I didn't see any Americans doing that. The British were more nonchalant about danger than we were. And the relationship between them and tea was mythic. A British officer at P.G. 21 whose job it was to retrieve abandoned and damaged German tanks told me he had the best bloody ORs in the Eighth Army. "Out of the lorry and a brew up in five minutes."

We were still a little distance from our boxcar when the sirens went off again and we heard aircraft in the distance. Almost as frightened as we'd been earlier, we pelted across the yards again, the young German right with us. He had a slight lead at first. His rifle weighed him down, so even burdened with a shirtful of apples I gained on him. We were dead even by the time we got back to the paved street. He seemed reasonably calm and it steadied me a bit. He led us to the cellar of an old apartment building. There were already a German soldier and two women in it. One of them was an ancient who sobbed hysterically. I'd never felt any twinges about bombing enemy shipping or harbors, but now I was ashamed that our planes were doing this to a helpless old woman. The cellar was divided by wood lattices but we all crowded together in one section. Fear loves company?

Bombs exploded outside. The prisoner who'd been hysterical in the boxcar ran in, wild-eyed with terror, bare-chested where his shirt had been ripped half off his body. We were so ashamed that the German soldiers and the two women saw an American in such a state we displayed courage we did not really feel. The Germans didn't seem particularly frightened. Being ground troops, maybe they were used to it. The old building shook with every bomb, bringing dust sifting down from the ceiling. We expected the apartment house to collapse on us at any moment. We made a show of talking nonchalantly, hoping it convinced the soldiers. Our terrified companion crouched on the floor, clutching the legs of a fellow prisoner, breathing hard and saying nothing. I was glad my fear was not as obvious as his.

When the bombing stopped, the older soldier ordered us out of the cellar. We went out and milled around in the street with other prisoners, all of us looking desperately for some avenue of escape. We were fearful of more bombing if we returned to the marshaling yard and didn't want to hide in any of the nearby buildings because we now believed if we were caught in one of them the people living there would be shot for harboring us.

A grim-looking old man came out of nowhere with a World War I rifle. He wore an armband marked S.O.D. He pointed his old but serviceable-looking rifle at us and barked out harsh commands. I couldn't understand his German, but it was obvious he he wanted us to line up. We did. He had angry eyes. He looked as if nothing would have pleased him better than an excuse to fire. We'd taken liberties with German soldiers because we knew they were veterans unlikely to shoot for some minor provocation. They knew just how far to let us go and made a sort of game of giving us a little leeway. But this old man seemed full of hate. Bloodthirsty. Instead of keeping his rifle slung over his shoulder, he pointed at our heads, moving the sights back and forth from man to man. He herded us like sheep back to the marshaling yards. He turned us over to some German soldiers who didn't seem to like him any more than we did.

We learned that the S.O.D. was a civilian auxiliary composed of over-military age Germans not widely admired by real soldiers and that one of them had killed Jerry Chambers, one of our most popular actors. Chambers had tried to escape on a stolen bicycle, and the S.O.D. had shot him in the head.

We climbed back into our boxcar and rounded up our belongings. Everything I'd left behind was there but my cup. It was of Gardinier's design, with a hollow tin handle. I'd put all my Sulmona money in it—several thousand lire in large bills and my Egyptian and American currency. I couldn't find it anywhere.

We were afraid more bombers would come and kept after

our guards to move us out of the yards. Padre Brach told us we were going to be all right and began haranguing the Germans. It worked. They had us gather our belongings and line up in the street in front of the station. And kept us there, fretting. We were still too close to the target. The sirens started up again. We broke and ran. We wanted as much distance as we could get between ourselves and the station and to find a building to hide in. I was better equipped to escape now because I had the jacket I'd left behind when I ran from the boxcar in panic.

Kennedy and I pounded straight down the street, front-runners in the stampede. The windows of a building up ahead had been shattered by concussion. Not reassuring. The few civilians out on the street didn't seem especially alarmed. We took that as a sign stray bombs didn't fall in the city when our bombers hit the marshaling yards. That was reassuring. The street forked. Kennedy and I took the right fork, and after we'd run a couple of blocks saw an S.O.D. waiting at the end of the street. We ducked into a walled yard that turned out to be a beer garden with iron tables and chairs and to one side a paved court and water fountain. A bunch of British Other Ranks had already taken shelter there and several Arabs, as well, the same Arabs I'd been sure weren't important enough to be moved out of Italy. The ORs asked us to pull rank if the Germans tried to make us leave. Kennedy out-ranked me, but we agreed I'd do the talking because he didn't know any German. We'd hardly caught our breath when a German private came in and ordered us to move. I told him I was an officer and would see that no one left the beer garden if he let us stay until the air raids were over. He left.

The ORs were apprehensive but not as much as Kennedy and I. If they'd had the makings, they'd no doubt be brewing tea. I still had my shirtful of apples. I passed them out among the ORs and Arabs. Kennedy took his clothes off and had a bath in the fountain.

It was pleasant in the beer garden. The last air raid warning had apparently been a false alarm. We relaxed. Kennedy tried to trade the proprietor of the beer garden cigarettes for beer but the man was afraid the Germans wouldn't like it. The Germans treated us better than they did Italians.

A German patrol came along and swept us up with a throng of other prisoners. They marched us back to the station. We didn't like that much but took comfort in the lateness of the day. If there was to be more bombing, it probably wouldn't come until hours after dark.

My water bottle and Red Cross parcels were missing. I wondered who'd stolen them. Italians or German soldiers? I doubted it would have been a fellow prisoner. The Germans formed us in long lines and marched us two blocks to an enormous apartment building. They herded us into its bare dirt courtyard, surrounded on three sides by the building and on the fourth by a brick wall. There was hardly room to turn around, but it wasn't as bad as the boxcars.

German guards were posted all along the building to keep us from sneaking into it and to prevent the occupants from coming out. However, they did let Italian children bring us water and oranges sent out by their parents. We'd found nothing but good will among Italian civilians. We sent the children back with gifts of chocolate and cigarettes. Apartment windows were filled with Italians looking out at us. We called out to them and waved, especially at pretty girls. How we craved to sneak past the guards and get to them. It probably was just fevered imagination, but we thought some of them looked as if they'd like that, too.

We must have gotten too rowdy to suit the Germans because they made all the occupants shut their curtains. German officers came among us and told us if anyone tried to escape they'd shoot every Italian in the apartment house. If the Italians we'd spoken with hadn't been so afraid of the Germans, we'd have thought it a bluff.

Now that the people in the apartment house weren't allowed to send out water, the only source was a single tap in the courtyard. And there were no toilet facilities. The Germans brought in picks and shovels and had ORs dig two latrine pits in the packed earth. We couldn't wait to get to them. All that fear and running had uncorked us. We waited our turns in two long, fretful lines, begging those ahead of us to hurry. My stomach was griping. I fought against losing control. If the man ahead of me at the pit had taken a second longer, I'd have lost the battle.

A friend from the boxcar came looking for me with my Red Cross parcels. He'd found them outside the station. And then, while roaming the courtyard in search of other friends, I saw a man with my water bottle over his shoulder. I told him it was mine. He argued. He said so-and-so had given it to him. I tracked down so-and-so and had him tell the man he'd found it in the marshaling yard. The man still wouldn't surrender the water bottle until I pointed out my initials on the cover. For a man penned under guard in a dirt courtyard thousands of miles from home I felt pretty pleased with the world. I had my Red Cross parcels back and my water bottle, without even having had to fight for them.

Kennedy and his friend, Lew Lowe, and I decided we'd share our blankets for warmth. While we were making our pallet, a loud disturbance at the back of the courtyard brought us running. An Arab who'd been lucky enough to have had too much to drink had jumped a soldier. The German had pushed him away and was looking for a clean shot at him with his machine pistol in the press of onlookers. An English OR named Chris, a huge young man, friendly and awkward as a puppy, tried to punch out the Arab to quiet him and save his life but the little Arab was just too tough and too drunk to go down. Instead, he turned his attention from the soldier to Chris. Chris didn't want to hit him again. He grabbed the squirming Arab but couldn't control him. The German moved right along with them as they struggled, his machine pistol still at the ready. The Arab got away from Chris and leaned drunkenly against the back wall. We got out of the German's line of fire. Even Chris. The German seemed just waiting for the Arab to make a belligerent move. Two of the Arab's friends rushed to the prisoner's side and argued with him in Arabic. One of the Arabs spoke some German. He promised the soldier they'd see their drunken friend didn't make any more trouble. The German saw humor in the situation and turned away, laughing. It was reassuring, confirming what we already believed. German soldiers were sure of themselves and didn't have to shoot us to demonstrate their authority.

With the customary mix of bungling and efficiency we'd come to expect of them, the same Germans who'd taken hours to get us from the station to the courtyard had hot soup made for us to go with our cold Red Cross food.

We bedded down for the night. Lowe had a German rain-cape. We put it down for a groundsheet against the cold and damp and spread two blankets on it. We pulled a third blanket over us and on top of that our greatcoats. We kept gloves, scarves and jackets on. The only thing we took off were our shoes. We lay talking about the bombing, the possibility of the RAF coming over that night, and our chances of getting away and making it to Switzerland, all the while alert for the sound of aircraft or sirens. We understood now why planes in the area always made Alvarado nervous. When we slept it was fitfully, waking to the sound of every aircraft passing overhead and listening in breathless fear until it was gone.

In the morning Padre Brach, who continued to be our liaison with the Germans, told us they'd informed him we'd have to march forty kilometers to the next town. The railroad bridges to the north of us had been knocked out in the previous day's raids. We were to lighten our loads, taking only what we thought we could carry. I burned what papers I had left except for a couple of notebooks and my packet of Italian toilet paper and discarded some of my food. An OR asked me if he could have it. I gave it to him. I would have left my books behind, but when Kennedy said he wanted them if I didn't, I put them back in my knapsack. Even if he carried them, I'd still have the use of the books and it would have amounted to him carrying them for me.

They gave us bread and hot water for brew. We ate heartily of the rations we'd brought with us. It was easier to carry in our stomachs than on our backs. I still had more possessions than I thought I could carry forty kilometers, so I put everything I thought most dispensable in a separate bundle to discard if I had to. We lined up out in the street and marched away.

Back to the same cars from which we'd fled. We never learned if the promised march had been only a ruse to get us to leave food the Germans could use for their own purposes or if the bridges had been hurriedly repaired. The only visible damage from the raid was to a building across the yard. It was still smoking. We learned that the bombers had been after the railroad bridge we'd crossed coming into Bolzano, a few hundred yards away, and had knocked it out. The bombs had slanted directly over our boxcars in their fall.

We were locked in again. And sat there. Noon came and went and still we sat. It was getting close to the time of the previous day's raid. We grew more frightened. We muttered among ourselves and called out the window. We got no answers. When a trainload of Hitler Jugend, which had pulled in after we were locked in our boxcars, appeared to pull out with unseemly haste we believed they'd been warned of approaching formations. We stopped all conversation to listen for the sirens. We knew it was common tactics for our planes to knock out a railroad bridge one day and return the next to hit the immobilized traffic in the marshaling yards.

The boxcar lurched. Blessed relief. Then nothing. At last we moved again and, slowly gathering speed, left the station. Past the roundhouse and over a bridge. And finally, into the Brenner Pass approaches. Fear dropped away, and I actually began enjoying the scenery, tailored, verdant meadows and backdrop of snowy peaks.

We stopped at a lonely siding. The door slid open and a German officer looked into our boxcar.

"You are now in Austria," he said in English. "Germany. Escape is now forbidden on penalty of death. If a soldier escapes, five occupants will be shot. Ten if an officer escapes."

The only one in the car who didn't appear to take that to heart was an Arab who'd somehow been shoved in with us and who didn't understand English. We tried to impress on him the officer's threat but got only an uninterested nod.

The scenery grew lovelier as we approached the Brenner Pass. Honeybear and I stayed shoulder to shoulder at the window, looking at it. Kennedy joined us occasionally but for the most part we had the view to ourselves. There were passages so narrow there was room only for the tracks, a small stream and a road. The frequent tunnels were all well guarded. We wondered peevishly why a few good bombings hadn't closed them. Where the pass widened, the green fields on either side of the stream looked manicured and the patches of trees parklike, without underbrush. There were herds of cows in the fields but not a cowpat to be seen. Puzzling, until we passed a farm and saw workers raking the stuff up almost before it got cold.

Roadside signs were all in German now. Depressing. But in a way exciting, as well. I was adding another new country to my list. The train stopped briefly in small way stations. We'd listen anxiously for aircraft. The pilots among us had learned to recognize the sound of German multiengine planes. They droned because the engines weren't synchronized. Allied engines were and had a smooth hum. We relaxed when we heard the drone.

Deeper within Austria the landscape opened up to present picturesque villages and rambling houses with fading "Gasthaus" signs painted on roofs. I resolved that after the war I'd bicycle through the Brenner Pass and stop off at one whenever I got tired. (I never did, but I did drive through the Brenner with my wife in 1967 in a British Triumph sports roadster.)

The tracks made a long curve, granting us a spectacular

146 · view of green slopes, a shining stream and emerald foothills against a background of snowclad peaks.

Honeybear said, "I wish my wife was here."

I stared at him. "What!"

"I just can't enjoy anything beautiful if she's not here to see it with me," he said. (At the 1984 Oflag 64 reunion in Las Vegas I got a chance to tell his wife what he'd said.)

The meadows gave way to fields of virgin snow. The guards let us out to one of them when the train stopped briefly. We scampered across the pristine surface and spread out to perform necessary functions, with no farmers around to rake up after us as they'd done for their cattle. Snowballs were thrown. I'd thrown one or two before in my childhood during Houston's very rare snowfalls, but I'd never done a squat in snow. An experience to cherish. The guards shouted, "Einsteigen!" We'd learned it meant "all aboard," and that "aussteigen" meant "get out," and "anstehen" meant "line up." We threw our last snowballs and clambered aboard, refreshed.

We spent the night locked in on a siding in a fairly large town, nervous the whole time and listening for engines that hummed smoothly. They let us out in the morning to use a public latrine in the yard. We learned a new word. "Abort." Toilet. Afterward we filled our water bottles and were led to a German Red Cross soup kitchen for thick, hot and delicious soup. Locked in again, we spent the morning listening for Allied aircraft and ogling young German women out the window. There were a lot of them in the station greeting German troops passing through. They could have been American office workers in their silk stockings and stylish dresses. Germans weren't supposed to be that prosperous-looking. We'd been lied to.

Still, we weren't sorry to get moving. Passing through the town, we saw a detail of Jews with Star of David armbands cleaning a street under armed guard. I couldn't identify with them. The boxcar was my identity.

We passed and were passed by troop trains. German troops traveled in boxcars like ours but equipped with rows of wooden benches. The floors were heaped with straw for them to sleep on. In one siding where we stopped the straw caught on fire and we pushed and shoved for places at our window to watch the Germans mill around and shout—no different from Italian soldiers.

Just after dark we were shunted onto a snowy siding. The

sign said "Innsbruck." The guards let us out of our cars to visit a latrine for German troops in transit and to fill our water bottles. Back in our cars, we were issued German biscuits and big cans of corned beef. The corned beef was fat and gristly and I couldn't get it down. I guess I'd have had to be starving.

Since a German had told us Innsbruck wasn't a regular bombing target and that anyway it was too late for day bombers and too early for night attacks, we weren't especially nervous about being locked in the cars. After sleeping fitfully in the crowded boxcar and waking to dim lights outside the windows, and hearing a guard call we were in Munich, I started listening for synchronized engines again. I wished I hadn't awakened so I wouldn't be listening in trembling fear. I didn't fall asleep until the train was rolling again.

We were shunted into a siding before dawn, rousing everyone. In the faint predawn glimmer we could see a dirt road, a few houses and in the near distance a vast, sprawling array of low buildings. We were stiff, cold and crowded but relieved to see nothing that appeared to be a military target. A guard told us we'd reached our destination, Stalag VIIA.

Saint George

AT FIRST LIGHT WE FORMED ranks in the muddy road beside the tracks and moved out. Despite having left some of our possessions behind in Bolzano after the false forced march alert, we were still heavily burdened and slogged awkwardly among the ruts and puddles. Charles Costanzo, a P-40 pilot, was just ahead of me with a friend of his, the two of them staggering under the weight of an immense Italian knapsack crammed to bursting with a harvest of food abandoned in the courtyard at Bolzano.

Over a small stream on a footbridge and we were there. Rows of long huts as far as we could see. Everywhere masses of prisoners. A tall wooden guard tower mounting a machine gun overlooked a sign on the gate reading, "Mannschaft Stammlager VIIA." Stalag VIIA.

We fell out inside the first gate and watched another batch of prisoners coming in. Italian soldiers. An American recognized an obnoxious guard from a camp he'd been in and jeered him. The Italian looked shamefaced and said something appeasing but the American refused to be mollified.

Guards patrolled among us with large German shepherd dogs on leashes. Our first encounter with military dogs. The prisoners would draw back when a dog came near. I didn't. I'd never been afraid of dogs. It made me feel kind of brave and helped make up for my abject fear during the bombing.

Padre Brach came around and told us the station at Bolzano had been bombed only a few minutes after our train pulled out. Men from the last cars said they'd heard the explosions.

German clerks passed out information cards for everyone to fill out. The drill was to fill in only name, rank and serial number, but Kennedy, Schoonmaker and I agree to fill in date and place of capture just in case it might one day be useful to prove we were Italian, not German, prisoners. After the cards we formed into lines for a personal search. The personal search was perfunctory but packs and blanket rolls got a thorough going-over. The searchers took our books and notebooks for a more leisurely inspection, but I persuaded the clerk to let me keep my two notebooks. One was Italian, with the names and addresses of all my P.G. 21 friends, and the other was the one I'd made from Red Cross cardboard, with a few French banknotes hidden in it and several pages of a secretly kept diary in such tiny letters that today I can read them only with the aid of a magnifying glass.

After the search, interrogation at long outdoor tables by German noncoms, almost as perfunctory as the search and on the whole friendly. When a tall, gaunt, scholarly-looking corporal wearing glasses escorted a party of us to the abort I asked him how the food was at Stalag VIIA.

"Pretty bad," he said in English. "But not as bad as ours. We get no Red Cross packages."

We would learn such frankness was not unusual among the better-educated noncoms of the camp staff.

After processing we were moved down the paved, center street between rows of long, dark, rundown one-story stucco buildings. Groups of huts were divided into separate compounds by barbed-wire fences, each compound gate with its own guard. The guards appeared slack and indifferent. Prisoners crowded the wire to watch us pass. Cries of recognition came from one compound. American aircrew sergeants, some from the crews of officers among us. Kennedy and I didn't see Barnes or anyone else we knew.

In our own compound we were turned over to a French "trustee" in civilian clothing though he was a POW. Each barracks had one. The trustees lived in little rooms at the end of barracks screened off by curtains of blankets. They issued bedding and rations and looked after things in general.

The Stalag VIIA barracks were even more crowded than those at Sulmona, with huge banks of twelve-man bunks, three high, two wide and two long and just enough space for a man to squeeze into, with the top bunk a couple of feet from the ceiling. Plain wooden tables and benches were end to end in the narrow center aisle. There weren't enough bunks for all of us, and we drew lots to see who would sleep that night on tables, benches and the floor. Kennedy and I didn't fare well in the drawing. That night we slept on the floor.

Padre Brach came in and told us he'd learned we were to

remain at VIIA only until we could be shipped out to permanent camps. We greeted the news with mixed emotions. The place was squalid but even squalor was preferable to another train ride sweating out our own bombers. He said the Germans had promised him that every man would have a bunk as soon as possible and that we were to give the barracks trustee an accurate count of our strength so the trustee could draw rations for us.

There were about three hundred of us in the back half of the barracks. Permanent personnel lived in the front half, separated from us by three rooms. The first room, the washroom, had a single water tap. The middle room, larger, with two windows, had an old-fashioned hand-pump instead of a tap. The other room was kept locked. We were told it had a big stove in it where permanent party did their cooking.

Our barracks was surrounded on three sides by other compounds with still other compounds beyond them. One of the adjacent compounds held Yugoslavs, another, Russians. The abort, a large, stinking cement building with broken brick steps leading up to its doorless entrance, was behind the barracks. Its rows of seats opened into a pit under the building. The urinals were gutters along the wall. Tarred, though, and kept sprinkled with lime. Our new hosts tried to do the best with what they had.

When we learned there were American enlisted men in our compound, Kennedy and I went looking for Barnes. And found him. He asked us to reassure him again that sergeants wouldn't be moved from Italy to Germany.

Next day we were issued American Red Cross parcels. The cigarettes in them were even more valuable than at P.G. 21. Here we could trade with the unexpectedly corrupt guards. For two cigarettes you could get out of the compound and back. It was said a pack would buy an all-night outing to the nearby town of Moosburg and if the price was right you could get a a pistol and ammunition. We weren't tempted by the pistol and ammunition.

We got one letter card each, with instructions to say we had no permanent address as yet but would write again from our permanent camp. It raised morale greatly. We no longer felt quite so cut off from everything.

We could see a smokestack from our compound and worried about it. A military target? An old hand assured us it was only a furniture factory. We hoped the RAF and the USAAF knew that. The old hand also told us there were fifty thousand prisoners in

VIIA representing twenty-two nationalities. The Russians, he said, were treated worst of all. No Red Cross parcels and worked like dogs.

Our second day in Stalag VIIA an American sergeant approached Kennedy and me and said he'd slipped out of his compound but hadn't been able to get out of the camp. And could he hide with our enlisted men and leave with them when they were shipped out? He seemed to be enjoying his outing. We took him to Barnes, who said he'd take care of it and see that the new man was added to their strength so he could draw parcels.

The sergeant entertained us with stories about VIIA. Especially the Russians. He said they were unbreakable and absolutely fearless. He'd heard one night they were so unruly in their barracks that the Germans had let two police dogs in among them. The dogs never came back out and next morning all that was left were their hides. The Russians had eaten them. The sergeant said there was a *strafe lager*, punishment compound, almost full of Russians on the other side of the Yugoslav compound. One night they started singing their national anthem, which was forbidden, and the Germans turned fire hoses on them. They kept right on singing.

At night we'd hear the Russians singing in the next compound. Powerful voices and strange, melancholy melodies. When we learned of their hunger we went to the wire to toss them bread. We had bread to spare, the German ration being better than the Italians' had been, with sausage, bread, soup and cheese. The Russians gathered at the wire, smiling at us and making V signs despite their appearance of grim deprivation. They caught the bread we threw but didn't scramble for it. A guard came to us and ordered us to stop giving them bread. We did, until we noticed he'd made no move to unsling his rifle. Then we threw what we had left. He drew close and asked us not to do it again.

"It is not because of me," he said in German I could somehow understand. "It is because I will get in trouble if an officer sees me letting you give them food. It is forbidden."

A detail of Russians came into our compound to repair a fence, two youths, one of them Asiatic, and a wrinkled old man. (Probably all of fifty, but in a POW camp that was elderly.) I tried to speak with him but he knew no language but his own. We might have been animals of different species for all the communication there was between us. I gave up and started filling my pipe. He made little whining noises in his throat and stretched his hand out toward the pipe like an infant, eyes tearing, underlip wet with drool. What could I do? I handed him the pipe and a match. He lit up and sat down on the ground, smoking with a concentration that shut out the world. I gestured to him that I'd come back for the pipe later but he ignored me, lost in the tobacco.

I went to talk to the German guarding the work detail, a kind-faced, middle-aged man with a limp. I'd noticed he never shoved prisoners as other guards often did and had helped the enfeebled Russians push their work cart over a stone. His German was textbook clear and he spoke slowly for my benefit. I understood most of what he said. He was Bavarian, he said, and not in sympathy with some of his country's policies. I believed him. He didn't mention Hitler. I was to learn that Germans we encountered often were inclined to tell us what they thought we wanted to hear but also there were others of his sort, so unlike my preconception of Germans. He'd got his limp on the Russian front.

The Russian finished his smoke and I retrieved my pipe. From the Yugoslav compound a voice said, "Hallo." (It took me a while to get used to being hailed with "hallo" instead of "hey.") A short, thin man with a stalk of a neck jutting from his Yugoslav uniform collar came to the wire. His long hair was bushy, his eyes sunken and his face lined. I couldn't tell if he was old or young.

"I see you give tobacco to Russian," he said in broken English. "You are kind man."

We talked across the wire. In English, though it transpired he spoke German as well as Russian, Serbian and Esperanto. He wanted to practice English and anyway his English was better than my German. He asked me all about myself. If I were an officer, when and where I was captured, was I getting enough to eat. He obviously really cared. I took an instant liking to him. And he to me.

His name was George Radovanovic. He was the nearest thing to a saint I've ever met and that included Padre Brach because Padre Brach didn't turn the other cheek.

He tried to interest me in Esperanto and threw me a grammar across the wire, also the first white bread I'd seen in many months and a German-English grammar. I'd told him I'd been trying to puzzle out German newspapers with so little success I'd thought "feind" meant "friend," only to learn it meant "enemy." He'd been a POW almost three years, taken only ten days after his mobilization when Yugoslavia surrendered to the Germans. He hated Germans collectively but not individually.

He said he could get in my compound for a visit for two cigarettes. I threw him two wrapped in a piece of paper. He said he'd repay them after he drew his parcel that night. He threw me some toothpaste and a packet of aspirins. He had access to such things because he worked as a dental orderly in the camp. I never had headaches but most of the other prisoners did and aspirins were precious. The toothpaste I needed badly. Radovanovic said some day soon he'd come for me and take me on a tour of Stalag VIIA.

That night Kennedy and I got bunks. We shared parcels and drew rations together and I still did our trading. He'd heard the guards would trade beer for cigarettes or chocolate, and he wanted some of that action. For chocolate. He wasn't a sweet-eater. An old hand told me the going price for an American D-ration bar was two bottles. I made the offer to the guard on our gate. He said he'd bring the beer in a couple of hours, on his next shift. Like all the guards, he wore a big, all-enveloping cape good for concealing beer, bread and even, sometimes, chickens. He came back on duty with only one bottle of beer. I offered half a D-bar. His dull face a picture of cupidity, he licked his lips at the sight of the chocolate but wouldn't settle for half. Kennedy, who'd been standing anxiously at my elbow, and who was eying the beer in much the same way as the guard eyed the chocolate, told me to break off negotiations.

Next day Radovanovic had me called to the gate of my compound. I gave the guard a cigarette and he let me out of the gate. Radovanovic took me to a sprawling courtyard in the middle of the camp between the cookhouse on one side of the paved center road and a canteen for permanent prisoners on the other. Both had been painted on the outside with vast, gaudy murals by French prisoners. Barbaric, striking, and totally unexpected in such a setting.

It was the Stalag VIIA black market.

One side of the courtyard was jammed with men on the move, circulating to display what they had to offer. Cigarette lighters, pocket knives, Swiss watches, gold rings, Red Cross food, clothing, medals, toilet articles, notepaper, wooden shoes. There were Russians trying to trade their shoes or pitiful bread ration for cigarettes. Prisoners who worked in the cobbler shop

154   displayed belts and shoelaces. I bought shoelaces and started to deal for wooden shoes. Wherever we went in Germany would be colder than P.G. 21 and I didn't want chilblains again. Radovanovic said not to buy shoes. There were plenty of them around, and he'd get me a pair.

The Russians dealt mostly through a chubby, jolly American private who spoke their language. A nonsmoker, he had a fortune in cigarettes. While I watched, he bought a Swiss wristwatch for a hundred cigarettes. It seemed a fearsome price, but I supposed he knew what he was doing.

Without warning, the guards let their dogs loose among the traders, and everyone fled for their compounds except Radovanovic and me. He told me the dogs wouldn't bite if we didn't run. We didn't and they didn't. Radovanovic said the black market was unofficially condoned, but the Germans often unleashed their dogs for the sport of watching the prisoners scatter. We walked back to my compound, where the guard let me in for a cigarette.

Radovanovic invited me to tea in his barracks. I hesitated. I could do nothing to reciprocate. He insisted. In a rare display of generosity, the guard let me back out. The Yugoslav barracks was less crowded than ours. One end was stacked with American Red Cross parcels "Packaged for Yugoslav Prisoners of War." Made me proud of my country. But I wondered why they weren't locked away in a storeroom. Radovanovic said nothing had ever been stolen from a Red Cross parcel and they were touched only on regular distribution days.

He fed me fried pork roll, sliced onions and tomatoes and white bread. My best meal in many months. And he gave me some garlic to take with me. The onions and garlic had come in parcels from home. The Yugoslavs, he told me, were not technically prisoners of war and, because their country was so near, got mail and packages promptly and frequently. Their families had little to send but produce from their gardens.

He'd received a letter from his wife saying he was safer where he was than back home in Sremska Mitrovica. Local Croatians had been killing Serbian men. Fortunately their two sons were too young to attract attention.

After tea Radovanovic wanted to give me cigarettes even after I told him I didn't smoke them. I made him take some of mine. He wouldn't accept them until I'd convinced him it was only proper for him to allow me to respond to his treat.

That night I gave the guard two cigarettes to let me out of my compound. Radovanovic had told me the one across from it was now occupied by Italians, many of them fliers. The guard said he was going off duty in a couple of hours and if I wanted to get back in without any trouble I'd better be back by then.

The Italians clustered around me asking questions. I didn't know enough Italian to answer them. Two of them persisted. One was a slim, handsome dandy in a well-cut civilian sport jacket, sleeveless sweater, shirt and tie, plus fours, wool socks over patterned wool stockings, and ski boots, the other a good-natured stocky, round-faced pilot. Both had a smattering of English. The civilian had been an attache at the Italian Embassy in Berlin. When he wouldn't repudiate Italy's surrender, he'd been interned.

I told them I'd been a prisoner of war in Italy, which they announced to the others. It drew an excited, boisterous crowd. The pilot fetched a distinguished-looking naval officer from a nearby bunk. His sleeve was laden with the gold braid of rank and his chest with rows of ribbons, obviously someone of considerable importance. He questioned me briefly and, learning I was only a first lieutenant with no knowledge of major issues, he shook my hand coolly and went back to his bunk. He wasn't the first senior Italian officer I'd failed to impress.

The Italians were out of smokes and I passed out a few of mine. I felt no resentment against them for P.G. 21 or for being shot down. I wasn't proud of that attitude. I felt it a sign of weakness to be so friendly. They hadn't any matches so I gave them some from a large store I'd found at Sulmona. When they saw the matches were Italian, the uproar started all over again.

The pilot had been taken in Greece when the Germans moved in on his unit before news of Italy's capitulation reached it. I told him I'd been shot down by a Macchi 202. He beamed. And told his friends. They clapped me on the back and shook my hand. I sort of enjoyed being a celebrity. The pilot asked me what I thought of the Macchi 202. I said they were very good planes.

I would have said more but he stopped me. "Why do you speak so slowly?" he demanded. You say, 'V-e-r-y g-o-o-d, v-e-r-y g-o-o-d.' I understand English. You must be accustomed to speaking to foreigners."

True. Ever since being captured I'd spoken very slowly and distinctly to Italians and Germans. I'd found they understood me much better than they did Kennedy, who spoke to them the way he did to everyone.

I told the pilot I'd been on bombing raids over Crete and Greece and asked if he'd ever attacked Liberators in the summer and fall of 1942. He had. Did he know of a mission over Navarino Bay when three Macchi 200s (not as formidable a plane as the 202) had attacked twelve Libs and two of the fighters had been shot down? He not only knew of it, he'd been there. When I said we knew the pilot hadn't gotten out of one fighter but we'd seen a parachute blossom from the other he said that was so but they'd never found the man who parachuted. His best friend.

We chatted without ill feeling, as if it were a game we were discussing. He said he'd been flying the third fighter, the one that hadn't been shot down. He'd scored hits on a bomber that day, between the inner starboard engine and the fuselage. Would that have pierced its gas tanks and eventually brought it down, he asked eagerly. I said we had self-sealing tanks (no secret; the Axis had intact B-17s and B-24s) and I doubted if the hits had caused serious damage. His face fell. So I told him I was only a navigator and didn't know that much about the combat-worthiness of our planes. All the planes from my outfit had made it back, but for all I knew a plane from another unit on the raid had failed to return. That cheered him up.

I hurried back to my compound before the guard went off duty, exhilarated and for the first time thinking how illogically war made men think they were different from each other because they were enemies in battle.

Radovanovic taught me how to manipulate the guards and I was soon moving between compounds at will. He'd given me the wooden shoes he'd promised—only the soles were wood, thickly studded with nails; the tops were leather in front and tire lining in back—and I acquired a pocketknife for a pack of cigarettes. A standard European design, apparently, it had a brown bone handle, one cutting blade, punch, can opener-screwdriver and cork-screw. It felt so natural in my pocket. I'd carried a pocketknife since childhood.

For another pack of cigarettes I bought a belt from a Russian cobbler. He came into our barracks with a display of belts, sandals and shoelaces. He didn't know a word of English and dealt through Padre Brach, whose vast knowledge of almost everything included a few words of Russian. All Padre Brach actually said in

Russian was, "Dobra, dobra," "Good, good," but it worked. It made the Russian laugh and easier to trade with. Padre Brach was a shrewd trader as well as our spokesman, protector, and major fount of information. A man who lived his religion but never proselytized.

Eventually all the prisoners from Sulmona who'd not hidden out or been in the hospital arrived at Stalag VIIA, including the Chetniks I'd been sure would be shot when the Germans pulled out. They joined the other Yugoslavs in Radovanovic's compound in a touching reunion.

In my explorations of the camp I visited the American flying sergeants' compound. The sergeants were even more crowded than we were and had less open space in their compound. Italian POWs lived in tents pitched behind their barracks. I asked around if there were anyone from the 98th in the barracks. I was finally guided to one. He was lying in his bunk and didn't even raise his head when I asked him if he were from the 98th.

"Yes," he said curtly, seeming to resent my asking.

I mentioned the names of some of the men who'd come over with me. He'd never heard of them.

"Must be replacements," he said.

The surly bastard was a replacement for *our* replacements.

A more friendly sergeant than the one from the 98th had told me the Italians in the tents suffered greatly from the frosty nights, being accustomed to a milder clime. He thought the Germans had put them out there on purpose as part of a campaign to get them to volunteer for the Eastern Front. Every day the camp public address system would sound a call for Italian volunteers, promising release from the camp, equal pay with German soldiers, furloughs home if they lived in areas not occupied by the Allies. The sergeant said that of the hundreds interned at Stalag VIIA, only one had volunteered.

When not prowling other compounds I spent my time with Kennedy or Radovanovic. With nothing to read, we talked a lot. When at last our confiscated books were brought in on a cart, my history was not among them. Just my Spanish grammar.

Brewing up, which we'd adopted from the British, helped occupy time. We didn't get enough issue hot water so we heated our own on little fires of grass, straw and shavings. Some of the more enterprising borrowed little blower stoves made of tin cans from permanent party. They'd heat a can of water in less than

158   three minutes with a minimum of fuel, and fuel was at a premium. We scoured our compound clean of everything combustible. With my new pocketknife I cut shavings from our bunks. We'd have cut up our bedboards but there weren't any. They'd already been burned in cooking fires and replaced with wire netting.

Padre Brach learned that ground and flying officers would be going to different camps, ground officers to Schubin, in Poland, and airmen to Sagan, ninety miles from Berlin in Upper Silesia. He'd even scrounged a map to show us where they were.

The rail route passed near the old Czech border. We wondered what the chances might be of escaping into Czechoslovakia. We didn't contemplate that as much as we did the prospect of being locked in boxcars in the marshaling yard in Dresden or Leipzig, two of the larger cities on the way to Sagan. Bolzano had made a lasting impression.

Padre Brach lodged a protest with the German commandant about being crammed in boxcars when the Geneva Convention specifically stated that officers must travel first class. (I've wondered since if it really did or if Padre Brach made it up.) Padre Brach said the commandant had apologized and said he'd try to do better for us when we left Stalag VIIA.

Even Padre Brach was unable to learn exactly when that would be. We were in limbo, sort of like we had been while waiting for the Allies to show up at P.G. 21, only without the promise of freedom. I spent a lot of time with Radovanovic. He'd worked on a German farm one summer and had tales to tell. He said German farm women were immoral, "like the other Germans under Hitler." With their young men off fighting, they took foreign workers for lovers, with dire consequences sometimes for the workers. He'd asked the seven-year-old son of the family he worked for what the child was going to do after the war. He wouldn't do anything, the child said. After the war Germans wouldn't have to work. As for himself, he would have a plantation in one of the conquered lands with the locals doing the work. Radovanovic said German children were told this in their homes, schools and churches. Germans, he said, had no morals, ethics or honesty. Hadn't I seen for myself how corrupt our guards were?

I hadn't bathed since the cold showers at Sulmona, weeks earlier. Radovanovic took me to the shower building one morning, a long room to hang clothes in and a large, square, white-painted room with overhead pipes pierced with many openings. (It was only after the war that I learned about the lethal showers in concentration camps.) There were a few other prisoners of various nationalities in the shower. We laughed and sang together while we luxuriated in the hot water.

After my shower I got a shave and haircut from a French barber who'd set up shop in an adjoining room. Five cigarettes. His barber chair was only a stool but he had clippers, hot water and a sharp razor.

Just as Radovanovic and I were walking out the door, up marched the whole group from my barracks. Kennedy said we were moving out and everyone was getting a shower. So I took another one. While we showered, our clothes went into delousers. I told Kennedy about the barber and he hurried through his shower and got a shave and a haircut. We were surprised at how different we looked with neat hair and clean faces.

Back at the barracks we said goodbye to Padre Brach. He was to add to his flock at Oflag 64 in Poland when the ground officers already there became as devoted to him as we were. In 1988 they dedicated a reunion to him in San Antonio, Texas. Instead of conventional name tags we all had our names on large round buttons with Padre Brach's photo on them. He wore one, too. His said "Himself" on it. Pope John Paul II sent him a congratulatory message. Suffering from Parkinson's disease, Padre Brach was in a wheelchair, but hadn't lost his feistiness or sense of humor. When he rose from a chair unaided to get into his wheelchair, he saw the surprise on my face because he'd needed help to do it before. He grinned and said, "You think I've been faking it, don't you?"

Through the wire I said goodbye to Radovanovic for the last time, so I thought.

In the administrative compound we lined up again at the long outdoor tables for a final search. Most of us had stores of Red Cross food from Italy. The Germans thought it might tempt us to try escaping so they were allowing us to take only two cans of food on the trip and promised to send the rest and other surplus baggage along with us in a separate boxcar. We didn't believe for a minute we'd ever see any of it again. We all took a little extra, hoping to slip it by the inspectors. Old hands in the camp had told us it would help to drop a couple of cigarettes by the clerk's foot.

The drill was to put everything one owned on a table for the scrutiny of the German clerk sitting behind it. Afraid the Germans might confiscate my pocketknife, I tied a string to it, tied the other end to a button on the fly of my longjohns and let it hang down in my crotch. I didn't expect a search personal enough to find it. The clerks were wilier than I expected and my hiding place not as original as I thought. They were making prisoners unbutton their pants. I retrieved my knife and put it in my pocket. Maybe if I just put it casually on the table with the rest of my stuff it would get by.

When I spread out my possessions on the table, including the knife, I slipped two cigarettes out of my pocket and held them where the German could see them. I dropped them on the ground on his side of the table. He looked around, saw no officer was watching, snatched up the cigarettes, put them in his pocket, pawed quickly over my property, and waved me on.

We loaded into third-class coaches. They weren't the first class accommodations Padre Brach had demanded but they were a long step up from boxcars. Wooden benches with backs to them, windows, a door at each end. We could sightsee without standing on tiptoe and, best of all, had our own toilet. The guards made us leave the door open when we used it lest we try escaping out the window.

We had two guards, one at each end. The one at my end was a sad-faced little fellow who smiled hesitantly whenever I looked at him. His eyes were red-rimmed and sorrowful. His uniform didn't fit and his rifle looked too much for him. Not a exactly a Wehrmacht poster boy.

The scenery was nothing memorable so I spoke with the guard instead of watching it roll by. My German vocabulary hadn't expanded much but my confidence had and we communicated reasonably well. Or maybe I just thought we did. He was from Munich. He didn't like the war or, although he didn't mention the Führer by name, Hitler. I didn't think he was saying it because he thought that was what I wanted to hear. I asked about his family. His wife and child had been killed in a RAF raid. He wasn't bitter. He blamed his own country for going to war. He could have been putting me on but I gave him two cigarettes and a little chocolate anyway.

He had a beer with his dinner ration of bread and sausage. Kennedy's lower lip glistened at the sight of the beer. He was obviously in torment. I bought half the bottle for two more cigarettes and a piece of soap. Kennedy downed it like a hound gulping a meatball.

We were on the train two days and nights, stopping in a

major city only once, fortunately by day and not for long. Chemnitz. We were frightened of bombers the whole time.

The nights were cold. We kept all our winter clothing on and those who couldn't stretch out on the benches slept on the floor, not that we slept much. The singing kept us up. Our guards'. There were two songs in particular they liked singing together. One was the lament of a young man going from bereavement to bereavement. Sadder than Vernon Dalhart's "I'm So Lonesome I Could Cry." The other one was a sentimental love song. "Mein Schatz." "My Darling." The guard who'd lost his family got tears in his eyes when he sang it. They hadn't good voices but they harmonized well, showing long practice.

As long as we couldn't sleep, we sang, too. "Fuck 'em All," which we'd learned in preflight as "Bless 'em All" before falling under the evil influence of the British; "Sixpence," also the unexpurgated British version; and whatever other rowdy songs we knew the words to. A friend who'd heard me singing Roosevelt (The Honey Dripper) Sykes' "44 Blues" in the washroom at Stalag VIIA requested a solo. I hadn't much of a voice but I knew all the words and liked to sing the blues, and it was too dark in the car for anyone to see me.

Weary from vocalizing, or maybe from listening, we fell asleep at last. A rude blow across the face woke me. I sat up with a curse. My assailant had fled, but there was a weight on my chest. A guard's rifle. He'd leaned it against the wall and gone to sleep. It had fallen on me. Grumpily I leaned it back in place and dozed off. It fell on me again. This time it occurred to me we could easily disarm our guards and escape. I didn't even consider it. Like most veteran prisoners, I'd have loved to escape if it were handed to me on a platter but when it came to planning one I found the obstacles daunting. As now. I didn't know where I was except that it was deep in enemy territory with no underground to help me, it was too cold to exist for long in open country, I was in the wrong uniform, and my German would never fool anyone. Maybe most important, when I was picked up, as I certainly would be, I'd have lost all the food and clothing I'd accumulated so painstakingly over the long months.

I woke the guard and shoved the rifle into his hand. He wasn't surprised, or even embarrassed. His attitude, and I suppose mine, was that we were all in this thing together. It was usually like that when none of their officers were around.

We were shunted onto a siding before daylight the next morning and heard the engine chug away. The guard said we'd arrived at our camp but would have to wait until guards were sent to fetch us. For a change we weren't afraid of bombers. It was too late for night raids and too early for day ones, and besides we could see nothing from the windows that looked like a military target.

At dawn my sad-eyed new friend from Munich slipped out of the car and returned with his pockets full of apples. He'd stolen them from a carload. He portioned them out to us, saying not to tell where we got them.

An hour or so later our guards arrived. Blue uniforms. Luftwaffe. The first we'd seen. Kindred spirits, I thought, remembering how well the Italian flyers had treated us at Naples. We formed lines outside the cars to be counted. Our baggage was offloaded with us, as had been promised. We walked through a pine forest with our burdens of food and clothing. The guards were friendly. Their officer spoke English. He told us our camp was Stalag Luft III, the best officers' camp in Germany.

Encouraging. A good camp, in a woods away from bombing targets. No more trains. We'd become reconciled to being prisoners again after our brief sniff of freedom and hoped for nothing better than safe, comfortable quarters. It was a sunny, beautiful day. Ideal for a walk in the woods.

Camping in the Woods

THE WOODS GAVE WAY TO A vast clearing with rows of long green one-story barracks behind barbed wire. No wall. Prisoners swarmed to the wire shouting questions as we marched to a building outside the fence. Who were we, what group, where based? Did we know so-and-so from such-and-such a group and was he with us? They called out their own names.

We were surprised they were so open in the presence of the Germans. We were more guarded. We told them when we'd been shot down and that we'd come up from Italy but didn't identify our bomb groups. The Germans didn't seem to mind the lively exchanges, a good omen.

We lined up for processing in front of one of the buildings outside the wire. Some American POWs were on hand to assist us. One of them told my bunch privately that the South Camp was best. When a German officer asked for forty volunteers for South Camp, Kennedy, Alvarado, Buckner, Schoonmaker, Bob Adams, Charlie Costanzo and his knapsack-toting buddy and I were among those rushing to the head of the line. Unfortunately, Charlie Jennette didn't come along.

We emptied our pockets on tables and stripped for the personal search. I put my knife on the table with my other things. It's hard to hide a pocketknife when you're naked. My German ignored it without looking as if he expected a cigarette. So knives were okay. This *was* a good camp.

We dressed, were fingerprinted and interrogated. Not much to the interrogation. Anything we knew was out of date. Kennedy and I readily told when and where we were captured. We wanted to establish our seniority in case of prisoner exchanges and to make it clear we were Italian, not German, prisoners. My interrogator turned jolly when I told him my name.

"That is a good German name," he said.

He wanted to know if my father and mother were from Germany. (My father was. My mother was from Russia.) I told him no but my grandfather was from Germany and that my mother was American for many generations back.

"We have an American Westheimer already in camp," he said.

I had three cousins that might be in the service. I hadn't seen them since before I went in myself. Wouldn't it be something to be a POW with Adolph, Sammy or I.B. Jr.?

"Oh," he said, "I am mistaken. He is Ostheimer, not Westheimer. He calls himself Osteemer. What do you call yourself? Do you call yourself Westeemer?"

"No," I said firmly. "*Westheimer.*"

He liked that and rushed me through my interrogation so I could gather my gear together. Knapsacks, GI watches (issue items were spoils of war), canteens, fountain pens (I was told Americans forged escape aids when they had ink), and money weren't allowed. My water bottle slipped by, probably because it was so crude it didn't look like a canteen, and I was allowed to keep my knapsack only long enough to carry my belongings into camp. The knapsack was noted on my record. I was given a receipt for my Italian fountain pen and the few coins I'd carried since Sulmona.

After interrogation, ID photos. We tried to look sullen and mistreated when our photos were taken. They weren't going to use photos of happy prisoners for propaganda if we could help it. Dirty-faced, unshaven and disheveled, we looked grim even though we were joking before and after the session.

Marching to our new home, we passed a group with Jennette in it. He was going to a different compound. We said goodbye and promised to visit if we got the chance. The South Camp was beyond a patch of woods, with rows of barracks like those we'd seen on the way in, and towering guardboxes mounting machine guns. The Germans in them looked relaxed but alert. There were two compounds in the clearing, separated by the usual double barbed-wire fences with concertina wire in between. Men came pounding to the wire from all over our compound, yelling. Above it all, a voice bellowing, "Purge in! Purge in!" All the questions we'd heard before, only now some of us recognized some of the questioners. Fervent greetings, always beginning, "So-and-so, you old bastard! What in hell are you doing here?"

Colonel Charles Goodrich, the Senior American Officer, and members of his staff met us at the gate. Our new companions engulfed us. It was like a homecoming. Jim Alexander, bombardier on Tex Newton's plane, the first one the 98th had lost in combat, grabbed me. We'd been on that mission, a shipping strike off Crete in August 1942, but had bombed before them and didn't see them go down.

"Am I glad to see you, boy!" he cried. "I keep telling these guys about the best group in the Air Corps and all they do is laugh. They're all from England and never heard of the Middle East. You're the first ones from our group to end up here."

The SAO assembled us at the cookhouse, the building nearest the gate, and his staff assigned us quarters. Kennedy, Adams, Schoonmaker, Alvarado, Buckner and I wanted to stay together. Told there was an eight-man room available, we got Costanzo and his friend, Luther, to join us. A host of willing hands helped us carry our belongings to our new home, Room 12 in Block 133, the second block in its row and next to the fence separating South Compound from the British North Compound.

The room was about twelve by fifteen feet, with two windows facing west. One wall was plaster. The block kitchen was on the other side of it. The other walls were beaverboard. The floor was rough pine. The room was empty except for a tall tile stove in a corner. We dropped our packs, borrowed brooms and started sweeping, with lots of help from prisoners who crowded in to ask questions and offer cigarettes and things we might need to set up housekeeping. We sensed an atmosphere of comparative plenty.

Our furniture arrived in a wagon, four disassembled double-deck bunks, ten bedboards per bunk, four double lockers, two benches, a stool and one table. All of wood. The German in charge of the detail was a youthful-looking noncom with straight blond hair neatly parted in the middle. Unteroffizier (Corporal) Hohendahl. He sounded upperclass English except for the merest trace of German accent. He had no armed guards with him and mixed freely with the prisoners while supervising assembling of the bunks. A far cry from P.G. 21.

For bedding we got empty palliasses, mattress covers, a rough sheet and two thin blankets. We filled the palliasses from huge bags of excelsior. Old hands advised us to cram all the excelsior we could into our palliasses because the stuff matted. We got them so swollen we needed help getting the covers on. When we'd taken all our palliasses would hold, the old hands scavenged what was left.

We were issued tableware, as well. Cups, bowls, and little brown crocks with the Luftwaffe emblem on them, and knives, forks and spoons. We all planned on taking Luftwaffe cups home with us for souvenirs but it didn't work out.

We lined the bunks against the walls and, as recommended by a friend, turned one of the lockers on its side to serve as a cupboard. Schoonmaker and Adams, Alvarado and Buckner, Kennedy and I and Costanzo and Luther were bunkmates. We filled the cupboard with the corned beef, pork roll, biscuits, margarine, cheese, raisins and prunes we'd brought from Italy. Prisoners came from all over the barracks to marvel.

Stalag Luft III was in Upper Silesia roughly midway between Berlin and Breslau, near the village of Sagan. The Bober River, a tributary of the Oder, was a few kilometers to the east. Although North Compound was just across the wire, Center Compound was hidden from view by woods. When the prisoners there were boisterous, we could hear them. South Compound's perimeter was about seven-tenths of a mile, a distance measured by countless feet on the wide track worn just inside the guardrail.

Our block was in one of three long, identical rows of prefabricated wood and beaverboard buildings. There were fourteen rooms in each block, including the kitchen, washroom and a latrine with the usual trough urinal and a toilet that actually flushed. We could use it only at night after lockup. Days we used the aborts between blocks. Outsize privies is what they were, but classy, with wooden lids for the holes and partitions, surfaces scrubbed daily with GI soap and the pit and urinal trough well-sprinkled with lime. A decent place for contemplation once you were hardened to the odor.

There were two-man rooms at each end of a block. The other rooms were for six or eight men except for a large room in the middle for the enlisted men who did camp jobs. The kitchen sergeants were in our block.

Each pair of blocks had its own incinerator for burning refuse. When we first got to Stalag Luft III, the incinerators had sheet-metal lids. They vanished one at a time. One ended up in our block, crimped into a frying pan. What wouldn't burn went into a fenced-off area to be gathered regularly by a young Polish prisoner with a horse and wagon. (Prisoners with gardens followed the horses everywhere with Red Cross boxes, hoping to get lucky.) He always had an armed guard with him.

We had volleyball courts between blocks and here and there chinning bars.

We cooked for ourselves, mostly, but some German rations came already prepared from the cookhouse, conveniently close to our block, which also provided us with hot water. Fetching hot water to one of the more distant blocks was a real chore after snow fell and the temperature dropped. There were storerooms at one end of the cookhouse and at the other classrooms and something called FoodAcco, where you could buy and sell goods based on barter points. After we got our camp public address system, it was turned on and off from FoodAcco but the main controls were in the German compound.

The parade ground was in the southeast corner of the compound. We were close enough that we got a few more winks before morning appel (roll call) than our friends in outlying blocks.

The high, double barbed-wire fences around the compound and the rolls of concertina wire between them were ugly but didn't block what view there was. There was a wooden guardrail ten feet out from the wire past which we weren't allowed except to retrieve an errant football or basketball. You could do that if you put on a long, sleeveless white smock with Red Crosses front and back. Even with the coat on it was scary in forbidden territory. What if you got a guard who didn't know the rules? It happened once. The guard was new. Fortunately he fired into the air. Everyone hit the dirt and stayed there until another guard told him the ground rules.

The camp had been carved out of a pine forest, with only a few trees left standing in the camp and for yards outside the perimeter. A tunnel would have to be damn long to reach the cover of the woods from South Compound. The compound was studded with stumps.

When we first arrived in South Compound work had just begun on a theater building in the southwest corner of the lager. So far they'd done some of the foundation excavation, a rectangle sloping from ground level at one end to eight feet deep at the other. The Germans supplied the materials and prisoners the plans and muscle.

In Stalag Luft III we were much more in control of our own affairs than prisoners were at P.G. 21. More room, more communal facilities, more internal administration left up to the SAO and his staff. Within limits, we functioned like an American military unit, with all its discipline. Living in small rooms instead of bays made for a familylike atmosphere.

Colonel Goodrich was a husky pilot we thought was getting on in years. Had to be well into his thirties. He'd had a B-25 Group in the Middle East (I learned we'd bombed through one of his lower-altitude formations on the Tobruk raid where we'd been caught in the searchlights) and was captured even earlier in the war than we were. Given his choice of a Senior Officers' camp or joining his juniors in less comfortable surroundings, he chose the men he'd flown with.

The Germans respected him as much as we did. He accepted no personal favors from them and didn't hesitate to confront them with the grievances of his junior officers. We saluted him as we would have a colonel anywhere but he was relaxed and informal with us.

Not so his second in command, Lieutenant Colonel Albert Clark. Not with me, anyway. A West Pointer who'd had to crash-land his crippled Spitfire in Occupied France in July 1942, he was tall and thin, with sandy red hair and pale eyes that bored into you. He never smiled at me when I saluted him, and when he spoke with me on the track for whatever reason he never gave me "At ease." So I always spoke with him at attention. We called him "Red" behind his back. (The next time I ran into him after liberation was at the Pentagon in 1951. He was a full colonel and I was a captain, editor of the personnel newsletter. I'd rewritten a hand-out from his office and he called me in to tell me it had to go as written. He didn't remember me from Stalag Luft III. I asked the colonel I worked for what I should do—everything in the newsletter had to be rewritten to cut the militarese—and he mentioned it to our general, who told Colonel Clark that was how it was going to be, which did not endear me to Colonel Clark. Years later, when I'd moved to Los Angeles and was on an Air Force-sponsored tour of the Air Force Academy, I saw his portrait hanging with those of other AFA superintendents. With three stars on his shoulders. And some time after that, when he started a Stalag Luft III section at the AFA library and I had correspondence with him, he signed his letters to me, "Bub," which had been his nickname all along although I hadn't known it. When I saw him face to face at a Stalag Luft III reunion I called him "General" and "Sir.")

Lieutenant Colonel Melvin McNickle, our administrative officer, was his exact opposite. Short, roundish, always smiling and trotting instead of walking. His was the most remarkable there-I-wuz story I'd heard. His fighter plane was hit, he was wounded, and he'd blacked out at eighteen thousand feet. He regained consciousness in a German hospital, where he was told he'd been pried out of his aircraft dug twelve feet into the ground. We called him Colonel Mac. (I didn't see him after the war until the 1985 reunion in Denver. He was still smiling, more roundish than ever, and a retired major general.)

In our room we were all experienced prisoners and quickly adapted to camp routine. Schoonmaker and Adams volunteered to cook for the room. Other daily chores were done according to roster. The man who did it was called the dog, for orderly dog. He swept the room, took out the garbage, peeled potatoes, washed dishes, built the fire and fetched hot water from the cookhouse.

Our day began around eight-thirty when we washed up and had breakfast, two paper-thin slices of toasted heavy German army bread smeared with a film of margarine and jam or canned fish (one of our later roommates made a sandwich of his two slices; we couldn't bear to watch him eat it) and coffee or tea. Usually coffee, just enough Nescafe to cover the tip of a spoon in a mug of hot water. The bread came in loaves. We took it to a slicer in one of the blocks. Thinness was all, but sometimes we overdid and a section disintegrated. Disaster.

Morning appel was at nine. When we first arrived we all fit next to the cookhouse but after the air war picked up we almost filled the parade ground. We didn't answer to names as we'd done at P.G. 21. We were only counted lined up by blocks in ranks of five with our block commander in front, with one guard to a block. The *Lager Hauptmann* (compound captain) came in after we'd formed. Our adjutant called us to attention. Except for the block being counted, which remained at attention, the other blocks were given "parade rest" by their commanders and called to attention in turn.

The lager captain and Hohendahl usually did the counting, one from in front, one from behind. Germans could really count. It was seldom that their numbers didn't tally with those they were supposed to, which meant we weren't kept standing around much. When they didn't tally it was usually because someone was still asleep in his sack unnoticed by his roommates, who were supposed to see things like that didn't happen.

After morning appel we made our bunks and looked for

things to occupy our time until afternoon appel. We had freedom of the compound until 10:00 p.m., when the bugle sounded and we were locked in. (One night Kennedy and I went to another block to look at a Patek Philippe catalog. We could order things from Sweden but I don't know if anything ever actually came. We didn't hear the warning bugle and, when we saw the time, knew we'd be shot at if we ventured out. We waited for the lockup guard to come around and I explained, in atrocious German, we hadn't heard the bugle and asked would he be kind enough to conduct us to our own block. He looked at me icily and said in flawless English, "You are rather optimistic, aren't you?" But he took us back.) Lights out at 11:00. During air raid alerts the lights were turned off earlier.

We fetched hot water from the cookhouse four times a day. Brew water and wash water, the wash water in a large, tapering lead-alloy jug labeled "Keintrinkwasser," "no drinking water." We called them keins. We fetched the brew water in blue ceramic jugs. Easily broken. You'd see a lot of them patched together with tar scraped from odd sources around the compound.

Much of our German ration was distributed by block ration officers, but for some of the cooked stuff, especially the daily soup, we had room service. The German issue was much more varied and abundant than the Italian had been. Potatoes, bread, barley, flour, cheese, fishcheese (cylinders of cottage cheese coated with something gelatinous, orange and smelly), margarine (better than American), kohlrabi, turnips, ersatz coffee and tea, millet, ruta-baga, pumpkin (not popular with those who'd come up from Italy), sausage (including a blood sausage as disgusting as the fish-cheese), sugar and fresh meat.

Overwhelmed by the abundance, we from Italy tried to eat it all, even the fishcheese and the vile-looking blood sausage. More seasoned Luft IIIers threw theirs away or buried it in their gardens for fertilizer. As far as I knew, it wasn't even good fertilizer.

Most rooms had cupboards full of potatoes accumulated dur-ing summer plenty. To us, potatoes were a novelty and a delicacy. We ate all we were issued and extras from outsiders, who mar-veled at our capacity. We couldn't find utensils big enough to boil them. What cooking utensils we had were made from tin cans, except for the sheet-iron skillet and the ubiquitous jam bucket. The buckets had wire handles and held about two gallons of dark

red turnip jam. The cookhouse gave them out after they'd been
emptied. Filled to the brim, a jam bucket gave each of us a bowl
full of boiled potatoes. We never thought it was enough. We didn't
have Doc Wynsen there to tell us we only thought we were
hungry.

Our Red Cross parcel issue was mostly American, with
British or Canadian only occasionally. Fine with us because the
American parcels were new, improved models, with name-brand
canned goods and cigarettes. Marge, corned beef, Spam (we
called all pork roll Spam), liver pâté, powdered milk, Nescafe (we
called all powdered coffee Nescafe), raisins or prunes, salmon or
tuna (at Camp Kilmer, New Jersey, when we first got back to the
States, I ordered salmon for lunch and the waitress snarled at me,
"Don't you know there's a war on?"), sardines, sugar, D-ration
chocolate, soap and outstanding jam. We did like getting the
occasional British or Canadian parcel. The Canadian for butter
and "real" (ground) coffee and the biscuits we'd learned to fry for
pancakes at P.G. 21, the British for tea, oatmeal, powdered eggs,
bacon and "condendo" (condensed milk).

We got the parcels twice a week, a half-issue at a time
because our hosts punched holes in the tops of cans so we couldn't
accumulate escape rations. We immediately sealed the holes with
margarine. At home I'd been taught once you'd opened a can you
had to empty it immediately or the food would spoil, especially
fish. Not so. Except in the hottest weather even fish kept for
several days.

When winter came we raised a corner of our ceiling and kept
food in the natural icebox of the attic. Early on, we were getting
more canned food than we could eat. I still thought constantly
about food but had lost my voracious appetite. Sometimes I'd
have to save my dessert until late brew. For a while the Germans
permitted us to draw only portions of the parcels and store the
rest in our names, as the maresciallo had at Poggio Mirteto. We
didn't believe they really would until Colonel Mac reassured us.
Before long we had more parcels than any other room in South
Compound—twelve. When times got harder the surplus quickly
melted.

Though officers couldn't work for the enemy, we were allowed to do things for our own benefit, improving dirt roads in the
compound, building our theater. Blocks furnished men by roster. I
began my construction work literally at the bottom of the ladder,

hauling buckets of cement to the bricklayers. We called cement "mud." The bricklayers, of higher status than the bucket brigade, harassed us constantly with cries for mud. Later I was promoted to mixing the cement and harassed carriers from the other end. The bricklayers and other artisans worked every day. We did it only when our turns came.

Improving roads and carrying mud was a breeze compared with stump pulling. The Germans had an enormous contraption made of six-by-sixes hinged at the top like a nutcracker that pulled pine stumps from the earth like monstrous wisdom teeth. They let us borrow it to amass firewood against the coming chill. Much too heavy to lift, it had to be walked to a stump site in giant strides of its six-by-sixes. We'd dig around a stump, exposing its roots, until Kennedy declared it pullable and selected the ideal place to set the giant iron hook dangling from the top of the nutcracker. The extractor was an iron rod attached to the top of the nutcracker and ending in the hook. Long timbers on either side of the nutcracker were attached to iron collars around the rod. Raising and lowering them alternately worked the rod upward. It took a lot of muscle and Kennedy saw that we applied it.

"It's gonna be a long, hard winter," he'd say. "Let's not stand short." We worked in teams. One team dug while the other pulled.

If Kennedy was our driver, Alvarado was our main muscle. Thanks to them, although rooms had equal time with the puller we had the biggest stack of stumps in the block, maybe in South Compound. More than thirty. Our hosts provided axes and saws for cutting them into firewood. We all took turns, but Kennedy and Alvarado cut more than the rest of us put together. Growing up, Kennedy had chopped wood on the family farm. Alvarado had done it for the family woodstove. We stacked the wood neatly in circular ricks and piled the chips for kindling.

We learned new slang in Stalag Luft III. "Dhobi" was still wash; gen either "pukka" or "duff"; we retained "bash"; but "buckshee," meaning extra, became "gash." Anyone superfluous or unwanted was a "gash hand." Instead of POWs we were "kriegies," short for *Kriegsgefangene* (war-caught); the Germans were "goons," not "Jerries." The sentry boxes were "goon-boxes." We didn't walk the perimeter, we "did the circuit." The Escape Committee was "X." Colonel Clark, who headed it, was "Big X." We never took a shuftee. We "ran a reccy." To fall down or be confused was "to spin in." When you couldn't eat another bite, which wasn't often, you "stalled out." To get mail was "to score," and to be vulnerable in bridge was to be "venereal" or "pregnant." In Italy, although we called the screwdriver-carrying Italians in blue coveralls "snoopers," we never had a regular name for them. The German version were called "ferrets." The guards who patrolled with dogs at night were called by their official name, *Hündfuhrer*. Then there was MEDP. Not slang but an acronym. We didn't get that until the daylight raids on Berlin began. One of our later roommates said he had been shot down on such a raid. An MEDP over Big B. A maximum-effort deep penetration over Berlin.

During our first few weeks our place in the pecking order was ambiguous. Old kriegies felt superior to new ones and at first the old hands tended to be patronizing. ("I got more time in the abort than you got in the bag.") Everyone was issued metal ID tags by our hosts, worn like dogtags. They were numbered. Theoretically, the lower the number, the longer the kriegie time. It wasn't uncommon to compare ID numbers. But our numbers belied our tenure. Mine was high for then, 2713. So we never missed an opportunity to mention how long we'd been POWs in Italy and got a reputation, deserved, for taking our seniority too seriously. They'd snicker when we theorized about being repatriated under some possible clause in the Geneva Convention, but we could see they thought maybe it was possible—to a kriegie no straw was too fragile to grasp at—and nursed a little envy.

Seniority had its practical side, too. Scarce items like shoes were distributed on the basis of time in the bag as well as need. Old kriegies got the best camp jobs and were more intimate with the senior staff. We displaced the old guard, the kriegies who'd been at the Wehrmacht camp in Schubin before Stalag Luft III was opened. Hardly anyone at Stalag Luft III before we arrived had the seniority of Schubin men. But now, because we'd been shot down before the air war heated up, only a few kriegies like Colonel Clark had time on us.

Schubin men wouldn't let any tale of hard times go unchallenged, saying how much worse things had been at Oflag 64. We mocked them. We'd say to complaining juniors, "You think this is tough? You should have been at Schubin. They didn't even heat the chains."

We argued a lot about which was worse, Oflag 64 at Schubin

or P.G. 21 at Chieti. Schubin was a lot colder than Chieti? But we had fewer blankets. They never got fruit or onions at Schubin? We never got potatoes at Chieti until the very last and most of the time were on half-parcels. At Schubin they'd hardly had room to turn around? Yeah, but at Chieti we'd had this big wall.

In addition to our tainted tenure, we had more food and clothing than even Schubin men. All that Red Cross food we'd come in with and had stored with the Germans and the thick Italian blankets warmer than three of the German issue. And we'd adjusted to camp routine quicker than was seemly, before the Schubin men could point out our mistakes or out-complain us when we spoke of past hardships.

Late in the war Schubin and Chieti men were drawn together by a shared disdain of pampered newcomers who arrived with special Red Cross POW kits issued at Dulag Luft, the main interrogation center, outside of Frankfurt. Towels, pajamas, cigarettes, chocolate. Tenderfeet with things it had taken veterans like us months and months to accumulate, if indeed we had them at all. Much too good for them.

Crew of B-24D *Natchez to Mobile, Memphis to St. Jo*, 344th Squadron, 98th Bombardment Group (Heavy), Kabrit Airfield, Egypt, on the Suez Canal, November 21, 1942, on return from Landing Ground 139 outside of Tobruk, Libya, after a night raid on Tripoli. *Left to right:* Staff Sgt. Frank Spindler, Staff Sgt. Matt Brazil, Staff Sgt. Albert Barnes, First Lt. Larry Kennedy, First Lt. Kent Leader, First Lt. Russ Gardinier, Staff Sgt. Norman George, the author, Staff Sgt. Armando Risso. Photo taken by Tech. Sgt. John Plavchak, who was out sick the day the plane was shot down and was replaced by Capt. Charles Jennette

Left to right: the author, Russ Gardinier, Larry Kennedy, Kent Leader. St. Jean, Palestine, 1942

The author in his "office" in the nose of
Natchez to Mobile, Memphis to St. Jo
on a bombing mission

The author (*left*) and Kent Leader on
leave in Beirut, Fall 1942

The author in electric flying suit.
Landing Ground 139, Libyan Desert,
Fall 1942

Left to right: Larry Kennedy (*in front of the Sphinx*), Kent Leader, the author
(*far right*)

The author (*far right, back row*) and unidentified British officers. P. G. 21, Settore II mess staff, 1943

The author posed with Italian officers in 1965, replicating 1943 mess staff photo. What was P. G. 21 is now an Italian army school. The school commandant is seated in the center.

Commandant and the author sharing a toast in the Officers' Club. Italian army school, 1965

Left to right: Zeak Buckner, the author, Alexander Alvarado, Larry Kennedy, Sam Fairchild, Ted Schoonmaker. Poker game in South Compound, Stalag Luft III, 1944

The author (*left*) with George Radovanovic. Stalag Luft VIIA, Moosburg,
May 1945. Waiting for British and Americans to load on trucks for
evacuation

General Dwight D. Eisenhower (*standing*) and the
author (*seated*) at Camp Lucky Strike, France,
Recovered Allied Military Personnel processing
center, May or June 1945

The author (*right*) and Chuck Williams.
Publication party for *My Sweet Charlie*,
Beverly Hills, 1965

Padre Stanley Brach (*left*) and the author in
Las Vegas in 1984 at a reunion of ex-POWs of
Oflag 64, at Wehrmacht (German army) camp
to which Padre Brach had been sent

SHARING A ROOM INSTEAD of a large bay, our group drew even closer together than we'd been at P.G. 21. I'd long looked up to Kennedy, but the man I came to know so intimately in Room 12 became one of the two I've most admired in my life. The other is Harry Truman.

Lawrence Clare Kennedy. You'd expect a Kennedy to be Catholic but he wasn't, nor even a practicing Irishman. He came from a long line of Missouri farmers but had gone to college and become a city man. He'd traveled all over the country as a salesman for a tire company and done well at it. (He had $10,000 in the bank, a fortune at the time.) Likely as not, when a new acquaintance told Kennedy where he was from, Kennedy would say, "Why, that's my hometown," and describe the place to him. Fairfax, Missouri; Salt Lake City; Des Moines; Austin, Minnesota; Los Angeles; Albuquerque; Phoenix; Tucson; St. Louis; Cleveland; Klamath Falls, Oregon; Omaha. He'd been there.

He liked a taste but wouldn't drink when there was flying to be done and certainly had no dependency. A joyful storyteller, spinning tales of life on the farm, selling tires, bartending his way through Tarkio College in Missouri, the women in his life. There'd been a lot of them. He had roguish charm.

I appropriated the moral of one of his stories in *My Sweet Charlie*, when Marlene, the protagonist, accepts a bologna sandwich from a storekeeper without asking the cost. When he was a child on the farm, Kennedy said, he'd toiled for weeks to earn his first dollar. When his father took him into town on a Saturday afternoon he went to the local restaurant to buy a rare treat, a candy bar. Five cents, the wrapper said. With the candy bar in one sweaty hand and his dollar in the other, he said, "How much?" The proprietor looked him in the eye and said, "One dollar." Kennedy said the bottom dropped out of his world. And that was where he developed the mistrust of humanity he still nursed. But a deal was a deal. He handed over his dollar and shuffled toward the door fighting back tears. The man called him back and gave him his change. "Son," he said, "never say you'll take something without asking the price first."

With it all he was a cynic and confirmed pessimist. For about six months his letters from home were all from his mother. Nothing would convince him his father hadn't died and she was keeping it from him. Nothing except the letter he finally got in his father's handwriting. He worried about his fiancée in Florida. Had he done the right thing? Getting engaged. Did he really want to rush into marriage after the war? (Turned out he did, but not to her.)

He found dark linings in silver clouds. When our bombers began pounding the heart of Germany, he said it would cut off our mail and parcels. If the Allies made a long thrust, the Germans had sucked them in to cut them off.

I called him Kennedy when I spoke with him, but when I spoke of him to others it was always "my pilot." I never took liberties with him as I did with other roommates, except about his ears. They were small, well-shaped and pink. When we had visitors I'd say, "Don't you think my pilot has the cutest ears?"

Alexander Alvarado. Alejandrito. Little Alvie. Quiet, a gentle giant, sweet-natured, raised poor but a man of instinctive courtesy. When kriegies argued they often exchanged taunts and insults. If you ridiculed Little Alvie, he might flush but he wouldn't respond. Almost impossible to anger, he never used his strength to dominate. Intelligent but not a quick thinker, he was sometimes underestimated by strangers. He underestimated himself, I think. He liked listening to us joking but seldom told a joke himself, yet he could send us into screams of laughter just by saying something he'd once heard spoken by a fellow worker at a San Antonio creamery. "Emmie, you knows you owe me dat dime." I don't know why we thought that was so funny. He doted on swing band music and liked singing blues. He was tormented by hemorrhoids. Sometimes he'd return from the abort pale and sweating in agony. He wouldn't say a word or groan, just climb in his bunk and lie motionless.

Zeak Buckner. He had the bunk under Alvarado's. Their friendship was as close as Kennedy's and mine. Buckner liked presenting himself in the most unflattering light. He adopted an air of offensive coarseness, disguising great sensitivity. The only married man in the room, he said the most outrageous things about his wife. If she was sleeping with other men and not charging for it he was going to knock her teeth out. And she better have every cent of it in the bank when he got home. (I met her after the war. A woman of taste and refinement with absolutely no sign of spousal abuse, physical or mental.) He boasted of dishonest things he'd done, of the suckers he'd trimmed at pool, and, after Kennedy taught him to play bridge, how he'd gotten by with a renege or tilted a score in his favor. He claimed he loved to lie and cheat, that it was just good business and everyone did it, yet we never caught him in a lie, he was scrupulously honest in all our dealings, and he shared his personal parcels freely. Except his cigars.

The only time he raged against his wife and sounded halfway as if he truly meant it was when his White Owls came. Five-cent cigars. He'd written her specifically requesting better ones. I was getting ten- and even fifteen-centers from my mother, selected by my cigar-smoking oldest brother. He claimed he'd allotted only $25 of his monthly pay to her because he didn't want to spoil her, which didn't keep him from asking of heaven, "Why don't she have brains enough to send good cigars?"

He could sometimes goad me to near-fury with his pretended vulgarity and a cynicism deeper and more biting than Kennedy's, but I could never get his goat. In fact, he enjoyed it when I tried. His face was like rubber and when I'd pull at it and tell him how repulsive he looked he'd grin. I pushed his bulbous nose and went, "Honk, honk." He loved it. When I got *Alice in Wonderland* in a book parcel, Tweedledum and Tweedledee looked drawn from him, and sometimes when I had a visitor I'd open the book to the picture and point silently at Buckner. He'd do a Tweedledum-Tweedledee pose. One night he sat on his bunk with Alvarado and read the Tweedledum-Tweedledee section to him aloud. I called him and Alvarado "my five hundred pounds of roommate."

Buckner hadn't gone to college and pretended a disdain for anything "cultural," yet when I started racing through books from South Compound's extensive (compared with P.G. 21's) library, he began reading, too. A man who had no acquaintance with *Gulliver's Travels* or *David Copperfield* was soon devouring Dickens, Thackeray and French and Russian novelists with a natural, discriminating taste. In a rare serious moment, he said he was going to college after the war. (He did. Although he served in the military twenty years, he got advanced degrees and, after retiring from the Air Force, became a professor of English at the University of Louisiana in Shreveport.)

He boasted of his laziness but was a willing worker. We never called on him to do anything requiring dexterity, though. He was absolutely inept manually and he couldn't play games. He couldn't even swim.

Robert Adams. Stubborn, an authority on almost everything. When you persisted in arguing with him he'd look at you pityingly and wag his head, which never failed to infuriate. That wasn't his purpose, though. He just didn't understand why you couldn't see it his way. We'd get insulting when he did it to us but he never responded in kind. He was an innocent, gentle soul with never a bad word to say about anyone. He adored his father and stepmother (his mother had died after a long illness), and we knew from the way he spoke of them he'd come from a loving home. He was engaged to a young woman in Texas he'd met at flying school. He talked of her as much as he did his parents.

We knew he hadn't graduated from college and one night after lights out he told us why. In his junior year he'd been seized with an idea for a radically new aircraft engine. He quit going to classes to work on the design. Working day and night, taking Benzedrine to stay awake, he completed the design only to learn it had already been patented by someone else. Despite being a good student, he was so far behind he failed his courses and never went back to school.

Though he got along well with his roommates most of the time, he eventually withdrew a little from the rest of us, finding friends in other rooms and spending many private hours in his curtained-off bunk, reading. No reflection on us, he said. He just needed new horizons. We gave him his share of our stumps, cut wood and food. He changed rooms several times after that, always still friends with those he left.

Theodore P. Schoonmaker. Toughened in the kriegie mold but still speaking with maddening pauses while searching for the proper word. Circumspect in speech, given to "shall we say" and "one might almost." He "simply dashed into" places or had "the merest bite" to eat. A Harvard man, and proud of it in his own diffident way. I dubbed him "The Harvard Fart." He relished the nickname. I called him that because he derived such great pleasure from passing gas at the table. He'd look around slyly, fart, and laugh. We knew it was something he'd never have done at home. His upbringing had been as properly Boston as you could get in Glen Ridge, New Jersey. (When my wife and I visited him while on our honeymoon in New York we found his parents warm and hospitable but very proper. When I wrote to him in later years I'd address him as "Dear H.F." His wife wondered what that meant. I told Schoonmaker to tell her "Harvard's Finest." He did. She believed it for years.) The Harvard Fart was only his summer name. In winter it was Hard Rock because of the icy stare he'd give me when I was his bridge partner and blundered. Sometimes, even when I was playing sensibly, I'd say, "Ted, look hard," and he'd entertain me with a cold, patrician stare. He was a better bridge player than I was and good at chess, which I didn't play at all. But he was terrible at poker. Now that I'd gotten away from the sharks at P.G. 21, I wasn't too bad.

How he loved to argue. Almost unbeatable, too. If you cornered him in one direction he'd switch you to another or baffle you with abstractions. If he really enjoyed an argument he'd keep it going for weeks, even after his opponent gave up. You couldn't pick on anyone when he was around. He'd rush to defend them. If you talked about someone behind his back, Schoonmaker would tot up his good points to you and minimize his faults.

He wasn't a good worker at anything that didn't involve intellect. He was willing, though. He'd do anything he was asked to but he'd stop in the middle of a room chore, a cigarette dangling from his plump lower lip, the only plump feature of his thin, sensitive face, and begin a long discourse on some favored topic. He'd forget what he was supposed to be doing until someone yelled him back to work.

He got masses of mail, some of the letters many pages long. His parents called his sister "The Wee One," and so did he. They wrote things like that in their letters. We'd get mad at Schoonmaker for tying up valuable censor time with his letters and holding up ours.

He even had an interview with the Protecting Power. His mother had been able to arrange it through the New York Red Cross, in which she was active. (My mother did volunteer work for the Houston Red Cross but hadn't the contacts Schoonmaker's mother did.) The Protecting Power made regular visits, but South Compound was so sprawling we often didn't see him arrive or depart and Schoonmaker was the only one in our room who'd been face to face with him. (The Protecting Power always made a point of visiting John Winant, son of the American ambassador to Great Britain. He'd deliver personal messages from the ambassador and ask Winant if there was anything his father could send him through diplomatic channels. Winant always refused special favors, which didn't sit well with his roommates because he shared his personal parcels with them. Winant finally surrendered to temptation and asked for something for himself. Tennis shoes and running shorts.

Schoonmaker, Kennedy, Alvarado, Buckner and I formed a family core throughout the rest of our internment.

Charles Costanzo. From New Hampshire, except for Mouse Rideout, who wasn't at all like him, the only New Englander I'd known. Costanzo had reached P.G. 21 after Kennedy and me and had lived in another bungalow so we hadn't really known him before. I'd been impressed by a lecture he'd given on the crumbling of the Mareth Line in Tunisia and the part his P-40 fighter unit had played in it. He was thin and wiry, with a Roman nose. He had a puckish sense of humor that never irritated. He described a new young singer we'd never heard of, Frank Sinatra, as "looking like seven kinds of consumption wrapped up in a zoot suit."

He could be obstinate but overall a good roommate, generous, fair and outgoing. Outside the room though, he was what Buckner pretended to be, a go-for-the-throat operator. He was a talented cartoonist, technically maybe only fair but with a whimsical eye that caught the humor in our situation—Italian guards going over the wall at P.G. 21, assembly line bathing under the cold water tap, the row of bare behinds showing under the boxcars at Florence, the flap during the bombing at Bolzano, and wry views of Stalag Luft III life.

He'd been on the ski and lacrosse teams at the University of New Hampshire. Sometimes he'd entertain us after lights out laughing and sobbing like an infant. He almost always talked in his sleep. I argued with him a lot, sometimes more seriously than with our other roommates, and there'd be periods of strain but we remained friends.

Luther. The man who'd carried the knapsack with Costanzo. His last name escapes me. Big, blond and handsome but seldom around when there was work to be done. He moved out before Adams did, taking an eighth of our pine stumps though he hadn't done his share of pulling them. None of us hated to see him go.

Settled in, we made improvements. Costanzo, the most enterprising among us, found the means to sling our palliasses onto
rope webbing. He got an iron spike, which we heated in our stove
to burn holes in our bunk frames through which to lace the rope he
got from our Red Cross parcel officer (who got it from the bindings
of parcels). The room stank with acrid smoke for days, but it was
worth it. Palliasses resting on a web of rope were more comfortable than those on bedboards, and we had the precious bedboards
for other uses like shelves at the ends of our bunks. Our hosts
considered such misuse of bedboards destruction of Reich property but never confiscated them or, as the Italians had done,
levied fines.

Adams and Schoonmaker were our first cooking team. They
volunteered. Adams started out boiling with enthusiasm. After a
few days of furious activity he did less and less until Schoonmaker
was doing it all. We weren't surprised when Adams announced he
was giving up cooking to study. Chemistry, history, astronomy
and economics. He went to the library that very night and
brought back a stack of books. He buried himself in one of them for
upwards of an hour but after that spent little time with them. We
knew he hadn't used study as an excuse to stop cooking. He'd
really intended to work at it.

Schoonmaker wasn't much of a cook. He'd combine complicated mixtures of incompatible ingredients. Author Elizabeth
Woody sent him an autographed copy of her cookbook but it didn't
help. We never complained, though. There was no such thing as a
cooking failure in our room. Alvarado told this story about three
hunters on an extended camping trip. They drew lots to see who
had to do the cooking with the provision that the first man who
complained about the food would have to take over from him. The
loser did everything he could to prepare such bad meals the others
would complain. It didn't work. So he went and gathered elk dung
and baked it into a pie in a nice crust. One of his friends bit into his
slice and exclaimed, "This tastes like elk shit!" Realizing the
consequences, he cried, "But cooked just the way I like it."

If the room was our core family, the block was our extended
family. As in any family, we liked some members better than
others and a few not at all. Being all Americans and all Air Forces,
we hadn't the diversity of P.G. 21. No Scots, kilted or otherwise,
except Church of Scotland Padre Murdo Ewen McDonald, who'd
volunteered to serve in South Compound, no University of Cal-

cutta professors, no London stockbrokers. We had one Englishman, Bill, in the block though he claimed to be American. We assumed he was there as liaison for the British across the fence in North Compound and worked for X (the Escape Committee) with his roommate, Casey. He borrowed my pocketknife once to use in fashioning a bow and arrows to shoot messages over the wire to North Compound.

Bill had been a commissioned gunner in the RAF. Casey was RAF, too, but a bona fide American from Maryland. They lived in the front two-man room across from the night latrine. Both of them were flight lieutenants, equivalent to U.S. captains. We knew they had secret, staff-authorized dealings with certain tame goons.

They often put in with friends on batches of kriegie brew. Kriegie brew was distilled from raisins, plums and anything else fermentable. When they got drunk, Casey would stand against their door and Bill would throw sharpened table knives at him. Bill never hit Casey but the door's glass center panel had to be replaced regularly. I was visiting one day when Casey was out and Bill asked me to stand in for him. I declined. He explained he wasn't the kind of chap willing to throw knives at just anyone. Only true friends, and since I was a true friend he couldn't possibly hurt me. I told him I appreciated that but still wouldn't do it. He said if I didn't trust him I could hold a pillow in front of my face. I said that wasn't the point. The reason I wouldn't let him throw knives at me was that it was against my principles to have knives thrown at me. But if it weren't, I certainly wouldn't hold a pillow in front of my face when he threw knives at me. That pleased him immensely. He wouldn't ask a man to go against his principles and he was glad I wouldn't hold a pillow in front of my face because if I'd held a pillow in front of my face when he threw knives at me he would have lost all respect for me.

Our block commander and the editor of our one-sheet camp paper, "The Circuit," lived in one of the two-man rooms at the other end of the block. The block commander was a large, blond-haired captain consumed with his importance. We called him "the boy captain" and tormented him at appel by not simmering down until he made threats. After it snowed the rear rank threw snowballs at him. He never caught a culprit. The editor was an earnest second lieutenant who posted a new edition on the cookhouse wall every week with items gleaned from new prisoners, letters and the camp staff. It even had a comic strip, "Penny." Penny was a shapely, semidraped American Red Cross blonde in London.

Two captains shared the other room. Another Bill, at forty-two maybe the oldest man in South Compound, who had been in Lindbergh's upper class at Randolph Field. An intelligence officer, he was also a qualified P-38 pilot. He'd been shot down riding in a B-17 as an observer. He was big in X and guardian of the the compound's clandestine radio. His roommate, Harry, was the block PX officer. The PX plan, we were told, was devised by Colonel Goodrich to keep our German POW pay from being charged against our U.S. Army Air Forces pay. Under the Goodrich plan, no one received his German pay directly. Instead, all German pay was pooled in a fund that went into camp projects or purchased razor blades, toothpowder and what similar items our hosts let us buy. We got them free, as needed, from the block PX officer.

A northerner originally, Harry now lived in the Rio Grande Valley but I didn't consider him a Texan. He was a serious type who didn't like being kidded, which I did whenever he came to our room to ask if we needed shaving things, toothpaste or such. I'd ask for an easy chair, a radio or a blonde. I thought I was pretty funny until he finally had enough and told me off. I realized I'd just been obnoxious. When I began treating him with the same courtesy he showed me, we became friends.

There were two men in Block 133 I'd known before. Ed Allen, in the room across the hall, I knew from Houston. Dorf, down the hall, I'd roomed with briefly in preflight at Maxwell Field. Allen had been shot down on his first mission and felt bad about it. It didn't matter that it had been a rough mission on which he'd seen more flak and fighters than I had on all my missions together. Dorf was a brooding, Jewish intellectual. A Communist, I supposed, which wasn't the reason I'd disliked him at Maxwell. He'd thought me a new boy and tried to push off all the housework on me. I'd had enough previous military service to know better and I pushed back. He was still a second lieutenant and bitter about it. At first, since we were Jewish and in the bag together, I figured we should get along so I'd do the circuit with him talking about the war, the world, and being Jewish, but even as fellow krieigies we didn't like each other any more than we had at preflight.

Another Houstonian heard I was in camp and came visiting. He said he'd known me back home. A towering, gangling, pleasant young man. I didn't remember him until he told me his name. Billy Kahlden. I remembered him as a little kid. I couldn't believe he'd grown into this giant. We became close friends. He was notorious in South Compound for two things, his racy photo of Susan Hayward and his cuckoo. He'd asked his mother to send him a pin-up and she'd sent the barest she could find. What a mom. He'd acquired the cuckoo as a flightless babe and fed it on bread soaked in Klim while he was teaching it to fly. It had messy habits and his roommates were glad when it left.

There was another Houstonian in South Compound I'd already heard of at P.G. 21. His copilot, navigator and bombardier had come in shortly before Italy got out of the war. Learning I was from Houston, they'd told me their pilot, Roger Smith, was from there and was in an Italian hospital with severe burns. I'd written my mother to tell his parents that. Later, when I wrote my mother from Stalag Luft III, they assumed he'd be there, too. They wrote to him using my address and POW ID number. He heard from them before they heard from him. We also became good friends. One evening before some disabled kriegies were to be repatriated and curfew was extended to midnight I was sure he'd be among them because of his scars and I went to visit him. On my way to his block a Hundführer asked me what time it was. I told him. He asked again, more insistently. I told him again. I was upsetting him and didn't know why. Finally he shrugged helplessly and went off with his dog. I was to learn he'd been telling, not asking me, the time. Smith hadn't made the repat list, but I stayed to visit with him until after eleven. When I stepped out the door a goonbox sentry challenged me. I tried to explain we were permitted out later that night. I could translate the military communique but a simple conversation was beyond me. I couldn't make him understand. Colonel McNickle, who lived in the block, heard the racket and came out to help me explain. Then Dick Schrupp, the staff interpreter, joined us to set things straight in his perfect German. The sentry let off a round into the air. The three of us were back inside the block before the echo died away. We looked into each others' frightened faces and suddenly began giggling. A roving guard who'd heard the shot and come to inves-

tigate told the sentry it was okay for me to be outside. I walked
back to my block whistling "Lili Marlene" as loud as I could, not
out of bravado but so no goon would think I was sneaking around.

Schoonmaker never served anything that tasted of elk and I
never complained, but when he tired of cooking, Alvarado and I
volunteered, Alvarado on condition I plan and cook the meals if he
did the drudgery.

Le Cordon Wild Bleu Yonder

COOKING WAS SERIOUS business. We almost always cooked on the kitchen stove because fuel was in such short supply. We didn't get enough coal to keep our room warm all day and even in the coldest weather, when the temperature sank below zero, we usually wouldn't start a fire until late afternoon. By judiciously using our stump wood, we built up a backlog of coal, which we concealed under our larder locker so the ferrets wouldn't report we were getting more than we needed.

South Compound's coal was brought in by wagon from a huge pile in some woods outside the wire and dumped in the road between blocks. We carried our issue to the block kitchen under the supervision of our block coal officer. A woodbox full of coal was a staggering load for two. The coal officer counted it out brick by brick to rooms, holding some back for the communal kitchen stove.

After we modified our room stove, we used it occasionally for cooking in extremely cold weather when we had a fire going anyhow, mostly for desserts, or to start potatoes boiling before moving them to the kitchen. The room stove, of fire brick and tile with a smooth metal top, was designed for heating, not cooking. Old hands showed us how to convert it. We took off the top, broke out the tile under it and lowered the metal grate to make a larger firebox. We switched the sheet-metal top for the washroom stove's cooking top. A cooking top had two holes with round lids.

Cooking on the kitchen stove was a good deal more complicated than cooking in the room. We shared its two-foot by three-foot space, minus that taken up by the chimney pipe, with the other rooms, about one hundred twenty kriegies worth. The top was scaly and buckled from the heat of our cooking fires and the weight of buckets of potatoes. It heated unevenly and unpredictably. A savvy cook always knew the best spot for his bucket. It was the same with the two-compartment oven.

Stove time was rigidly scheduled by rooms and regulated by a complicated set of rules posted on the wall as well as unwritten laws governing who cooked when and where and the order of precedence for various dishes. Two or three rooms shared the stove for forty-five-minute periods. Potato boilers got the choice sites until the water bubbled, then had to slide over, to be supplanted by fryers. Men from stove-time rooms could toast bread if they could find the space. Cooks surrounded the stove, poking, prodding, stirring, testing, moving aside only to let a helper reload the firebox from the untidy heap of briquettes at the back of the kitchen, all in a flux of kriegies coming to draw water from the kitchen tap, offer advice or, in dead of winter, just looking for warmth.

Until the Red Cross sent us pots with lids and other proper utensils, we improvised. Jam buckets for boiling, the incinerator-lid skillets for frying, and a shallow, rectangular pan made from tin can strips hammered together with clever self-locking folds for everything else. Though they were almost watertight to begin with, accumulated grease made them completely so. We made rolling pins and potato mashers from sections of peeled birch and cheese and breadcrust graters from the jagged side of tin can strips punched with holes. We used a mug to grind hardtack into flour on the rough wood top of the table where we ate, wrote letters and played cards.

Alvarado and I began with a well-stocked larder but knew it wouldn't last, so we skimped. FoodAcco had some Red Cross and parcel food but we didn't trade there often. FoodAcco also stocked cigarettes, toilet articles, clothes from personal parcels and, occasionally, cigars. Most rooms had an account there, buying goods with points accumulated by contributing goods. Prices fluctuated as in any barter system. Some kriegies used FoodAcco to speculate, buying short or selling long. Some guessed right, some wrong, just like commodity traders outside the wire. Run with honesty and efficiency, FoodAcco made a profit by levying a small surcharge on all transactions. The funds went to various camp projects.

Our goal was to serve what gave the illusion of "enough" while varying the monotony. I invented dishes and used recipes tested by other room cooks. If a recipe didn't work, we ate the dish anyhow. And no one mentioned elk. Portions were exactly even, measured by spoonful if necessary. Some rooms measured solids like cakes with a ruler but Room 12 relied on the cooks' judgment. We had to be accurate. We got last pick.

The potato was central to our diet, the anchor of the day's major meal at night. During our long stay at Stalag Luft III we probably had no more than a dozen evening meals without potatoes.

As at P.G. 21, we had several small meals throughout the day. The two slices of goon bread at breakfast, two more for lunch with canned fish, cheese or jam. Lunch might have soup or other cooked German rations from the cookhouse. Some rooms took afternoon tea but we had dinner early and had our tea or coffee later with bread or hardtack.

Dinner was Spam or bully beef and potatoes in as many variations as didn't require special ingredients or prolonged cooking time. Sometimes we had vegetables—kohlrabi, swedes, turnips, rutabaga or cabbage. I'd never had any of them but turnips and cabbage at home.

We served the potatoes boiled, usually, and french-fried on the occasional Saturday night. We had a communal pot of fat in the block, used over and over again. Everyone in the room pitched in to peel and slice. I fried, Alvarado scooped them out in batches, drained them on copies of the *Volkischer Beobachter* newspaper in our wash basin, and hustled them piping hot back to our room. As a matter of honor we never ate a fry except at the table in front of everyone. And I never tasted anything as I cooked, either. If anything needed tasting, I got someone else to do it. Protocol.

Kennedy would take over his specialty, pan-fried potatoes, when we accumulated enough dried onions from personal parcels. He piled them above the brim in the block's skillet and stirred and prodded them mercilessly without ever spilling. He cooked as he did everything, at fever pitch. (Once when my wife and I were visiting his family in Phoenix he cooked pan fries for us. His technique hadn't changed.)

We got fresh meat every ten days to two weeks. At least it was supposed to be fresh. Arthur A. Durand in his book, *Stalag Luft III*, quoted a South Compound cook as saying the meat always arrived covered with maggots. We usually got it as cooked hamburger. I tried to draw it on Saturday for Sunday dinner. In cold weather when we had our stove going I'd surround it with boiled potatoes and baste it for hours with a mixture of water, margarine and bouillon cubes. More rarely we got a piece of pork or beef. When it was beef, Alvarado sliced it into "steaks." Small, tough, delectable.

Spam was our meat of preference. Our first Thanksgiving I poked George Radovanovic's garlic brought up from Stalag VIIA deep into it. I'd seen my mother do that with turkeys.

I'd try to make bully beef look and taste like something else, kneading hardtack flour into it with chopped raw turnips or dried onions and whatever spice was available from personal parcels— sage, curry powder, allspice or cloves. When it was curry powder I cooked Kennedy's portion separately. He didn't like curry.

And my bacon and eggs. I was famous for them in every corner of Room 12. We didn't have them often. It took a while to accumulate enough powdered egg and canned bacon. The way you cook Bacon and Eggs Room 12 is first soak your egg powder overnight and add a thick mixture of Klim and water with a touch of hardtack flour for stiffener. Shred your bacon and give it a shot on top of the stove before mixing it with the eggs and shoving it all in the oven. You get it just right, it comes out with the texture of light cornbread.

When I was lazy, Alvarado and I gave our roommates soups and stews. Pretty plebeian, except for my stewed chicken. What made it a challenge was that we never had any chicken, just dried noodle soup, diced potatoes, chicken bouillon cubes and a can of finely shredded Spam.

We used a lot of margarine in Room 12. We craved fats and it was abundant because a lot of men in the block wouldn't eat it. In the States they'd been brought up to believe only butter was good enough. Margarine traded low.

Sunday brunch had yet to catch on in the States but we had a version of it in Room 12 we were perfectly content with—a large bowl of steaming oatmeal or barley, or the two mixed, sometimes with raisins in it. Barley took longer to cook than oatmeal. I served the cereal with margarine, Klim and sugar.

While we always ate whatever showed up on the table, some of my experiments were so unsuccessful I never repeated them. Baked fishcheese, for example, for which our room was taunted, and pumpkin, baked or boiled, and fried turnips.

Everyone liked desserts, but when Alvarado and I first took over we were so preoccupied with just trying to get something edible on the table we sometimes didn't make one. When we didn't, if anyone asked, "What's for dessert?" Alvarado did the answering. He'd say, "Desert the table." When we started doing desserts regularly, we began with the simplest and most economical. Gedoing. It was already a South Compound staple and we never learned where it got its name. Bread scraps and crusts mixed with Klim, sugar, and raisins, cocoa or shaved D-bars, boiled to gummy consistency and served with cream made from Klim.

After a while we graduated to cakes and pies. A level spoonful of Red Cross tooth powder made a cake rise a little. It was the bicarbonate of soda. Cakes were fine but we liked pies even better, with crusts of hardtack flour and margarine. The rarest and best-loved pie was condendo—parcel lemon crystals stirred into condensed milk until it set. Costanzo would make individual pastry shells for it.

Sometimes we topped dessert with "whipped cream" made of equal parts of Klim and marge blended into a smooth paste and beaten fluffy with a fork while you added water drop by drop. A delicate operation—too much water, the marge settled out in lumps. Not enough, it wouldn't whip. It could take an hour to get the whipped cream exactly right. With cocoa whipped into it, it was our supreme dessert. I looked forward to making some when I got home, with condensed milk instead of Klim, real butter instead of marge, the finest cocoa. I did, at my sister-in-law's. No one but me got past the first bite. Pride dictated that I eat it all but I managed only a spoonful at a time over a period of days.

Sometimes when I'd spent half a morning planning a meal and Alvarado and I worked an hour or two executing it only to see it wolfed down in minutes I'd wonder if it were all worth it. The answer was always yes. There were few enough opportunities to spend time productively in the bag. Not only did cooking break the monotony but also it got the cooks out of room chores and camp work details. When Alvarado's name or mine came up on a camp duty roster roommates took our place. When outside work didn't interfere with cooking, though, we'd often take our turn anyhow because it used up time.

Cooks didn't wash dishes or clean up after meals. The orderly dog did that. The dog's day was longer and harder than the cook's, like K.P. in the army, the ugliest detail in the service. Mornings, the dog rose before anyone else. In winter he started the fire in the room stove. He fetched brew and wash water from the cookhouse, he swept out the room, emptied the garbage (never anything edible in it), opened cans for the cook, peeled potatoes, ground hardtack and, after dinner, washed the dishes. He had an assistant dog for that. One dog washed, the other dried. They did the dishes in the same basin we mixed cakes and gedoing in.

The dog's most important job was slicing bread. He had to go to a block with a bread slicer to do it. The bread slicer had a dull, circular blade turned with a crank in the middle. A dog took pride in the number of slices he got from a loaf of bread. Forty was on the upper end of normal. Dogs tended to visit the slicer at the same time and enjoy a cigarette and a chat waiting in line. It was a kind of social event.

With the first smell of winter, the machine guns came out of the goonboxes, leaving the sentries only rifles. We attached significance to this, as we did to everything not routine. It told us German arms production was slipping and that our machine guns were needed against a coming Russian onslaught. When the machine guns reappeared in the spring, we realized it was only because our hosts had wanted them out of the weather and didn't expect any massed assaults on the wire in the winter cold.

About the time the machine guns left, a German photographer was allowed to shoot pictures in South Compound for propaganda purposes and for a proposed picture album for kriegies. Wings Kimball, a fighter pilot who lived down the hall, worked with the photographer, who was paid out of camp funds. Wings was to get the negatives from the photographer after the war and have the albums made up. (He did. *Clipped Wings*, a handsome hardcover affair like a college yearbook which is still in print.) Costanzo arranged to have the photographer visit our room and shoot us playing poker. Each of us was given two prints. I sent one of mine home stitched to a letter form. My mother had copies made and sent them to all my roommates' next of kin. She'd never seen me in a mustache and thought Alvarado was me. The picture ran in all our hometown newspapers, in the Red Cross bulletin, and in *Liberty* and *Flying* magazines.

Sports were more varied than at P.G. 21. Besides basketball and softball, we had touch football, fencing, weightlifting, horizontal bar and even swimming and ice hockey. We swam in the firepool, a brick affair about fifty feet on a side. For hockey, we dammed an area between two blocks and flooded it. Winters, freezing it was no problem. The International Red Cross provided clamp skates, which came off army boots a lot, and sticks. Hockey season ended abruptly when all the sticks were broken.

The weightlifters made their weights out of cans of cement at either end of poles. Most of them gave up their body-building when we went on half-parcels. Earl Guyette, who'd replaced Adams, was a weightlifter. Guy was not a new boy. He'd come to us from another room and we never learned why he'd left it. He was wonderfully obliging. If someone asked him for a light while he was lying in his bunk smoking, instead of waiting for the man to come to him, he'd spring up and take the light to him. If I said I was going for water or to slice bread he'd offer to do it for me. He was a true innocent and thought well of everyone. We walked the circuit a lot together.

I didn't participate in any of the organized sports. I'd played ice hockey at Rice but didn't go out for a South Compound team because I'd been a poor enough goaltender even before I got nearsighted. I skated though, on the firepool and on a pond we froze by our block, the first time I'd ever skated on natural ice. I walked a lot, did calisthenics, and when the weather warmed swam half a mile daily in the firepool. It was a lot of laps. The water was still icy when I began the routine. I was considered a little eccentric for swimming on cold, gusty days.

Most of us tried to keep in decent physical shape. Playing games and exercising not only killed time but also made us more escape-ready if an opportunity presented itself. Some kriegies could trot the circuit several times but I was never able to do it even once without slowing to a walk.

Sam, a Jewish San Antonian with a flashing gold tooth, and one of our best softball players, fielded YMHA (Young Men's Hebrew Association) basketball, softball and touch football teams. You didn't have to be Jewish to be on one. He'd post game notices on the cookhouse bulletin board. We never knew if our hosts knew what the initials stood for but relished the idea of a Jewish organization flourishing deep in Naziland.

Sam was as flashy a gambler as he was an athlete. He was one of those setting up an outdoor crap table layout when the weather got nice and a gambling craze struck South Compound. The SAO allowed it as long as kriegies played for cigarettes and chocolate, but when they began giving money IOUs he decreed that gambling debts were not to be considered debts of honor and were invalid, even IOUs for chocolate D-bars. No food was to be bought or sold in South Compound except by barter.

Kriegies would bet on anything, especially on when the war would end. Before the invasion I was pessimistic and won bets from optimists; money IOUs, a watch with a broken mainspring, chocolate bars. After the invasion I joined the optimists. And lost chocolate bars, my wristwatch and a box of cigars.

There was one kind of bet the whole compound would follow as closely as we followed the war. That was a man betting he could eat a whole Red Cross parcel in the span of twelve hours. A parcel had eleven pounds of food in it, which didn't seem like a whole lot to someone always hungry. None succeeded but one man came close. He downed the meats, fish, and cheese and combined the milk, margarine, sugar, hardtack, chocolate and prunes in a cake which he couldn't finish. Goodrich eventually banned eating orgies because they wasted food and were a health hazard.

Sam ran a crap table at our daylong 1944 July Fourth celebration, which offered carnival games, hula "girls," sports competitions, and an evening outdoor concert by the Luftbandsters in a week also highlighted by a rare issue of onions.

Later that month we celebrated more enthusiastically than we had July Fourth, though out of sight of our hosts, when Count Claus von Stauffenberg tried to kill Hitler. At first we firmly believed Hitler had died in the explosion and the Germans were covering it up. We thought the war was as good as over, but after hearing him speak to the nation on the radio and seeing new pictures of him we were forced to admit he'd survived. We took some small comfort in noticing that in all the new pictures he shook hands with his left hand, indicating his right had been damaged, and greater comfort the week after the attempt when he announced the formation of the *Volksturm*, the people's army of every man, woman and child, to defend the Fatherland to the last inch, from every window and every ditch and from behind every bush. He sounded even more hysterical than usual and to us the thundering "Sieg heils!" that interrupted him were last hurrahs.

A Walk in the Rain

THE END OF JULY, KENNEDY and I made the parole walk list. We borrowed uniform blouses and real insignia so we would be a credit to the Air Forces while out among German civilians. We assembled at the theater to wait for our guards. They came promptly but one parolee didn't. We waited. We fretted. We waited some more. And cursed. Our precious minutes outside the wire were frittering away. Someone went to fetch the man. He was sick in bed and hadn't bothered to tell anyone. We hoped he wouldn't recover. All present and accounted for. Ready to move out. It started to sprinkle. The guards suggested we postpone the walk until next day. We'd already lost a precious hour and now we were getting wet but we refused. Kriegies didn't trust tomorrow.

We set out. Six kriegies and two guards. We stopped in the outer compound to sign our paroles. Out of sight of barbed wire for the first time in months, we walked a country lane to the outskirts of a village where cherry trees bordered the streets. The fruit was still green. There were no civilians around to admire our uniforms. We crossed the Bober River on a little wooden foot-bridge and ran for cover in a nearby wood as rain pelted down. We wished we'd postponed our walk. The rain let up and we headed for Sagan. Kennedy kept after me to ask our guards to let us stop in a tavern for beer. I did and was told, with regrets, this was a beerless day. Taverns were closed by decree. Houses now, and a few people. The houses were all two-storied with lace curtains at the window and their backs to the street. Their flower and vegetable gardens were flourishing.

We followed the Bober through well-tended green fields, which Kennedy viewed with a critical farmer's eye and gave high marks. Then along a paved road to a little village. Cobbled streets and hardly anyone about. Up ahead a meadow strewn with girls.

They shouted at us and waved as we passed. Foreign workers? Children? I hadn't brought my glasses and couldn't see well enough to tell. Children, I decided. Kennedy asked me to tell our guards we wanted to go back and talk to them. I wouldn't do it. It really pissed him off. When I learned they'd been young women, not children, I wished I'd done as he asked.

Farther along, we saw a ragged woman leading a dirty little boy by the hand. She had a paper sack in her free hand filled with what looked like edible garbage. Could they be Germans? We gave them chocolate. They seemed stunned by it. More children, these clean and well dressed, playing with dolls, riding bikes, doing what American children did. Our uniforms impressed them. We gave them chewing gum and chocolate. We gave our guards cigarettes, hoping to soften them up to let us do some trading. We'd brought barter goods with us. They wouldn't let us. Probably had orders not to but one of them did get me a few apples. A guard looked at his watch and said it was time to turn back. We'd come to a railroad track and he led us along it. He didn't seem too sure of himself. After a quarter of a mile he asked a trackside guard for directions. We were heading for Berlin. The wrong way. We turned back, hurrying now. He had his orders about when to get us back. Flatcars passed on the tracks, loaded with wrecked American bombers. We hurried through foreign worker settlements. Some of the workers lived in boxcars on sidings, others in little lagers surrounded by barbed wire. We exchanged greetings and threw them cigarettes. A handsome, dark-eyed woman smiled at us from a boxcar, invitingly we thought. Lust engulfed us. There were other women among the workers, some of them frustratingly pretty.

Into the heart of Sagan. A real town. Lots of foot traffic. A file of German soldiers, Stalag Luft III guards, maybe? Russian prisoners returning from their work. More children. Old people. A fierce, stringy old man glared at us and bawled out our guards for bringing us through his city. The guards listened respectfully but as soon as we were out of earshot laughed and made fun of him. All through the town painted white arrows marked the way to air raid cellars. Just outside Sagan, slit trenches along a dirt road. We didn't like the implication of air raid cellars and slit trenches so near Stalag Luft III. Beyond the slit trenches, the POW cemetery in a cleared space surrounded by woods, well tended, peaceful, beautiful. The guards let us stop a while to pay our respects. We took off our caps when we entered. The memorial to the British prisoners murdered after the mass escape from North Compound was of stone, long, low, impressive. Men from our own compound were buried there—the one who'd gone around the bend and another whose appendix had ruptured.

We put our caps back on and took a shortcut through the woods to the camp, where our roommates were waiting for every detail. I passed out my apples and Kennedy told them about the women, the air raid cellars and the slit trenches, the things that had impressed us most. What we'd seen allayed any fears we'd had about angry citizens from Sagan storming the camp. There'd been no young men around except soldiers, other prisoners and foreign workers.

Escape and undercover activities were more complex and highly organized than they'd been at P.G. 21. The SAO and X staff allowed only a few designated kriegies to speak with goons and even fewer were allowed to trade with them, and then only for designated items like radio parts and German money. Corruption wasn't nearly as flagrant or rife as it had been at Stalag VIIA, but some guards would bend rules for cigarettes and there may have been some who secretly sympathized with us.

South Compound had a flourishing escape industry: tunnel digging, map making, forging German IDs and making wooden pistols and German uniforms. Almost everyone assembled emergency rations and made packs and water bottles. My Italian knapsack was confiscated after I'd brought in my belongings and my water bottle didn't last long, either. *Lagerfeldwebel* (officer compound sergeant major) Hermann Glemnitz made a surprise visit to our room once, saw it, and said, "I am not on a search now [he spoke excellent English] but I will come back soon and take that bottle." So I hid it. Really well. He found it on the first search. Glemnitz was a stiff-backed German and scrupulously correct.

I was never invited to join a tunnel gang but often served as a lookout, or "stooge." My usual job was to guard one end of a block and shout "tallyho" when a guard came into view. When a German came into a block the first man to see him cried, "Goon in the block," and the call was relayed from room to room. The guards complained about that, saying "tallyho" or "goon in the block" whenever they showed their faces was embarrassing. So we varied our warnings.

Sometimes I'd stooge for one building from a post in another. From a designated window in one block I'd watch a designated window in the other block and when a German approached the block I'd hold up a handkerchief in a signal for whoever was doing what mischief to suspend operations and cover up.

The really serious X operatives we called "the cloak and dagger boys." There were those among them who took what they did so seriously it showed. We knew by their furtive ways when they were on a job and assumed the Germans did, too. The most obvious was a major from P.G. 21 who'd been so security-minded there he hadn't even opened up to an officer he knew. You could tell he was a man on a mission from halfway across the compound. We thought maybe he was a touch around the bend and he may well have been. Despite the obvious few, security in South Compound on the whole was excellent and more went on under German noses than ever was sniffed. In fact, a lot went on that most kriegies never guessed at. There are things revealed in Durand's *Stalag Luft III* of which I never had an inkling.

I was a courier for X for a while, carrying spoken or written messages for known X men so closely watched by our hosts that they couldn't communicate openly with their teams. The Germans suspected that Colonel Clark was heavily involved in escape activities and assigned guards to tail him constantly. They called it off when kriegies began falling in behind the tailers and following them wherever they followed Colonel Clark. I had to report to him once and discovered he was not as unbending as I'd first believed. Not sure whether it was expected or not in prison camp surroundings, when I reported to him in his room I followed all the procedures for reporting to a superior drilled into cadets at pre-flight and felt a little silly going through them. The crisp salute, the "Lieutenant Westheimer reporting to Colonel Clark," the clipped report, the salute, the about-face hoping at the end of it I'd be facing in the right direction. What made me wonder about my evaluation of Big X was the twinkle I'd have sworn was in his frosty eyes when he solemnly returned my salute.

I was always on the outer fringe of X and never knew what kind of activity I was stooging or carrying messages for, even when Casey or Bill down in the end room gave me an assignment informally. Costanzo was closer to the inner circle. He drew maps and may even have known how they were intended to be used. We never discussed it.

Although a few men managed to get out of South Compound,

none ever made good an escape from Germany. A fighter pilot got out in a load of garbage after several failed attempts but was caught immediately. "Silent Death" Sage, an undercover type masquerading as Air Forces, a bearded, menacing fellow and an escape artist, describes being out for days in his book *Sage*, but even he was picked up eventually. One of our interpreters came closest to going all the way. A small man, he tucked himself into the running-board toolbox of a truck that came into the compound and when the truck left the camp hid there until after dark. It had been carefully planned. He had forged foreign worker papers and German money. He spoke fluent German and traveled openly by train. He looked very young, almost waiflike, and strangers on the train befriended him, treating him to beer and bread and sausage. On a train to Vienna he attached himself to a young couple with a child and evaded the Gestapo in the Vienna station posing as a member of the family. He was doing fine until he ran out of money. He had to sell his watch, and when the proceeds were gone he had nothing to eat and no place to rest. He threw himself on the mercy of a priest in a church. The priest gave him food but couldn't give him shelter. Desperately cold and hungry, he stopped an old woman on the street and told her he was an escaped American prisoner. She furtively gave him some money and hurried away. He decided to "hardass it" (strike out cross country on foot) and hope to make it into Czechoslovakia and hook up with the underground. Near the border, completely used up, shoes worn out, feet bleeding and frostbitten, weak from cold, hunger and exhaustion, he stumbled into a house and asked its sympathetic occupant for help getting across. He'd picked just the man who could give it, except that he was a border guard. The border guard fed him and turned him in. After the kriegie got out of the cooler we filled the theater to hear him describe his experiences.

Preventing escapes preoccupied our hosts as much as planning them did us. They'd mount searches day and night. Once when they uncovered a tunnel and evidence of widespread X activity in a block across from us, they evacuated everyone from it into our block while they dismantled the interior.

Sometimes the Germans did a block-to-block search. Those took hours. Usually they'd do the search while we were at morning appel. That way the surprise would be complete, with no stooges to shout a warning "tallyho!" The first we'd know of the impending search would be guards marching in the front gate while we stood helplessly in ranks on the parade ground hoping that whatever was hidden remained that way. If it was just one block being searched, after roll call its occupants had to stay out until the search was over. When the search was block to block we were confined to the parade ground for the better part of a day. Sometimes our hosts combined a personal search with the block-to-block. We'd know that was coming when we hit the parade ground because there'd be tables lined up for us to empty our pockets onto. The tables would be there for "picture appel," too. For picture appel instead of being counted we'd file past an officer as our name was called and he'd compare our mugs with those in our IDs.

It was usually hungry out on the parade ground during all-day searches, but occasionally Colonel Goodrich got advance warning from a tame goon and tipped us off. When we showed up with lunches for morning appel the Germans knew we'd been warned, but I don't think they ever learned by whom.

Sometimes there'd be surprise roll calls at night. The guards would enter blocks and check us out room by room. On a serious visit they'd search us individually and then turn us out and scour our rooms at their leisure looking for tunnels and radios. They'd be pretty decent about it, leaving block lights on and letting us take refuge in other blocks until they were done. They weren't always neat, not bothering to put things back the way they'd been. Sometimes there'd be an unexpected kindness, though. During a room search when the occupants were allowed to remain, a kriegie got upset when a guard prepared to rip his wife's picture out of its frame. The officer in charge stopped it.

Our cigarettes, coffee, tea and soap were highly prized outside the wire, but there was very little pilfering by the searchers. When kriegies complained of missing food and cigarettes the Germans began searching the searchers. The pilfering stopped.

We had some fairly secure hiding places behind the beaver-board paneling of our walls that usually went undetected, but the searchers were expert and we sometimes lost maps, handmade saws and other verboten items. They never found our radio, though. Only the operator and a few others knew where it was located and when it was used. The rest of us weren't even sure we had a radio in our compound. For all we knew, the BBC news was coming from North Compound or tame goons.

At first we got the news from a kriegie who slipped from

block to block and read it to us in the hall or washroom. My first news staff job was to get the time of the reading from our block X man and inform the room commanders. The Germans knew we were getting BBC communiques from somewhere and grew more vigilant. The same man going from block to block was too obvious. Each block got its own news reader. I got the job in ours. Hadn't I claimed to be a newspaperman? Readers were told to report to a certain room in a certain block at a certain time, never the same two days in a row. We'd arrive separately a few minutes apart so as not to be seen converging on the block. There we'd be given mimeographed news summaries. I never knew where the duplicating machine was and never tried to learn. The mimeographed sheets were barely legible and the man who passed them out would read the material to us in a low voice to fill in the gaps, then give us the time and place for the next meeting. Back at our blocks we'd tell our block Xs when we'd be reading the news and they'd tell room commanders and set security.

I read the news in our washroom, with stooges at both ends of the block and the kitchen window. Afterward the audience would depart in small groups.

After a while reading an entire summary was considered too risky and the news was condensed even more and divided into main topics—Russian Front, Italian Front, Air War. When the Germans tightened the screws we began reading room to room instead of to a washroom assembly. Even that got chancy as the Germans strove to eliminate our source of information. We had to memorize the five to eight most important bits and go from room to room repeating them. Each room had its own security, a man at the door and another at the window. At first we began reports with "Hohendahl says," to confuse and mislead any goons who might be hiding under the blocks or in attics, but when it occurred to Big X that the Germans knew we disliked Hohendahl and he wasn't fond of us and he'd never tell us anything we switched to "The cookhouse goon says." Before long the cookhouse goon was transferred out of South Compound. We liked to think we helped.

I assumed North Compound had its own radio but never knew for sure and never asked. I did know that Bill at one time was responsible for getting news reports to North Compound. The bow and arrow he'd made with the help of my pocketknife hadn't worked and he got Maxie, a strapping fellow, to throw the report over the wire wrapped around a rock. It took a strong arm.

Maxie had to stand well back from the wire around the corner of
our block out of sight of the goonbox and peg the rock over two
fences with concertina wire in between. He had a couple of mis-
fires that gave Bill fits, once when the rock landed inside the
guardrail on the North Compound side. An English officer risked
his life to fish it out. The other time was worse. The rock landed
between the fences and lay in the concertina wire tormenting Bill
until the report weathered away. Bill tried to signal the news at
night in Morse code with a margarine lamp and tin shutter but
without success.

Stalag Luft III wasn't exactly a home away from home but
we were more comfortable there than at P.G. 21. There were
small things we yearned for when we thought about them, things
we'd taken for granted on the outside. A rug to step on when we
got out of bed instead of a rough floor, clean underwear every day,
a warm room, a real stove to cook on, a radio, hot water gushing
from the tap, a hot shower or a bathtub on the premises, padded,
comfortable chairs. Sometimes we'd think about other ordinary
experiences we were denied: driving a car, riding in an elevator,
using a telephone. We missed simple privacy. We were never
alone, even in the abort. Once when I had a touch of the flu and
was allowed to miss morning appel, the minutes of solitude I had
in the room were almost as good as freedom.

As the war on the Eastern Front progressed, we could
surmise how things were going from the air traffic. Stukas and
fighters streaming east, the Russians were starting a major attack; transports flying west, the Russians had broken through and
casualties and high-ranking officers were being brought to safety.
Late in the war we saw a twin-engine fighter that mystified us
with its speed and strange-sounding engines. It was a jet. And we
saw a V-1, the first German *Vergeltungswaffen*, "Vengeance
Weapon," the unmanned rocket raining terror on London. It was
riding piggyback on a Heinkel bomber. The German radio had
boasted of terrible new weapons that would turn the tide of battle
but we'd dismissed it as propaganda. During the Russian advance
that was to bring our evacuation from Stalag Luft III we saw
everything the Luftwaffe could throw into battle, from first-line
fighter and bomber types to obsolete stuff we'd never seen as well
as primary and basic trainers.

We sought diversion looking through the wire. Civilians took
shortcuts past our camp and in winter went by on horse-drawn

sleds. Army recruits, self-conscious in new uniforms, marched past, and groups of Hitler Jugend. We'd hear the Hitler Jugend coming, singing. They threw out their chests and sang louder and marched more crisply when they saw us watching; and they could sing. When they passed close enough we'd hear someone in their ranks cuing the pauses, diminuendos and crescendos.

The female mail censors occasionally took the path along the wire on the southern perimeter. They didn't sing but we gave them our full attention. Once an especially shapely young woman walked the path slowly, pausing for lingering glances into the compound, and then turned and did it again. Before she'd finished the return trip, the whole camp had turned out except for a handful of warped souls who refused to give a German the satisfaction of knowing she was driving them crazy.

We even watched our British neighbors in North Compound. In decent weather, and sometimes in bad, they played fierce soccer and rugby. They had a track meet that included a mile run. We couldn't imagine where the runners got the stamina.

Russian details sometimes worked in and around the camp, some of them regularly. We got to know several Russians on sight. They were in much better shape physically than those at Stalag VIIA. A wagon driver, handsome, well over six feet tall and powerfully built, told us he was a major in the Russian army. Entirely possible. We'd heard the Germans didn't recognize rank among Russian POWs. When he saw three American officers struggling to carry a heavy pole they'd been given to put up a clothesline, he climbed down from his wagon, took it from them, and carried it alone. Another time he accidentally backed the wagon into a four-by-four supporting the cookhouse overhang and knocked it from its concrete base. Guards converged on him, shouting and making threatening gestures. He shrugged indifferently, said, "C'est la guerre," squatted, and heaved the support back onto its base.

A detail of three Russians came in frequently to do casual labor and work on the plumbing. They were friendly types and although our hosts didn't like us speaking with them they always drew a crowd. We gave them cigarettes, which they smoked while they worked with their guards looking on enviously. Sometimes the guards stopped us because they'd be in trouble if Russians were found with American cigarettes so we'd sneak them to the Russians. We tried not to upset guards but the Russians ignored them. They worked at their own pace and if a guard tried to speed them up they'd just stare at him blankly even if he threatened them with his weapon.

The Russians liked Americans and we liked them. They didn't get Red Cross or regular personal parcels so sometimes Colonel Goodrich would have us take up collections of tobacco or clothing to send to their camp. Kennedy worked for a while in the parcel room in the outer compound and said packages sometimes straggled in for Russian prisoners from relatives in German-occupied areas, a little moldy bread, a few onions, a ragged coat. He was always depressed after seeing one of them.

Civilian workers came in to do jobs not trusted to Russian POWs. The chimney sweep was as skinny as a rail—I guess it was a job requirement—and wore a sooty tophat over what looked like black longjohns. We had a carpenter in our block for a while making extensive repairs in anticipation of an inspection by the Protecting Power. He was skinny, too. We figured civilians weren't eating well. He loved to talk with us and while never saying anything overtly subversive hinted he wasn't too happy with the way things were going in Germany. We gave him hot coffee, which he drank greedily, coffee being much rarer outside the wire than in. And we gave him cigarettes. He couldn't take any out with him because he was searched at the gate so he chain-smoked furiously while he worked. He smoked himself giddy. He always left with a buzz on.

A civilian who came to repair the roof was young and well fed. We wondered what aberration had kept him out of the Wehrmacht. He worked on our roof all day with two kriegies detailed to help him. The first day, Maxie the message-heaver was one of them. Next day, when two different kriegies showed up, the roofer refused to continue until he got Maxie. Maxie was a hell of a worker. Colonel Goodrich, considerably amused, put Maxie on the job for the duration. My German was a little better than Maxie's so when he and the roofer had a conversational impasse Maxie would call me to the roof to interpret. It was my first view of Stalag Luft III from that high. Impressive but depressing—endless barracks stuffed with shot-down airmen all neatly done up in barbed wire. Before long the two were chatting like old buddies and didn't need me any more.

Unauthorized trading was strictly forbidden but Maxie was dying for some onions and asked me if it was okay for him to make a deal with the roofer. For some reason he thought I really understood such things. We had a sort of *Of Mice and Men* Lenny and George relationship, not that he was backward like Lenny but because he was so big and uncomplicated while I was smaller and devious. I told him it was fine as long as he kept his mouth shut about it.

Once we saw a party of Jews repairing the wire east of our compound, all of them gaunt and weak, and working slowly. Sometimes a guard kicked or pushed one of them. The victim wouldn't even look up from his work, just shied away in a reflex action like a feeding animal poked with a stick. It was the first time since coming to Stalag Luft III we'd been exposed to that side of the Germans and it angered and disturbed us.

Anything drew spectators. During our residence in South Compound we watched three generations of cats grow up. Mating cats drew cheering audiences. The foraging certainly wasn't much, but cats were there, even in winter, when they'd lurk outside in the snow and wait for windows to open after lights out so they could jump into warmth. They scared the hell out of us sometimes, leaping in out of the darkness.

People- and cat-watching did not take nearly enough of the time that went on twenty-four hours a day, seven days a week. We occupied the rest as best we could. Cards, books (the longer the better), interminable talk, marathon arguments, writing strictly rationed letters. We liked card games that took a long time to play. When the cards became speckled with grime we'd scrape them clean one at a time with a table knife, slowly, meticulously. We were meticulous in most things. It made the task last longer. When I darned a pair of socks, if the rows weren't machine perfect I'd take them apart and do them all over. Dapper Dan Story even learned to knit. He'd sit outside, burly in a tightly buttoned battle dress jacket, looking like a scowling Mongol warrior with his shaved head (he shaved it hoping it would grow back thicker but shaving didn't help), knitting socks, scarves and ditty caps.

The one place we didn't drag things out in cold weather was the block washroom, where we shaved, bathed and washed clothes. It had wash basins but no hot water. We rigged up a shower by tapping into an overhead pipe and attaching a tin can punched with holes. Winters, most kriegies didn't have the stomach for icy showers on the cold cement floor. They heated water in *keintrinkwassers* and had sponge baths from wash basins. We hardy souls from P.G. 21, showing off, took showers. On Saturday nights, usually. Saturday night was when we had a fire in the washroom. There was a stove in the washroom but no coal allowance for it. For Saturday night each room would contribute a few briquettes for communal warmth. The stove didn't heat the room, but it was terrific to stand by while you were drying.

Cold water made whiskers stand up to the razor, and I declared that when I got out of the bag I would continue to shave in cold water and to use a paste of soap chips instead of expensive lathers, a promise broken from the moment I gained access to hot water and foamy lathers.

Books, Books, Books

AFTER WE'D BEEN AT STALAG Luft III a while we got an occasional hot shower outside South Compound premises. We walked to the showers on a road between the new West Compound and South and North compounds. We'd have shouted conversations with men in West Compound who'd escaped after the evacuation of P.G. 21 and been recaptured. We learned our ground officer friends were at Schubin and that the doctor we'd disliked at P.G. 21 had been recaptured while attending a wedding in Florence. Larry Allen had been recaptured, too, and was at Schubin. (The Germans later repatriated him.) Gardinier had made it but hadn't contacted any of our families. We deeply resented that. (In 1988 an ex-kriegie friend of mine told me he'd run across Gardinier in West Texas and would I like his address. I said no.) Mouse Rideout and Claude Weaver had made it, too, but Weaver had gone back into combat and been killed. When we yelled across the wire our guards would start worrying about their officers hearing us and make us stop.

Although we were allowed to soak in the shower for almost as long as we liked, after the novelty wore off and the weather warmed up we didn't take advantage of every chance. Eventually South Compound got its own shower building, and we were allowed hot showers once a week all winter. We'd bundle up in our warmest clothes and trudge to it through deep snow. Though we were crowded cheek to cheek beneath the rows of nozzles on either side of a duckboard walk, we never missed those showers. They were not only warm and cleansing, they were also social events. And in all the times I trudged back through the snow all flushed and rosy, I never caught a cold.

The shower building shared premises with a cobbler shop run by an officer who'd been a shoemaker in real life. The one time I needed him he couldn't help me. My GI shoes had served me faithfully for years and still had wear in them when I lost a heel in the deep mud outside our block. I raked through the muck fruitlessly. The cobbler didn't have any heels. To get shoes, or any other clothing, you had to put your name on a list. I wasn't on the shoe list because I hadn't needed any. When I went to put my name on the list, fearing weeks of waiting in which I'd be walking on one heel, the clothing officer told me he had one pair in stock. Too small to fit anyone in South Compound. They were just my size. Six-and-a-half E. I wear a seven in civilian shoes.

After parcels began arriving from home, I never wanted for clothes. My basic needs had already been supplied from Red Cross stores because of my seniority, and eventually I owned two each of wool GI pants and wool GI shirts, a khaki uniform shirt and pants, a battle dress jacket, a greatcoat, two sets of wool longjohns, three sets of cotton underwear, several handkerchiefs and pairs of socks. Except for socks and underwear, I never kept more than one change of anything. When I got a shirt or a pair of pants in a parcel, I gave an old one away. Winters I bundled up in longjohns, shirt and pants, turtleneck sweater, battle dress jacket, stocking cap pinned to my sweater to stay down over my ears, scarf, Red Cross gloves and greatcoat. It might have been easier to roll than to walk.

I had a spare blanket, too, a GI blanket issued to oldtimers whether they needed it or not after every needy case had one. I took it to the theater with me for a seat cushion.

Washing clothes was less a chore than at P.G. 21. Our washroom was cozier than that at Chieti, and no one left his washing to soak overnight in the basins. We washed in jam buckets filled with suds from cut-up GI soap (the Red Cross lavished that and toilet paper on us), agitating our laundry with dhobi sticks, cleverly punched concentric tin cans at the end of long handles. Dhobying didn't work for wool pants and blouses. You had to spread them out on a table and scrub.

We'd have long discussions of our postwar plans. When we learned of the GI Bill of Rights, the talks were about continuing our educations. Guy the weightlifter, who hadn't finished high school, said he was going to get his diploma after the war and go to college. He wanted an aeronautical engineering degree. Privately, we didn't think he had a knack for math. Schoonmaker had received *Mathematics for the Millions* in a book parcel and tried to teach him algebra from it without getting very far. I'd majored in chemistry at Rice and ended up a newspaperman and figured I was deficient in liberal arts studies, so I was going to get an M.A. and maybe even a Ph.D. I couldn't make up my mind if it would be at Oxford, the Sorbonne, or both.

Homesteading in Alaska had a longer run than the South America bug at Chieti. We scoured South Compound for men who'd been to Alaska and plied them with questions. My Alaska plan was to marry a statuesque brunette who'd share the back-breaking work and my bed and help me make my fortune farming. As a child, I'd grown and harvested a two-dozen stalk stand of corn and there'd been nothing to it. I made a list of what I'd take with me—Klim, powdered eggs and other staples for food, books for instruction and recreation, and records. Lots of records.

Then a kriegie received a book about subsistence farming on small tracts while holding down a city job. That's what I was going to do. I read everything on the subject I could find. I'd buy a tract on Clear Creek, a stream outside of Houston I'd always loved, and if I couldn't live off it take a job to eke out. I wasn't interested in making a fortune, just in living in peace and comfort.

Postwar schemes came and went, but while I was in the throes of one I was always sure it was exactly what I would do. None of my plans included going back to my old life. Most kriegies felt the same. We all believed that after the war all things would be possible.

Postwar planning was only sporadic. Cards were constant. We played for hours on end, even days. My card games were poker and bridge. I was better at poker. We played for cigarettes. A lot of men learned bridge while kriegies. Schoonmaker taught anyone who asked. He was a good teacher and a good chess player as well, advancing far in a South Compound tournament. He offered to teach me chess but I passed. I wasn't even good at checkers. We played hearts, too, and blackjack and games new to us.

I started whittling again. Time passed unnoticed when I had a pocketknife and a piece of wood in my hands. Using birch, which wasn't hard to come by and carved well, I did small carvings of large animals—a hippo and a giraffe, among others—and gro-tesque human heads. I gave them all away and later regretted I hadn't saved at least one to bring home for a souvenir. None of them had much artistic merit, but they were displayed at the occasional arts and crafts shows in the theater. The South Com-

pound craft shows tended to be better than those at P.G. 21 but
not the arts. Apparently there were more American craftsmen
than artists and more British artists than craftsmen in the bag. It
might have been that the average age of American kriegies at
Stalag Luft III was three or four years younger than the average
age of British POWs at P.G. 21, and we matured later than they
did. American kriegies had an interesting attitude toward age. In
South Compound the age range was nineteen to forty-two, yet
every man I ever spoke with there said he was wasting the best
years of his life in the bag, leading me to believe ever after that
the best years of your life are those you're living. Everyone told
anyone younger, "If I were your age I'd absolutely go back to
school," when news of the G.I. Bill of Rights, with its educational
advantages, reached us. (I was to use it for summer writing
courses at Columbia and the "52-40 Club," forty dollars a week for
fifty-two weeks, while writing my first novel. I got an advance on
the novel before my fifty-two weeks were up, and when I reported
to the Houston unemployment office that I wouldn't be coming in
any more we had a little celebration.)

Books were the best escape. You vanished into whatever
world was theirs and hours fled by. On the South Compound
library shelves I found some of the old Literary Guild selections
I'd read in my big brother's easy chair when I was a boy. The
library was divided into two sections, one for reference, the other
for lending. The lending library was the smaller of the two, an
eight-man room lined with shelves full of fiction, nonfiction and
poetry, mostly fiction and, under the circumstances, an excellent
selection of classics and fairly recent novels. An advantage of
being shut off from book reviews was that sometimes you could
discover for yourself a gifted new writer or a fine novel that
readers outside the wire had been led to by the pundits. I came to
The Heart Is a Lonely Hunter that way, and until I came home
thought Carson McCullers was a man. The reference library filled
two adjoining eight-man rooms, one of them fitted with packing-
case armchairs and settees. There was a fairly good selection of
textbooks and technical works on history, banking, law, chemistry, math, foreign languages and literature but nothing on map
making, radio, navigation, or any other subject that might prove
useful in escape and evasion. A few regulars, maintaining strict
study schedules, could always be found in the reference library
preparing for their return to college after the war. (Kriegie Nick

218   Katzenbach, who one day would be the United States Attorney General, continued his law studies with a program of disciplined reading and after the bag got his degree.)

The books in our library came from the International Red Cross and YMCA and from personal book parcels. The Red Cross and the Y also sent books to individuals. We could apply for books on forms supplied by the agencies. I received a book parcel from the Canadian Red Cross and some art magazines and a history of English literature from the Y.

I read to kill time and for entertainment, mysteries and other light novels, but I also read books I thought I might never turn to outside the bag. Some of those I found hard going but others brought unexpected pleasure. I'd already developed a crush on Dickens with *Dombey and Son* and now I had *David Copperfield* and *The Pickwick Papers*. I discovered Thackeray, too. *Vanity Fair, Pendennis, Yellowplush Papers, The Great Hogarty Diamond.* I read the whole of *The Faerie Queen, The Divine Comedy* and *Canterbury Tales* and Boswell's *Life of Johnson, The Compleat Angler, Tom Jones, Roderick Random, Moby Dick, Lord Jim, Pride and Prejudice, Jane Eyre, Wuthering Heights, The Mill on the Floss, A Passage to India, The Vicar of Wakefield, Madame Bovary, Crime and Punishment, Penguin Island, Growth of the Soil.* The only novel I started and didn't finish was George Meredith's *The Egoist.* Too mannered for a lowbrow no matter how bored.

In the bag, books often conveyed vivid images undreamed of by their authors, a richness beyond anything experienced by a casual reader in an easy chair in a comfortable room with a well-stocked refrigerator in the kitchen. "Sir Thomas and Nigel lunched at the club." Lunch. The narrative stopped while I visualized the setting—the comfortably appointed room, the table, always round and roomy and set with flowers, the starched napery, heavy silver, attentive waiter, but most of all the food. If the author didn't specify, and I thought it incompetent of him not to, I visualized a menu of my own choice. (Now when I write, and there's food, I let you know exactly what it is. My longtime literary agent, Dorothy Olding, believes I overdo it.) "As Millicent ran along the path, twigs brushed her legs." Legs. I saw legs, all right. Bare legs. And everything above them, also bare.

Costanzo, as block library officer, was sent German, Russian and other dictionaries, which he kept in our room and loaned throughout the block. As block news officer, I was delivered the German newspapers. At first every room received newspapers but as the supply dwindled only designated individuals got them. In the beginning there was the *Pommerische Zeitung, Volkischer Beobachter, Kolnischer Zeitung* and *Wien Tageblatt.* Eventually there was only the *Volkischer Beobachter.* Though I was reasonably fluent with military German, I had problems with speeches and editorials and suspected a lot of German readers did, too. We got German magazines, as well. *Simplizissimus, Die Illustierte Zeiting, Der Adler (The Eagle,* the Luftwaffe magazine), the Wehrmacht magazine, and a publication written and ostensibly edited by American POWs. I wondered if the staffers were turncoats or had been misled by the Germans into thinking they would be helping kriegie morale, and I suspected they were men who so wanted to be in print that they'd write for friend or foe. We all wondered if they'd be court-martialed after the war for collaborating with the enemy.

The magazines were supposed to be passed from room to room, but as they circulated they lost pictures to kriegies who wanted them for their walls or War Logs. The War Logs were handsome hardcover scrapbooks distributed to kriegies on the basis of seniority a few weeks after our arrival from Stalag VIIA. We old hands from P.G. 21 got them. We wrangled a lot over mutilated magazines, so block news officers started rotating first pick by roster. A handful of kriegies subscribed to Swiss movie magazines on credit, payable after the war. They were in French and German but featured American as well as European stars.

We adorned our walls with three types of pictures, in descending order of popularity: maps, voluptuous women and airplanes. Some were cut from the magazines and some were handdrawn. The most popular pinup was a German ballet dancer named Gisella.

Kennedy read, too, but without my need to escape into books. Not that he wasn't oppressed by confinement. It bothered him more than it did me and as time went by much more. At first he worried about not hearing from his father or his fiancée. As winter deepened, so did his mood. He was pessimistic about the progress of the war and our prospects. Confinement weighed more and more heavily upon him. He seldom laughed or joked any more. He didn't look his old self physically, either. His eyes lost their sparkle and his face was drawn. One day he asked me to walk the circuit and confided he thought he was going crazy. I responded with the popular wisdom of the day, that if you thought you were going crazy you couldn't be because people losing their minds never knew it. Later he told me it had done a lot to ease his mind. I wasn't comfortable with this reversal in our roles. He was the steadying influence, not me. When he began hearing from his father and fiancée, he brightened along with the weather and became tanned and fit. I was relieved to have the real Kennedy back.

Kennedy escaped not in reading but in learning Spanish. Buckner caught the bug from him and the two of them spent hours in Spanish conversation with Alvarado. When Kennedy and Buckner played bridge with Schoonmaker and me, although they were considerably better than we were, they'd try to increase their edge by talking across the board in Spanish. I knew just enough Texas Spanish to catch them. Some of the time.

As in Italy, mail was even more important than books and almost as important as food. Letters sometimes took as little as five weeks to reach South Compound, but usually two to six months was more like it. Our hosts asked us to write our correspondents and suggest they ask the U.S. government to provide special letter forms for POWs as the British did for their captives.

We were allowed to send three German letter forms and four cards a month. All my letters went to my mother. The cards I divided among my other correspondents.

I was the first P.G. 21 transfer to get mail in South Compound. Larry Allen had given me the name of the Associated Press man in Portugal, Luis Lupi. As soon as we were issued our card and letter forms I sent him a card asking him to contact my paper in Houston, the *Post*. He cabled the paper, a friend there called my mother, and she sat down and wrote me at once, airmail. Mailed November 20, her letter arrived three days after Christmas along with mail forwarded from Italy. It was the letter that let everyone from P.G. 21 know that our families knew where we were. Every P.G. 21 transferee in the compound must have come to my room to verify I'd actually gotten a letter from home.

My letter didn't portend a flood of them. Other mail was a long time coming and when it did, it came in fits and starts—bags of it, then none at all, then bags again. Some kriegies got stacks, others few. Sometimes we blamed the mail drought on our censors. Specific censors did certain letters of the alphabet. Every censor had her own number. I suspected mine, whom I identified by her number, must have had other duties because it seemed to me I was often slighted. When I heard letters with her number were in the compound my hopes soared, occasionally justifiably.

We watched the progress of the mail from arrival to distribution in the same agony of suspense as at P.G. 21. There was always someone who saw it come in the gate and counted the bags, a statistic quickly spread throughout the lager. It might be a limp bag slung carelessly over a guard's shoulder or, much more rarely, two or three bulging sacks on a pushcart. The mail room was in another block. After morning appel, when mail was sorted, kriegies crowded outside the window to see which letters of the alphabet predominated. That information quickly made the rounds. Every block had its own mail officer to bring letters from the mail room. They lined up outside the mail room, harassed by kriegies demanding to know if they'd scored. We hated the bastards who did that. They were delaying our letters. Birddog Johnson was Block 133 mail officer. When he was even a few minutes late going after our letters, we hated him.

Just having Birddog come in the door with mail, even a stack of it, didn't mean you'd scored. It might all be for only a couple of your roommates, or even just one, and you had to wait until Birddog read out the name on the last letter to know. We rejoiced with a roommate who got a spate of mail after weeks or even months without, but we fumed at one who always got lots of letters, especially long ones, even at good old Schoonmaker, who got sheafs and took them to his bunk to chuckle over. Correspondents were encouraged to send one-page letters to speed up the censoring process, but not all of them did, especially those who wrote to Schoonmaker. Kennedy got lots of mail, too, but Alvarado got few letters. He didn't write many, either, except to his mother.

Waiting for Birddog became so agonizing for me I sought refuge in the library trying to get lost in a book at mail time. Then I'd race back to the room to see if I'd scored. Some mail could be disappointing. A long-awaited letter might not tell you something you'd been burning to hear, or your lone piece of mail might be a long-delayed Christmas card with no personal message.

We'd get letters from people we didn't know who'd read about us in a newspaper story, or mail from acquaintances long forgotten. I got a letter from someone I'd known for years and dated for a while but who'd gotten married while I was in the service. I wondered what she, a married woman, was doing writing to me. (I found out only after I got home. My mother, in her white aide's uniform, had run into the woman at the bank and told her I liked getting letters from friends. After liberation, I learned her husband had been killed in the Battle of the Bulge. Dody and I married two months later.)

We didn't answer people we didn't know because our letter forms were so limited but sometimes we'd write cards to strangers we thought might be helpful, as I had done to Luis Lupi. Several kriegies got Rolex and Patek Philippe watches from Switzerland for IOUs payable after the war. I ordered a Hermes "Baby" typewriter but never got it, only a card saying government regulations prohibited the sale of typewriters to individuals. I wrote Lupi and the AP man in Sweden to open accounts for me in local department stores. When they went unanswered I suspected they hadn't left Stalag Luft III.

I kept a careful record by date of all outgoing and incoming mail. Sometimes I'd get photos with letters. I put them on the wall by my bunk in two groups. One family pictures, the other girls. I lettered a sign over the pictures of girls. "Domani." Tomorrow.

"Dear Lieutenant" letters, those breaking engagements or announcing the marriage of a kriegie's sweetheart, were common, and devastating. Caged men with nowhere to find consolation took broken engagements and news of infidelities hard. One kriegie collected the discarded photographs of those sending "Dear Lieutenant" letters and covered the wall beside his bunk with them. Dusty Runner, the Luftbandster trumpet player, wrote a song called "Dear Lieutenant." It was an instant hit.

Though girlfriends sometimes proved fickle and wives refused to send parcels, ran through their husbands' savings, or even asked for divorce, most women stood by their men and helped them through dark hours with their letters.

Costanzo got the saddest letter of all. He got lots of what we called "sugar reports" from young women smitten with him. He'd read portions of them aloud for our entertainment. He was reading one such letter mirthfully when he paled and stopped abruptly and just stood there. We quit laughing. Alvarado went to him and, reading the letter over his shoulder, said gently, "Fellows, Charlie's mother has passed away." No one but Alvarado could have handled it so delicately.

Costanzo's mother had died several months earlier, but his father, not wanting him to learn of it while a POW, hadn't told him. The friend, assuming Costanzo knew, had casually mentioned attending his mother's funeral.

Buckner's mother also passed away while we were at Stalag Luft III. He was summoned to our adjutant's office and informed by Red Cross cable. He never told us why he'd been called, and we learned of her death weeks later from Alvarado.

Some kriegies wrote letters to Swiss and Swedish women whose pictures they'd seen in magazines. Some of the them answered, sending photographs. Dapper Dan Story got an unsolicited letter from one in Switzerland. Guardedly, it concerned Ed Griffin, his bombardier. She reported Griffin was having a lot of fun skiing, skating and taking pictures with his new camera. It was a while before Dapper and the rest of us stopped feeling more sorry for ourselves than usual.

Some letters brought gems of such exquisite irony they were published in "The Circuit" for the whole compound to read:

A mother was sending a money order so her son could do some shopping.

Another advised her son to be sure to take in the Bayreuth Festival; it would be a shame to miss it when he was in Germany.

A mother wrote that the requested toothpaste was on the way but until it came try baking soda (baking soda being scarcer than diamonds at Stalag Luft III).

A wife informed her husband she still loved him even if he was a coward and a prisoner.

Another wife told her husband that if he wanted her to send parcels he should increase her allotment, "and don't you know there's a war on?"

Musik, Musik, Musik

FOR OUR FIRST CHRISTMAS dinner in Germany, Alvarado and I prepared a repast augmented with special issue food. We'd taken over as cooks right after Thanksgiving, about the time of the first snowfall. Complicating our job, the dog dropped and broke four of our ten bowls (room strength had risen by then) and we had to borrow four bowls from other rooms every evening meal.

Block parcel officers drew our Red Cross parcels and distributed them from their rooms. Sometimes there'd be a special issue of Red Cross bulk food. The parcel officers divided it up by room strength. On occasion some of the more desirable items were in short supply and room leaders would draw cards for them. It was especially true before Christmas, when special Argentine and Turkish shipments started arriving. For some reason we sent Schoonmaker to represent our room for a drawing and he brought back canned stew. We railed at him in room strength for upwards of half an hour. I went to the next drawing myself after getting a consensus on what I should try for. I drew lucky. Room reps crowded around the heaped tables like shoppers at bargain counters and resented it when something especially desirable went before they got a pick. I had enough early choices to get my pick from a spread of condensed milk, canned pork sausage, canned steak and onions, pork and beans, a sweet called Milkjam, chocolate, jam, Irish stew and canned meat and vegetables. I went for sausage, steak and beans and didn't have to settle for stew until the end. It was days before I let Schoonmaker forget it.

My haul contributed mightily to the Christmas feast— Canadian pork roll baked with English bacon, New Zealand peas, potatoes au gratin and chocolate pie. (I fantasized a pork roll studded with cloves and baked in brown sugar like a ham. I cooked one that way after the war. It was okay, I guess.)

Except for a few finishing touches, the theater was completed in time for a pair of Christmas record concerts. Of brick and wood, it was more like the real thing than the one at P.G. 21 and a lot roomier. There wasn't a lot of leg room but the seats, made from Canadian Red Cross parcel crates, had backs and armrests. I went to both concerts, almost six hours of music, and heard a lot of tunes for the first time, "Brazil" for one, and several records we'd had in our St. Jean collection in Palestine, including the Mills Brothers' "Paper Doll." (I liked it so much I bought a copy in New York on my honeymoon.)

In time the theater got curtains, sets and costumes. Admission for events in the theater was by ticket, the tickets distributed by our block entertainment officer. The British performances had better acting, but Americans were better swing musicians. The Luftbandsters' leader was a major who played clarinet. A couple of trumpet players soloed and did vocals. Dick Jones's trumpet was hot but sweet. Dusty Runner played a wild, screaming trumpet and we screamed wildly when we heard it. (After the war I heard that Runner, a bombardier or navigator, had gone to Randolph Field for pilot training and been killed in an accident in his convertible.) Ed Allen, my Houston friend from across the hall, was an early vocalist with the Luftbandsters. Not much of a voice but plenty of enthusiasm. We'd stamp the floor and cheer when he did an original called "Honeywagon Blues." The honeywagon was the tank wagon that periodically pumped out the aborts. Allen lost his job to a flyer who was so pretty in makeup they made him wear an evening gown singing. Al Batik, smooth-skinned, blond, with a sweet, clear voice close to contralto, in his evening gown a vision of female loveliness. Until he moved. Then all farmboy. So they made him stand still when he sang. On occasion he'd come to individual rooms with a guitar and sing cowboy songs. He was much more comfortable doing that than pretending to be female.

Sometimes instead of Batik and his guitar we'd listen to records. South Compound had a portable phonograph from the International Red Cross in Switzerland that was passed around from block to block and room to room. We hardly noticed the needles were dull and the records scratchy from so much use. When it was our turn the phonograph was never off. Overnight was best. We played it long after lights out. One man would volunteer to stay up to wind it and change records while the others lay in their sacks listening, blissful and yearning, to the same records over and over again. "Rosalita," "You Are Always in My Heart," "That Old Black Magic" and a dozen or so others.

One night a Luftbandster concert had to be canceled after we were already in the theater when it was discovered someone had stolen the saxophone. A mystery never solved. Nor was the greater mystery—how did one hide or use a saxophone unheard in such close quarters? The Germans got us another saxophone a few days later and the show went on.

We hadn't been long in South Compound when, to the chagrin of some Schubinites, we were included in a group of old hands permitted to visit North Compound for a production of *Macbeth*. North Compound's theater was like Rockefeller Center, with professional-looking sets and costumes and armchairs made from Red Cross packing crates. Fine acting, too, even the female parts, but we left long before "Out, damned spot!" We'd really come to see the British P.G. 21 friends from whom we'd been separated. We were expected, and several of them laid on a grand tea for us. We'd brought along a gift of tea from our growing surplus, and they had Nescafe for us to take back. Some occupants of the room in which they entertained us had been kriegies since before the U.S. entered the war. You couldn't tell the room was in a POW camp. The walls looked paneled, there were drapes and cushions and framed pictures. Friends from P.G. 21 were in and out throughout the afternoon, among them Tweedy, the South African who'd unlocked our boxcar door at Bolzano, and Arnold Feast, the cynical Canadian. Feast told us how he'd run into the town during the raids, been cut off by an SOD, one of those bloodthirsty overage civilians with guns, and ducked into an imposing building to evade him. With his usual luck, he said, he'd picked the local Gestapo headquarters for a sanctuary. The Gestapo turned him over to guards from the train.

Our actors wisely didn't attempt Shakespeare. The nearest they came was a parody of *Julius Caesar* called *Julius Smolensk*, when the Russians were giving the Germans fits at Smolensk. Mostly they did Broadway hits like *The Front Page* and *The Petrified Forest* or original musicals and comedy skits. We liked Daniel Xavier Murphy, who did Irish dialect jokes, and a Jewish flyer who did Yiddish accents and straight comedy. A team reminiscent of the music hall types at P.G. 21 did vaudeville skits with soft shoe and patter.

The theater was equipped to show movies, too. Usually

American, including decent prints of recent ones, with German or
sometimes French subtitles, the Cary Grant–Katherine Hepburn
Bringing Up Baby and the almost-new 1942 *Orchestra Wives*,
featuring the Glenn Miller band and some familiar tunes.

German films could be fun, with lots of audience participation
in *Hello, Janine*, a musical starring the "German Ginger Rogers,"
Marika Rokk. Large, blonde, hippy, not exactly twinkle-toed. Her
little voice didn't match her proportions. We cheered when the film
broke. It did that often. When a policeman knocked on a door we
yelled, "Tallyho!" the warning cry for goon coming. We talked
back to the screen in fractured German. It did have a catchy tune in
it, though: "Musik, Musik, Musik."

I was unexpectedly affected by a German news film with the
German view of the Dieppe raid. It showed bewildered prisoners
and beaches littered with bodies, abandoned equipment and
smashed tanks. The only actual combat footage was in the air. I'd
have thought that after being shot down, and later scared out of
my wits by a bombing, the sight of flak bursting and bombers
bombing and being attacked by fighters would reawaken my terror. Instead my adrenalin flowed, and I wanted to be back among
them.

The theater was the center of camp activities. In addition to
the auditorium, there were several rooms at the rear. Some were
classrooms and one was the newsroom, considerably more elaborate than Larry Allen's bulletin board at P.G. 21, with maps of all
fronts, including the Far Eastern, kept up to date from German
sources (we usually knew more than the maps showed from BBC
communiques we were getting); copies of the German communiques; translations of articles and speeches from German newspapers and miscellaneous news.

Our "radio station" operated from the theater, "broadcast-
ing" a regular schedule of record concerts, plays, quiz programs
and newscasts over the compound public address system. Developed by kriegies with civilian radio experience, it sounded pretty
professional to us. A man from our block was a producer-
announcer.

A couple of notorious crimes began in the theater. One involved a lightbulb, the other a trombone slide. The lightbulb: a set
of roommates stole it from the theater because they wanted a
stronger light. They were caught, officially reprimanded and reported to higher authority in the States, presumably to be court-

martialed after the war (I doubt if that happened). It was one of the few cases of theft in South Compound and one of the few times a kriegie was put on charges. (A former boxer who decked a fellow kriegie after an argument was also put on charges. Fighting in general was frowned on, but when men wanted to settle things they put on boxing gloves. Grudge matches had few casualties. The combatants usually didn't have enough wind to keep at it. We sparred for fun, too.) About the trombone, some kriegie brew-makers borrowed the slide to use as a condensing coil for a batch. That was fairly common but in this instance the timing was awful; just before a Luftbandster concert, which had to be cancelled.

I never made or drank any kriegie brew, but I knew how it was done. The usual mixture of sugar, raisins and prunes out of Red Cross parcels was allowed to ferment and then was strained and distilled. Distilling was the most complex stage. After lockup at night, the kriegie brewers built a hot fire in the kitchen stove using their own briquettes. They cooked the brew in a jam can connected to a trombone slide in a wooden trough bathed in water flowing from the kitchen tap. They divided the output in proportion to the share of ingredients contributed.

This could hardly be kept secret but the yield was so small neither the SAO nor the Germans took serious steps. When a kriegie brew craze hit South Compound, it did create problems that couldn't be ignored. Kriegies began trading food and clothing for the makings. Willie the ferret got drunk and was robbed of his flashlight and screwdriver. Jerry "Silent Death" Sage led a drunken group through the wire into North Compound. Our hosts got tough and confiscated all dried fruit from personal parcels and threatened to do the same with Red Cross fruit. Colonel Goodrich agreed to prohibit all kriegie brewing. The few desperate types who flouted the ban usually saw their fermenting casks discovered and destroyed. Before long we were allowed to keep our personal parcel fruit.

The theater was central to our entertainment but was only a part of our recreation. As at P.G. 21 there were classes, lectures and sports. We may not have had a University of Calcutta professor among our speakers, but we had Lieutenant Colonel Richard Klocko, a West Pointer and very Air Corps. His handle-bar mustache quivered with enthusiasm. He sprinkled his talks with cadet slang and said "hubba, hubba" a lot. We called him the Boy Colonel. He was fearless. During the occasional all-day searches of our quarters we were confined to the parade ground until they were over. One cold, rainy day during such an operation field officers were permitted to take cover under the eaves of a nearby block after they'd been searched. A guard approached Klocko, who was standing alone under an eave, and ordered him back out among the rest of us. Klocko, leaning back against the side of the block with his hands in his pockets, said conversationally, "Nicht verstehen." "I don't understand." And didn't move. The guard unslung his rifle, put a round in the chamber and motioned with it for Klocko to get moving. Klocko ignored him and just stood there leaning against the wall with his hands in his pockets. We looked on, fascinated, hoping he'd obey. We didn't want an atrocity to happen before our eyes. The guard, flustered, lowered his rifle and while he was thinking over what to do next a German officer sent him packing.

Night Fright

WINTER CHANGED THE FACE of Stalag Luft III. Snow blanketed its ugliness in white, covering the trampled ground and softening rooflines. Ice sheathed the barbed wire in sparkling diamond strands and mantled the birches in crystal. We made a mess of the parade ground and stitched the South Compound with dirty, ice-crusted paths. The paths were often dangerously slick. A navigator who'd been decorated for landing his wounded bomber in England when both pilots were casualties slipped while walking the circuit, hit his head on a stump, and fractured an eardrum. After he returned from the camp hospital he went around the bend and was taken back to the hospital, where he died. A hospital orderly said he'd killed himself.

I tried walking the circuit in my wooden shoes but they were clumsy and gobs of snow clung to the hobnails. I had to stop frequently to knock them off so when I walked for exercise I'd change to my GI shoes. The German winter was much fiercer than the Italian, but with the wooden shoes and the inner slippers I made from scraps of an old blanket my feet stayed warm, and I never had a chilblain.

My first personal parcel in Germany, mailed in November, arrived in February. It contained a pair of glasses and well-selected, carefully packed food and clothing, much better than my Italian parcel. Some of my roommates had received parcels transhipped from Italy, and I had hopes of receiving one myself. And in March I did, two cigarette parcels and a book parcel. (Two months later I got a book that had been confiscated in Italy, *Music for All of Us*. Why I got it now was as big a mystery as why it had been confiscated in the first place.)

March was a month of daily thaws and nightly freezes. It was in March that escape, paramount despite the odds against getting out of Germany, lost its element of gamesmanship. Of seventy-six men who escaped from a tunnel out of North Compound, forty-seven of those later captured were shot by the Gestapo (chronicled in the book and motion picture, *The Great Escape*). North, South, Central and West compounds assembled with their chaplains in appel formation for memorial services. We stood at attention. From Central Compound, faint and mournful in the distance, a bugle played "Taps." When the last note died, a bugle in our compound took up the call. We saluted until it ended. Then a North Compound bugle took it up. Padre MacDonald preached a short funeral sermon and we were dismissed.

Next day the British in North Compound gathered on their parade ground and auctioned off the personal effects of the murdered men for the benefit of their survivors at home. They paid their bids with chits, redeemable after the war. What was so British about the affair was its festival air. They may have been seething with anger inside and lusting for revenge, but they weren't going to let it spoil their good time.

A few days later they gathered in appel formation to hear a group captain, a very senior RAF rank, give a farewell speech. He was being repatriated because of his wounds. His speech was fiery and bitter. He promised to spread the word about the murders and report conditions in the camp where it would do the most good and assured everyone he'd see to it that all aircrews were briefed on our exact location. There'd be no accidental bombing of Stalag Luft III. Cheers on both side of the wire.

After the escapes but before the executions, the Germans reacted with lengthy extra roll calls. Colonel Goodrich informed us he did not consider extra appel just or reasonable and therefore we needn't keep our usually good military order. We assumed, correctly, that he meant us to be naughty. We took our time getting to the parade grounds when the appel bugle sounded. It was half an hour before the last straggler arrived. We slouched in ranks and smoked and didn't come to attention as we normally did when counted. One man deliberately blew smoke in our Lager Hauptmann's path. After counting two blocks the Lager Hauptmann broke off abruptly and said something we couldn't hear to Colonel Goodrich. We were dismissed. We broke ranks cheering our victory.

Within the hour the appel bugle sounded again. Every guard and office clerk marched into the compound armed with rifles, machine pistols or pistols and cordoned off the parade ground. The

Lager Hauptmann informed us he would now proceed with appel and it would be orderly. We became lambs. We snapped to attention when he counted and no one blew smoke at him.

A purge (a shipment of new prisoners) had arrived just that morning, and we'd been assigned two new roommates from it. They'd been bombed out of Dulag Luft, the interrogation center outside of Frankfurt, and were as traumatized as Schoonmaker had been when he arrived at P.G. 21. The "strafe" appel was their first roll call at Stalag Luft III. They assumed all appel were like that and wondered if they'd ever get out of South Compound alive.

The Lager Hauptmann had intimidated us but lost his credibility because he'd had to make a show of force. He was replaced next day by a new Lager Hauptmann, Gallatowicz, a transaction greatly to our advantage. The former Hauptmann was a cold, haughty man who had as little to do with kriegies as possible and seemed barely to tolerate us at appel. Gallatowicz, on the other hand, always had a big smile for everyone, flashing a gold tooth, and had an embracing sense of humor. He always opened appel with a warm, cheerful, drawn-out, "Goot mornink, zehntlemens." One morning soon after his arrival the count was a man short, and we fumed restlessly while guards conducted a room-by-room search. They found the missing man asleep in his sack. His roommates hadn't noticed. He came across the parade ground sheepishly under our hostile gaze. Hauptmann Gallatowicz beamed and gave him a merry "Goot mornink, zehntlemens." It broke our surly mood.

Some days after his takeover he came to appel looking as if he'd been weeping. A rumor swept us that his family had been killed in an Allied bombing of Vienna. It wasn't until Colonel Goodrich announced the executions of the forty-seven escapees that we understood the real source of his grief.

Among us were men who'd been in North Compound before being moved to South Compound and had close friends among the dead. After a moment of shocked silence, they called for revenge but of course there was nothing anyone could do about it.

Later the German commandant, a decent man, called a conference of senior Allied officers to extend his sympathy and offer his apologies for the murders. He said they'd been committed by the Gestapo on Gestapo orders, and the Luftwaffe had not been involved. He warned that escape was a deadly serious business.

A red-bordered leaflet was distributed among the kriegies. In large, bold print at the top it began, "To All Prisoners of War!" and continued, "The escape from prison camps is no longer a sport! An urgent warning is given against making future escapes! The chances of preserving your life are almost nil!" The chill was only temporary. X activities continued.

Even before Gallatowicz's reaction to the deaths of the North Compound escapees we'd considered him a friend. We'd taken to him at once. He was dark, plump and jolly, friendly but never in an ingratiating way. He laughed with us when his broken English amused us. We never failed to greet him and give him a smart salute.

The gen was he was Austro-Hungarian and had suffered an abdominal wound in World War I and still had to be careful what he ate. He told us Americans ate like pigs and smoked too many cigarettes. He'd smile when he said it and poke you in the ribs. We wondered how he kept his job when he was so friendly with us; somehow we knew he wasn't deliberately ingratiating himself to serve the Reich. When other Germans did that we could always tell. And Casey, who came to know him well because Gallatowicz came to him for English lessons, said he thought of us as youngsters who needed looking after (shades of Colonel Gooler at P.G. 21) and not as bloodthirsty luftgangsters.

During a block search and roll call, when he read my name he chuckled and read it aloud again. "We make you mayor of Sagan," he said. While making a surprise inventory of German-issued property, he found several table knives missing. He wagged a finger at us and said, "Yesss, zehntelmens, so you zay zey are lost. You cannot fool me. You make zaws out of zem." He did funnier dialect than the Jewish comedian in our theater skits, and without even trying.

We considered Sergeant Glemnitz, who wasn't jolly at all, okay, too. He was a middle-aged man with a strong, seamed face and close-cropped salt and pepper hair. We didn't think he loved us, but he was always fair. The only time he said anything unseemly was when he came into our room for a search and said with unfamiliar joviality that after Germany won the war he was going to have an American colonel for his chauffeur. If we hadn't known Sergeant Glemnitz was too good a soldier to drink on duty, we'd have thought he'd been into the schnapps.

He looked on our subversive ways pretty much as most of us

did, a battle of wits between us and him. You hid or did it, he found it or stopped it, and no hard feelings. It was against our own regulations to give a goon a cigarette, but there was an occasional decent guard or ferret we'd sneak a smoke to when he came into our room. During a room search, only Glemnitz would never accept a cigarette from us. There were kriegies whose job it was to cultivate our keepers and who'd offer him cigarettes. On rare occasions he'd take one, but when he did I think he was playing a game—his, not theirs.

Nobody liked Hohendahl, the perfect Nordic corporal who spoke English with an Oxford accent. He was suspect because he seemed to have unusual authority for a corporal. We thought perhaps he had a rank in some Nazi unit considerably higher than his grade in the Luftwaffe. On top of everything else, we thought him a snob. He treated the run of us with a hint of resentful condescension but fraternized with our senior officers when he could.

Though Gallatowicz, Glemnitz and Hohendahl were around a lot, ferrets were the Germans we saw in our midst most regularly. They were always around with their long screwdrivers and baggy coveralls. We became so accustomed to their presence we hardly noticed some of them as persons, only as potential threats to our illegalities. Most of them were just ordinary men doing their jobs without animosity toward us and a few were even friendly. The one we knew best and liked least was Schnozz, so called for his large nose. Schnozz was a Pole who claimed he was only serving the Nazis under duress and was our friend. While other ferrets prowled mostly outside and when they did come into a block went about their business looking for tunnels, Schnozz would come into rooms in search of conversation. Since the SAO didn't allow unauthorized conversations with Germans except for the return of greetings, he didn't get far. Schnozz lost what little cachet he'd had as a friend with the handful who believed him friendly when he caught a kriegie from our block using a hammer. Hammers were verboten for kriegies. When Schnozz tried to confiscate it, the kriegie dashed into our block and hid it. When Schnozz couldn't find it, he turned our blockmate in and the kriegie went to the cooler.

There was another ferret we called California because he claimed to have been an oilfield cook there before the war. Like all German soldiers we encountered who'd lived in the States, he claimed to have been caught by the war when in Germany on a visit and given no choice but to join up. He told a pretty credible variation, though. He'd come to Germany to spend an inheritance in marks, fallen in love with a Fraülein, and married her. We tended to believe he considered himself more American than German because he seemed more comfortable around us than among his fellows. When he tried to engage us in conversation about the States, all he seemed to care about was what was going on between the Democrats and the Republicans. When we had a mock national election he followed it eagerly. I never learned which he was.

Sometimes it was better for a ferret's own good to be an enemy than a friend, as was the case with Willie. Willie was a young fellow so subsidized by Dick Schrupp, the South Compound interpreter, that he'd report to Schrupp when he came on duty. He was a useful contact for us until some bored, irresponsible kriegies got him so drunk on kriegie brew he passed out. They stole his screwdriver, flashlight and pass and left him in the abort, where he was discovered by a guard. It was a dumb thing to do. It ruffled the SAO's relationship with the German authorities, lost Schrupp a valuable contact (we heard poor Willie was sent off to the Eastern Front), and didn't gain us the screwdriver, flashlight and pass. The SAO made the pranksters return them because if our hosts had come in looking for them, they might have found hidden treasures far more important to us.

Some kriegies resented not being allowed to speak and trade with ferrets although all agreed it was better for security and access to things useful to X if only authorized kriegies fraternized. It was rumored the favored few sometimes traded on their personal behalf. I never knew if they did and even if they had it wasn't enough to interfere with their official duties. But I grumbled right along with those who complained. I'd have welcomed a chance to practice the skills I'd honed at P.G. 21 and Stalag VIIA.

The purge arriving the day of the strafe appel that brought us Gallatowicz also brought us a new block commander to replace the unpopular boy captain. Major Bill Beckham, a skinny little fighter pilot with a mustache like mouse whiskers and a friendly drooping grin. He looked utterly harmless but with eighteen victories he was the leading ace in the European theater, not that he ever mentioned it himself. But gen like that got around fast. He didn't work at being a major. When other senior officers weren't around we called him Beck. He'd let us horseplay in ranks a little but if we grew boisterous could stop us with a gesture. He held a loose rein but we knew who was in control. He was an instant hit.

He could be odd. Someone said a cat smelled with its whiskers and having nothing better to do Beck figured he'd find out. He lured the cat that hung around our block to his room and summoned me there as a witness. He blindfolded the cat, rubbed a piece of cheese on its nose, and hid the cheese. The cat went straight to it. "That proves he can smell cheese," Beck said gravely. He snipped off the still-blindfolded cat's whiskers with scissors, rubbed its nose with the cheese, and hid the cheese again. "Observe," he said, releasing the cat. It went straight for the cheese again. "That proves a cat does not smell with its whiskers," he said. "I want you to be my witness when I report this to the troops."

Spring came at last. Time to get out of longjohns and wooden shoes. We shed garments as the weather warmed. From being bundled in many layers, including an olive-drab wool turtleneck sweater and cap my mother had knitted for me, I went to just shorts.

We started gardens with seeds from the Red Cross. Onions, radishes, tomatoes, lettuce. Though we cultivated ours meticulously, plucking out every weed and pebble, pulverizing every clod by hand, and watering abundantly, the soil was acidic and we got little for our efforts. Only the radishes flourished. The pitiful yield of green onions, tomatoes and lettuce was just enough to tantalize. We might have had more were it not for the hares, who crept in by night to nibble. We tried a little fence made of twigs and roots to no avail and then a trap, which caught nothing except Padre McDonald's cat.

Summer brought birds—cuckoos, thrushes, woodpeckers, crows, plain and fancy warblers and sparrows. Sometimes we'd ask a guard to identify an unknown species for us even though talking with them was verboten. Most of us had never heard a cuckoo and were surprised that they really sounded like cuckoo clocks. We liked listening at first, but after a while their monotonous "cuckoo, cuckoo" drove us crazy. We called it "striking a thousand."

Important to us who'd come up through Bolzano, Stalag Luft III was a haven from Allied bombers. We'd asked if there were any military targets in the area and been assured there weren't. The regular daytime *Luftlagemeldung*, "air situation report," over the cookhouse speakers usually said, "Uber dem Reich Gebiet finden wir keine feindliche Flugzeuge." "There are no enemy aircraft over German territory." We could hear night bombing attacks on Leipzig, southeast of us, and even on Berlin, ninety miles to the north, and though on cold, clear nights the distant skies lit with flashes and we could hear the rumble of explosions we weren't frightened even when the RAF dropped such big ones on Berlin that our windows rattled. It was no threat to us and even if thousands of civilians were dying, no concern of ours. We relished hearing German cities being bombed. There'd be obituaries for bombing casualties and soldiers on the Eastern Front in the German papers. We read them and called them "the funny papers." The best view of Berlin raids was from Bill and Casey's room, and sometimes they'd let selected groups come in to watch. All the lights at Stalag Luft III went off during night raids. For illumination we used margarine in English cheese tin lamps.

In the spring of 1944, the U.S. Air Forces began daylight raids. The air situation report got longer. Until the first daylight raid on Berlin we hadn't heard American bombings because sound didn't travel well by day. But the Berlin raid was a big one, wave after wave, and we could hear it. We ran outside and stood around in groups enjoying it. After the Berlin raid the Germans installed a siren in the administrative compound and when it sounded we had to return to quarters.

Bolzano veterans still weren't worried. We weren't a target. We listened to sirens as to a concert. Faintly first, in the distance. Then more of them, ever nearer. Louder, more enveloping. Now the Stalag Luft III siren joins them, three blasts when Allied aircraft approach our air defense region, changing to a continuous rising and falling if they approach our air defense district. No targets, no sweat, until shortly after the announcement of the Gestapo murders.

April 11, 1944, my twenty-seventh birthday. I was in the kitchen during an alert. An explosion closer than I'd ever heard before made me a little nervous. Men ran in and crowded at the window. I heard others rushing to windows in other rooms on my side of the block. Shouts of "Look! Look! They're coming this way!" I couldn't squeeze through to the window to see for myself. Terrified, I crouched by the stove. They said the safest place inside was by a chimney. Weren't chimneys always standing after a bombing? I got up and ran to my room. Schoonmaker was on the floor with his palliasse pulled over him.

The other Bolzano veterans were pale and shaken. Kriegies from other rooms were at our window. I wedged myself into a place among them. Here they came, right at us, B-17s, silvery in the sun. I'd never seen silver bombers before. Most had been olive drab, ours desert pink. I relived Bolzano. The two new roommates who'd been bombed out at Dulag Luft were terrified, too. Those who had never been bombed laughed and cheered. I could have strangled them. Tinsel floated down from the bombers. "Chaff," someone said knowingly, tinsel dropped to confuse ground radar. The formation made a ninety-degree turn at our camp and back where they'd come from smoke rose in the distance. A military target perhaps ten miles from South Compound, twenty at most. We were told later it was a small aircraft factory and that a French POW had said it lay between another prison camp and a hospital and neither had been hit in the bombing.

Though we were assured by later arrivals that bomb crews were briefed on Stalag Luft III's location, I never drew a peaceful breath again during an alert, nor did Kennedy or any of those who'd known bombings. Never again would we lie safe and snug, listening blissfully to Berlin's torment. What if a crippled, off-course British bomber jettisoned its load just when passing over?

To sleep through an alert was a boon. Unfortunately for me, I almost always woke with the first distant siren and trembled in mounting fear as other sirens took up the call ever closer and I could hear the labored breathing of men all around me as frightened as I was. Two strong responses to terror are flee and pee. We couldn't flee. But we could and did take what we called a "nervous piss." First Alvarado, then Schoonmaker and Bob Bessee, the roommate shot down on an MEDP over Big B, and in no particular order, Kennedy, Buckner and me. Costanzo was never as frightened as the rest of us.

We tried to pry up our floorboards and dig a slit trench but couldn't budge them. Colonel Goodrich thought South Compound should have slit trenches and asked the commandant to let us dig some. Permission denied. The commandant said there was no danger of Stalag Luft III being bombed.

Other kriegies in our block ridiculed our fears and thought us cowards. None had ever been bombed. We resented their response to alerts and wouldn't let men from the other side of the block into our room to look out our windows for bomber formations. We said we didn't want to give a guard an excuse for shooting into the room. A cookhouse corporal standing in the door watching for planes had been killed at long range by a guard firing from the perimeter.

Day alerts were more endurable than night ones. The cookhouse radio gave warnings every half hour. "Achtung! Achtung! Wir geben die Luftlagemeldung." "Attention! Attention! We give the air situation report," followed by a description of the type and size of the aircraft formations, the province they were flying over, the direction they were heading, the province they were approaching. Every week there were more Allied planes over more of Germany.

At the first mention of Upper Silesia, our province, in an air situation report, I'd hurry back to my block and tell the others. I also listened to *Der Heutige Bericht*, "The Day's Report," which was the official German communique. When it came on while we were confined to the block during an alert, I'd go to Bill's room and try to catch it through an open window.

We saw American bombers again but they didn't frighten us as much as they had the first time. Once it was a plane dropping leaflets and another time, in the distance, one in trouble. Its crew later joined us. And once we saw a whole formation. It turned east instead of west toward England, a shuttle raid heading for Russia.

We welcomed German aircraft overhead. They provided diversion, especially when a German fighter pilot gave us a show. There was a fighter field not far from Stalag Luft III—far enough, we thought, not to make a tempting target for our side—and they'd drag the area and stunt. Early on, they'd come in barely skimming the wire but then they started flying a bit higher. Maybe it was because we threw rocks at them.

Singly they'd dive at us, slow-rolling, and break off into a steep, rolling climb. One pilot did it while we were at appel, streaking right at the block formation next to ours. Everybody hit the dirt. One day a Focke-Wulf 190 almost augured into North Compound. I heard it winding up and saw it just as it was pulling out of the dive. I could have sworn it was below the top of the ten-foot wire fence and sinking when it streaked behind a British block and vanished, to reappear with a mighty roar against a cloud of dust billowing from the ground in its wake.

Sometimes Me 109s or Focke-Wulf 190s would rat-race over the camp, doing follow-the-leader aerobatics or mock dogfights. They were good, as a lot of kriegies in Stalag Luft III could testify. The fighter pilots among us would ache with frustration, wanting a turn in the cockpit.

MY MYOPIA INCREASED AND the spectacles I'd received from home in February no longer corrected it. I went on sick call, hoping to get new ones from our hosts. Germans were great with lenses. Didn't they make Leica cameras? Those on sick call gathered at the cookhouse to be marched under guard to the outer compound. We waited in the anteroom of the little hospital there until called by name. English orderlies saw us first, dressing wounds or dispensing medicine to those needing it and sending those requiring treatment to a British or American POW doctor. There was no eye specialist around and I had to make a second visit. This time I was checked by a German doctor. He wore pilot's wings and several decorations. He spoke fair English. There was no eye chart. He had me look at a calendar across the room. I couldn't read anything. "But I thought you were an airman!" he exclaimed. I said I was. "But how? Your vision is too poor." I said it had been good enough to pass the tests when I joined up.

"That is impossible," he said firmly. "You are nearsighted. That happens only in adolescence, never when a man is older."

He wrote out a prescription and told me I'd have to send home to get it filled. I said it was strange that they couldn't make glasses for me in Germany when they'd been able to do it in Italy. It made him sore, which made me feel better. He didn't wish me well or even say goodbye when he dismissed me. I sent the prescription to my mother and our own medical officer sent another copy to Switzerland, but I never got new glasses.

I was lucky I hadn't been ill when I went on sick call. If you were well enough to stand you had to march to the hospital with the group. Kennedy got very ill one night and went on sick call in the morning. He could stand, barely. With the others he stood in the snow to be counted and marched away. At the hospital the American doctor found he had a severe case of flu and said he had to be hospitalized at once. The head of the sick call guard detail wouldn't permit it. He had to return with the same number of men he'd brought out, he said. The doctor demanded an audience with the hospital commandant. The commandant said he was sorry but he couldn't countermand the guard's orders. Kennedy would have to go back with his group and return with a medical orderly and a guard. The American doctor stayed with Kennedy until he was marched away, demanding to the last that the Germans take him back on a stretcher. When Kennedy got back to our room he looked worse than he had when Barnes pulled him out of our downed plane. We put him to bed to wait for his escort while we got some of his gear together. The hospital detail arrived without a stretcher. We asked them to get one. Not permitted, they said. He had to walk back through the snow. After a few days in the hospital he looked better than he had before he fell ill. He said it was worth being sick just to have a little peace and quiet.

Our hosts weren't totally unreasonable about illness. If a man wasn't mobile they'd send a stretcher, but two other men on sick call had to carry him. If an emergency arose at night we could switch on a red light above the block door and the first Hund-führer or goonbox sentry who noticed it would phone the outer compound and a patrol would come to investigate. Not a speedy process.

Personal parcel day was the major event in South Compound. Kriegies came running from everywhere when shouting from the cookhouse loiterers announced the posting of the parcel list on the bulletin board. If you saw a friend's name on it and he wasn't in the crowd that gathered, you'd run to tell him after looking for your own. Early on, personal parcels were brought into the compound and handed over intact. With tightened security, they were delivered to a storeroom outside the wire beyond North Compound and we went to fetch them, making parcel day even more of a treat. Until parole walks began months after our arrival, the only other way out the gate was escape, sick call or the cooler.

The lucky kriegies getting parcels lined up at the gate to be counted and marched off. The storehouse was about a quarter of a mile away and everyone enjoyed the outing, even the guards. They talked and joked with us. X never chided us about parcel day fraternization.

Before you got your parcel a clerk opened it and examined

the contents. Some clerks made a big production of it, scattering your goodies on the table and poking through everything. Others were more casual. I didn't try dropping a couple of cigarettes at the foot of a slow clerk. This wasn't Stalag VIIA.

We had an informal agreement about sharing personal parcels. Anything that had to be cooked or brewed went in the communal larder. We'd usually divide hard candy and when there was gum everyone got a stick. Some of us shared all sweets except chocolate. Chocolate was strictly personal, as were toilet articles and clothing. We tried to make sugar communal but some men used so much more than others we stopped pooling it except for the German ration. It was common practice to write home for larder items. Spices, flour, baking soda, powdered eggs, saccharine. We used saccharine in brews. It saved sugar for important things like desserts.

Although most next of kin mailed parcels promptly every three months, the parcels didn't arrive with any regularity. You'd figure out when your parcel was due, sweat out the list, maybe two or even three, and not see your name. Then you'd get two at once. The same with book and tobacco parcels. Once I got three tobacco parcels the same day. Six cartons of cigarettes, a pound of pipe tobacco and four boxes of cigars. I'd asked for cigarettes because of their trading value. The cigarettes were the major brand names, which I understood were scarce at home but for which next of kin got special certificates at cut-rate prices. I was rich and would have been richer if a lot of other cigarette parcels hadn't arrived with mine, depressing the market.

Our hosts limited the number we could have on hand to two cartons per kriegie when they began pouring in faster than the worst nicotine heads could smoke them. We accumulated so many the Germans feared we might do some serious bribery with them. All over two cartons were stored in a block by the theater, theoretically in the charge of a kriegie cigarette officer. I had six cartons in storage. After unusually large shipments of cigarette parcels arrived, we figured the storeroom had as many as two million cigarettes in it. That included English cigarettes meant for issue with British Red Cross parcels. We could have bought Sagan for two million cigarettes.

Cigars kept their value, but I wouldn't sell any of mine. I did give a few to the kitchen sergeants who lived in our block. They were usually off at work and didn't fraternize with the officers but

I saw them frequently, the block commander having made me their commanding officer. That didn't mean much. They seldom asked me to do anything for them, and I never gave them any orders. I'd have felt funny trying. They were ground soldiers, combat types. Their top sergeant was older than I, a seasoned veteran who reminded me of the 344th's Sgt. Fred Leer, who'd flown from West Palm Beach with us and of whom I'd been in awe. (When I saw the real Leer after the war, at the Las Vegas reunion, he was Col. Leer, U.S. Air Force-Retired.) Ground soldiers were more formal with officers than aircrew sergeants were, but once they saw I knew my place as a mere flyboy they were friendly enough to kid me about my singing in the washroom shower. Their room was next to the washroom. (The sergeants were my only command in World War II. I got another during the Korean War when I was put in charge of a supply room technical sergeant at the Pentagon. When he wanted an afternoon off I had to clear it with his real boss, a warrant officer.)

One day Kennedy and I were playing poker in the room across the hall when a kriegie named Downing ran in white-faced and breathless, so shaken he had to lean against a bunk.

"The invasion's started!" he gasped.

We jumped to our feet, hearts pumping, demanding details. We'd been expecting it for weeks because of the relentless Allied bombing of communications and defense installations. Every conversation, no matter what the subject, always ended with speculation about when. When Downing was able to speak rationally he told us he'd seen Schnozz, the ferret, listening unusually excited to the cookhouse speaker. Downing didn't know any German. Schnozz told him the Americans had landed in France. Someone had run for Schrupp, the staff interpreter, but he didn't get there until the tail end of the broadcast. Schrupp didn't trust Schnozz's account. The ferret had been known to start false rumors before.

While Downing spoke we heard kriegies running and shouting all over the compound. We ran outside and joined them. There was a shoving crowd around Schrupp, wanting to know if it were pukka gen about the invasion. They harassed him into a rage when he wouldn't confirm it. Wild rumors about all sorts of things had swept the compound before but we tended to believe this one. Kennedy and I, unable to sit still, walked the circuit with scores of others in the same state, talking, speculating, trying to control our excitement.

At the next scheduled broadcast more than a thousand men stood shoulder to shoulder and back to front before the cookhouse speaker. The first sentence confirmed Schnozz's information.

"That's it!" Schrupp cried.

The uproar drowned out the broadcast. Schrupp shouted for silence so he could hear the rest. But he couldn't, nor could I. We heard enough to know the Germans either weren't sure about the scope of the landings or were holding back details. They claimed the invading forces had been contained and it was only a matter of days before the enemy was thrown back into the sea.

Broadcasts continued to draw a crowd until the Germans returned to their former practice of reporting war news only in the regular official military communique. I hung around the speaker anyway, hoping for bulletins. Colonel Clark assigned a group of us to monitor all broadcasts.

We'd followed the war avidly before the invasion, especially the Russian Front after it became fluid and the air war when it heated up. We had accurate maps from German newspapers or copied from books in the library. Many of us could draw the frontline positions from memory, naming every important city and town. I came to know Russian geography, the part of it where my fate was unfolding, better than I knew American. I could locate every strategic city and rail junction and rejoiced when one fell to the Russians. Even when Russian forces were still hundreds of miles from Stalag Luft III, we knew exactly how far the most advanced spearhead was from us.

After D-Day we had new maps to draw and new names to memorize. I learned the geography of France almost as well as that of Russia. Sometimes localities were mentioned I couldn't find on my maps and I'd fret until they were pinpointed, only to be disappointed if they marked no significant advance. After the breakthrough at Avranches we'd sometimes be unable to locate an advance point because it was deeper in France than we'd dared hope. We kept drawing new maps, following spearheads, measuring distances, predicting strategies.

After D-Day the news got so hot the senior staff feared some kriegies wouldn't be able to hide their enthusiasm and thus reveal to our hosts we had secret sources of information. The more sensational Allied successes were kept from the reports. We had to learn of them from German sources. We didn't like that but understood the necessity for it.

Though the glamor was gone from summarizing the BBC

communique for my block, I was assigned another duty that more than compensated for it. I'd taught myself military German by studying the daily official communiques in the newspapers and was able to translate the communiques verbatim as they were broadcast over the camp public address system. It was not as masterful an accomplishment as you might think. The official communique was repeated two or three times a day, once at dictation speed, the vocabulary was limited, and stock phrases abounded. "After the heaviest of artillery preparations, the enemy began its long-awaited attack" meant the Russians had a big one going and were driving. "Despite the gallant resistance of our heroically fighting troops" meant the loss of another major city was about to be announced. They would string words together into one long one, though. My favorite was *flussubegangverkehrsicherungpunkt*, which meant "river crossing traffic security point."

I was assigned to monitor one of the less important daily broadcasts and enter any important news in a log kept in a room across from FoodAcco. When a lot was happening I'd write out summaries and post them in my block.

For months after the invasion I haunted the cookhouse speakers, listening to every news broadcast and not just the one I was assigned to. A crowd of kriegies always gathered at the cookhouse when the fighting fronts were active. The ones who didn't know German listened intently for a town name they could recognize. When the news was especially good they'd know it from our reaction and bombard us with frantic questions, which we'd shrug off impatiently, straining to catch the next words.

Sometimes the dictation speed communique came during appel, a frustrating time for me. As soon as we were dismissed I'd race to the cookhouse to catch a rebroadcast or read the posted translation. The South Compound staff translator himself did the dictation-speed communique and when it came during appel was excused from the formation to do so. When he complained that at off-appel broadcasts kibitzers distracted him with their questions, Colonel Goodrich persuaded our hosts to let us bring a speaker into FoodAcco, where he could have more privacy. As a radio monitor I was allowed to listen in. I really appreciated that when winter came and it was bitter outside. One of my assignments was to return the speaker to the theater after the communique, climbing a shaky ladder to the loft to reinstall it.

I'd hung around the cookhouse for news broadcasts even
before the invasion along with several other of the faithful who
never missed one. Among them was a quiet young American,
Fahnestock, who had what sounded to me like a British accent and
who understood hardly any German. We had only a nodding acquaintance until after the invasion, when I had trouble with the
names of French towns. It turned out he'd wintered with his
family on the Riviera and spoke fluent French. He'd stand with
me during broadcasts and identify the French towns for me and
I'd give him a running translation of the German. I looked forward to our conversations.

After a broadcast I always stopped by to tell what I'd heard
to Bill, the RAF flight lieutenant I wouldn't let throw knives at
me. It was a courtesy, not a duty. He was high up in the chain that
got BBC news to us, and on occasion in the past he'd tipped me off
to important developments even before I was given the news
summary for my block. And after the senior staff began editing
sensational news out of the summary he'd sometimes give me the
deleted gen. He'd call me to his room, check outside the door and
window, his face creased in a wide grin and his eyes shining, and
say, "Westy, hold on to your hat!" It was strictly against regulations for him to do that and he always swore me to secrecy, which I
followed faithfully, except with Kennedy. I had no secrets from
him. I'd invite him for a walk around the circuit and pass on Bill's
news where no one could overhear. Kennedy was a close friend of
Bill's and sometimes already knew.

After reporting to Bill I'd give my roommates the news.
After late news broadcasts I'd take copies of the highlights to the
theater and an ex-announcer named Lee Pilert would put them on
the air. He had a marvelous voice and made the news sound
exciting even when it wasn't.

It wasn't coincidental that many members of the news staff
and some members of the camp staff had German names. Who was
more likely to know some German? One was actually German-
born, though few of us knew it. Certainly our hosts didn't. He'd
been brought to the U.S. as a child.

A kriegie who wasn't on the news staff could have been the
ideal Aryan poster model for the Third Reich. John Grunow,
Major Beckham's roommate. He was tall, husky, blond, blue-
eyed, erect, with a magnificent Heidelburg dueling scar across his
cheek. Only it wasn't a dueling scar. It was from an automobile

accident. Germans running across him for the first time would stare at him. What was this Teutonic knight doing in an enemy uniform? Grunow sometimes borrowed a mandolin and if you asked him would come to your room to play for you and your roommates.

Discipline in South Compound tightened appreciably after D-Day with the fluid situations on both the Western and Eastern fronts. We were organized into squadrons by blocks. As a senior first lieutenant (I would have preferred being a junior captain), I was given a squad. Because I knew some German I was also designated squadron interpreter and put in charge of a scouting party that was to reconnoiter outside the wire if we were liberated by paratroopers and became a true military force. I sincerely hoped Allied strategy did not include liberating POW camps deep inside the Reich with troops dropped from the skies. I had no stomach for ground combat. Few airmen did. In the air they were shooting at your plane. On the ground it was more personal.

Schoonmaker, who'd been a chemistry major as I was before the war but whose education had been interrupted by it, was assigned the job of investigating ways of making explosives and incendiaries from materials at hand or obtainable from corrupted guards. He enjoyed everything about it, the secrecy as well as the research. He didn't seemed nearly as disturbed as I was by the prospect of attacking a German Tiger tank with a bottle of kerosene with a wick in it.

To prepare us for an orderly evacuation by air if we were liberated by peaceful means we were assigned loading numbers based on time in the bag. Kennedy was number 49 and I was 50. We figured we'd be in the first planeload if it were a four-engine aircraft and the second if twin-engine. We pushed that estimate back a little when we decided senior officers and the disabled would go ahead of us, but the thought of being among the first flown out gave us quiet comfort.

Tightened discipline included Saturday morning room inspections. Immediately after Saturday appel we scrubbed floors, cleaned windows, wiped down the walls and the door and made our bunks with square corners. The enlisted men whom I theoretically commanded swabbed the halls. By this time our rooms were so crowded we had to put our lockers along the walls in the hall, leaving only a dark, narrow aisle. Owners stood by to move their lockers so the orderlies could mop under them.

U.S. BOMBERS POUNDED THE heart of Germany in ever-increasing strength. So many downed airmen poured into South Compound we'd have thought we were losing the air war if we hadn't known Germany was reeling. And still they came, filling long tents thrown up along the wire by Russian prisoners between South and North compounds. The new prisoners were assigned to rooms only to take meals. To make room for the tents, the Germans took down the wooden guardrail, permitting us to approach the wire. The new ground, untouched by our trampling feet, was so resilient we took off our shoes to walk on it. When the weather grew cold, the tents were struck and their occupants moved into rooms. By the end of the summer of 1944 South Compound was oppressively overcrowded. So many prisoners poured into Stalag Luft III that the new West Compound, with a capacity of two thousand, filled up. Two-man rooms went up to three and, eventually, six-man rooms to ten and eight-man rooms to fourteen. Men went into rooms that had been used for purposes other than living quarters. When Room 12 reached fourteen men, we went from the original four two-decker bunks to three three-deckers reaching almost to the ceiling and three two-deckers. I was in a two-decker, not from seniority but luck of the draw. As always, we let cards decide. I retained a side of a locker to myself the same way.

We went from eight men to fourteen by twos. Our first new men were Sam Fairchild, a B-17 copilot, and Mac, his navigator. Sam was a courteous, considerate, sharing type, but I argued with him unmercifully trying to make him admit to what I thought were factual errors over a wide range of subjects. Sam, on the other hand, often annoyed me by claiming I was the one who would never admit I was wrong. I confess I had a reputation almost as bad as Sam's for not admitting when I was wrong.

Mac was bright but boastful, and a reckless liar. I rode him unmercifully, and unfairly, because I was older, an experienced prisoner and never lost my temper in a dispute, as I could goad him into doing. Over my months in the bag, months when the only surcease from boredom was interminable, sometimes petty arguments, I'd developed a mean, sarcastic tongue and a delight in attacking anyone who offended me or whom I thought needed deflating. At one time or another I'd alienated, although only briefly, every one of my roommates except Kennedy with my sarcasm—even gentle, patient Alvarado. I never showed Kennedy anything but the respect he merited and on occasion, when I got too spiteful with others, he'd call me aside and tell me quietly to knock it off. Which I always did. It wasn't uncommon for roommates to fall out. Constantly together in close quarters, we'd sometimes grate on each other's nerves. Kennedy and Alvarado were perhaps the only men in our room that no roommate ever fell out with, although Schoonmaker, despite his delight in keeping arguments going, rarely made an enemy.

One night when Mac and I were sparring playfully with borrowed boxing gloves, he tagged me a good one. You weren't supposed to do that when you were just messing around. I retaliated with a pretty left hook. A mistake. He pounced on me raining punches so thick and fast I had to crouch and cover up, backing into a window and breaking a pane. I was in serious trouble with my roommates. It would have been better if I'd have just taken it on the chin. I wasn't accepted back into the fold until I replaced the window with one stolen from the indoor latrine. After Mac eventually moved to another room I regretted the way I'd ridden him and visited him in his new room. We got to be friends.

Two later roommates arrived with capture parcels and to our chagrin in some ways were better equiped than we oldtimers. One of them, Bob Bessee, who'd been an undertaker in civilian life, was a prize, a marvelous storyteller who entertained us with tales of his fearsome (he said) mother-in-law and the lighter side of funerals. We came to dislike his fellow arrival because he refused to share personal parcels, as we did, and tried to pick a fight with Buckner.

We added a temporary roommate, Erwin Feld, a big fellow from Oklahoma, who came to us from the German hospital where he'd been held while his broken pelvis healed. He was an opera singer but, while he whistled arias and sang snatches of songs to himself, he wouldn't sing publicly in the theater or even for us. He confided to me that he hadn't sung for more than a year and wouldn't take the chance with his voice. He left us when men in over-strength rooms were moved into a lecture room converted to living quarters in another barracks. (Forty years or so later, another Stalag Luft III ex wrote me that Feld was living in Hollywood and I should get in touch with him. Feld wasn't in the phone book. I wrote our mutual friend. The friend wrote that he'd forgotten Feld had changed his name to something more theatrical. He'd had a successful career on the musical stage in the States and later in opera in Italy. I phoned the former Feld, and now he and I lunch regularly, but he still hasn't sung for me, though when he warbles Italian to a waiter, it sounds like an aria to me.)

After Feld, came two twenty-year-old P-38 pilots, barely out of high school, bringing the room strength to twelve. They joked a lot about shooting up church bell towers on strafing missions. One of them, I'll call him Mike, was worldly wise beyond his years and always spoiling for a fight. Failing to start one with Guy, he started on me. It always began with a harmless argument, which he would escalate until I had to fight or flee. I'd flee. Poetic justice I guess for all those I'd vanquished with sarcasm instead of fists.

We only thought we were crowded with twelve men in the room until a new purge brought us to fourteen with the addition of Georgie "Bogie" Boege and Ralph Eisenach. Bogie was always laughing, singing and dancing, and he was a good cook to boot. A treat for us all. Eisenach was a quiet, good-natured fellow who surprised me by objecting vehemently when I suggested some goodies in the special parcels distributed for our 1944 Christmas be turned over to the room cooks instead of being shared out. When I insisted on knowing why, he said it was because one of our roommates was stealing from the larder, about as serious a crime as you could imagine in the bag. Bogie was cooking for the room by then, with Guy as his assistant, and I knew they were above suspicion. I got into a shouting match with the normally low-key Eisneach and was stunned when Alvarado and enough other roommates sided with him to veto my suggestion. It was only months later, when we'd been moved from Stalag Luft III, that Alvarado told me Eisenach had spoken the truth and Mike was the culprit.

Only room commanders remained in the rooms during inspection. Kennedy had been moved from our room to a former two-man room, and I was now room commander. Kennedy was reluctant to move even though the end rooms, which held only three occupants, were much more desirable and open only to camp staff or captains and above and even though our room had grown terribly overcrowded and there were newcomers he disliked. He continued to spend more time with us than with his new room-mates.

I tried to be away from the room on news business during inspections, with Schoonmaker or Costanzo taking over for me. Colonel Clark was usually the inspecting officer and he was tough. It was like being in preflight all over again. We'd always tried to keep a clean room, but there were those in South Compound who hadn't bothered, to such a point that the Germans complained to Colonel Goodrich about it. The Saturday inspections took care of that.

The virulence of German propaganda against us intensified with the increase in massive American daylight bombing raids. Airmen were *Terrorfliegers* or *Luftgangsters*, their planes *Terror-bombers* and their attacks *Terrorangriffs*. The newspapers ran photos of bloodthirsty nose art on shot-down bombers, and one of them had a story attacking our former squadron commanding officer, now commander of the whole group. "Colonel John R. Kane, with the lovely nickname, 'Killer'." I clipped it out of the paper, hoping one day to give it to him, but it was one of the things I unloaded on moving day. A journalist learned of a satire kriegies sang and quoted it to show that barbarians though we were, we were also cowards of low morale. "I wanted wings 'til I got the Goddamn things, now I don't want 'em any more. You can leave all the Zeroes to the Goddamn heroes, I've had a belly full of war." He missed one that I liked better. "There's a combat theater where the boys hate to go, to see Hermann the German and his Luftwaffe show. Shoot 'em down, shoot 'em down cried the boys in the rear, let's go home, let's go home, that is all you could hear."

The fury of the daylight attacks mounted. Goebbels declared open season on downed fliers, saying there were no longer enough military and civilian police to protect them from the righteous indignation of the populace. New prisoners brought in horror stories of rumored lynchings and their own rescue from blood-thirsty mobs by German military. They said civilians in the Balkan countries were worse than Germans. If Germans didn't arrive quickly to pick up downed airmen, they'd beat the fliers or even kill them. Negroes and fliers suspected of being Jews were killed out of hand, the new men said. The consensus was the Hungarians were the cruelest.

Propaganda, the Reich's declining fortunes and perhaps war-connected personal problems made our guards increasingly surly. Shootings into the camp, very rare in the past, increased. A guard might fire at a block he thought too noisy after lights out. The only person hit in a block that I knew of for a fact, though, was a Colonel Stevenson, shot in the leg during a night bombing alert by a guard who claimed the colonel was sending out lamp signals. Some of the more timid souls, I among them, feared that if enraged civilians tried to storm the camp our guards wouldn't try to stop them.

The guards grew so short-tempered we were ordered never to look directly at one after an air raid and were not to smile at one ever lest he think we were gloating. When nerves on both sides of the wire were stretched tautest, Brigadier General Arthur W. Vanaman turned up at Stalag Luft III. The rumor spread quickly that he'd bailed out of a B-17 over Germany, which later got back to England with all its regular crew unharmed, and that he spoke fluent German, was a prewar acquaintance of Hermann Goering, and had been sent to defuse the situation. (I learned years later from Arthur Durand's *Stalag Luft III* that, on the contrary, his capture was a near disaster; he'd just been briefed on Project Ultra, the breaking of the German cipher code; but he did speak fluent German and had known Goering when Vanaman was an air attaché in Berlin before the war.) Whether he was sent there for that purpose or not, tension did ease considerably after his arrival.

For months Stalag Luft III was exclusively white. The news raced through South Compound when we got our first black officer, a P-51 pilot from the all-black 332nd Fighter Group. The Army Air Force we knew had been completely segregated and few among us had ever seen a black pilot. Most of us hadn't even known they existed. Segregation was so entrenched that when another officer and I nominated Lena Horne as our favorite Hollywood actress in a poll, we'd been asked by the pollsters to pick another candidate. There was talk the new pilot might be quartered with one of the senior officers, but several rooms asked for him.

Within a few days he was just another kriegie, only in a darker shade. He had a degree from Northwestern and when it was learned he was a philosophy whiz, men studying the subject on their own went to him for help.

When more black officers arrived they were awarded, almost as a privilege, to rooms that had requested them. A kriegie who objected when his roommates asked for a black officer was forced to move when they turned on him in outrage. The black officers were all pilots from the 332nd and uniformly better educated than the general run of new prisoners because they'd had to be better qualified than white applicants to get flight training.

For many of us it was our first contact with blacks on an equal footing. Having been born and raised in a strictly segregated environment, I'd never had an opportunity to meet a black person socially. As a boy I'd swum in the bayou with black kids and wrestled with them on the bank, but we never knew each others' names and left separately.

Now that I could remedy that deficiency I wanted to do it casually, without betraying the nervousness I felt at the new experience. The way a virgin feels, maybe. One morning I saw a light brown officer about my size, with a thin mustache and an important nose, examining a flower in a garden by his block. Charles "Chuck" Williams, P-51 pilot. I went over and looked at flowers, too. Waiting. He spoke first and, after a period of mutual shyness, we got to talking like any pair of kriegies, except that I found myself being educated. Emancipated would be more like it. Coming from an immigrant family, I hadn't been raised with the deep-seated prejudices of the usual Southern white, but I had thought white and colored water fountains, back-of-the-bus seating, and being called "Mistuh David" by a yardman old enough to be my grandfather perfectly normal. After my first conversation with Williams I'd never think so again. When we got to know each other better and he saw how eager I was to learn, he'd talk of the black experience in white America more in sorrow than in anger. Things like hesitating about going into an unfamiliar restaurant in Los Angeles, where he lived, lest it be one that didn't serve Negroes and, after he was a commissioned pilot wearing his country's uniform, going into a drugstore with some white officers and the clerk refusing to serve him. The white officers had wanted to wreck the place but he persuaded them to leave. He wasn't the type to look for a fight, except when he was in his P-51 protecting bombers with white crews from German fighter planes. He roomed with John Winant, escape artist Jerry Sage, and the officer who briefed block representatives on BBC news.

We became fast friends and bickering bridge partners. We often played with another "mixed" couple, the black half being Richard Macon, from Alabama. Macon had arrived at South Compound in such deplorable shape we were indignant that he'd been sent to a POW camp instead of a hospital. There was no obvious wound but his neck had been injured when he was shot down. He held it at an awkward angle and walked tentatively. Very dark, his skin had developed a dusty blue pallor. He'd return your sympathetic looks with a smile. Colonel Goodrich got him sent off to the camp hospital and he was back in a few days looking fit and without the blue pallor.

Macon was an excellent bridge player. I was average. Williams and Macon's partner were atrocious. (I can still get a rise out of Williams by telling him he was the worst bridge player in Stalag Luft III.) Macon was also one of the best minds in South Compound and more deeply resentful of racial prejudice in the States than Williams. I was glad I'd hit on Williams to educate me. It was easier to pal around with an average type like myself than a superintellect. (I was to learn Williams wasn't as average as I thought. In Los Angeles he'd been a postal worker. After the war he hooked up with a Fortune 500 corporation and eventually retired as a vice president. When he first joined the corporation he sometimes came to Houston on business. Houston was still segregated, and we couldn't take him to a restaurant. So he came to our house.)

A colonel who came in with Williams' purge created a sensation like the arrival of the first black officer. When the purge came in, there were shouts of, "It's Luper, it's Luper!" from our ranks. James Rhea Luper, the notorious commandant of cadets at Maxwell Field preflight, the one I'd quizzed Colonel Agee about at P.G. 21. Even those who hadn't gone through Maxwell knew of him, his reputation as the coldest, strictest most inflexible man in the Air Corps having been spread by those who had. (I wasn't so sure Luper was quite as heartless as advertised. One Saturday after daily parade—we had seven a week—three of us cadets were heading for the gate to go roller-skating in Montgomery. We encountered Luper as we rounded our barracks. I was in uniform but my friends had on sweatshirts and we all had suckers in our mouths. We snapped to attention. I snatched the sucker from my mouth. We saluted. Luper demanded to know where we were going. To town, we said. He asked my companions coldly if they considered sweatshirts the proper attire for visiting Montgomery and ordered them to report themselves for being out of uniform. Adding, just as coldly, "And don't you know better than to salute an officer with a lollypop in your mouth?" I could have sworn there was a twinkle in his hard eyes.)

I'd heard before going overseas that Luper had been reassigned from Maxwell Field to command the Officer Training School at Miami, but here he was, a full colonel. Junior officers in the purge with Colonel Luper said he had been in a spot of trouble, though, for flying his piano to England in his B-17. They said that after capture they'd been held in a building with a piano in it and Colonel Luper had played it for them. Well, too. And when one of them diffidently mentioned they knew him by reputation he'd replied, "I used to be a hard man but I've softened up some."

Field grade officers were no longer a rarity in South Compound. There was no friction between them and junior officers until the eggshell scandal. When enough colonels and lieutenant colonels had been shot down to have their own mess, they ate in a private room in the cookhouse. They pooled their parcels and the cook prepared their meals. It was a completely legitimate application of Rank Has Its Privileges. But some junior officers resented it, saying the senior officers were dining in luxury, and did you know eggshells had been found in their garbage? It was never proved.

In August I had a book bonanza, parcels mailed in February, March and April, and Dapper Dan shaved his head for the second time. Kennedy and Buckner had been concerned about losing their hair, too. They'd take turns sitting on a stool while one massaged the other's scalp vigorously. I, with my thick, curly hair, made fun of them and remembered it when in the sixties I started losing my own hair until I had less on top than Kennedy. That month we saw our first mail written on the new U.S. letter forms and Kennedy and Buckner won the seven D-bar first prize in a block bridge tournament. After some major Allied successes in September I wrote myself a card, thinking I might be free by the time it arrived in Houston. It's all I wrote that month. In October, no longer so euphorically optimistic after the Allied failure at Arnhem in Holland, I started writing letters home again.

When the headlong Allied advances slowed I lost some of my addiction to the radio but continued to monitor one daily newscast as a duty and was always there for the daily communique when it wasn't on during appel. There were always ferrets among the kriegies listening to the radio. You didn't even need to hear what was said to follow the tenor of the news. We smiled at every report of Allied successes. Their faces fell. They took heart at reports of weapons which would turn the war around—the devastating new terror weapons, the V-1 and V-2, their air- and ground-launched rockets; one-man submarines, torpedo sleds and demolition swimmers—but we scoffed. One ferret claimed to know for a fact Hitler had a new weapon that would sweep us from the skies. We laughed at him. He was talking about jet fighters. Had they been developed earlier and in large numbers, he might have been right. There were broadcasts from the fighting fronts and even from holdout German garrisons under siege in Channel ports. Whatever the German claims, our faith in Allied arms was boundless and our expectations of a quick end to the war unshakable, until mid-December and the Battle of the Bulge. I heard the bad news before it was reported on the radio. Bill called me to his room and told me about the German breakthrough. Optimist that I was, I analyzed the situation as clever Allied strategy to lure the Nazis out of the Siegfried Line as Montgomery had once drawn the German armor into the defenses at El Alamein in the Western Desert. Even after I understood the gravity of the situation I thought it only an aggravating delay to the inevitable ending of the war, and I took great comfort from Russian successes on the Eastern Front as the Soviets pressed ever closer to Stalag Luft III.

Autumn deepened and great skeins of ducks and geese flew over Stalag Luft III. We watched them pass beneath the lowering skies by day and, filled with nostalgia and longing, listened to their quacking and honking by night. Soon they'd be in far-off lands and we'd still be behind the wire.

When my second winter in South Compound approached, I made myself a sleeping bag. I folded my sheet into a sack and stuffed it with my summer clothes, shredded newspapers and rags. I sewed my two small German blankets into one wide blanket and sewed that to my warm, wide Italian blanket. I folded the Italian blanket into a larger sack around the sheet sack, which became a rustling inner mattress. With one of my two pairs of longjohns for pajamas, I'd slip deep into my sleeping bag and sleep warm and cozy on the chilliest nights.

Christmas Eve I stuck my head in every room in the block and demanded, "Where were you last Christmas?" Mostly the kriegies had been in the States. Some had been in England or North Africa. None had been in the bag. I told them where and how I'd spent my last two Christmases, ending with, "So kiss my ass," and was met with jeers, laughter and a derisive "Ha-ard luck!" followed by "Merry Christmas" all around.

Christmas. My third in the bag. We were issued American Red Cross Christmas parcels with canned turkey, nuts, cherries, dates and cookies as well as playing cards and other gifts in them. The Argentine and Turkish Red Cross sent cheese, pork sausage, canned beans, nuts and dates. As we had the previous Christmas, we drew cards to determine the order in which we made our selections. Our hosts provided extra rations, too, including a half-keg of nonalcholic beer per block and a drink like root beer.

Alvarado and I were cooking for the room again. We served canned turkey, candied carrots, mashed potatoes au gratin and a variety of desserts, including a date-nut cake and individual cherry tarts. The date-nut cake was a masterpiece even if the tooth powder didn't work enough magic and it fell in the middle. We filled the depression with an icing invented by Costanzo—sugar, marge, shaved D-bar, Klim and chopped raisins boiled to caramelized smoothness. Bogie made the crusts for the tarts and the cookhouse sergeants baked them.

We also prepared a sumptuous tea and had the sergeants in to share it. We set out dried fruit, nuts, candy, tea, coffee and the date-nut cake. Later they invited me to their room for cherry ice cream made with snow.

As a Christmas treat, several kriegies from Center Compound were allowed to visit, among them a Houstonian I knew, Charles Forney. (After liberation and processing at Camp Lucky Strike in France, I went on a three-day pass to Paris and ran into him. He had some blank passes. We forged two more passes and spent six more days at the Hotel Crillon for ten francs, twenty cents, a night. When my wife and I checked in there in 1965 and I told the desk clerk the last time I'd stayed in the hotel I'd paid twenty cents a night, he said now it was dearer.) Jennette, our flying adjutant, had been passing notes to us through book and mail officers who sometimes moved between compounds but didn't get over with Forney's group. The former broadcasters among us did a marathon record show with disc-jockey patter all day and everyone wallowed in nostalgia.

A Hard Day's Night

WE BEGAN HEARING DISTANT explosions day and night in the east. Was it artillery or demolitions? Colonel Goodrich ordered us to assemble emergency rations and to make packs and be ready to march should the Germans decide to move us ahead of the Russian advance. Every kriegie was required to have a minimum emergency ration, and there were showdown inspections to check on compliance. Most of my roommates had already saved the minimum or more but a few hadn't and wanted to divide our communal supply of food. As room commander I refused and went a step further by holding back their Red Cross chocolate and keeping it for them. They didn't like it but they put up with it. As it happened, I should have shared the larder out.

With a great surge, the Russians established a bridgehead over the Oder River at Steinau, only a few miles from Stalag Luft III. At night we could see and hear them bombing Breslau, ninety miles away, the distant overcast flashing red moments before the rolling thunder of explosions. We feared the Russians might mistake Stalag Luft III for a German installation and bomb us and hoped they would make a lightning strike to liberate us.

Even as we prepared for evacuation we held on to that hope, we from P.G. 21 not so strongly as most of our fellow kriegies, who sang that familiar old refrain, "They haven't got the transportation." They ridiculed us when we said the Germans would move us even if they had to march us out. There were others who took the threat seriously enough to begin knocking together sleds from bedboards and making packs. Kennedy planned to leave with Alvarado, Buckner, Schoonmaker and me if we marched.

I made a knapsack out of a khaki shirt, sewing the tail closed and sewing the cuffs to the sides to make shoulder straps. I'd learned on the trip up from Italy that a bedroll was handy for carrying things, too, except that when you unrolled it to use the blanket everything in it was lying around. So I cut the legs off my khaki pants and sewed them into bags with drawstring tops. If we had to move I'd put my gear in them and roll them up in my blanket.

January 27, 1945. A chilly night, heavily wrapped in snow. We were getting ready for late brew when the lights went out. We hadn't heard any sirens but the block air raid officer came down the hall shouting, "Air raid, check your shutters!" The lights came on. We could hear shouting and doors slamming in other blocks. Now the front of our block was erupting. Major Beckham, the block commander, stuck his head in the door and said, "We've been ordered to evacuate the camp. Be ready to move in half an hour. As soon as you've got your kit together, fall out in the road in front of the block. Take only what you can carry. We're going to march." He was off to the next room before we could ask questions.

We were petrified for a moment, then we ran for our lockers, pushing, elbowing, swearing. Panic has no manners. I had expected to be calmer if and when. My emergency rations were already assembled—chocolate, sugar, dried fruit, cheese, margarine and saccharine—and I had my shirt-pack and carrying bags. Once I started packing I settled down some. I took all my socks, two cartons of cigarettes, my cigars, some pipe tobacco and laid out everything I intended to wear on the march. With what I already had on, that meant two pairs of socks, wool longjohns, wool shirt and pants, sweater, battle dress jacket, stocking cap, muffler, greatcoat and two pairs of gloves—one GI, the other thin knit wool from a personal parcel. For my blanket roll should I rip the thick Italian blanket from my sleeping bag or settle for the lighter GI blanket? I hesitated and opted for the easy way.

Some of my roommates scrambled for food in the larder. I hadn't thought about that. Alvarado and I joined them and took what we thought we could carry. From all over the block came the sound of frantic movement, breaking dishes and rolling canned goods. I knew I should eat all I could hold and tell the others to do the same, but I couldn't have forced down a bite and hadn't the will to advise the others. Some room commander. Kennedy came from his room at the end of the block to tell me we'd fall out together with Alvarado, Buckner and Schoonmaker and that Tom Brooks, one of his roommates, wanted to join us. Brooks had escaped from Stalag Luft I and been sent to our camp when recaptured. Someone had the presence of mind to mix a pitcher of thick Klim and I forced down what I could. When I made my bedroll after packing my shirt knapsack I found I had only enough clothes left for one pantleg bag. I gave the other one to Alvarado, who was even less prepared than I and in more of a flap.

He needed help in making a bedroll. Irritable and self-centered in the face of sudden change, I was angry with him for not being prepared. I realized I'd failed to measure up in the face of other emergencies and been ashamed of myself later, all the way back to when we'd been shot down and I'd have been of no use to anyone if Gardinier hadn't told me what to do. I settled down a little and helped Alvarado. Buckner had been standing around helplessly and I helped him, too. I was no longer rattled and didn't even feel rushed, and felt a little smug about it.

I looked ruefully at the discards on my bunk. Pictures, clothes, books, letters, the War Log I'd assembled so religiously, my warm Italian blanket. My nest egg two years in the gathering. Here we go again, I thought wryly. Another escape from freedom. Someone stuck his head in the door and said Major Beckham said when we fell out to form in squads but after roll call we could rearrange any way we wanted.

I went up the hall to see how Kennedy was coming along. Every door in the block was open. Inside every room kriegies were milling around in wild confusion. Block 133 was like an ant heap poked with a stick. I stuck my head in a room where men lived who'd been particularly raucous with me when I said the Germans would march us out if they had to and yelled, "So they haven't got the transportation?"

Kennedy and Brooks were just about packed. I went back to the room and they joined us shortly. With a last look at our room, our cozy world, littered with dumped bedding, clothes, papers and food too heavy to carry, we shouldered our packs and fell out in the snow. Some men had rude sleds made of bedboards or upside-down benches with nailed-on runners. All of us were swathed in layers of clothing and festooned with packs and bed-rolls in a scene repeated in front of every block. We still had no clue why we were moving so precipitously or where we were going.

Maybe the Russians were driving and would overrun Stalag Luft III before the Germans could get us out. No Russians appeared. And for a while, no Germans either. We just stood there in the cold. We loosened packs and let them fall to the snow at our feet. Someone cried, "Get these men in out of the hot sun." I wished it had been me. A courier brought Major Beckham orders and he marched us toward the west gate, by the theater. The sound of boots crunching on frozen snow hung over the converging blocks. We stamped numb feet and hunched our shoulders in ragged parade to be counted. Colonel Goodrich addressed us. He didn't know where we were going or how far we'd be walking but said to keep our spirits up and keep our heads. We marched out behind him.

I didn't see anyone turn for a wistful parting glance at South Compound. I felt a curious mixture of depression and excitement. Depression because once again I was being snatched from liberation, leaving behind comparative comfort and security for unknown hardship. Excited because I was outside the wire and on the move. Going somewhere. The "anywhere but here." And with it all something utterly unexpected. "God damn, isn't this romantic? A flight by night in the snow, destination unknown?"

The long line of columns of five accordioned along the road between the compounds in fits and starts and came to a dead halt. West and North compounds were silent and dark. Why were we the only ones freezing our butts off? I asked a guard where we were going. He said he didn't know. Another guard said the name of a town I'd never heard of and that it was two hundred miles away. I didn't believe him.

The guards were as charged up as the kriegies. It was an adventure for them, too. It wasn't going to be any easier for them than for us, either. They had huge packs and their weapons. For once I was happy they had the guns and not us.

Moving again. And now we were really outside the wire. Another halt. This time longer than before for another head count. It took a while. I asked a guard if I could step out of ranks to urinate. I'd never peed in snow before. I wondered if it were true you could write your name in it if you had the bladder power. I barely finished my first name and rushed to button up. Anything exposed, the cold nipped. I felt strong, confident I could walk as far as the next guy if my feet held up.

I don't think the Germans ever got a count that pleased them but they started us moving anyhow. It was as cold for them as it was for us. The first yards of the road were familiar to Kennedy and me from our parole walk but when we turned west, away from Sagan, it was unknown territory. It was snowing now. We walked heads down, wrapped in our private thoughts. What do you think about at times like these? If you're single and unattached, mom. How would she take it when she learned I'd been moved again? How long before we reestablished contact? And, presciently, I thought, this is an adventure I could tell my grandchildren about. (I tried, after I'd acquired some, but they weren't terribly interested.)

Almost midnight. Could it be less than two hours since we'd been debating what to have for evening brew? Kennedy, Alvarado, Schoonmaker, Buckner, Brooks and I stayed close together in ranks. We'd marched in good order at first but now the column had settled into a monotonous, plodding gait. We stumbled often in the rutted snow but we had it better than our guards. They had to plow through drifts on either side of the column.

Cold as we were, as dispossessed and encumbered, we took pleasure in a small, silent drama unfolding beside us. A German sergeant handed a heavy ammunition case to a corporal. The corporal struggled along with it for a while and passed it to a private first class. The PFC soon had enough of it, too, and unloaded on a small private. The private was already bowed down by his enormous pack. The added weight of the ammo case bent him further. He'd stop to ease his pack and shift hands with the ammo case, then plow through the snow to catch up, all the time under our grinning scrutiny. Our faces were so muffled he couldn't see the grins but he knew we were watching. He was in great distress but there wasn't anyone of lower rank he could dump the ammo case on. At last, desperate, after looking around to see no superiors were watching, he heaved the ammo case into a drift. Before the night was over he'd thrown away his pack, too.

We stayed on back roads, plodding past fields blanketed in white and groves of trees dripping snow. There were no lights in any of the scattered houses along the route. We trudged along mechanically, interminably, with an occasional ten-minute break. After a while I lost all sense of time.

The first breaks we put down our packs and stood and talked. Where were they taking us? How long would we be doing this? Was there any sense in trying to make a break for it? As the night wore on we lost the energy for it. When we stopped we'd lie down where we stood, still encumbered by packs and bedrolls. And the snow kept falling. We were chilled but not freezing. Too many layers of clothing and all that healthy exercise.

Kriegies started lightening their loads, discarding food, clothing, even tobacco. In the morning there were going to be some surprised and happy German civilians passing this way. I'd left behind more than I really needed to and began picking up food within easy reach. We'd be eating on the march and lightening our loads that way.

A German staff car patrolled the column, making periodic sweeps back to front, front to back. Motorcycles with guards in sidecars did the same. When they passed we got off the road into the drifts to let them by, moving dumbly as cattle. Hohendahl was one of those in a sidecar. He'd climb out of it and exhort us to keep up the pace and maintain good route order in his most superior way. We'd never hated him more. Word drifted back along the column that Colonel Goodrich had been offered a ride in the staff car but had declined and was still leading us.

We'd been on the road maybe four or five hours when we got a half-hour break. Guards came along distributing bread and margarine. We ate that instead of getting into our own rations. A bite of bread, a bite of margarine. We couldn't have spread the margarine if we'd wanted. It was too cold. Biting into a chunk was like biting into an apple, without the juice and good taste. A kriegie in front of me opened his pack and dumped out cans of food. He started doggedly throwing them out into the snow as far as he could. I yelled at him to stop. He ignored me and reached for a can of bully. I asked him to give it to me. Instead he threw it after the other cans. Now his roommates were yelling at him, too. We were furious. "If you don't want it, let someone else have it!" I cried. When the frenzy left him he'd thrown away most of his food but I'd salvaged a can of bully. I'd started into the field for more cans but gave it up when I sank to my knees in snow.

Kennedy's bunch lay huddled on our packs near one another. The others lit cigarettes and I started my pipe. A wagon drawn by a drooping horse powdered with snow came by loaded with the baggage of kriegies who couldn't carry it any further. There were a few exhausted kriegies sitting on the pile. A courier came down the line saying when someone couldn't make it to drop out and wait for a wagon to pick him up. The courier urged us not to do that if we could possibly keep going. We resolved we'd never drop out. We wouldn't disgrace Colonel Goodrich in front of the Germans.

After the break we walked on into a dawn made bleaker by a solid overcast. Snow was still falling, blown about by a chilling wind that had sprung up. We were colder than we'd been at night. "Wind chill factor" was a term that had yet to be invented.

The column stopped at last in a huddle of barns and cottages. The Germans counted us again, taking their time as usual. We were told arrangements were being made to bivouac us in barns. We waited. And waited some more. We grew loudly angry and rebellious. Some of the guards tightened their grip on their weapons. They needn't have bothered. We weren't that rebellious.

Eventually we were split into groups and led away, our bunch to a large barn in a cluster of farm buildings. The kriegies in front filed in. When Kennedy's bunch neared the door all movement stopped. The barn was full. Several of us pushed in anyway, desperate for a place to lie down out of the cold, but we could see there wasn't even sitting room.

We shuffled back a few steps, complaining bitterly. Guards arrived with a farmhand and a ladder. He propped the ladder against the barn and a guard said there was room in the loft. Weary and burdened as we were, we could hardly make it to the top, but everyone helped the next man after getting there.

The floor of the loft was thick with hay. We were warned not to smoke. Kennedy, Buckner, Alvarado and I opened our bedrolls and made a pallet for four. We were too tired to eat and too hungry to sleep. Someone said hot water was available for brews. Kennedy and I climbed wearily down the ladder to fetch some. Young women were smiling and waving to us from windows. We wondered what would happen if we went inside. The shape we were in, probably nothing much.

We took the hot water back up the ladder and made tea, the four of us drinking it gratefully between mouthfuls of bread, margarine and chocolate. We climbed onto our pallet and stretched out side by side. Warm and comfortable at last, but still unable to sleep. We couldn't relax. After a couple of hours we gave up trying and started repacking our kits. We pooled some of our food in the bag I'd given Alvarado. We fashioned a carrying handle for it. We'd been in the loft maybe five hours when we were told to prepare to move out. We assembled our gear, and waited. I won a guard's undying gratitude with the gift of a cigarette, which he put away carefully. I asked him where we were going. He didn't know but he did know the Russians were advancing rapidly. Kennedy and I wondered if we should try leaving the group and hiding out somewhere to wait for them. Not a good idea. We were exhausted and wouldn't last long in the freezing cold. We had no maps and no idea where we were. And we remembered waiting for another army to reach us, in Italy. We'd stick with the column and maybe the Russians would overtake us.

We had a better idea. Why not sneak into one of the farm buildings and get the girls to hide us? Even if the Russians didn't get to us before we were found, having female company for a while would be worth it. We climbed down the ladder, this time more enthusiastically than our earlier trip, and spoke with some farm-workers. They were foreign labor, not Germans. They said the women were all Polish and the things they would be willing to do for us did not include hiding us. They could be shot for it.

So we did the next best thing. We got hot water and had a brew. After we fell in again it took the Germans a while to rout the last kriegie out of the warm barn. We moved out to the road and formed our column to be counted. The Germans couldn't get a number to suit them no matter how many times they tried. And they tried for hours. We cursed them, tucking our hands into our armpits and shivering. It was almost dark before we were on our way again, stiff, sore, and colder and wearier than we'd been before the rest stop.

We walked on and on into the night, half-asleep, falling behind the rank ahead, then overrunning it and treading on heels, with the rank behind doing the same to us. Our food bag was heavy. When one man tired, he passed it to another. Intervals between transfers grew shorter. Alvarado would say, "Take it for a while, Westy?" And I'd take it for as long as I could and say, "Take it for a while, Zeak?" Buckner and Kennedy were having the roughest time, Buckner because he never exercised and was out of shape, Kennedy because he couldn't relax even during breaks.

Rumors of extraordinary Allied successes swept up and down the column. I wanted to believe them even though I knew flux bred them. We'd been through it before at Sulmona.

It started snowing again. It congealed on our mufflers at our mouths and froze in our eyebrows, but we were grateful it wasn't rain. The infrequent ten-minute breaks only left us colder and more exhausted. Discarded prizes marked our route. I picked up two cartons of cigarettes and a box of cigars, wedging them between the tied ends of my bedroll and holding them there with one free hand. Sometimes I carried the food sack in the other hand but never for long. It seemed to grow heavier each time it passed to me.

We couldn't walk another step. But we did. Stolidly, dumb as posts. We protested sullenly to our guards. They kept assuring us we had only a few more kilometers to go. My left knee began aching. I limped. But at least my feet didn't hurt.

We grew parched and scooped up handfuls of snow from the side of the road to melt in our mouths. It didn't help much. Alvarado had been passing around a can of Klim and sugar he'd thought to mix just before we evacuated our room. We all had our knives and spoons in our pockets and ate it by the spoonful. It had a sharp, searing taste my senses were too dulled with fatigue to identify. We'd almost finished the can before Alvarado realized he'd mixed salt instead of sugar with the Klim. That's why we'd been so thirsty. We stopped eating the mixture but didn't throw it away. Salt was too precious.

Everyone was stumbling now, complaining mindlessly. Some dropped out to wait for the wagon. We yelled at Hohendahl when he came by and demanded we stop and sleep. He answered with sarcasm or not at all. I was sorry we'd even acknowledged the son of a bitch's existence.

The road slanted up ever so slightly but still enough to make walking more laborious. Buckner spoke of dropping out but we wouldn't let him. A Kennedy man couldn't quit. We discussed just stopping and refusing to go on but realized sitting down in the cold without shelter would be worse than walking until we dropped. Our steps got shorter and slower. The column contracted and expanded raggedly as the ranks blundered together, stumbled, fell back. Just putting one foot ahead of the other took great concentration and willpower. Word came back from the head of the column that we were approaching a village and would bivouac there. The pace picked up a trifle. My left knee was aching more and the right one hurt some. We reached the village. A sign said Muskau. I'd never heard of it. We trudged through the center of the silent village. And kept going. We slid into dull and bitter despair. We agreed we'd go no farther. There were buildings here where we could take shelter from the bitter cold. Let them shoot us if they wanted to. All that mattered was warmth and sleep. The head of the column was turning off the main road into an industrial area! We really would be stopping! It was about two in the morning. We'd been on the move almost two nights and a day.

The column collapsed on itself as the front ranks halted and those behind kept moving blindly forward in a solid, whimpering mob. A kriegie in front of me, a frail man who'd kept going the last few hours on sheer nerve, began to sway. With my last strength I put one of his arms across my shoulder. Light though he was, I almost collapsed. I locked my knees. Studs, one of his roommates, a powerful man, took his other arm and most of his weight. Suddenly he leaned and retched, almost dragging us down. Men were reeling and vomiting all around us. Studs leaned him against a wall. After what seemed like an interminable wait, the mob moved toward an open door streaming light. Just inside, we ran into a solid wall of bodies and could go no farther. The mob pressed against our backs, groaning. Goodrich appeared from nowhere and said there was room in another building. Dazed kriegies ignored him and kept trying to crowd in.

The wall of men in front of us inched forward as those who'd dropped to the floor just inside were prodded to their feet and herded toward the back by guards and our senior officers. They moved reluctantly, groaning and complaining, dropped again after a few steps and had to be urged to their feet once more. We were in a glass factory. The floor was layered with supine bodies. It was like the scene of a massacre without the blood. We were inside but with nowhere to lie down, or even sit. Scores of us still clotted the entrance.

Von Ryan Takes Charge

COLONEL LUPER EMERGED from a huddle of men and climbed the steps to a platform around a furnace. Where did he get the strength? He asked the men on the floor to move back as far as they could to make room for us. The few who tried to obey couldn't get over the bodies tangled on the floor. The Luper I remembered from preflight surfaced. With a voice like a whip he ordered everyone to move. And they tried. Someone complained, "There isn't anywhere to move to." Colonel Luper, hard-eyed, surveyed the throng. "Who said that? I want that man to come up here!" No one did but under the sheer force of Colonel Luper's presence the mass found somewhere to move to.

I got separated somehow from Kennedy and the others when they wedged themselves among the bodies on the floor. I crawled toward the back over the quivering mass until I found a tiny opening and squeezed myself into it. The men I disturbed complained querulously without waking. There were arms and legs laced over and under me and I was twisted in an uncomfortable position but I was warm at last. Pain stabbed through both my knees. I was too wedged in to straighten my legs. I couldn't stifle my groans. Embarrassing. I endured the pain as long as I could before asking for help, even more embarrassed that I needed it. A kriegie I didn't even know wrenched himself from his stupor and disentangled us both from the mass. He helped me straighten my legs. I embarrassed myself further by moaning. He half-dragged me over the bodies and helped me up to the furnace platform, where there was a little standing room. Colonel Luper had allowed only emergency cases to remain there. Now that my legs were unlocked and I massaged my knees in the warmth of the furnace they felt better. Colonel Luper came to me and when I explained what I was doing there gave me a smile and a friendly word. It did wonders for my morale. (Colonel Luper became the model for Colonel Joseph Ryan in *Von Ryan's Express*.)

The furnace was at the back wall, round, encircled by the platform. You could look into it at several points and see dancing flames. Its brick wall and the platform were wonderfully warm. A conveyor belt system threaded the floor. Steps like a country stile crossed it near the furnace. Colonel Luper had ordered them kept clear so men could cross the conveyor to go outside to urinate. It was the only clear space in the factory. The floor, the conveyor, a little room in one corner, every ledge, projection or tiny niche was overlaid with entwined bodies. One man was balanced perilously on top of a small cabinet against a wall, his head pillowed on a knapsack. As I watched, a kriegie separated himself from the tangle and tugged at the knapsack. The sleeper held onto it dumbly. The man kept pulling. The man on the cabinet clutched it convulsively, facing his tormenter, eyes open wide now but unseeing. The knapsack came free. He sank back down, the hand that had clutched the knapsack hanging limply. Neither man had uttered a sound.

My knees were much better but I knew if I lay down and bent them they'd lock again. Men worse off than I, some feverish, were clamoring to get on the platform. I walked over bodies to the conveyor steps and sat there with my legs outstretched. Colonel Luper asked me sharply if I'd heard the order to keep the steps clear. I explained my problem as diffidently as if I were still in preflight. He smiled again and said I could stay. (I never saw him again after liberation, and he died in the wreckage of his aircraft on February 28, 1953, on a snowy night at Offutt Air Force Base, Nebraska.)

I hadn't slept for two nights and three days. I did so fitfully now, sitting. When I fell off my perch into the men below, they'd groan and mutter and push me away with arms and legs without opening their eyes. The steps were so narrow that when men crossed the conveyor I had to cling to their legs as they squeezed by.

The mass on the floor seethed, the interlocked bodies turning and twisting. Deep in exhausted sleep, kriegies sobbed, groaned, moaned, sighed, muttered. A German workman came in to adjust a flue Colonel Luper had reported was leaking fumes but couldn't get to it through the press.

Day came. Men sat up. I was able to knead my way through them to find Kennedy and the others nested together. When the area cleared a little he spread blankets against the conveyor and tucked me in like an infant. I fell asleep at once. He woke me an hour or so later to feed me oatmeal mixed with Klim, margarine and sugar. He'd cooked it in a tin can held against a furnace door. It was rich, sweet, scalding hot. Ambrosial. I slept again. When I awoke a few hours later my knees were stiff and sore but without the night's agony. My cap and a glove were missing. I had no idea where I'd lost them.

Some kriegies had gone outside and there was room to move around. Men were clustered around the furnace, cooking. Kennedy and I went outside into a space of dirty, beaten snow bounded by the glass factory and some other buildings and a railroad spur track. Several men were building sleds from heaps of scrap lumber but we were too tired to do the same. I questioned our guards. They thought we'd be leaving soon but still didn't know where we were going.

Captain Daniels, a tournament-class amateur boxer, South Compound's first-aid officer, organized a sick parade on the furnace platform. He lanced blisters, massaged cramped muscles and did what he could for men running fevers. He thought some of them had pneumonia. I hadn't been on sick call in South Compound, but I knew him from giving him German communiques or BBC news summaries when he hadn't had time to listen with the others. He asked for volunteers to bring hot water from a building at the back of the courtyard. I joined them, not just because he'd been friendly back in South Compound but also, maybe chiefly, to make up for my collapse the night before. I thought it might help my knees to stay on the move, too.

We fetched the hot water in vessels like overgrown test tubes from taps in the factory's packing plant. The workers stared at us as we stood in line at the taps but didn't make eye contact. Afraid of getting in trouble maybe, or just afraid of us? We looked hard and raunchy. Between trips I massaged my knees and legs near the furnace heat. Colonel Luper, the South Compound Luper, not the Maxwell Field one, grinned at me encouragingly. My fatigue fell away. He knew when to be the strict disciplinarian and when to be the dutch uncle.

Daniels asked if I'd like to stay on and help him with the sick men when the column pulled out. His legs were bothering him, too, and we could tend our own aches while taking care of the more helpless. It was tempting, and flattering, but I wanted to leave with Kennedy and the others. I told him if I found I wasn't up to it I'd stay and work for him.

There was a latrine and cold water tap in a low building by the spur track. We weren't allowed to visit either without a guard at first but gradually the Germans relaxed and we went at will. We didn't know if the water were potable or not but we drank it anyhow and brewed up with it in the big test tubes.

Later in the morning the man who'd briefed block news officers in South Compound looked his people up one by one to give us the latest BBC communique. Where could he have gotten it? From a German? But listening to enemy radio broadcasts was punishable by death. We'd read of executions in German newspapers. Kennedy found out the news had come from the regular South Compound radio man, a slim, taciturn type who hadn't mingled much. I'd seen him many times in South Compound alone on the circuit in a French military greatcoat. The greatcoats were ankle length but he'd cut off the bottom of his to make an attached parka. What I hadn't known until Kennedy told me was that the radio's earphones were sewed into the parka and connected by wires running down the sleeve linings to the radio and batteries in the overcoat pockets. He'd monitored the BBC and German radio the whole time we were on the road.

The news was encouraging, especially behind us, where the Russians were driving. Maybe they'd overtake us yet. But kriegies needed something to worry about. Our side was bombing German industry. Did they know this plant at Muskau was only a glass factory? And we worried about having to hit the road any minute. Colonel Goodrich relieved us of that concern. He told us the Germans had intended to pull us out early that morning but he'd refused to transmit the order to us. We cheered. We learned he'd told them they could shoot us if they liked but he wouldn't order us out. He'd said angrily we were in no condition for another forced march so quickly and if we weren't allowed to regain our strength many would die on the road.

We didn't think he'd been bluffing, or that he'd had to. We didn't think the Germans had the stomach for a massacre with the Russians so close on their heels. Anyway, they were Luftwaffe, not SS.

Colonel Goodrich returned later to tell us the Germans had agreed to let us stay in the glass factory until the next morning. He asked for volunteers to go to a nearby building in the village to ease the crush in the glass factory. The other place was at least as good, maybe better. He didn't get many. Colonel Luper was more persuasive. He got as many volunteers as Colonel Goodrich needed.

We were still crowded but no longer a disorganized mob. Kennedy's bunch was in a group of nine men allotted about ten feet of space between a wall and the conveyor, with room to stretch out but not enough to leave space between us. We made a comfortable pallet with our pooled blankets and repacked our gear. I divided my possessions into two bundles, one to discard along the way if my knees started giving out and the other to carry as long as I could.

Late in the afternoon Colonel Goodrich announced we had a hard march ahead and should get down to bare minimums. Even safety razors. Just keep one for every three or four men. Was it Bolzano all over again, where I'd needlessly left so much behind? But I knew my knees wouldn't let me carry very much very far. I pared down ruthlessly. Short stories I'd written in Italy, most of my shaving gear, all my pictures except one of my mother and the two taken at P.G. 21 and Stalag Luft III. I gave the box of cigars and two cartons of cigarettes I'd salvaged and clung to on the march to the sergeants from my block, keeping only one carton I'd brought the whole way.

Colonel Goodrich advised us to eat well and retire early. We made a hearty meal of our emergency rations and bread and margarine issued by the Germans. We bedded down at dark, keeping on all our clothes except our shoes. There wasn't enough room for us to lie down on our backs so we lay on our sides, alternating heads and feet. Somebody's feet were in my face and mine were in his. We lay awake talking escape and, as at the barn bivouac, concluded we hadn't a prayer. Somehow I was in excellent spirits and, except for my stiff knees, felt strong. We slept fitfully because when one of us wanted to turn over we all had to. And when I lay in one position too long my knees would ache and my legs contract. I'd have to reach down between my body and the next man's to push them straight.

Once I was on my feet in the morning my legs didn't hurt at all. Colonel Goodrich said we'd be leaving later in the morning and that the owner of the factory had told him to take what lumber we needed for sleds and any glassware but not destroy any wantonly or damage equipment. We thought that pretty decent of him. I've wondered what happened to him and his factory.

After we ate the last of our emergency ration oatmeal, I

found a stout stick to use for a cane and rummaged through a heap of discarded clothing to replace my lost cap and glove. Kennedy and I visited the latrine, not knowing how long we'd be on the road and not liking the idea of squatting in the snow.

Inside the factory we learned Colonel Goodrich had returned to announce the Germans now said we had only twenty-eight kilometers, about seventeen miles, to walk and would do it in two easy, daylight stages. So it was Bolzano all over again. I felt like a fool. I poked through the litter for some of the things I'd discarded but couldn't face asking the sergeants for the cigars and cigarettes. I still had a handful of cigars, some pipe tobacco, and more than a carton of cigarettes.

We moved out as soon as we formed up. No head count. The senior German officers had vanished, and the junior officers left with us seemed almost to defer to Colonel Goodrich and Colonel Luper. It was said General Vanaman, Stalag Luft III's ranking officer, had been flown to Berlin to report on our health and morale and had promised to protest our treatment. Kriegies who'd bivouacked elsewhere joined the column as we moved through the town. I felt lively. After what we'd been through, twenty-eight kilometers in two days was a stroll. Muskau was jammed with civilians and German troops. They stared at us and we stared back at them. Men who looked like prisoners filled the windows of a huge building that looked like a prison. They waved at us and called out. We responded. We never learned who or what they were. We went through a park. Children were sliding down its slopes on sleds. I tried to buy a sled from a little boy, displaying chocolate and cigarettes, but he wanted more than I could afford.

Beyond the park, an *autobahn*. It appeared we'd no longer sneak along back roads, taking the long way round. The Germans' attitude had changed and so had ours. We didn't plod silently, head down but, setting our own pace, looked around us like tourists, talked a lot, and joked with our guards. Kennedy began describing a racy passage in Ayn Rand's *The Fountainhead*. We kept treading on the heels of two men in the rank ahead of us. We apologized and fell back. But we still kept treading on their heels. They'd fallen back with us. They looked around at us, smiling sheepishly. They'd been staying close to Kennedy, listening.

We had company on the snow-covered autobahn, a line of wagons longer than our column pulled by horses and oxen. All piled with straw and loaded with bedding, furniture, and well-nourished, rustic-looking families, mostly fair-haired, with lots of children. I asked one of the men where they were from. Poland, he said. Back at Stalag VIIA George Radovanovic had told me of the little boy who said when he grew up he'd be a landlord in one of the conquered lands. That's who these people were, Germans who'd dispossessed Polish farmers and now, just like us, were fleeing the Russians. They looked like decent people—most German civilians did—but I felt no compassion for them. They had it coming to them.

A woman called from a house at the side of the autobahn, asking who we were. A guard near us called out gaily, "Prisoners from the Russian Front. We made a big drive and have plenty more." I laughed, more with him than at him. "Oh, what a liar you are!" I shouted in German. He laughed with me. After that it became kind of a game. He'd tell onlookers we were Russian prisoners and I'd say he was a donkey, we were Americans, and our guards were running from the Russians. And everyone would have a good laugh, guards, prisoners, German civilians. It was fun.

My knees were stiff but didn't ache and I wasn't at all tired. I didn't sit down at rest stops lest my knees lock when I cooled down—it wasn't snowing but it was cold—but instead circulated, visiting friends. During one stop I fell into conversation with a Hundführer who'd given me a friendly smile. I told him I had cigarettes to trade for any bacon, ham, bread, onions or cheese he might scare up along the way. He promised to see what he could do. I gave him a few cigarettes and a cigar. He took some small apples out of his greatcoat and gave them to me. It came to half an apple per man for all of us in Kennedy's group. We ate seeds and all. Sweetest apples this side of Heaven.

After that I visited with the Hundführer every stop. I gave him a full pack of cigarettes and some cigars from my dwindling hoard to trade for me. I wasn't sure I could trust him to, but I thought it worth the smokes to subsidize a guard. You never knew when it might come in handy to have a pet German. He didn't get me much in the way of food but at every stop he looked me up to tell me how far we had to go. Late in the afternoon, toward the end of the day's march, he told me to move up a bit in the column to be sure of getting a good billet.

We stopped in a farming hamlet crammed with German transport. My Hundführer told me he'd see what he could get for me in the hamlet and would look me up in the morning. We were split into small groups and marched off. Our guards took us to a farmyard and ordered the farmer to open his barn for us. The farmer was cooperative and it didn't seem out of fear. He opened doors and showed us where to find straw, asking only that we not light matches or smoke in his buildings. I took a package of Canadian coffee to the farmhouse kitchen. There were other kriegies ahead of me cooking on the stove and bartering for produce with the farmer's wife. The whole top of the stove was occupied. I showed her my coffee and told her if she made a big pot for me she could keep the rest of the package. She clutched the coffee to her bosom like a baby and shooed a kriegie away from the stove to make room. When I rejoined the Kennedy bunch I had a big can of strong, scalding coffee.

Schoonmaker had made a pallet for us in the straw. We'd split up into groups of two or more to sleep together. With only one blanket per man, we needed to for warmth. When I took the can back to the kitchen several kriegies were washing their feet in hot water provided by the farmer's wife. She poured some into a basin for me. It was an exquisite sensation, sitting with my feet in warm water. My whole body relaxed.

It was dark by the time I returned to the barn, and I had to feel my way to the pallet. Schoonmaker and I stayed awake talking for a while. Near us the others were doing the same. The farmer came out and gave us a lantern to hang from the rafters, cautioning us not to let it fall into the straw. A guard shut the door and locked it from outside. We shouted in protest. What if the straw caught on fire? No answer.

My legs would draw up and my knees ache as I slept. The pain would wake me. When I pushed my legs straight with my hands the pain would stop. I was so close to Schoonmaker it woke him every time. He'd mutter but never cursed me.

In the morning the farmer and his wife had a huge kettle of water boiling on the stove and all of us got enough for a good brew. Several of us gave the farmer cigarettes. Just before we fell in for our march I ran back and gave him a cigar. He stared at it and fondled it. Tears glistened in his eyes as he seized my hand and tried to kiss it. He said it was the first cigar he'd seen since the war began. He followed me all the way to the formation, laughing and clapping me on the back.

My Hundführer looked me up after the column formed. He had some apples, cheese and bread for me. Not much. I suspected it was his own ration and he was keeping the trade goods for himself. I didn't care. If he stayed on as a Hundführer wherever we were going I'd have a good contact. And his dog knew me. He promised me that if he was detailed to our permanent camp he'd look me up.

Only another nine kilometers to go. A breeze. The previous day's holiday mood prevailed. We straggled, we talked, we looked at the sights. Civilians asking our guards where we were from were surprised to learn we'd come so far in so short a time. Our guards took credit for it and basked in their admiration. We stopped near some houses and I left the road to knock on a door. The man who answered was afraid to trade with me.

Hohendahl, who hadn't appeared in a while, came along in a staff car checking the column. He stopped to order a kriegie sitting with his back against a tree, legs no longer able to support him, to rejoin the column. The kriegie refused. Hohendahl said something sarcastic about flying gangsters not being able to take it and stalked away. We marked him down for the blacklist, a record of bad guys we'd been told the British in North Compound were keeping.

We had a rest stop near a *gasthaus*. Kennedy and I went in with our Hundführer but had to hurry and rejoin the column before I was able to make any trades or get Kennedy beer.

My Hundführer told me we were going to Spremberg, a city on the River Spree, and that it wasn't far away. I passed the news along the column, feeling smug about having such a good contact.

Spremberg was the largest town we'd seen. It had a sprawling marshaling yard crammed with rolling stock. A good target. We didn't like that. We marched through the outskirts to some buildings and garages surrounded by a high wall. It looked like an important bivouac and motor pool. Also a fine target. We were called to attention as we approached the gate and entered the compound in good military order. Some high-ranking German officers reviewed us as we passed. Among them was a major from Stalag Luft III we'd liked because he restrained room searchers when they got too rough with our property. He smiled and nodded at kriegies he recognized. When a guard threw him a Nazi salute, which had replaced the military salute after the attempt on Hitler's life, he responded with a flick of his hand, as if reluctant to Heil Hitler.

We fell out in the snow to await instructions. Wherever we

were bivouacking we hoped it wasn't here. Too good a target. No such luck. We were marched to some tremendous garage buildings and given bundles of excelsior to make into bedding. Leaving the others to take care of it, I went out to do some trading. I'd lost my pocketknife and wanted another and a cigarette lighter for Kennedy. Matches were in short supply these days. German soldiers were desperate for cigarettes. I heard some kriegies had gotten SS rings for them. I got the cigarette lighter but couldn't find anyone with a pocketknife to trade. Tea and coffee were also hot trade items. Some soldiers offered gold rings in trade but gold didn't interest kriegies. You couldn't eat it. A civilian—what he was doing in a military compound I couldn't fathom—offered a gold watch for ten pounds of coffee, with no takers. I wanted a messkit and a canteen but most had already been traded for and the few left were too high.

We were told to line up for soup at a building near the entrance, the biggest building in the compound. Long lines of kriegies stretched from steaming tubs set up beside it. With nothing to put the soup in, I looked frantically for a container. A kriegie at the head of the line said I could use his jumbo test tube from the glass factory after he ate his soup. I grew desperate as I neared the tub with nothing to put my soup in. He showed up just in time. The soup was thick and hot, full of potatoes and meat. My glass container was burning hot, but I endured the discomfort to wolf down the soup. It was great. Wehrmacht cooks sure knew how to make soup. Kennedy and I got back in line for seconds. I'd had to give the test tube back but Kennedy had borrowed one and we shared.

After soup call we went exploring. No one seemed to be paying us much attention. Kennedy saw a truck with no Germans near it and asked if I knew that urine rotted rubber. So we peed on the tires as an act of sabotage.

Guards came around ordering us back to the garages. We learned we were going to Moosburg. Moosburg, we said. Oh, Stalag VIIA. We knew it well. We were surrounded immediately by kriegies demanding to know all about Stalag VIIA. We loved it. Even the kriegies who'd been at Schubin now had to admit we were special.

We would travel in boxcars. In Berlin General Vanaman had insisted that we move on foot no more. Those of us with boxcar experience didn't like that. We'd rather have walked, even if it

280   took weeks. I went out and traded a cigarette each for two large empty German corned beef cans. We weren't going to be caught without containers at another soup call.

We were marched to the boxcars the next afternoon. On the way we passed *Volksturmers* being trained. Old men being taught to run and flop on their bellies in the snow, boys with outdated infantry weapons in mock attack on an equally outdated tank, and more tottering old men and young boys marching with *Panzerfausts*, "Tank Fists," an antitank weapon, on their shoulders. Few had uniforms. We weren't too impressed with the People's Army that was going to save Hitler's Reich.

Memories of discomfort and terror enveloped those of us from Italy when we saw the waiting boxcars. The best we could hope was that they wouldn't crowd us thirty to a car, the way we'd traveled before.

The column moved along the string of cars. Through their open doors we saw that many of them still reeked with manure that had been only partially flushed out and their floors were still wet. The Germans counted us into cars. Fifty to a car. Impossible. Thirty had been barely endurable. At least we were lucky enough to draw a car that hadn't been hauling cattle.

We had less baggage than when we came up from Italy but the press was intolerable. There wasn't enough room for everyone to sit and even the standees were crowded together. We piled everything but our food on the floor. The food we tried to keep near us, away from trampling feet. We didn't leave until dusk. We'd rearranged ourselves so everyone could sit, though wedged in. There were the usual windows high up at each end of the car. They were hard to get to.

We couldn't have all lain down were it not for the lesson of the glass factory. We slept in a tangle of arms and legs. When my legs drew up and my knees locked there'd be men lying on them and I'd have to wake them to extricate my legs.

One man had a little space, a rank-conscious major, a latecomer to our block. A tall, snobbish Bostonian, Harvard to the core (Schoonmaker was a Harvard man, too, but he was *our* Harvard man). He'd pulled rank on Kennedy and Buckner in South Compound when they caught him cheating at bridge, and now he pulled rank again to claim a private preserve under the window at our end of the car. Sometimes he'd condescend to let one of us look out his window.

The journey was a blur of crowded days and nights. Sometimes we were given hot soup in big cities. In Chemnitz we who'd endured Bolzano were frightened out of our wits when an early-warning siren sounded. We asked the major to let us remove the window so we could leave in a hurry if the area went to full alert, but he said we were cowards and refused. He'd never been bombed. The full alert never came and some workers passing by assured us Chemnitz wasn't a popular target. We offered them cigarettes for pocketknives or onions. Most of them were afraid to deal with us but several kriegies acquired pocketknives passed through the windows. I couldn't strike a deal for one.

Kennedy had lots of chocolate, his share of what he and Buckner had won in the block bridge tournament and ten bars he'd won guessing closest to the invasion date in a block pool. We lived mostly on that and the bread and margarine the Germans distributed from time to time.

Sometimes we'd have relief stops in the countryside. The doors would slam open, the guards would shout, "Aussteigen!" and we'd pile out to scatter and squat in the snow. We'd scarcely have our pants back up when they'd be shouting, "Einsteigen!"— "all aboard." We'd shout "einsteigen" to each other as we raced for our boxcars. The relief stops were the only exercise and fresh air we got.

Several kriegies plotted to bail out of the car when we got as close to the Alps as we were going to. Most of us thought it futile. None of us was strong enough for a cross-country hike even if we'd had the food for it and knew the country. Even the few who'd considered it abandoned the notion. We knew from the shouts and shots up and down the boxcars that men from other cars had tried.

The third night out, someone hung a blanket in a corner for a hammock and others followed suit. Kennedy went to put one up in the major's corner, but the major wouldn't allow it. He said he might put one up himself. He never did, though. It turned out sleeping in a hammock was worse than sleeping on the floor. It was much colder away from warm bodies, and under a man's weight the blanket encased him as tightly as a straitjacket.

Our third afternoon we were shunted into a siding in the marshaling yard at Regensburg. We knew from news reports it was a hell of a target and now saw the evidence with our own eyes. Bomb craters everywhere, and all in view bombed out and devastated. Even the Danube was drab and muddy, as if constantly roiled by explosions. What a relief that we were there too late for the USAAF and too early for the RAF.

On the fourth night our cars were shunted into a siding. I looked out the window to see if we'd arrived at Stalag VIIA but saw nothing familiar. Before dawn what sounded like hundreds of marching men woke us and we heard snatches of conversation and song in English. Someone beat me to the window to ask where we were. An American voice demanded who wanted to know. We told him who we were and voices shouted back we were at Stalag VIIA and they were a work commando marching to work. We exchanged information as the work commando streamed past. It was oddly silent afterward. I assured anyone who'd listen we were in no danger of being bombed because there weren't any targets in the area and anyway it was the wrong time for either night or day raiders.

The Snakepit

283

DAY CAME BUT NOT OUR wardens. It was more than an hour before the doors were opened and, stiff, weary and pleased to be rid of the cars, we formed the usual column of fives on the road. Hohendahl was there. We'd hoped we were rid of him. He went down the column dividing us into sections. Kennedy and the rest of us shifted positions to be sure we'd be in the same section. Hohendahl didn't like us moving around and said something sharp. When our section moved out Kennedy stayed put. He'd thought we were the first rank in the section behind us, not in the last rank of the one in front. Hohendahl gave him a shove from behind. I was outraged. No German had ever laid a hand on one of us before, and certainly not a snobbish corporal. (Later, when I compared experiences with ex-Japanese POWs, I realized how lucky we'd been.)

We were herded into an area of Stalag VIIA I'd never seen, a muddy, barren, temporary-looking compound surrounded by a single barbed-wire fence well manned by the guards who'd made the trip from South Compound. I didn't see my Hundführer among them. We remained outside the gate while Colonel Goodrich told us there wasn't room for us in the regular compounds and we'd be here a few days before being moved to a permanent camp. Such was our low state of mind we assumed that meant another march or long train ride and morale plummeted. Mine wasn't helped when captains and above were called from our ranks to move out immediately, Kennedy among them. It helped some when I learned they were going no farther than another Stalag VIIA compound. Kennedy assured me I'd be there, too, in a few days and that he would save a bunk for me. We divided our food and cigarettes and he left with the others.

I felt abandoned and, even in the crush, alone. Except for the few days he'd been in the hospital at Stalag Luft III, it was the first time we'd been separated in more than two years.

We were assigned to the buildings by blocks. My block got the last building and, we learned, the poorest. The other buildings were divided into rooms with benches and tables in them. Ours was a shed with a dirt floor, its only furnishings a few benches and tables and two five-foot-tall stoves that didn't give off much heat. Roof supports divided the room into thirds. We were counted, split into groups, given group numbers, and assigned spaces. Straw was brought in, and bundles of blankets. We spread the straw and made pallets of the blankets. There wasn't enough room for all of us to lie down at the same time so we divided into two sleeping shifts.

Daily thaws kept the compound slushy except at night, when the ground froze. Our only water came from two outdoor stand-pipes. The latrine was a a slit trench with an arrangement of peeled pine logs over it, like one the 98th had in Lakeland, Florida. You had to hook your knees over the bottom log and brace your back against the top one. One end had collapsed and it slanted. Though it was deep winter in Upper Silesia when we left Stalag Luft III but already thawing in Bavaria, the wind was still nippy to a bare behind.

Someone dubbed our compound the "Snakepit" and the name stuck. Life in it was irregular and disorderly, like camping out. We ate when there were rations, slept when it was our turn on the pallets, and roved in the slush to kill time. With no books or other diversions, we talked endlessly, mostly speculating about the progress of the war and our impending move, whenever and wherever that might be. We did have one diversion. It was quickly evident that Moosburg was at the center of Allied air activity. Not as a target, thank God, but as a rendezvous or turning point for formations from Italy and England striking targets in southern Germany. We knew Regensburg, Schweinfurt, Nuremberg and Munich were popular and tried to guess from the lines of flight which they were after, not easy because our view was restricted. We had to go inside during alerts and when we heard the mighty drone of large formations we'd rush to the small, dirty windows set high up to try and get a glimpse. There would be as many as four air alerts in a single twenty-four-hour period when the weather cleared and never less than two. The Stalag VIIA alert system made the alerts seem faintly ridiculous, just the feeble wail of sirens mounted on bicycles pedaled down the street. Maybe that's why I was no longer so frightened by

alerts, that and the fact rooftops were painted with POW identification and the dispensary across the street from our compound
had a huge red cross on its roof.

We were hungry all the time, except for a few combines
who'd reached the Snakepit better supplied than others. A group
from the room across from ours in Block 133 had built a sled before
the evacuation and traveled in style. They had food, bowls, and a
big cooking pot from the block kitchen. They always had an audience, more admiring than envious, when they cooked. The stove
they cooked on, one of the two in the shed, was fueled with
bundles of twigs brought in by the Germans and with bedboards
from dismantled sleds.

The rest of us survived on the German ration, distributed
daily. Soup, a little bread, sausage and cheese, ersatz tea and hot
water. Not nearly enough. I wished Doc Wynsen were there to
explain it was good for us.

After my first shift on the pallets, well-rested from sleeping
undraped with arms and legs, I bathed from the waist up at an
outdoor tap, a raw wind raising goosebumps, and shaved, using a
dull, borrowed blade. It didn't exactly glide over the scummy film
of cold water and hand soap, but when I was done I felt as clean as
I'd ever been in my life and refreshed enough to troll the compound for friends from whom I'd been separated along the way.
There were several I hadn't seen for a while, men who'd escaped
and been recaptured and brought to the Snakepit, among them
Jack, the man I'd become friends with at Sulmona after begrudg-
ing him some bouillon cubes.

I wasn't terribly surprised when the South Compound news
officer who'd briefed us in the glass factory put his block news
officers back to work. He gave us bulletins several times a day.
We'd post lookouts at the doors and go from section to section in
our block areas giving the news in a low voice to small groups. I
was delighted to have something to do and loved the expectant
hush when I knelt by a section and the angry shushes when
someone across the way talked too loudly during my delivery. It
made me feel important.

We learned we'd soon be moving out, to our relief only into
the main camp. We were divided into numbered groups for the
movement, which was expected to take several days though it
would go on twenty-four hours a day. My group's number was a
high one, and it would be a while before we went.

There was a limit to how many cigarettes and how much tobacco we could take. The Germans feared too many cigarettes threatened camp security. I had more than the allowable. I gave Jack, who'd left everything when he jumped from the train, most of my English cigarettes and agonized over choosing between pipe tobacco and cigarettes to get down to my allowable. I still didn't smoke cigarettes but they were better for trading. I settled on a combination. A little pipe tobacco for pleasure and the balance in cigarettes for business. But, as Kennedy always advised me, I wouldn't stand short. I packed a tin and half of Players pipe tobacco into a single tin, filled my New Zealand chocolate tin case with cigarettes and stuffed extra cigarettes into full packs to pass them off as packages of only twenty. Everyone was doing it.

We had room to spread out as the shed emptied. We lolled around waiting our turn. We calculated it would be late that night. The order came after midnight. We were taken in small groups to another building in the Snakepit where we formed in lines to be searched. The search room was warm. I slipped an overstuffed pack of cigarettes in my greatcoat pocket and dropped the coat on the floor when it was my turn to be searched. The search tables were hidden from view by a screen of blankets so those waiting in line couldn't observe the procedure and maybe find ways to beat the system. The clerk at the table had me pick up my coat. He kept up an easy line of talk as he went about his business. What had the march been like, what did I think of German scenery? No probing. I displayed the customary two-cigarette bribe but he shook his head. I assumed he'd be getting his share of confiscated tobacco. He was quick and thorough, even leafing through my homemade P.G. 21 notebook. He counted my cigarettes and put the overage in a separate pile. He divided the pile into two equal parts, pushed one back to me and added the other to a growing heap of confiscated tobacco. It was all out in the open so I supposed he wasn't getting a rake-off after all. He shrugged and said sympathetically, "You have more than allowed but I let you keep some of them. All right?" I thought it more than fair and thanked him.

After being searched we filed out through another door and waited under guard outside until we had a full complement. We entered the main camp through the gate I remembered from my previous visit. This time the interrogation was indoors, in a long, low room crowded with end-to-end tables. The interrogators were American sergeants, not German clerks. They sat at the desks with stacks of questionnaires at their elbow. They asked the usual questions about name, rank, serial number and date and place of capture as well as others we didn't choose to answer. The sergeants cooperated by deliberately slurring. They had to make a show of asking because there were Germans present. The newcomers asked as many questions as they were asked. About living conditions, parcels, showers, mail.

When my sergeant learned I was from Houston, he looked up and said, "I know you." His name was Bob Wright. He was married to the sister of a high school and college classmate of mine. After he was captured she'd written him I was a prisoner, too, and to be on the lookout for me. This contact from home, and already having a friend inside the camp, cheered me immensely.

One of the questions was about religion. Wright told me not to say I was Jewish. At one time the Germans had harassed Jewish prisoners there by moving them into a separate barracks and letting them wonder why. They hadn't been harmed and were moved back to their regular barracks just before a Protecting Power visit but Wright thought I should play it safe.

We'd have gossiped longer but men behind me muttered impatiently. From interrogation we went for showers and fumigation. Glorious as the hot shower was, I hurried through it to trade for a pocketknife, not knowing when I'd get another chance. A French shower attendant sold me a cheap, wooden-handled one for a pack of cigarettes. Highway robbery but I hadn't time to bargain.

After the showers we were marched through a misty rain in the raw, chilly predawn to two old stucco barracks in one of the warrens of compounds. I'd been cheered by meeting Wright but when I saw the inside of a barracks my spirits ebbed. It was worse than I remembered from my first stay. The air was dank and the floor wet, as if from a leaky roof. The place was dirty and looked long unoccupied. Two weak bulbs in the ceiling seemed only to add gloom to the cheerless scene. Instead of bedboards, the twelve-man bunks were strung with screening, most of them ripped and not looking as if they could support a man's weight. A grumpy old soldier with a limp grunted for us to follow him. He unlocked a door at the end of the barracks and issued everyone a bowl and spoon. He pointed to a pile of blankets and said to take two each. We took palliasses from a tottering stack. They were thin, hard and lumpy. We scrambled for the better ones and for bunks with the least-torn screening. Schoonmaker, Alvarado, Buckner, Brooks and I stayed close but exchanged few words. We were too depressed at finding ourselves in such a miserable place after expecting something better. Weary from a sleepless night, everyone spread their blankets and fell into their bunks with their clothes on. I was climbing into mine, dispirited, when I remembered the many dreary times I'd been thrust into other seemingly intolerable situations and soon become accustomed to them. In time, this would be no different. I went outside.

It was early morning, gray, cold and rainy. I found piles of boards, some with nails in them, strands of heavy wire, and an even greater treasure—a pinch bar some workman must have lost. I pried a double handful of rusty nails from the boards with the pinch bar and took a piece of metal grating and as many boards and as much wire as I could carry back to the barracks. I hid the pinch bar and nails in my belongings, slid the boards under my bunk, and turned in. I'd scarcely fallen asleep when ersatz tea was brought in. We rose and washed our faces at the kitchen tap. After I drank my tea I went outside. The other barracks was filling up with men arriving from the Snakepit. Ours was still half empty. Learning captains and above were in the next compound to ours, I went to the wire and asked someone to find Kennedy. He came to the wire and we filled each other in on what had been happening with us. He said things weren't too great in the captains' compound, either, but he expected conditions to improve after we settled in. There hadn't been a Red Cross parcel issue yet.

Back in my barracks, I went to work setting up housekeeping. I made two shelves, one with a plank nailed between upper bunk supports, the other with the piece of metal grating hung on wire. Schoonmaker and Alvarado made themselves shelves with some of my leftover boards. Others went out for boards and nails and when it became general knowledge I had a pinch bar so many of them wanted to borrow it I had to lend it out by roster.

While waiting for the Snakepit to empty we were organized into combines of six to draw rations. Without Kennedy there were only five of us. Lennie, a cheerful, agreeable guy we all liked, asked to join us. We were happy to have him.

The first rations were the usual German issue. When everyone from the Snakepit was aboard we got Red Cross parcels again. Two men to a parcel, plus an allowance for the days spent in the Snakepit. We were told Colonel Goodrich had tried to wangle a partial issue for the days we'd been on the road without them but had been turned down. We'd been so long without parcels even half-parcels seemed an abundance.

At first orderlies, English Other Ranks, brought our soup and brews and dipped out individual portions in tin cans. There was so much bickering among us about short portions or thinner soup that we turned to our solution for everything which was, setting up a roster, in this case to rotate the first combines in line. Later they left the soups to be ladled out by one of our own. Blood sausage, cheese and bread were issued in six-man portions to be divided within combines. Parcels were issued in combine lots as well by a parcel officer from a table in the barracks.

In a redistribution of kriegies from South Compound our barracks was asked for volunteers to move across the wire to the compound with the captains' barracks. My combine talked it over and volunteered in a group to rejoin Kennedy. We took our nails, boards and wire with us.

Even without Kennedy it would have been a good move. In our new home the bunks had bedboards instead of sagging screens and the palliasses were newer and plumper. And the rear half of the barracks, beyond the kitchen and washroom, had an interesting mix of nationalities—British, Indians, Serbs, Russians and Italians.

As soon as we'd moved in I went to Kennedy's barracks. I found captains lived better than lieutenants. More space and instead of three-decker bunks reaching almost to the ceiling, double-deckers that made the barracks much brighter and airier. The back half was unoccupied. The captains used it as a mess and recreation room. Kennedy was messing with John Grunow, the big mandolin-picking, perfect Aryan-looking captain, and another huge captain.

The first night in the new barracks I went to the kitchen, where officers from the rear bay were cooking. They were mostly longtime residents. I introduced myself to a tall Yugoslav officer and asked him if he knew George Radovanovic. He was very friendly but I had a feeling I'd committed a faux pas when he said he didn't know any Yugoslav enlisted men. He never saw them except at the chapel on Sundays and then was too busy looking up friends (obviously other officers) to have much contact with them. His name was Radomir Vidakovich. He introduced me to his friend, Ivan Andrejevich, who spoke no English. Rad, as I came to call him, interpreted for us.

Our Luftwaffe guards from Stalag Luft III weren't with us

long and I never did locate my Hundführer. When the camp's regular Wehrmacht guards replaced them I immediately began trading for bread for our combine. I knew it was only a matter of time before Colonel Goodrich banned all fraternization. Alvarado and Buckner and Schoonmaker and Brooks had paired up on the march. With Kennedy gone, I teamed with Lennie to share parcels. We bunked next to each other in the bottom layer of the aisle end of our triple-decker.

I was unable to contact Bob Wright with any regularity but found a friend from P.G. 21, British corporal Victor Skipp, who'd been a messing orderly. He'd brought German rations to our compound from time to time and had asked if I were there. I started waiting at the gate for the ration party and one day he was among them. We'd been friendly at P.G. 21 but not what you'd call close. Now we greeted each other like brothers. Sharing P.G. 21 was like a blood tie. We talked without pause the whole time he was in the compound. I gave him a pack of cigarettes and he said he'd bring me bread his next time in. It wasn't a trade. It was an exchange of gifts. It continued that way. When I had cigarettes to spare I'd give him some and when he had extra bread he'd do the same. He did trade for me, though. As I'd expected, when we'd settled into a reasonably normal routine, Colonel Goodrich ended trading with Germans and our noncoms were our only trading partners. Officers besieged the orderlies to trade for them but Skipp always saw to it that I had first refusal for food up for trade in his compound.

Skipp and his fellow orderlies were eventually moved to our compound, making our trading easier. We visited back and forth frequently. Often he'd sit and talk while I played cards, and once when I visited him he drew me into a darts game with homemade darts. He ran out the game before I scored a point, delighting our gallery of orderlies. Skipp's favorite pastime at home had been playing darts in the neighborhood pub. He'd carried his personal darts in a little leather case, the mark of the pub crawler, he said.

Skipp had escaped from Sulmona and liked to talk about his adventures as an evader as much I liked to hear about them. He'd lived a good while with an Italian family. He learned the language and went openly to movies with them. When we talked he peppered the conversation with Italian words and phrases. He loved speaking Italian and said when he got back home he was going to teach his wife. He was a construction worker in civvy street but intended getting a job where his Italian would be useful when he got back. His Italian idyll ended when he and several other English ORs were informed on by an old woman. Skipp wasn't bitter about that. He said the Italians were so wretchedly poor under German occupation that the reward money the old woman got was a fortune to her.

We had to stop openly exchanging gifts. Trading with Germans was already prohibited and now Colonel Goodrich decreed we couldn't trade with the orderlies, either. It could only be done by those authorized to do so for the benefit of all. It was his considered opinion, which turned out to be correct, that we could get more for our cigarettes that way. We were forbidden even to accept gifts from orderlies. I'd always been reg-happy, someone who followed the rules to the letter, but this one I disobeyed. Skipp and I were friends and if I had cigarettes to spare and he had surplus bread or saccharine it would be a shame not to help each other. We did it secretly, of course. Everyone deeply resented illegal trading if they weren't in on it. Skipp would visit my bay when I was out and hide things in my bunk, where sometimes I'd leave cigarettes. He'd slip me the saccharine as we walked around the parade ground. Only my combine knew what was going on. We shared the illicit spoils. There were others doing the same but, like me, trading only for bread and saccharine and never with guards and so not undermining the authorized trading committee.

The trade committee officer for our barracks was in the next bunk to mine and had me on his staff—was it delicious irony or because he knew I was trading illicitly with Skipp and must know the ropes—assigned to check a particular guard for bread and saccharine every night when he came on duty. Other kriegies checked the other guards, all of whom were kept under twenty-four-hour surveillance to be sure no unauthorized kriegies got to them. The bread and saccharine were distributed to messing combines in rotation, the combines repaying the cigarettes paid out by the committee. The committee got its start-up funds by assessing every combine five cigarettes. The privilege of buying more serious items—flour, macaroni, dried beans and sugar—was first determined by drawing cards. The merchandise was spread out on a table and combines made their selections in the order determined by their cards. When a purchase wasn't enough for all six members of a combine, the two-man teams drew cards for it. Combine members bickered a lot about what to choose. The decision in mine was unanimous when we had a shot at a particularly rare delicacy, a pound of dried beans. The committee flourished and eventually many things were distributed by roster rather than card-drawings.

Our news organization fell into place as well. We had no news of any kind our first few days in the camp. The German commandant wouldn't allow us to have newspapers and there was no public address system airing radio broadcasts. Papers bought with cigarettes from guards went from hand to hand and we throve on rumors. After I made contact with Skipp he often brought me news. The ORs, obviously not as strictly monitored as officers, had radios. Our South Compound news-briefer soon re-established his network and I was in business again.

We thought there might be informants among the foreign officers and gave the news to Americans and British only. I felt guilty not telling Rad but fortunately he'd learn the important stuff at chapel. I had the feeling he attended chapel so religiously not so much for the good of his soul as to visit with friends.

In my barracks I'd quietly notify the British and Americans among the other nationalities in the back half and they'd slip out in twos and threes to listen in the American end. In the beginning two of us shared the news job but the other man found better things to do with his time and I did it alone. The drill was to give the news at the noon meal when everyone was together eating. I went from table to table giving a summary of the BBC communique and repeated it to successive groups of eight or ten men from the back bay. The last official report was to Doc Cox, a first-aid officer from South Compound, and his patients in the dispensary but after Skipp came off duty I'd give him the highlights while we walked around the parade ground. After the fences that split South Compound kriegies among three different lagers came down to reunite us, the news officer briefed block news officers in a group. Stalag VIIA security was laxer than Stalag Luft III's had been and we were allowed to take notes, relieving us of the burden of having to memorize everything.

Before the fences came down, there was little to do in our cramped compound but visit between barracks. The frequent rains kept us inside with no books and no organized entertainment. I lingered over meal preparation and visited Kennedy or Rad a lot. Schoonmaker and I teamed up against Lennie and Brooks at bridge occasionally and once I dared join a pot limit poker game with Sam, the organizer of the Young Men's Hebrew Association athletic teams in South Compound, and some others who played every night. I'd watched them often and knew Sam was good. I'd been a competent player myself but not among players of his caliber. I didn't play for the fun of it. I played to win cigarettes. I'd heard desperate men always lost but I didn't dare lose. Lennie would never forgive me. I never played better, or maybe with more luck, before or since. I folded weak hands immediately and bet strong ones boldly. I took a good pot from a player who, on the face of it, had me beat and a bigger one on a bluff, benefitting from that trait that left my face frozen and inscrutable when I was so quaking inside with fear I could hardly breathe. Sam, who was sitting to my left and whom I'd rather have been my right so he'd bet ahead of me, had dropped out early. If he hadn't I wouldn't have run a bluff. He committed the cardinal sin of peeking at my hole card. When my last opponent threw in his hand I was too relieved to point that out. All he said, was, "I see you've played this game before," highly flattering, coming from him, and he never told anyone I'd bluffed. I won seven packs of cigarettes that night, a small fortune. I kept four packs for Lennie and me and gave one each to Skipp, Rad and Ivan. At the time Kennedy wasn't in need.

Even after Colonel Goodrich's command was consolidated, we saw little of our former roommates except Bogie, the irrepressible singer-joker-tap dancer. He was of Greek extraction and a great favorite of the Greek POWs and their unofficial trade representative among us. While he didn't stand short for himself and his compound he also served all our interests with the Greeks. Mike, our belligerent former roommate, visited us once. After he left, Alvarado admitted Mike was the one Eisenach had meant when he wouldn't pool our Christmas goodies because we had a food thief in the room. Mike had stolen bread and when he and another roommate, Pete, volunteered to bake a batch of cookies for us, Alvarado had caught them gobbling cookies as they took them from the oven. I got sore at Alvarado and asked why he hadn't told me back then so I could have had Mike moved out. Alvarado said he hadn't wanted to cause trouble. I couldn't stay mad at him, but I avoided Mike, and Pete, too, after that.

In our new bay, the front part was all closely packed bunks. The rear part had bunks on one side and wooden tables on the other, where we ate, read and wrote letters, just enough tables to give each combine assigned seating space three to a side. The table side was also used for FoodAcco auctions of trading committee items and as a distribution point for Red Cross parcels.

FoodAcco never achieved the heights it had in South Compound. With no influx of personal parcels its sources of supply were limited and more variety was available through the trading committee than the store. The store idea was abandoned in favor of a daily auction. We received points for items we provided for the auction and used the points to bid for items provided by others. We'd gather at the auction table even when not in the market to keep our fingers on the pulse of commerce or just for the sheer entertainment of it. The auctioneer would hold up a box of prunes as if it were an objet d'art and accept shouted bids. Sam, who was everywhere and into everything, was frequently the auctioneer.

Scarcity fed paranoia and sometimes we'd mutter darkly that the FoodAcco types were pocketing huge profits and on occasion suspected members of the trading committee, parcel officers and cooks of benefitting personally from their positions. That was seldom true. On the whole, considering the temptations, kriegies were a scrupulously honest lot. Occasionally a parcel officer was caught tampering with the parcel issue to upgrade one for himself or a friend. When that happened, his name was read out at appel and charges were drawn up to be forwarded to the War Department. With one exception the parcel officers never did anything really evil. The exception was a lieutenant colonel block commander who issued German rations and Red Cross parcels from the privacy of his room. He seemed always to get one of the good parcels and to have an abundance of food. A lieutenant in his block called on him and asked that parcels and rations be distributed in the open by junior officers. The lieutenant colonel said, "RHIP," and threatened him with court-martial for insubordination. The lieutenant reported him to Colonel Goodrich, who immediately removed the block commander of his command. We heard that Colonel Luper, now adjutant, gave him the kind of racking back that had made him notorious throughout the Air Forces, he was shunned by his fellow field officers, and charges were drawn up for the standard operating procedure post-liberation court-martial.

Closer to home, a popular kriegie was caught stealing food from his own combine. After everyone was asleep he'd eat desserts left out to cool. He got away with several before his combine partners lay in wait, caught him in the act, and beat him up, after which the senior staff put him under barracks arrest and had his name and crime read out in every bay. He was "sent to Coventry," as the British called being treated as if he weren't there, and had to cook and eat by himself. He was obliged to report every day to Colonel Goodrich. We figured he'd get a dishonorable discharge for sure. He stopped caring about his appearance and his eyes grew red-rimmed and frantic. Some kriegies wanted to bet even money he'd either go around the bend or kill himself. He did neither, and after his release from barracks arrest, some of us started speaking to him again.

We started a primitive library in the FoodAcco-trading committee auction area. It never amounted to much. The demand for the more popular books was so great that a waiting list could have hundreds of names on it. *Barnaby Rudge* not being very popular, I was able to borrow it as well as an unusual memoir by an obsessive balletomane titled, appropriately, *Balletomania*. I dug into *Tristam Shandy*, too, a book I'd begun and not finished at both P.G. 21 and Stalag Luft III. This time I was determined to stick the route but was only about a third through it when its owner was moved out of the compound and took it with him. (I bought a copy of my own some years later but have still to read it through.)

Breaking the Trade Barrier

KENNEDY AND THE OTHER captains were moved into our bay but we couldn't team up again because we were already firmly partnered. The American sergeants from our block at Stalag Luft III were moved into a barracks in our compound to take over many of the British OR's details. We had a lot of catching up to do. Like the British orderlies, they were working when block news officers gave the noon reports. Every day at their lunch break one of the sergeants would look me up to get the news for them. I was pleased, flattered, I guess, that they came to me instead of their own block news officer. I still had that old notion it was sergeants who really ran the army.

Early on we ate and cooked as a combine. I did most of the cooking and was the dessert specialist. We ate much of our food cold at first, but when we settled in we prepared innovative cooked dishes. We soon found cooking for six impractical without large enough utensils and began cooking instead in two-man teams. We made tiny, surprisingly efficient stoves of two tins wired one atop the other and stoked with twigs and bedboard shavings. The inventor called them smokeless cookers but they threw off so much smoke we changed it to cookless smokers. With dozens of us cooking at the same time the smoke in the bay was so unbearable that cookless smokers were banished outside by day and to washrooms and kitchens by night. To escape the miasma in washrooms and kitchens, some kriegies moved their cookers to the miasma of the aborts.

It took two men to operate a cooker, one to tend the food and fire, stoking the fierce little flames through slots cut near the top, the other furiously cutting shavings from a bedboard. Our fingers were perpetually scorched and blackened, our faces sooty. At night in the blackout, after shutters were opened, we crouched over our cookers coughing and hacking in the crowded vestibule, brewing up. I did more serious nighttime cooking in the kitchen, where the lights were on all night.

Lennie and I saved food from regular meals for snacks to go with the evening brew. We were often there until after midnight cooking, eating and drinking coffee. Later on, after Kennedy moved into our barracks, he'd join us. He'd contribute his share of wood slivers and the makings. And after the Allies crossed the Rhine, Kennedy and I would stay up after Lennie left us and sit with our backs against the still-warm side of the stove planning our futures. One night we were up until dawn planning a trip. I was to bring my mother to Phoenix to meet Kennedy's and then we were all going to Santa Fe together. (I didn't, we didn't, and our mothers never met.)

Despite the efficiency of the cookers, fuel was a problem and available almost exclusively only from forbidden sources—bedboards and excelsior from palliasses. We slung our sacks to free the bedboards, differently than at Stalag Luft III. The bedboards rested on long planks nailed lengthwise along the side rails of the bunks. We pried them off, slipped them into the palliasses on either side, stretched the palliasses over the sides of the bunks, and nailed them to the outside of the rails. However tight we stretched them, the palliasses sagged but were still more comfortable than when resting on bedboards. Palliasses themselves were a fuel source. We pulled out excelsior by the handfuls to feed into our cookers.

The Germans provided a limited supply of wood for the kitchen stoves. There was no individual cooking on them. Instead we brought prepared dishes to volunteer cooks at strictly scheduled periods, much as at P.G. 21. Volunteers cooked for all at our scheduled stove times. We prepared our dishes in tagged containers and when our team numbers were called lined them up on tables in front of the stove in the order called. A member of the team would hang around to make sure no one from another team usurped his place in line. We hadn't the handmade tin-strip utensils developed at Stalag Luft III and performed our culinary tricks in tin cans. The stove top was a forest of them with not enough room between them for a cook to burn a finger. The cooks would bake things in the embers for you if you brought a sealed can and did your frying for you in huge skillets provided by our hosts. If you didn't have a representative in the kitchen looking out for your interests, you'd be summoned there by number when your food was ready. Most of us liked standing around and watching the cooks work.

Sam was the quickest and most entertaining cook and naturally the most popular. I tried to work it so my containers got to him. He took special pains with them. Sam was barracks ration officer, too, speedy and precise dividing the German issue. The soups weren't as easy as the solids. He had the same problem with us as the English orderlies had. He'd call combines to the kettle by number, so we'd all have a chance at being first, and ladle soup into our bowls. We'd take them back to the table to eat, looking about us to see if other combines had thicker soup than ours. Someone was always complaining his soup was thinner, despite the fact Sam stirred the kettle vigorously between dips. Though he had the mind of a measuring cup, when the ration was shorter than usual he'd run out before the last few men were served and had to levy on those who'd already gotten their soup. We resisted so strenuously he cut down to be sure there was soup left for the last man. On occasion there'd be a little soup left, which permitted seconds, by roster.

Except for cooking and drawing parcels, our combine stuck together as a unit. We shared our German rations and ate together, sometimes pooling our resources for a major dessert. I'd put my shelves back up and kept our food, cigarettes and drinking cups on them. We kept our bowls and spoons in a cardboard box at the end of our tier. Our most prized possession was the pinch bar, which I kept hidden in my palliasse.

My parcel-mate, Lennie, trusted me to manage our food. He didn't complain when I began saving a small reserve even though it meant being constantly hungry. He smoked cigarettes only occasionally and I not at all so we had a supply to pool for trading. I had more cigarettes than he, but he contributed such harmony to our partnership I didn't quibble. And he never objected when I gave cigarettes to Skipp or my Yugoslav friend, Rad.

Such was the nature of parcel-sharing that I spent more time with him than with Kennedy. Scanty though our meals were, we spent hours preparing and cooking them. We could have done it faster, but time was not of the essence. We'd lie awake at night in our adjoining bunks talking. He'd grown up on a farm and I'd make him tell me about the huge meals they'd eat. It wasn't *Of Mice and Men*'s "Tell me about the rabbits, George," but "Tell me about breakfasts, Lennie." We agreed that when I came to visit him after the war (I never did), all we would do was eat and fish. He'd watch while I cooked and when I prepared desserts of sickening richness, he'd get to lick all the spoons and pots.

We seldom argued and when we did I never unleashed my evil sarcasm. Lennie was just too damn good-natured to pick on. The whole combine got along famously, more so than most combines, where the scarcity of food, the cold, and the cramped quarters fostered bickering. We had one serious argument, about the merits of restaurant versus home cooking, me pro-restaurant, he pro-home cooking. We both lost our tempers, were embarrassed by it, and continued the argument on a more temperate level. We never did reach a compromise.

Appels were held between barracks when we first arrived but later were moved to a crushed-shell parade ground behind the compound. The parade ground was separated from the compound by a barbed-wire fence and warning wire, but its wide gate was unguarded and we had free access to it and its deep, long slit trench lined with a mat of interwoven small branches.

We shared a reeking abort with an adjoining compound, a strafe lager for Russian prisoners. Our half was walled off from theirs but we could communicate across the barbed wire outside. For men who weren't supposed to be getting Red Cross parcels they seemed to have ample food to trade for cigarettes. Knives, too, and belts, wooden shoes, slippers, cigarette boxes made from airplane aluminum decorated with colored Plexiglas, and other handcrafted things. A Russian would stand on his side of the wire holding what he had to trade until he caught the eye of a prospect on our side. He'd hold his goods up and if the American was interested he would nod his head and ask the Russian how much, the only English most of them understood. The Russian would signal the price in cigarettes with his fingers. If it was too much, the American signaled back a lower offer. Negotiations continued with hand signals. If asked, the Russian would throw his merchandise over the wire for inspection. When a deal was struck the Russian would toss the merchandise over the wire and the American would weight the cigarettes with a rock and throw them to the Russian. Sometimes the guards ignored our barbed-wire market and other times they'd run us off. When they did that we'd trade less obviously. If they chased the Russians inside before a deal was consummated we'd throw cigarettes over the wire anyhow. The Russians would run out to pick them up under the guns of the

Germans. Apparently finding us easy marks, the Russians raised their prices. We resisted by sticking to a set price list, with anyone paying more being reported to the block commander. It worked. No kriegie was going to break the price barrier under the self-righteous gaze of his friends.

What I needed was clothing. I came in with nothing but the clothes on my back, two extra pairs of socks and three hand-kerchiefs. I got felt slippers and wool socks from the Russians for Kennedy and me. The slippers were for indoor wear only but a great relief to feet swollen from the damp cold.

After a couple of weeks I dared take a bath in the washroom. It was as cold as the P.G. 21 washroom. I took the opportunity to wash my longjohns. I'd worn them continuously for almost a month and they were too ripe to put on a clean body. It took them three days to dry in the damp bay, three days in which I was miserably cold with nothing under my uniform. After that, until the weather got warmer, I washed only feet, hands, head, socks and handkerchiefs.

Although we were on half-parcels, we were told Stalag VIIA was running out of parcels entirely, Allied bombings having inter-rupted traffic from Switzerland. The camp was running out of sugar and salt as well. I wasn't much concerned about the sugar. I'd brought a lot of saccharine from Stalag Luft III, and my combine had been using it and saving our sugar. We were ahead on bread, as well, through trades engineered by Skipp. We had both the coarse army type and a finer sort that was almost white. Maybe German officers ate it.

Anticipating the day we'd run out of parcels, I was pretty stingy with Lennie's and my rations until one evening I had an irresistible reckless urge. I said, "How about a bash?" Lennie's face lit up. He admitted that he hadn't been completely happy with the way I'd skimped but had trusted my judgment and not complained. So we sat down and ate our entire emergency ra-tion—jam, biscuits, chocolate, Klim and prunes—giggling like fools. While we ate I hummed a song I'd liked on the phonograph at Stalag Luft III but never learned the name of. We went to bed happy and when the camp ran out of parcels two weeks later, finding us with no reserve, we had no regrets.

Things got worse. As predicted, Stalag VIIA ran out of salt. Even the most appetizing-looking thick soups of barley and po-tatoes or stringbeans were flat and unpalatable. Soups were the best of the German rations, on which we were now utterly dependent. It was worse for Kennedy than for me. He'd always salted his food heavily and he found the soups revolting.

In the depths of the shortage, Rad got two pounds of salt from a friend of his at chapel and gave me a pound. It is the most valuable gift I've ever received. I gave some to Kennedy and the men in the combine but kept the bulk for Lennie and me. If Kennedy ran out I would give him more. No one would believe a prisoner would give away salt, and I was accused of trading with Germans. I had to get Rad to vouch for me.

During this particularly inappropriate period a German general and his staff made a tour of inspection. We stood at attention sullenly, muttering "How about something to eat?" "Where the hell's the salt?" It didn't improve our lot but we weren't penalized for our insolence. We even got hot showers. When we took off our clothes and saw each other naked for the first time since the move from the Snakepit, we were embarrassed by our bodies. Protruding stomachs, thin arms and legs. We tried to joke about it. Squeaky clean, we put on our filthy uniforms and marched back to our compound.

It was likely the general hadn't reported us to the camp commandant, a cruel, arrogant man who, unlike the commandant at Stalag Luft III, had no patience with or sympathy for terrorfliegers. It may have been merely a difference in personalities, but it might also have represented a difference in Luftwaffe and Wehrmacht attitudes. We'd been told that when Colonel Goodrich went to the commandant's office to complain about living conditions or some new abuse, the commandant would let him cool his heels for a while before giving him an audience and then insult him to his face.

After two weeks without parcels we were all weakened and undernourished (though nothing like concentration camp inmates or Japanese prisoners of war) and were pretty sorry for ourselves. We fell easy prey to illness, chiefly diarrhea and dysentery. Diarrhea was common, and men who couldn't wait squatted where they were. Every day men were carried fainting through our barracks to the dispensary in a back room. An Indian doctor ministered to patients there, assisted by Luther "Doc" Cox, a first-aid officer from South Compound. He wasn't a doctor but was knowledgeable and competent. (I thought surely he'd study medicine after the war but instead he remained in the service until he retired. In 1990 he published a book about his World War II experiences, *Always Fighting the Enemy*, Gateway Press.) There were a few bunks for the more serious cases but not much in the way of medicine. Standard treatment for acute diarrhea was rest and starvation until the intestinal tract could tolerate food. Among the more seriously ill was Guy, our South Compound roommate. He'd jumped the train and was brought to Stalag VIIA half dead from cold and hunger. He'd drunk ditch water and wasted away to skin and bones from dysentery, his eyes burning feverishly, before someone took him to the dispensary. He never groaned or complained even after his parcel-partner cheated him on their food. A remarkable man.

When we pared down for the evacuation from Stalag Luft III, he'd asked Schoonmaker if he was taking *Mathematics for the Millions* with him. Schoonmaker shook his head impatiently and said, "Of course not," as only Schoonmaker could say it. Guy said he'd carry it for him so he could continue studying algebra. Schoonmaker said he could have the book. Guy said no, he'd carry the book for Schoonmaker and give it back when we got where we were going. He carried it to Spremberg and had it in his pack when he jumped off the train, and still had it when they brought him to our compound. When he was strong enough to return to us he traded a Rolex Oyster Perpetual watch he'd ordered from Switzerland for twenty-five D-bars and lived on them until he was free of dysentery.

Luckily, despite an infestation of parasites, we never had the epidemic of infectious diseases our senior staff and doctors feared might sweep through our overcrowded ranks. The three-tier bunks were the special preserve of lice and bedbugs, which kept the more sensitive among us awake at night. If you'd stripped one of us you'd have known he was a kriegie at once from his welts and lumps. Apparently bedbugs didn't like my flavor because I seldom felt a bite and the only marks I bore were a lump or two at my ankles and wrists where my longjohns were tightest.

Everyone in our combine was sick at one time or another, and everyone but me had long bouts of dysentery, though I did have three or four bad days of diarrhea. Alvarado, the largest and strongest of us, was the first to fall ill, and precisely because he was so big. He needed more food than the rest of us to keep going but got only what we did. He never complained, and it was only when he reeled in the appel line and almost fainted that we knew something was wrong. Schoonmaker, who was standing beside him, held him up and got permission to take him inside and put him to bed. He didn't get his strength back until we went on full parcels. He was embarrassed by his weakness, and during the days he had to keep to his bed he worried about Buckner doing all their housekeeping. We all helped out. The men in our combine looked after each other.

I had fever and nausea with my diarrhea and was surprised that, like Alvarado, I was embarrassed to be ill. Schoonmaker had to bully me into going to the dispensary. Doc Cox kept me there a few days, more as a favor to me than anything else, I thought. Patients generally got the same food as everyone else, but it was quieter in the dispensary than out in the bay, and we had almost unlimited brews. While I was taking my ease among the more deserving, Lennie cooked and gave room service. Doc was permitted to break the regulations against tapping into the electric wires and made a loop of naked wire that heated a Klim tin of water to a boil in a couple of minutes. (We could tell someone was operating a hot wire illicitly when they caused a short circuit and our lights failed. Skipp and the other orderlies had a hot wire they used regularly after lights out.)

Doc Cox ran the dispensary for the Indian doctor with the help of volunteers from our bay. Schoonmaker and Brooks volunteered for a night shift, and after Doc Cox took care of me I did, too, out of gratitude. We worked two-hour shifts between eight P.M. and dawn, the going-off shift waking the coming-on shift. There were never more than ten or so patients in the double-decker bunks and not much we had to do for them, or could. Doc left written instructions every night for taking temperatures and giving medication and we'd record what we did on the patients' charts—five-by-seven cards. If a patient was too weak to visit the latrine bucket, we brought him a tin can. If he had to move his bowels, we'd help him to the bucket and steady him on it.

The light in the dispensary was dim but always on and I'd often read there, which didn't do a lot for my myopia. A curtain of blankets shrouded the patients from its weak glow.

Dispensary duty had its perks. Doc let us use the dispensary relief bucket even on our off-nights and on-duty nights he left us the makings of a brew on the table. On occasion he'd leave a surprise from a comforts parcel, condensed milk for our brew or a bouillon cube. On occasion, with Lennie's concurrence after we went on full parcels, I'd share one of our special desserts with him.

We hungered almost as much for word from home as we did for salt. We wondered if anyone knew where we were, or even if we were alive. We faithfully wrote our cards and letter forms but had little faith in them getting out of Germany. My first letter was to Luis Lupi, the AP man in Lisbon who'd helped me before. I asked him to cable my paper telling them where I was and that Kennedy and I were in good shape. We longed for personal parcels as well as letters. We were all encouraged when one personal parcel was forwarded to a South Compound kriegie, but another never came. A cigarette parcel would mean wealth because even in this period of acute shortages cigarettes bought food. And we wondered if our cigarettes stored at Stalag Luft III would be forwarded. I'd had six cartons in the warehouse when we left. They weren't, of course. I've wondered many times what happened to that staggering fortune in cigarettes. I hope the Russians got them.

A rumor raged through the compound. A shipment of parcels had arrived. Hundreds, some said. Thousands, said others, enough for full parcels. I wanted desperately to believe it but didn't until it was confirmed by our senior officers. A string of boxcars full of Red Cross parcels was on a siding outside the camp. We were expected to go on full parcels within a week. We celebrated that evening with what little we had and were restless far into the night.

Parcel day. We counted the boxes as they were carried in on shutters. Only enough for half-parcels. No need to worry. The rest were on the way. But they weren't. The German commandant said all cans had to be punched so we couldn't accumulate escape rations and he didn't have the manpower to punch enough for full parcels. Colonel Goodrich offered his word no Red Cross food would be used for escape rations and if the commandant wished, American volunteers would punch the cans. The commandant refused. There was talk of hanging him from the latrine with barbed wire from his own fences after liberation.

Half-parcels were enormously better than none at all, and it wasn't long before we were on full parcels. It was rumored that the commandant had been directed by higher authority to free them. Some parcels were better than others. The old-style British parcels were considered the poorest because of the food substitutes. The new ones were considered at least the equal of American and Canadian and sometimes better. We always hoped we'd be getting one when we lined at the tables to draw them. The name of the packing center was stamped on parcels and we quickly learned which center shipped the best and which the poorest. We'd count parcels to a good one and try to arrange a place in line that would get it. Or we'd try to influence the draw by sending a man from our combine we thought lucky. A lucky man was the one who'd last drawn a good parcel. If someone drew a good parcel in a batch of poor ones, the block officer was accused of favoritism. We were pretty childish and unreasonable where food was concerned.

On the way back to our table Lennie and I would tear open our parcel for a quick look before spreading everything out for a full check. Everyone did it. There'd be cries of delight and sour muttering. Lucky kriegies bragged, unlucky ones complained. All a lucky one had to do to enrage an unlucky one was to say, "Oh, I don't see where you got such a bad parcel." They did that a lot. When Lennie and I got a bad parcel we sulked until we got a good one. We got one so bad everyone admitted it was a lousy draw, which was some consolation. A can of turnips—we already had more turnips in our German issue than we liked—and a can of damsons (English plums) instead of jam.

American parcels were more consistent than British but still varied enough to keep them interesting. As at Stalag Luft III, we preferred raisins over prunes and tuna over salmon and almost any jam over grape. Some parcels had the usual two D-bars but others had one D-bar and something new, chocolate pellets with brightly colored candy coatings, called M&Ms. We preferred two D-bars. D-bars were the best emergency ration and were good for making desserts. M&Ms were for immediate bashing. We divided them equally. Toward the end a new type of American parcel outshone all others. Dehydrated corned-beef hash, powdered eggs and, most precious of all, dried onion flakes. Lennie and I never got one of the new and improved parcels but Schoonmaker and Brooks and Alvarado and Buckner did. Sometimes when Lennie and I were eating, Schoonmaker or Brooks would casually sprinkle onion flakes into our bowls, an act of whimsical generosity.

We grew more daring and creative on our cookers as we learned our instrument. I did Spam Wellington, chunks of Spam in dough, and whips in sardine can piecrusts. Piecrusts were even more labor-intensive than at Stalag Luft III. We mixed flour made of ground hardtack and dried bread cubes with margarine and water, lined the sardine cans with it, and baked late at night over the dying fire in the stove after regular hours. Kriegies were elbow to elbow there long after the barracks slept, shuffling their sardine tins to what they perceived to be hotter spots.

Everyone loved whips, with or without crusts, mixed with jam, coffee, cocoa, prunes or raisins and sometimes with M&Ms for a crunchy surprise. Sam was the king of whippers. He always had lots of Klim. He made his whips with a whole can of it in a washbasin. He'd stir for hours. Then he and his parcel-mate would bash the whole thing at a sitting with an appreciative audience.

Indian officers and the British ORs did most of their cooking out-of-doors whatever the weather. Indian Red Cross parcels contained lentils, flour and extra fish and sweets instead of meat. The Indian officers made their flour into thin pancakes that looked to me like big tortillas. They molded balls of dough, which grew larger and larger and rounder and thinner as they were tossed from hand to hand. The process always drew an audience. They baked the pancakes on a sheet of tin. It was about the only time we saw much of them. They kept to themselves and most of the British officers avoided them.

The ORs' cookers went a step beyond ours. They had blowers on them for quick, hot fires. ORs didn't fool around with elaborate desserts, preferring heavy British fare. Their most elaborate dish was Yorkshire pudding. Because they worked and had better contacts than officers, they had greater abundance and variety than we did. Skipp once fried half a dozen fresh eggs before my very eyes. The first I'd seen in more than a year.

Soon after we went on full parcels a bashing craze swept the compound. We vied spreading the most elaborate feasts and trying to see how much we could eat in a single meal. It meant going hungry other days but we thought a good bash was worth it. We bashed ceremoniously, laying everything out nicely and making sure we had an audience before tucking in.

After we bashed we'd lie in our bunks feeling carefree and idiotically happy even when we knew we'd be on short rations for days. Only our emergency ration was inviolate. Schoonmaker and

Brooks resisted the craze. However much we tantalized them with ostentatious bashing, they would not be swayed. When they finally succumbed they went the whole hog, devouring everything in their path and surviving on the scanty German ration for several days.

Lennie and I bolted down our food when we bashed. It gave us a brief sensation of boundless plenty. Others bashed slowly, prolonging the pleasure but, we thought, diluting it. One kriegie ate with incredible slowness, taking a tiny dab on the tip of his spoon and lifting it to his lips in slow motion. It took him up to an hour to eat a sardine can of whip I'd destroy in a minute or two. I'd watch him with fascinated loathing.

A Rumanian in Kennedy's barracks was reputed to be the prewar concert master of the Bucharest symphony. He walked with two canes on a shattered leg. He'd been wounded first by Russians when Rumania was a German ally and more seriously by Germans when Rumania switched sides. He gave a violin concert in Rad's end of the barracks. Men came from other barracks to listen and he played to standing room only. Rad and Ivan saved a place for me on Ivan's top bunk. He played with his eyes closed, his feet spread wide to favor his bad leg, painfully thin, face pinched, clothes ragged and dirty. I thought he played like an angel. We applauded ferociously after every number and he bowed with a tired, sick smile. When he tried to stop we applauded him into two encores, after which he said his leg would support him no longer. Before he left, several officers came around collecting donations of cigarettes and gave them to him with the delicacy of someone presenting a bouquet. He accepted with tears in his eyes and stumped out on his cane.

Usually when I visited Rad we'd sit on Ivan's top bunk. A three-way conversation, with Rad interpreting. We talked about politics—officer-class Rad and Ivan were fiercely anticommunist—and the war and a lot about our lives in our own countries. We had a long discussion about our foods. When Rad spoke of his favorites, all accompanied by slivovitz, which I'd never drunk but knew I wouldn't like, his eyes would sparkle with the memory and he'd smile, smack his lips and kiss his fingertips with a spontaneity you wouldn't expect of one with such patrician bearing. They were always feeding me. The first time they pressed an American biscuit spread with jam on me I refused. Food was too scarce to give away. Rad reminded me he'd accepted cigarettes from me and I must allow him to give things to me. Like many Europeans I met in the bag, he repaid favors many times over and cigarettes were more precious to him and Ivan than mere food. So after that I followed my baser instincts and wolfed down whatever they offered.

The Circus Grounds

AT STALAG LUFT III, what I'd feared most was friendly bombers. At Stalag VIIA, it was my nighttime sorties to the abort. It was the trickiest navigation I'd done since the square-search convoy missions that got me lost over the Mediterranean. Our bay was at the front of the barracks, the abort was behind it. There was never a glimmer of light anywhere. It was always an emergency run because you never left your warm bunk until your bladder absolutely insisted. It was a tortuous grope in the pitch-black darkness along the narrow aisle between sharp-cornered bunks, through the small washroom, left into the big washroom, right into the kitchen, left into the back bay and, feeling your way, down another black aisle to the rear vestibule— watch out for the door—left to the exit door. Outside, your troubles were just beginning. First the water hazard—a deep mud puddle—then the incinerator and the heap of tin cans beside it and the smaller puddles on the way, and finally, if you overshot, the barbed wire of the parade ground fence where it anchored on the abort. The abort, at last, was as dangerous as the journey getting there. Its crumbling brick steps were a menace. Many kriegies, dazed with sleep, numb with cold and reckless with urgency, fell there. You felt your way past complaining bodies for a place at the urinal trough and put you hands against the wall to measure your distance and to steady yourself. Sometimes you missed, and were cursed, or the kriegie next to you missed and you cursed him. It was too dark to identify the guilty so no lasting enmities developed. When you returned, though easier in body, you had the same obstacle course to negotiate and your own bunk to locate. I sometimes went past my bunk and didn't realize it until I reached the front door. You knew a bunk wasn't yours if there was someone already in it, complaining.

Everyone made night runs, sometimes more than one. It

was the cold and the liquid diet. We missed the inside abort in Block 133 and I even longed for the inside latrine at P.G. 21.

We weren't allowed out during alerts. Our hosts left a large pot, like the one from which our soup was ladled and we hoped it wasn't, to accommodate us in the vestibule. We weren't to use it except during alerts but there was a lot of furtive cheating. During alerts you'd find a line at the pot whatever the hour. A posted notice proscribed using it beyond its capacity. When it was full we were to collect at the back door and get a guard's permission to visit the abort two at a time. Guards were surly in the small hours and slow to respond to our calls. We often couldn't wait. There came a time every morning well before dawn when you had to stand clear of the pot and aim in the darkness to keep out of the overflow. It was only after I started helping out in the dispensary occasionally and Doc Cox let me use its pot that I stopped dreading the night.

We cooked more after we went on full parcels, making fuel an ever-increasing problem. The German fuel issue wasn't enough to keep the kitchen stove lit for even one meal a day for everyone. Someone discovered our barracks had subflooring, and a colonel who'd been in charge of road building and stump pulling details in South Compound organized wrecking teams in every block. Every day, in a different block, we moved bunks in front of windows, against entrance doors and around the area to be plundered. We told the Germans we were mopping the floors and housecleaning. One team pried up the floor while another ripped out the subflooring and a third broke the boards into kindling. The first team replaced the top flooring right behind the second team so only a small section of subflooring was ever exposed. If the Germans came in, we made a great show of shoving bunks around while the top flooring was nailed back in place and the broken boards shoved under bunks. By the time the Germans were among us we were sweeping and mopping industriously. We acquired a hell of a reputation for cleanliness, and despite our sagging floors, our hosts never caught on.

When the South Compound kriegies were fully established in Stalag VIIA, parole walks resumed. Since they continued the old South Compound priority list and Kennedy and I had already had ours, we weren't included. We were damned bitter about that, too, as only veteran kriegies jealous of their tenure could be. We resented seeing men we perceived as upstarts returning from walks with food they'd traded for and tales of eating at an inn. We whined to whomever we knew who had a shred of influence, but it didn't get us a walk. (Our seniority wasn't entirely ignored, however. We were near the top of the list when a limited number of GI comforters were issued and we got one each.)

As a kind of consolation prize for missing the walk, Kennedy gave me my lighter back. He had plenty of matches now. I gave it to another kriegie on his promise to get me a Russian-made aluminum and Plexiglas cigarette holder. I intended converting it to a pipestem. He returned it when he couldn't get one, and I gave it to Buckner.

Our Stalag VIIA compound had a barber, an English orderly who plied his trade all day long at two cigarettes a head. Alvarado had cut my hair in South Compound, but here he couldn't get hold of scissors and I welcomed the barber's services. There was always a long waiting list for haircuts but because we had a mutual friend in Skipp, the barber took me at my convenience. We'd become pretty good friends before we learned from Sam, to our mutual surprise, that the other was Jewish. I wasn't active in the faith and I suspected he wasn't either, but it added to the bond we already felt as fellow kriegies.

The weather improved earlier than it had in Upper Silesia. When we began having sunny days we took the shutters off the windows and lay on them against the side of the barracks out of the wind, stripped to the waist, reading, playing cards or talking endlessly about the progress of the war and when it would be over for us.

During barracks searches we were moved out to the parade grounds until they were over. There was an alert during one of them and we watched a huge force of American bombers pass over at high altitude. A bomber with a smoking engine started lagging behind its element. All of us knew the dangers of falling behind the formation. There were German fighters waiting to pick you off. We watched breathlessly, sweating it out, as it fell farther and farther behind. Suddenly, with a last great burst of smoke, the engine quit streaming vapor and the aircraft began catching up with its element. A spontaneous sound, half sigh of relief, half cheer, drowned out the muted roar of engines. We were still on the parade ground when the planes returned from their target. I was sitting with my back against a post supporting the guardwire near a blanket draped over the wire. I heard the fearsome swish of a falling bomb. I lay flat and rolled behind the blanket, as if its thin folds would protect me. The sound died away. No explosion followed. It must have been an empty fuel tank jettisoned by an escorting fighter. I crawled sheepishly from behind the blanket and joined a huddle of men in the slit trench. I didn't come out until the all clear.

I no longer trembled in my bunk at the sound of engines in the night even when British night raiders flew over the camp. Mosquitoes on nuisance raids, I assumed. One night a plane came over so low its racket woke the compound, followed by a crackling burst of its guns, a sound like wood splitting. We figured it was strafing boxcars on a Moosburg siding. Next day we learned we'd been right and were grateful it hadn't happened the night we were held in boxcars outside the camp.

We waited impatiently while the Allies massed for the assault on the Rhine, and when the Americans secured the bridge at Remagen and poured across we rejoiced wildly. But we worried that we might be moved again. To Hitler's redoubt or into the Alps in the Brenner Pass area, to be held as hostages by fanatical, last-ditch Nazis without the facilities or desire to feed or shelter us. Kennedy and I agreed that if that happened we would try to escape at any cost.

John Winant, son of the ambassador to Britain, was, in fact, moved out. Colonel Goodrich later learned from the Protecting Power that he and other VIPs, including generals and a relative of the British ruling family, were in a group kept constantly on the move lest the Allies locate them and send a spearhead to rescue them.

Our senior staff began preparing us as they had at Stalag Luft III. We were ordered to assemble emergency rations and were organized into disciplined, manageable squadrons by twelve-man tier. As an aged-in-the-bag first lieutenant and the senior officer in my tier, I was automatically squadron leader. Fortunately for all of us I had little to do but check the roll before the German appel and report absences to the block commander. Groups of squadrons were commanded by captains or majors. We got a commander we liked, a Captain Atlas, because of his size appropriately named. He was a big, blustering but good-natured fellow.

Anticipating a late-night move to take us by surprise and force us to leave radios and other contraband, our senior officers ordered us to be ready to move on a moment's notice with everything we intended taking with us, a sort of permanent stand-by alert.

After the British and Americans drove into Germany we drew a huge map on the wall by the mess tables and marked their progress. We were careful to show the front as described in German reports while picturing for ourselves the actual front according to BBC reports. A translation of the official German communique was posted daily by another map elsewhere in the barracks. Though the Americans were some distance away and the Russians even farther, we entertained hopes of one day being liberated by a fast-moving column, preferably American.

Trigger Downing, an American in the rear half of our barracks, built himself a radio from parts he'd illicitly bought from a guard and one night invited me to listen to it and translate the German communique for him. Crouching with him in the darkness, listening to the radio with neither the other kriegies nor the German guards aware of our secret, I had the same special, privileged feeling I'd known when I was a child hiding in a tree house with my best friend and looking down at the world.

Our morale soared, and not just from the war news, when the Luftwaffe moved in to take over the administration of Air Forces prisoners. While the Wehrmacht colonel was still Stalag VIIA commanding officer, Colonel Goodrich now dealt with Luftwaffe officers and with much more success than he'd had before. Appel were shorter, food better and more plentiful, and we were allowed to keep a blackout light on all night.

With no organized entertainment, our mess tables were the center of social life, the only place with light enough to read, write letters or play cards. Before, all such activities ended with lights out, now they could go on as late as we liked with the last man up turning off the light. Almost as late as we liked. Sometimes when a guard found us playing cards in the wee hours he'd think it a cover-up for something nefarious and send us off to bed. As in our room in South Compound, when we played cards we spread a blanket on the table and folded another under us for a cushion. Bridge partners sat side by side instead of across from each other. Kennedy and Buckner played bridge for cigarettes and never wanted for smokes. Lennie and a partner got into a game with them against my advice. Naturally Lennie lost his cigarettes.

Red Cross parcels began reaching Stalag VIIA directly from

Switzerland. There'd long been rumors that the Red Cross was dickering with the Germans to bring supplies to prisoners of war in trucks provided by the U.S. Army driven by POWs on parole. We'd thought it too good to be true. Allied air power had paralyzed German rail transportation, and days went by when we heard no traffic on the main line to Munich outside our camp. If the Germans couldn't satisfy their own needs, why would they bother to satisfy ours? But one day I heard an uproar and ran out of the barracks to the wire overlooking the outer compound. And there was a white-painted American truck with Red Cross markings. A detail of enlisted men was off-loading parcels into a storehouse. Stalag VIIA was to be the distribution point for Red Cross supplies to POW camps everywhere.

Some of the old parcels had to be distributed to make room in the storehouse for the deluge of new ones. We were offered the option of drawing an Indian parcel instead of the usual British or American. For variety's sake Lennie and I volunteered. There were lentils in the parcel, and tiny pebbles in the lentils. We had to pick them out one at a time. I'd bought some noodles from the trading committee and intended cooking lentil soup for us just like my mother used to make.

That night Captain Atlas interrupted my preparations by calling his command together. "Fellows," he said, and we grinned, as we always did when he called us fellows, "get ready for some bad news." We stopped grinning. "We're going to be moved." Consternation. Our worst fears confirmed. He went on to explain we were moving across the street in a consolidation of Stalag Luft III personnel. We were too relieved to learn we weren't taking to the road again to hate him.

Kennedy and I stayed up late reviewing the situation. We agreed that in the new lager if it were okay with Lennie we'd team up again. No one slept much that night. We lay awake expecting to hear, "'raus!" It didn't come.

In the morning I took my lentils to the kitchen to preboil them on my little stove. Lentils needed a lot of cooking. They were boiling nicely when a hubbub reached me from the bay and Lennie rushed in to tell me we were moving out. I left the lentils and ran back with him to find everyone demolishing bunks and tables for firewood to take along, oblivious to the hardships we might be creating for the next occupants. Our senior officer put a stop to it, saying we were to leave the furniture, such as it was, and bedboards. We stole the bedboards anyhow and pried what wood we could off the bunks without actually wrecking them. Though we hadn't accumulated nearly as much as we had in South Compound, with our bedding, food, clothes, eating utensils and firewood we had more than we could carry easily, even across the street. Lennie and I had long since emptied our palliasses of excelsior for fuel so we made litters of them with side boards from our bunks. Many kriegies did the same. With nothing left to be done, and still no order to move, I finished cooking our lentil soup. There was a lot of it but Lennie and I wolfed it all down. One thing less to carry.

It was afternoon before we moved. We lined up alphabetically between two barracks to be checked off by name. The Germans said we'd have to leave our palliasses. They were adamant until one of the brighter kriegies among us promised we'd return everything that belonged in the old barracks after we were settled across the street. Being Luftwaffe, they were reasonable and simply marked down the names of those with returnable items.

What a procession we made in our hundreds. Raucous, ragged and dirty, dragging palliasses like Indian travois, with one man proudly trundling his worldly goods in a borrowed wheelbarrow. In the distant background, Munich was being bombed. Smoke rose from countless fires, bursting flak peppered the sky and the attacking planes glinted silver. There were two great bursts of flame in the air which could have only been exploding bombers. It took some of the shine off the festivities.

We moved into the same compound we'd been in when we came up from Italy, but into tents, not barracks. We'd called the holding lager the Snakepit. We were to name the tent area the Circus Grounds. We milled around looking for friends while we awaited instructions. I'd gotten separated from Kennedy and was looking for him when we were ordered to reassemble by combine for tent assignments. We were to sleep in the tents in three long front-to-rear rows. The least desirable row was the one down the middle, where anyone negotiating the two narrow paths between rows could stumble over your head or feet. Lennie and I drew the middle row.

We brought armfuls of excelsior from bundles dumped outside the tent and made a nest of it and our blankets. When everyone had done the same, the only open spaces in the tent were the foot-wide lanes between rows. We didn't expect ever to be comfortable there but had learned from experience it was better to adjust than brood. Our space was between tent poles, its only advantage. We strung rope between the poles and hammered nails into them with my pinch bar to hang our equipment on and piled our firewood on either side of our nest to protect our territory. That done I went looking for Kennedy. He found me first, with Charlie Jennette, our flying adjutant, in tow. Charlie had been living in the lager with other kriegies from Center Compound and was established in a barracks. He invited us to use the facilities there at will.

Kennedy and I agreed that now was the time to leave our parcel-mates and team up again. Lennie was a little hurt when I brought up the subject but was aware how close Kennedy and I were and agreed to change if we could find him another partner and place to sleep. Being a captain, Kennedy had been offered a favored place in a barracks vestibule. He let Lennie have it and Lennie soon hooked up in a combine of old friends.

Being back with Kennedy made the move worthwhile, tents and all. Though the thought of living without eating, washing and shaving facilities dismayed us at first, the war news kept our morale high, we slept comfortably on excelsior between blankets and GI comforters, and we quickly accommodated to Circus Grounds life. More quickly, in fact, than our hosts did. It took them a few days to hit on a workable system of issuing hot water and rations. Initially the hot water lines were so long we tired of waiting and heated our own water on our cooker.

Being back with my pilot wasn't untrammeled bliss. He couldn't start the day without his brew, which meant we had to rise early before morning appel instead of lolling in the comfort of our warm nest until the last minute. He was usually decent enough to get up first and start the brew going while I gathered my resources to rise and shine in the raw morning air. He worked on the timing until we were just having the last sip when the appel bugle blew.

The compound was so crowded appels were massive but, in a way, merry because Gallatowicz, our jolly lager captain from South Compound, was in charge. During our first appel on the Circus Grounds, South Compound kriegies crowded around him to shake his hand. We came to like another German just as much, a flying corporal who'd lost a leg in combat and was now reduced to earning his pay counting kriegies. To him we weren't terror-fliegers, just a crowd of fellow airmen. He would hang around after appel bantering with us and talking flying in picturesque broken English.

We came to prefer our tents to the barracks even though we had to walk across the compound to Jennette's quarters laden with tin water cans and other paraphernalia to wash our faces and brush our teeth or to shave, which we did only two or three times a week, using a window for a mirror, and to wash ourselves and our eating utensils at a cold water tap in the dank washroom. When we visited Jennette in the crowded, smoky bay with its dirty floor and accumulated grime in every crack and crevice, we missed the cool, clean air of our own quarters. Once our hosts achieved their celebrated German efficiency, life in the tents ran as smoothly as in the barracks.

They brought our rations to the mouths of our tents for distribution, hot water lines moved expeditiously, appel were orderly, and parcels, full parcels, arrived on the dot. For our own part, we made what open space there was outdoors our kitchens and living rooms, kept our twelve-man squads but readjusted from six-man combines to two-man teams, and got the trading committee and news organization going again. Kennedy was now the senior officer of the squad but it was a while before I could persuade him to take over. He didn't like telling people what to do except in an airplane.

The only thing we continued to do as a combine was to draw rations and parcels. Schoonmaker usually took care of that for us. It was not too onerous a job except when bulk food from the Red Cross stores was distributed in lieu of regular parcels. It was brought in daily, with not enough of some items to go around, condensed milk, for example. One can for sixteen men. Combines drew lots for things like that, and when our combine was lucky the two-man teams drew lots for it.

We were just beginning to settle in when it was announced at appel that our hosts were most displeased with the condition in which we'd left our barracks across the street. Where were the bedboards? Our senior staff said we'd better give some back or they'd come confiscate them and maybe find things they shouldn't. We were all to take a few bedboards to the front gate and maybe head off a general search. Most of us did. They made a pile impressive enough to keep the Germans out of our hair.

The Germans pretty much left us to our own devices. Stalag VIIA was crammed with prisoners from all over and getting fuller by the day, just too many of us to control. There were no more searches, and except at appel the only Germans in the compound were the usual roving guards. And what guards. Old or partially disabled men armed with Italian rifles or captured British weapons. One of them told me he'd been too old to serve in the First World War.

We spent a lot of time at the center road wire watching new arrivals being marched to lagers all around us. Among them was a large contingent of kriegies from West Compound and several from South Compound who'd been unable to march out with the rest of us. Some were assigned to the next lager over. I knew Erwin Feld, the opera singer, had been left behind because with his combat injuries he couldn't have kept up. I went to the wire and asked if he was among them. Someone went for him. He looked in fine shape. He and the West Compound kriegies had walked to Stalag VIIA all the way from Nuremberg, more than two hundred miles away. Their prison camp had been near a marshaling yard the RAF bombed almost every night. Although the pathfinder planes marked off the camp with flares, they'd all feared a near miss would do them in. The bombs fell so close to the camp they shattered windows and buffeted the prisoners about. (A kriegie who'd made fun of me in South Compound for being afraid during alerts and who had been at Nuremberg later called out to me from across the wire to apologize for it.) Feld had brought two French POW parcels with him. He said they had more sweets than other types and threw me a slab of concentrated jam that could be eaten like candy or mixed with water and spread on bread.

And still they came. A group of British navy men was brought into a lager behind ours. There was an American among them who shouted his "there I was" story to us across the wire. "You're the first Americans I've seen in years," he yelled from a pack of Britishers. "I'm sick of these Goddam Limeys." He'd been a sailor on a private yacht converted to Coast Guard duty that was torpedoed one hundred fifty miles off the South Carolina coast soon after we entered the war. He and his surviving shipmates had been picked up by the submarine that sank them and brought all the way to Germany.

There were Indian enlisted troops in a compound adjoining

the one with the navy men in it. While watching them one day, I saw a kriegie I'd known in South Compound. He'd tried to escape several times at Stalag Luft III, then had jumped off the train to Stalag VIIA, been recaptured and brought to the Snakepit, and escaped from there, too. I started to yell at him but figured he had his own reasons for hiding among the Indians. Officers often slipped into OR camps hoping to go out with a work party and escape. He saw me staring and made a surreptitious gesture of recognition. Then, deciding to abandon secrecy, he yelled to me to tell Colonel Goodrich he was with the Indian ORs, his feet were in bad shape, he had dysentery, and he needed medical attention and food. He had been caught at a railroad station in the Alps. It took a while but Colonel Goodrich got him back with us.

We news officers got our briefing in the British section of the lager. It was a long way from the nearest guard post and we could talk freely. Two of us gave out the news in our tent, starting from opposite ends and working toward the middle. There were so few guards patrolling the compound we didn't even have to keep our voices down. The news continued to be remarkably good but the only map we could follow it on was painted on an inside wall of a barracks all the way across the compound. After every news summary there'd be a parade of kriegies from the tents to the barracks.

In Happy Expectation

IN APRIL 1945, TWO DAYS after my twenty-eighth birthday, we got the news that President Roosevelt had died. We were supposed never to reveal our emotions after sensational news lest it tip off the Germans to our secret source, but none of us could hide our shock and dejection. When I gave the report, after the initial shock kriegies would ask, "Who's president now?" and I'd say, "Harry Truman," and they'd ask, "Who's Harry Truman?" The same questions I'd asked at the briefing. German propagandists gloated over Roosevelt's death. They said it was God's punishment for his many crimes. It really pissed us off.

Our appetites and our cookers were insatiable. We foraged constantly for twigs and scraps of wood, hundreds of us, all relentless as predators. Wheat, which we bought from the trading committee when our number came up, took hours of boiling to be plump, soft and edible. We ate it with Klim, margarine and sugar. I'd never eaten boiled wheat before. (When I found it on the menu many years later at the Nut House Restaurant not far from Travis Air Force Base in California, I had some for sentimental reasons. Pretty good, too.) For a while I had a private source of fuel. Our tent ropes were anchored to big stakes, a good foot of which extended above the ropes. I'd slip between the tents out of sight of guards and my fellow kriegies and hack away at them with my knife. The blade was dull and the wood hard. It could take as much a half an hour to split off one good sliver. But I never considered it wasted effort. Fuel was dear and time was cheap. Soon everyone was doing it.

Kennedy and I hung back when kriegies started tearing at the twigs lining the slit trenches. Without the lining there might be cave-ins and we thought some day we might need those slit trenches. The kriegies at first stole the twigs only after dark but as German supervision lessened they did it in broad daylight, ripping out not only twigs but also the heavy posts and crosspieces supporting them. Kriegies toiled at the logs with pocketknives until two axes, source unknown, appeared. It was only when the slit trenches had been despoiled beyond repair that Kennedy and I joined the assault. The twigs were disappointing, green, damp and usable only when mixed with drier fuel.

A potentially major source of fuel was tantalizingly out of our reach. The unmanned pillboxes that overlooked slit trenches were made of heavy sandbagged logs but were protected by such thickets of barbed wire we couldn't get to them.

After the slit trenches we attacked an interior fence. There was already an opening in it cut by Russian prisoners when the Germans combined adjoining lagers. The assault began at dusk. The noise brought a sentry, who asked us to stop. When we didn't he leveled his rifle at us and we ran, so many of us we made a great clatter. When the panic subsided, we decided he was bluffing and resumed the attack. He had been bluffing. Now he ran off and fetched a German officer. The officer pleaded with us to stop, promising to have fuel sent in the next day if we stopped the destruction. We didn't believe it but were so tired from our efforts we went back to our tents. In a few days only tangles of barbed wire marked the line where the fence had stood.

We sometimes got raw potatoes from the trading committee. They were far superior to the boiled ration potatoes, which were soggy and often bitter. The committee made most of its deals over the wire. Some ORs had the run of the road and would assemble outside our lager to do business. As the Russians had done in our previous lager, they'd toss things over for inspection. German guards after cigarettes often joined the ORs. That's where the raw potatoes came from, also bread.

German influence continued to deteriorate. We were far too many to be guarded by so few and they were well aware of it. With Allied troops pressing ever closer, we were aware they would do nothing to us for which they'd be held accountable. They came into the lager only for the two daily appels. They no longer even brought in the parcels and other Red Cross supplies trucked in daily to the outer compound. Prisoners did it.

We lived each day in happy expectation. It could end any time and this might be the day. Living in tents contributed to the feeling we'd not be here much longer. We weren't being held prisoner, we were camping out. The crowding and the squalor were to be expected. We liked cooking and eating and playing cards and gossiping out in the open, and even though there was hardly room to turn around in we had more true freedom than we'd known since capture.

With no Germans around to object, we stayed outside during alerts, even at night. We gathered for daylight raids as if they were for our entertainment and cheered the fighter planes that regularly patrolled the tracks outside the camp and sometimes flew over us at low altitude and rocked their wings in greeting. The guards manning the machine gun in the goonbox at the main gate never fired at them. Most mornings, before the American fighters came, a German single-engine jet fighter would buzz us. To frighten or entertain us? It flew so low its slipstream made our tents strain at their ropes. We called it "Whistling Willie" because of the sound it made.

One day our flying friends hit four targets simultaneously— Munich, the nearby rail junction at Landshut, something in between, and Regensburg. We couldn't see the Regensburg planes on their bombing runs but we watched them going and coming and saw the billowing smoke from their marker bombs. The smoke from those marking the other three targets seemed almost close enough to touch.

Over Munich, the bursting flak was like a fantastic fireworks display, but for us the most spectacular attack of the four was that on Landshut. We heard the bombers before we saw them, a distant, throbbing roar of countless engines. Then they swarmed into view at high altitude, small as metallic bees. As the formations rumbled closer, we saw their covering fighters weaving over and under the bombers. The bombers came in elements of seven, one behind the other, in an endless wavering line, hundreds of them. The first elements marked the target with smoke bombs. Those that followed reached their initial points and wheeled toward the target, dropped their bombs, and flew away in another endless line. The visibility was so good that despite their altitude we could see the bomb bay doors were closed as they passed, reassuring to those of us who were a little alarmed on their first approach. The planes seemed to avoid flying directly over the camp except for one stray group and some fighters who came over low to say hello. Smoke billowed from the target long after the all clear sounded. We hadn't seen a single German fighter challenging the bombers.

Raiders sometimes dropped propaganda leaflets as well as bombs. A guard gave one to a kriegie. It reported Allied military successes and urged the Germans to give up their hopeless struggle.

During the almost nightly RAF bombings of Munich, when we heard explosions Kennedy and I would leave our tent to watch the sky light up. We felt nothing for those under attack. Our only concern was that a bomber might stray off course and, seeing the scatter of lights in the camp, think it an imperfectly blacked-out city.

Other than bombings, our only group entertainment was an occasional impromptu concert for as many kriegies as could push their way into a barracks kitchen. Some bandsmen from South and Central compounds had gotten instruments from somewhere. Most often it was only trumpet, accordion and bass but sometimes there'd be as many as six jamming away without written music but with boundless enthusiasm.

We still hated having to go to the outdoor abort after dark. The journey was even more treacherous than in the barracks. The way ran a perilous course between tent ropes and a slit trench, and finding your way back to your own sack was tricky. The lane between the rows of recumbent kriegies was narrow and there were no bunks you could feel your way along in the pitch dark of the windowless tents. I'd slide my feet along and change directions when they encountered a head or feet. The only way I could get back to our pallet was to whisper Kennedy's name when I thought I was close. He'd whisper back and I'd home in on the sound. Once I stumbled over a leg in the aisle and my steadying hand pushed flat against a face. I felt the nose in my palm, the eyes at my fingertips. The owner of the face cursed me. I cursed him back and crept away, grateful for once that the darkness was impenetrable.

Kennedy and I visited back and forth with Jennette. Usually he preferred coming to the tent area because visitors weren't encouraged in his jampacked barracks. He did invite us to a spread there once, under the circumstances an act of splendid generosity, when he'd gotten his hands on some Canadian coffee. He cooked for us on a sort of shelf fastened over a horizontal section of the kitchen stovepipe. Fried Spam, mashed potatoes, a whip and the first noninstant coffee we'd had in months. A memorable repast made more so because for the first time in weeks we sat at a table. We brought him a bag of Canadian sugar and almost had to fight him to make him accept.

Jennette's hospitality didn't end with the meal. He broke out a new razorblade he'd been saving from a long-ago personal parcel and let us shave with it, providing a wash basin of water and a real mirror.

With our lagers filled to bursting, the Germans took down interior fences separating American and British prisoners to create one huge compound, creating barracks space for the Circus Grounds people. The German staff, as if washing their hands of us, let our own senior staff handle all arrangements. On moving day we gathered with our belongings and waited for the signal to move out. We'd been assigned to specific barracks by squads with no detailed instructions on how to arrange ourselves. Our space was in the rear half of a barracks directly across the road from our present lager. Kennedy and I agreed to try for a bunk next to the kitchen wall for its comparative privacy.

At the signal, Circus Grounds kriegies surged across the road. It was like the Oklahoma Land Rush scene from the old Richard Dix movie *Cimarron*. The entrance to our bay was at the back of the barracks. Instead of using it, Kennedy and I climbed in the first open window and staked a claim to a choice kitchen wall tier for our combine. The six of us brought our gear in through the window and drew lots for bunks. Kennedy and I won first choice and took the middle bunks at the window end of the tier. Mine was in the corner, Kennedy's by the window. Later we regretted not taking the top bunks. They were a climb to reach but closer to the ceiling light and out of the constant traffic through the window.

There were four times as many kriegies in our compound as there'd been in a comparable area at Stalag Luft III, some of them sleeping on the floors of barracks that hadn't any bunks and some spilling over into tents. Shoehorned into quarters as we were, we nevertheless had almost as much outdoor space as in South Compound even if there were more kriegies roaming it. The compound was U-shaped, embracing the cookhouse square. We were all Americans in the rows of barracks on both sides of the main road all the way to the square. The barracks on one side of the square were RAF and RCAF and those on the other British army. Our sprawling lager was hemmed in on three sides by a German outer compound and other lagers occupied by what we considered "foreign" prisoners—not American or British. Beyond the wire on the fourth side we now had a glimpse of the outside world—a cheese factory, trees and grass.

German presence was minimal. Except for the occasional roving guard, who almost never came into a barracks, the only time we saw Germans was at appel, and even appel was left largely in the hands of our own senior officers. No one even considered escape. We had orders from above not to try. We assumed that liberation was near. It didn't entirely reassure those of us who'd been moved from both P.G. 21 and Stalag Luft III.

Except for that small concern, we were content. We came and went as we pleased, we watched air raids, we were reunited with British friends we hadn't seen since Chieti. We even had firewood. There were bedboards in our new barracks. Kennedy and I immediately slung our palliasses and appropriated them.

American ground officers from Schubin, including those moved from P.G. 21, moved into the compound. We were astonished. We thought they'd long since been overrun and liberated by the Russians. They'd walked all the way from Poland and been months on the road but looked fit and healthy. Lew Lowe, a particular friend of Kennedy's, gave us a full account. The first stages of their evacuation ahead of the Russians in bitter weather had been frightful, worse than our march. But the tempo slowed when the Germans became as exhausted as the prisoners and they settled into a leisurely pace, sheltering in barns and towns along the way, trading for food at every stop until they reached the town of Hamilburg and its POW camp. They'd been there only a short time when an American spearhead broke through and plunged sixty miles to liberate the camp. Lowe had been among those who'd climbed aboard tanks and trucks for the dash to freedom. The column was ambushed by German troops. Some prisoners died in the attack and others were retaken. Of those who weren't, some set out for American lines and others returned to the prison camp to equip themselves for the sixty-mile walk. Those who went back found the camp back in German hands. When a new American advance threatened the camp, the prisoners were marched out and allowed to set their own pace and to leave the column to trade for food. Red Cross trucks had regularly patrolled the column distributing food parcels. The Schubin men said they'd been much better off on the road than here in Stalag VIIA. It had been fun and they missed it.

When the Center Compound kriegies came in, their SAO, Colonel Darr Alkire, who was senior to Goodrich, had taken over. When the Schubin contingent arrived their senior officer said, "Are there any generals here?" Told there weren't, he announced, "I'm your new SAO." He was the U.S. Army's ranking colonel. His West Point classmates were all generals. The new SAO was a sterner disciplinarian than Colonel Goodrich and immediately organized us into companies and platoons, with orders to salute all officers superior in rank. When the order reached us down the chain of command, our own senior officers said it would only be necessary to salute colonels and above.

In the pleasant anarchy of our days Kennedy and I stopped having meals at regular times, cooking when the mood took us and as frequently as we had food. Other teams did pretty much the same. There were far too many men in our bay to be accommodated at tables and we usually ate outside or sitting on bunks.

We also cooked outside. Even without smoke the air inside the barracks was rank with the smell of sweat and dirt and at night the dim bulbs in the ceiling were shrouded in fetid haze. Despite the odors we carried with us, the smell of the barracks hit us when we stepped in the door. Usually we cooked in a plot around the slit trench behind the barracks across a shell path from the abort. There was a little rise along the path and we dug pits into it and built our fires there under flattened tin can grills. Often the six men of our combine cooked side by side and squatted on the ground to eat together. On windy days we'd brew up in the washroom, coughing. The floor was a constant litter of cookers, ash, cinders and wood scraps.

A kriegie traded his watch for a Red Cross parcel and he and his partner ate the whole thing. It started a new bashing craze. Almost everyone with a watch or a gold ring wanted to do the same. A Rolex Oyster Perpetual went for as much as two and a half parcels in trades with foreign prisoners in compounds across a double-wire fence from ours. Their demand for gold and watches was as strong as the kriegies' was for a good bash. They were concerned about an uncertain future when watches and gold might mean survival. We never knew where they got the parcels. As with the Russians, deals were made by shouting across the wire. A handful of men on the other side seemed to have cornered the market in trades for rings and watches. Often they didn't deal directly with us but through a runner. A kriegie after a trade would wrap his item in a handkerchief, stuff it in a cocoa tin with a tight lid and toss it over the wire. The trader would examine the merchandise and, if it suited him, go into a barracks and bring out payment. The German guard patrolling the space between the fences, whose job it was to prevent such trading, would pass along goods too heavy to toss over the fence. He usually got a cigarette or two for his services.

Watching the trading and bashing, Kennedy and I got caught up in the frenzy. Wouldn't it be great to have a big bash before we were liberated and it was too late to really appreciate it? I had my broken hack watch and the cheap working one Kennedy had traded me for a broken Gruen I'd won in South Compound. Someone who knew watches had told me the hack watch was easily fixed. I figured there should be a market for it. There wasn't, not in the compound with the active traders or in the Indian compound on the other side of our lager. I even contrived to slip out of the compound and canvass other nationalities. We put the working watch on the market. We wanted two cans of Klim, two cans of jam, two cans of meat and sugar for it, more than enough for a major bash with all the whip we could eat. I tossed it over the fence to a runner for a major trader. He took it to his principal in the barracks and came back with an insulting offer. I asked for my watch back. He went back into the barracks and returned with an offer not much better. I refused again and demanded my watch. He wanted to negotiate further. I said if he didn't return my watch I'd report him. To whom I wasn't sure. He wasn't, either, but knew if he stole the watch he'd be out of business. So he threw it back, with a mocking smile.

A kriegie who'd come in with the Schubin contingent had been a watchmaker before the war and had traded for a watch-repair kit during the march. He'd traded for a wheelbarrow, too, and came in trundling his possessions in it. I took Kennedy's broken Gruen to him. It was gold and fifteen-jewel, the traders' minimum requirement for a two-and-a-half parcel deal. He said it would be easy to fix if he had the part, which he didn't. When he learned we had a mutual close friend and I hadn't had a fresh egg in more than two years, he gave me one he had left from the march. I wanted to share it with Kennedy. It was his watch that led to it. He said it wasn't enough for two good bites and neither of us would benefit. So I had the egg for breakfast. Best egg I ever ate.

A likable, boyish Scot from my bungalow in P.G. 21 came to my barracks looking for me and we brought each other up to date. We visited back and forth often and drifted into business together. The British preferred bully to Spam and tea to coffee, the Americans quite the opposite, so I handled his people's Spam and coffee and he made trades for my side's bully and tea. It added considerably to our popularity within our own circles.

Those of us who'd been in P.G. 21 together, British and Americans, shared particularly strong bonds. British officers I'd known only slightly greeted me with affection I hadn't anticipated, having been accustomed to English reserve. My closest friend among the British, an officer named Harry Fincham, hadn't been sent to Stalag VIIA. We didn't reestablish contact until after the war and then only by mail. (We corresponded regularly until he emigrated to South Africa and our letters gradually trailed off.)

SPRING CAME MUCH EARLIER in Bavaria than it had in Upper Silesia. There were days when it was warm enough to bathe without flinching at the washroom pump or kitchen tap, but getting dressed in the same filthy garments took much of the pleasure out of it. We discarded our filthy longjohns but lived in our equally filthy wool shirts and trousers. The trousers rubbed the hair off our knees and the grime peppered them with blackheads. No one was ever offended when we'd pull up a pant leg and casually squeeze them during a conversation.

Eventually the Red Cross brought in summer uniforms and most kriegies got one set of cotton underwear and a khaki shirt and pants. We got blue barracks bags as well, solving what had become a serious storage problem. The barracks were so packed with bunks and tables there'd simply been nowhere to put things.

There was no official announcement but a rumor spread that the Red Cross had taken over most of the Stalag VIIA administration and the Germans were guarding the camp as much to keep their own people out as to keep us in. Our own fighter planes seemed to be keeping us under surveillance because they flew over frequently and not only buzzed us and rocked their wings but also on occasion entertained us with aerobatics. We heard a fighter had shot up a Stalag VIIA honey wagon that ventured out of the camp onto the highway.

We believed that story, and that the Red Cross had truly taken over, when the next honey wagon that came in to pump out our abort was painted white, with Red Cross markings. It did as much for our soaring morale as any stunting fighter.

There were still a few pristine strips of grass between barracks preserved by fences. In one of their few positive acts, the Germans pulled down those last interior fences. As soon as I learned of it, I hurried to a spot between two neighboring barracks and picked a Red Cross box full of dandelions I'd seen growing there. Knowing nothing of dandelion greens, and being greedy, I picked everything in sight, favoring the larger, mature plants. I boiled them up with half a can of Spam for Kennedy's and my first green vegetable in months. The greens were bitter, but we ate them and shared with Alvarado, Buckner, Schoonmaker and Brooks. Apparently other kriegies knew even less about dandelion greens than I did because when I went back to my plot it hadn't been picked clean. This time I took only young and tender plants and boiled them with a whole can of Spam, a delectable dish which we devoured to the last morsel. We could feel the vitamins rushing to all the places starved for them.

Throughout the turmoil at Stalag VIIA the parole walks continued. All the older kriegies had their walks and now they were being granted based on service to the camp as well as seniority. Kriegies returning from the walks said civilians were eager to trade for cigarettes, coffee, tea and soap and displayed their goodies in evidence. Kennedy and I wanted desperately to get outside the camp to taste uncrowded air but even more to get in on the bonanza. Even though we knew we'd soon be free and have access to such things, as with parcel bashing we wanted some of the good things in life while we could appreciate them most.

Kennedy kept after the parole walk officer to get us on the list, saying if he couldn't go I deserved to because of my work for the news staff and occasional jobs for the trading committee.

We didn't get on a parole walk but we landed something just as good. The wood-gathering detail. Our senior staff complained of the shortage of fuel for our cooking needs and persuaded the wavering German commandant to permit small parties of kriegies to go out on parole, under guard, to forage for wood. Kriegies were selected for wood-gathering on the same basis as for parole walks. Kennedy and I were assigned to one of the early details.

About twenty of us gathered at the lager gate with our blue barracks bags to receive instructions and be checked off the list by name. We endured the delay restlessly, eager to be off. We could keep half the wood we gathered, the other half was for the cookhouse. And we were to spend our time gathering wood. No trading. Kriegies who'd ignored the rule on previous details hadn't been penalized but we knew that could change any time. We intended risking it.

A single guard accompanied us out of our lager, through two more interior gates and the main gate. We were counted at all the gates but without a roll call. We took the dirt road past the Snakepit. The Snakepit was as crowded as ever. A solid rank of men at the wire held up trade goods. We shouted greetings but didn't stop. Indian prisoners from an unfenced tent encampment lined both sides of the road offering Red Cross canned meats. We slowed down to dicker with them despite our guard's urging but didn't buy. The price wasn't right. Straw-lined trenches along the route were heaped with potatoes. We broke ranks to paw through them, upsetting our guard. The potatoes were soft and had a bad odor. We didn't take any.

We passed little heaps of withered carrots and turnips on both sides of the road. How had they gotten there? Fallen from Heaven? They weren't worth stopping for. The road entered a wood. The guard sat down under a tree, lit a cigarette we'd given him, and told us to be back at three-thirty. We couldn't believe our luck. The other kriegies scattered into the woods. Kennedy and I and the kriegie who briefed me and the other barracks news officers headed for a clearing where a civilian was chopping on a felled tree. I asked him if he had bread, eggs or potatoes to trade. He took an end of bread out of his pocket, obviously his lunch, and offered it to us, asking nothing in return. His face was weary and defeated. We were embarrassed. We ate better than he did. He insisted. We divided his bread in three. We ate it and each gave him two cigarettes. He made an almost courtly bow and went back to work.

Beyond the clearing a stream with a log across it ran through marshy ground. We hesitated. Should we waste time looking for another crossing or take off our shoes and socks and negotiate the marsh? Why waste any time at all? We kept our shoes on and walked through the mud. We pushed through a thicket beyond the marshy area to a clear, brawling stream we thought must be the Isar River. A lovely spot.

A detail of prisoners whose scraps of uniforms we didn't recognize was toiling on the bank under the sour gaze of a German soldier. They knew we were American officers and wanted to know what we were doing walking so openly. They were amazed to learn we were prisoners of war, too, and more amazed when we told them we'd left our guard sitting under a tree. Their guard barked at them to get back to work and ordered us back the way we'd come. We said goodbye to the prisoners and crossed the stream on a footbridge to a path running along the other side.

Drunk with freedom, we hurried along the path breathing virgin air, the limpid, musical stream on one side of us, sweet-smelling woods on the other. We snatched at leaves and buds as we passed. Our stream merged with a broad, swift river, the real Isar. We trotted beside it toward a long wooden bridge. There was a cluster of houses on our side of it and a big farmhouse on the other. We agreed to hit our side first. A combat-equipped soldier guarded the bridge and it was mined. The big charge attached to its supports looked like a bomb. The guard gave us a hard look when we went by but didn't challenge us.

The first house belonged to the mayor. A sign in front said "Burgermeister." An Italian prisoner of war in a white smock answered my knock. He said he worked there and could trade nothing. I told him I had been a POW in Italy, but before he could tell me how much that impressed him, if in fact it did, Kennedy rushed me away. There was trading to be done and I was not to stand short. The gate of the next house was invitingly open but there was a sign saying "Bose Hund." "Bad Dog." I saw no dog. Maybe the sign was to scare off kriegies and other undesirables. Anyhow, dogs were one of the few things I wasn't afraid of. But I was very nervous at the prospect of addressing a civilian. We went to the back door. There was a dog but he only raised his head to look at us. The gray-haired woman who answered my knock looked like all the grandmothers in the world rolled into one. My nervousness vanished.

She was puzzled by my appearance but not frightened. I bowed the way the woodchopper had and spoke the German words I'd been rehearsing in my mind since leaving the wood-gathering detail. "How are you this morning? We are American prisoners of war and have soap, tea and cigarettes to trade. Have you any eggs, potatoes, jam or bacon?"

She smiled, maybe at my brand of German, and invited us into the house. It was obvious we were her first scroungers. We followed her down a cool, dim, clean hall—how strange to be in a real house—to the kitchen. Spotless. Even the wood-burning stove. It looked like the parlor and dining room as well as the kitchen. There were three other Germans in there, a wary old man and two women, one middle-aged, the other younger but plain and tired-looking, sewing on a foot-operated machine. We all shook hands as I introduced myself and my friends. I chatted companionably before we produced our trade goods.

She was impressed by the soap and tea and wondered where we'd gotten such treasures and was greatly impressed when I told her they'd come from the Red Cross. I gave her a bar of GI soap and a large package of Canadian tea and asked for eggs. I told her the soap was very good, strong and meant for clothes. She nodded eagerly and hurried out the back door to return with nine chicken eggs and a duck egg. She asked if that were enough. I said it was. We got out more tea, a can of coffee and some hand soap and asked for potatoes. She brought in a wash basin filled to the brim with clean, firm, beautiful potatoes. Kennedy emptied them into our barracks bag and I was about to thank her for her generosity when she left and brought another basinful. And a third. I wanted to throw in some cigarettes but she refused. I gave them to the old man, who quit being wary and became jolly and voluble. I tried for saccharine. The old lady said sadly that rationing was so strict they didn't even have enough saccharine and sugar for their own needs.

The three of us felt comfortable with the Germans and drawn to them as they apparently felt drawn to us despite, or possibly because of, the bizarre circumstances of our meeting. We'd been enemies of these nice people. Damn the Nazis for setting us against each other. I wanted to prolong the moment. I told them about Stalag VIIA. They clucked sympathetically. I told them my father had been born in the Rhineland. They liked that. I wanted to keep on but Kennedy signaled it was time to go. We still had trade goods. Outside he said, "You were good with that old lady." I thought so, too.

We went back to the bridge to try the farmhouse on the other side. The guard blocked our way. I told him we were gathering wood on parole. He demanded our parole papers. We showed him our POW dogtags. He let us pass. We waited until we were well away from him before we let ourselves laugh. What a war. If we didn't run into SS or Gestapo, we could probably go anywhere on the tags that were meant to show we belonged behind barbed wire. We were nearly to the farmhouse when we realized it was almost time to rejoin the wood detail and we hadn't gathered so much as a twig. We hurried back, burdened by the barracks bag bulging with potatoes and nursing our eggs, plucking at low branches and underbrush without slacking our pace.

The soldier guarding the detail working on the river bank scolded us, saying our guard had been looking for us. That didn't bother us. What did was that if our detail was late getting back it could jeopardize future wood-walks and we'd be in deep trouble with everyone. We paused at the clearing where we'd seen the woodchopper just long enough to forage a few sticks. Our detail had already formed on the road. We could see they weren't happy. They yelled at us to hurry up, scowling when they saw the swollen barracks bag and our pitiful bits of wood. They all had more wood than we did, and we felt guilty about it until we discovered that one team had barely beaten us back and almost everyone had a bundle they hadn't started out with. We headed back, Kennedy, my friend and I, taking turns with the heavy barracks bag; the other kriegies dragged loads of twigs and branches and made sarcastic comments. Whichever two of us weren't carrying the barracks bag kept darting from the formation to snatch up branches, hoping somehow to have enough wood for a respectable showing when we got back. We paused at the little heaps of carrots and turnips to rake through them for edibles while our guard railed at us. A cart loaded with vegetables approached. A prisoner riding on it was furtively pushing carrots over the sides for other prisoners to find, which explained where the mysterious heaps by the road had come from.

The closer we got to the camp, the greater our apprehension. The ponderous barracks bag was a dead giveaway. We fixed on a plan. I'd split off from the detail with our plunder before we got to our lager, and Kennedy and my friend would take our wood in while I went to the fence between the lager and the cookhouse. Kennedy would hurry around to the wire and I'd hand everything across to him and try and talk myself through our lager gate.

When I found a gap in the wire behind the cookhouse I thought our troubles were over, but it wasn't big enough for me to squeeze through. When Kennedy didn't appear, I began looking for someone I knew well enough to take the bag and mind it for me until Kennedy showed up. A roving guard came by but when I ignored him he kept going.

Someone called my name. I looked back. George Radovanovic was rushing toward me with a keintrinkwasser in his hand. I'd tried to find him from my first day in Stalag VIIA but no one, including the orderlies who went everywhere, had heard of him, so I assumed he'd been moved. I ran to meet him. He dropped the kein, spilling boiled potatoes all over the ground, and grabbed me. He'd been looking for me as earnestly as I'd been looking for him. Words spilled out as we brought each other up to date. He'd never left the camp and was still working as a dental orderly. He couldn't understand how Rad could not know him. I forgot about the potatoes and meeting Kennedy. We were still at it when Kennedy came to the other side of the fence. He let us talk. Radovanovic and I picked up his potatoes and exchanged barracks numbers. He wanted me to take the potatoes. I told him I didn't need them and made him look in the barracks bag. He insisted and forced a scarce packet of saccharine on me as well. I said only if he'd take my cigarettes. He did, reluctantly. Kennedy at last grew tired of our Alphonse and Gaston act and Radovanovic helped me pass the barracks bag to him. He came through my lager gate with me, telling the guard I'd stopped to speak with him when the wood-party came back.

My combine welcomed him. I'd talked about him a lot and they knew how I'd been looking for him. After we'd talked a good while he tore himself away reluctantly, saying he'd be back.

It was only after he left that I thought about the treasure Kennedy and I had brought back from the wood-walk. Kennedy hadn't forgotten about it for a minute but, though impatient as always, he'd deferred to my euphoria at finding Radovanovic.

We emptied the barracks bag in what we thought was the privacy of Kennedy's bunk, but word of our haul spread quickly and we drew a crowd. It was the biggest score yet on a wood-walk. Some of those we'd kept waiting on the road renewed their complaints, one of the most vigorous among them being a kriegie I knew had barely beaten us back to the formation. We didn't mind. We'd all gotten back to the lager without incident, so no harm had been done. The kriegie who'd gone with Kennedy and me was embarrassingly supportive. He told anyone who'd listen I'd been so incredibly smooth with the old German lady he couldn't believe it. I really couldn't, either. In civilian life I'd been inept at bargaining and nowhere near suave and I'd expected being in the bag so long would have made me even less prepared to deal with strangers. He was happy with the way we divided the loot. He'd tagged along with us because I was his only friend on the detail and I'd done all the trading. Since Kennedy and I were a team and he was only half of one, we proposed he contribute a third of the barter price and take a third of the goods. His parcel-mate was as pleased with the arrangement as he was. The potatoes filled four Red Cross parcel boxes. He got a box and a third and three of the nine eggs. We offered to draw lots for the duck egg, but he said to keep it, we'd already been more than fair.

Another crowd gathered when we fried our six eggs with Spam and fried a mound of potatoes but followed kriegie etiquette and didn't stand around watching us feast on them and huge helpings of Klim pudding. We gave the others in our combine enough potatoes for a good bash and the kein full of boiled potatoes from Radovanovic. Until our fresh potatoes ran out, we gave them our boiled German issue.

Fresh potatoes were too precious for just eating. You could make better trades with them than with cigarettes. Most kriegies hadn't tasted one for months and panted for them. After we brought ours back they besieged the wood-walk officer for places on his list. We particularly wanted dessert ingredients for our potatoes and traded a Red Cross box of them for the makings. Before we were shot down Kennedy hadn't been much of a sweets eater, but now he was as mad for them as I was. (My craving has persisted; his didn't. My addiction is a source of amusement to my grandchildren.)

I talked my way out of our lager to return Radovanovic's keintrinkwasser. It wasn't too hard. I told the guard I was visiting a friend and pushed by him while he was deciding whether to let me or not, hoping he wouldn't come after me. I was willing to risk it because most of the guards were thoroughly demoralized by now. It took no special boldness on my part. I'd acquired a little brashness in my years in the bag and even, when it was safe, insolence, but not a whole lot of physical courage.

It was the first time I'd been in the Yugoslav enlisted men's quarters. The men were all uncommonly friendly though at first glance some of them were intimidating—fierce-looking men with sweeping mustaches. There were two factions, pro-Tito and anti-Tito. Radovanovic didn't take sides. He was pro-anyone who'd get the Nazis out of his country. The Yugoslavs had been in Stalag VIIA for years and had created homes away from home, screening their bunks into little private cubicles with blankets, wood or cardboard and putting up shelves and storage boxes.

I visited him frequently after that though ordinarily only those doing camp business left the lager so freely. The most noticeable of these was the parcels officer, who went every day to a storehouse set up in the cheese factory across the road dressed as if reporting to work in a stateside headquarters. Pressed blouse and pants, shirt and tie, all shaved and rosy. It was rumored he visited Moosburg when he liked. We felt he created a good image of kriegies until he got fat. Then we didn't like the impression he gave that we were all well fed.

I learned a good deal more about Radovanovic's incredible selflessness. Though apparently not a communist, he shared the pro-Titoists' empathy with Russian prisoners. With him it was more akin to pity. Cruelty upset him and he cared deeply for its victims, which was no doubt why my careless act of sharing my pipe with a Russian prisoner my first time at Stalag VIIA had drawn him to me. As a dental orderly, he helped treat Russian generals brought to VIIA. Many of them still suffered from wounds and all were malnourished. He pitied them particularly because he thought as ranking citizens of their own country they deserved greater respect and consideration. He told me he'd given them the cigarettes I'd given him when he gave me his potatoes. He'd shared his food with them, too, and had their autographs. His pride in the autographs revealed a boyish side to him I hadn't known.

As a long-timer, he knew all the guards and had the run of the camp. He was ideally situated to make trades for our combine but I quickly learned not to ask him to do it. If I told him we wanted something, he'd buy it with his own food or tobacco and refuse repayment.

He took me to the French barracks once to help me trade a broken watch. The place smelled like a bakery. Everyone seemed busy making cakes and pastries. Radovanovic said they were good cooks and traded much of their food for the ingredients. I could understand that, but I wasn't in their league as a dessert-maker.

Radovanovic later introduced me to a Swiss who'd lived in the U.S. long enough to be in the American army and get captured. Charles Disch, formerly of Zurich. He'd been a salesman for a Swiss chocolate firm. Yearning, I made him describe everything on his list.

I was living in a hive, by civilian standards in abject poverty, in every physical sense deprived, yet the electric feeling that freedom was close enough to touch kept me absurdly happy, shadowed only by the fading specter of another precipitous move.

Even that vanished when word came down that the Red Cross
and the Allies had been assured by the Germans we would not be
moved under any circumstances and that Stalag VIIA was "open
territory," not to be defended when friendly troops reached us.
(It was only later we learned Hitler had ordered all POWs to be
killed rather than surrendered, but fortunately for us he no longer
inspired unquestioned obedience.) And further, through secret
contacts with Allied commanders, our senior officers had learned
an airborne division had been alerted to move in and protect us if
any attempt were made to move or harm us. The titillating question now was not only when but also by whom we'd be freed.
Patton's Third Army was driving south toward us though Nuremberg, and the Russians were sweeping toward us from the east.
We hoped, and believed, it would be Patton. The Third Army
seemed headed straight for Stalag VIIA, as if bent on liberating
it, which didn't surprise us. Kriegies had an inflated sense of their
priority.

We had accurate, current news from radios operating almost
openly. I no longer read it furtively from bunk to bunk but in a
loud voice from the middle of the bay. Old habits were hard to
break and barracks news officers continued to post lookouts at
every entrance.

We understood the strategy but didn't much like it when the
Third Army wheeled east, as if to link up with the Russians. It
made sense to split Germany in two at the Danube but not at our
expense.

Though our fighters had interdicted all daytime road and rail
transportation in the area, at night road traffic was heavy. We
could hear it. Over the normal sounds of trucks was a labored roar
as if heavy vehicles were moving backward and forward in a small
area. Bulldozers, we surmised, throwing up roadblocks. But
hadn't we been told this was open territory? A kriegie who
seemed to know what he was talking about said it was the sound of
motorized columns downshifting to climb a hill, and we felt better.
The sounds continued all night, every night.

Wood-gathering parties left the camp more frequently. Enterprising kriegies were mingling with them on their own. Out of
potatoes and most other edibles, Kennedy and I agreed I should
try to attach myself to a detail for a trading expedition. Maxie,
who bunked near us, overheard us planning and was eager to go
with me. He'd seen the potatoes we'd brought back and heard the
news officer boast of my trading prowess. I didn't much want a

trading companion, especially one as skittish as Maxie, but he persisted and I agreed.

When we saw a detail of British officers forming at the gate, we grabbed our trade goods and barracks bags and tacked onto the group. Witnesses to this misdemeanor looked indignant rather than supportive, and I thought they might even give us away. There was a lot of petty jealousy among kriegies when they thought someone might be getting more than their share. I was like that myself when I wasn't on the receiving end. But they said nothing, nor did the British officers we'd joined, and the guard on the gate didn't even count our party.

The detail took the road mine had taken but went to a wooded area closer to the camp. The guard sauntered off and the senior of the British officers instructed us not to wander too far to hear the call to reassemble when it was time to go back. The British scattered and started foraging for wood. They'd actually come out just to gather fuel. Maxie and I headed for a railway embankment between the woods and an open field. Off to our right the railroad bridge crossing the Isar was mined and guarded, like the one I'd seen on my previous excursion. Our guard asked us what we were doing. We said we wanted to urinate and went back to the woods. We hid until he blew his whistle and our detail moved to a new area. We ran to the embankment and hesitated a moment between the bridge and the open field. We opted for the field because the guard on the bridge might turn us back.

We considered going into Moosburg but decided not to. The Senior American Officer had issued strict orders against it. Of course we weren't supposed to be doing what we were doing, either, and would be in trouble if we didn't get back in time to tag onto the British detail. There were strict orders against leaving the camp except on authorized parole. The Senior American Officer didn't want us escaping at this late hour and risk being killed by German soreheads.

We were nervous crossing the field, worried that the wood-detail guard would see us or the bridge guard might take a shot at us. Neither happened. We approached a farmhouse sitting by itself on the river. There was a fence around it. We looked for a back gate but there wasn't one so we walked through the front gate and knocked on the farmhouse door. An old man answered and held the door open a crack when he saw us. "I have nothing," he kept repeating. "You keep coming here and we have nothing." I gave him a cigarette and he let us in, still saying he had nothing to trade. His wife was peeling potatoes in the kitchen. They were simple peasants, not at all like the family I'd traded with before. Even their German was different. The others had spoken it the way I'd been taught in school. As the old man had said, they had nothing to trade but I said if they'd heat water on the stove I'd make coffee for them. They resisted at first, thinking I must want something in return. When the water boiled I made coffee for all of us, spooning pinches of Nescafe into glasses. They'd never seen soluble coffee before and were profoundly impressed. A boy who looked perhaps twelve came in while we were drinking our coffee, his face expressionless. The old man explained it was his son. He was twenty and not right in the head.

When we'd drunk our coffee the old man followed us into the hall, wanting to give us the potatoes his wife had been peeling, but even kriegies wouldn't take food out of the mouths of a couple with a retarded child. We struck off along the river toward Moosburg. We encountered an Italian prisoner of war who was also out foraging. He said there was nothing along the river. Maxie hovered close by, nervous and impatient for us to be on our way. He was worse than Kennedy. When I told the Italian I'd been a prisoner in Italy, he shook my hand warmly and shook it again when I said goodbye.

We kept close to the river anyway until we reached some farm buildings with ducks and chickens in the yard. That meant eggs. The woman who answered our knock said she had nothing to trade but invited us inside. She led us to a bright, airy parlor at the back of the house. The room made us painfully aware of how dirty and unkempt we were. A pretty young woman and an older one were sitting there. A kettle boiled on a little stove. I had fantasies about the young one, imagining Maxie wasn't with me and she was alone in the house. Prisoners I'd talked with who'd worked on farms said German girls were often friendly. Two children came into the room and stared at Maxie. He was so big and he looked German, though he was actually of Dutch extraction. The housewife had a few eggs she was willing to part with but wanted too much for them. We gave the children a little chocolate and made coffee for their elders with hot water from the kettle. We looked at framed pictures of young men in uniform. The housewife said they were the young woman's husband, brothers and cousins. The man of the house came home and we left after talking with him long enough to be polite.

MAXIE WAS UPSET. We'd lost a lot of time and accomplished nothing. Maybe we should go back. It wasn't hard to persuade him to keep going. He was desperate for eggs and potatoes. We came to a paved road and another bridge over the Isar. Two burly, stern-visaged German military police checked the papers of everyone trying to cross it. Instead of armbands like American MPs, they wore metal breastplates suspended from chains around their necks. We screwed up our courage and walked past them. Kriegies apparently had greater freedom of movement than German civilians. The MP on the other side challenged us, though. I fished out my POW tag and showed it to him, telling Maxie to do the same with his. The MP waved us on. He stopped the civilian who'd come up behind us and demanded his papers, a man in a dusty but well-cut knicker suit and a porkpie hat, with an expensive-looking briefcase. The MP inspected his papers and questioned him before letting him continue. I knew from other foragers that German civilians often had food in their briefcases. We asked him if he had any to trade. He didn't, but volunteered that he'd been an office worker at a Krupp plant in the Ruhr and left just before the Allies closed the Ruhr pocket. He'd ridden all the way on his bicycle.

Parties of foreign prisoners of war were foraging along the highway on this side of the bridge. We headed down a rutted road for a promising cluster of buildings across a field in the other direction. The field was full of wildflowers. A German soldier on a motorcycle went by and went through a gate into the building compound. We followed, thinking nothing of it. The courtyard was full of troops and military vehicles. Alarmed, we turned to leave before they saw us. A Catholic priest in a shiny black suit and a black hat came up and asked us what we were doing there. He was bespectacled, short, clean-shaven and friendly. He laughed when we told him we were prisoners of war looking to trade for food. He said we'd landed at a convent which was also the temporary bivouac for a German detachment. He spoke some English and we had no problem communicating.

He led us through the back door of one of the larger buildings out of sight of the troops, not one of whom seemed to have paid us the slightest attention. He deposited us in a high-ceilinged vestibule with a wide stairway and told us to wait. The most agonizingly tempting odors of cooking food drifted from a huge kitchen out of which passed hooded nuns and white-coated orderlies bearing trays laden with fried eggs and other marvels. We stared at the trays.

An exceedingly tall and thin Luftwaffe corporal wearing thick-lensed glasses came through the back door and stopped short when he saw us before approaching to ask if we weren't from Stalag VIIA. He thought he recognized me. He spoke excellent English. He said he'd been in our lager several times. He was a clerk in the records section of the administrative office. He said he sometimes came to the convent for lunch because there was so little food in the German mess. He asked us please not to tell any of the other Germans in the camp we'd seen him at the convent because Catholics weren't popular in Nazi Germany. I assured him we wouldn't, relieved he didn't intend reporting us, either. Hesitating, he asked if I could spare a cigarette. I gave him two. He was embarrassingly grateful, saying he missed cigarettes more than anything else. He said if I wished he'd try to make trades for me with a civilian family he knew who might want soap, tea and coffee. I gave him more cigarettes and he promised to visit me in my compound. He said he wouldn't forget my name because it was German. Maxie, who was shy despite his strength, hung back while we spoke. The corporal left us when the priest returned with a jolly nun almost as tall as Maxie. The priest introduced us. She was the Mother Superior. Maxie and I were embarrassed and intimidated. We hastened to assure the priest we wouldn't presume to barter with a Mother Superior. That amused her. Her eyes twinkled behind her glasses. She asked us what we wanted most. Eggs, potatoes, jam and onions, we said reluctantly, not daring to ask what she wanted for them. She stopped a passing nun, who left and returned with eight eggs wrapped in newspapers. Another nun brought a box of potatoes and the Mother Superior herself fetched a pint of jam. We put the eggs in a tall Scottish biscuit tin we'd brought with us and the jam in another. We brought out soap and English tea in exchange. The Mother Superior's face lit up when she saw these things that were so rare and precious in Germany but she refused them. She said the food was a gift from the convent. We insisted. Now she was as sheepish as we were. The priest looked on, amused. When we told her we'd be embarrassed if she didn't accept the soap and tea as gifts, she took them and left us with the priest. (Soon after I got back home I was guest speaker at a Kiwanis Club luncheon with Morris Frank, the newspaper colleague who'd written to me in P.G. 21, as master of ceremonies. I told the gathering about the episode in the convent and when I sat down Frank said I'd failed to admit the Mother Superior had been angry with me. "He kept calling her Mother Shapiro," Frank explained.)

We offered the priest cigarettes. He said he didn't smoke and wouldn't take them. He invited us into a little hideaway fitted out as a dining room and study. There was a table in it set with a fresh white cloth, gleaming china, silverware and a bowl of flowers. We insisted he take a pack of cigarettes. He could trade them or give them to friends. When he took them it was obvious he did so only to please us. He was so remarkably caring we wanted to give him something for himself. I spread out everything I'd brought on a table for him to see. Among my trade goods were two Red Cross toothbrushes, which drew his attention. He willingly accepted one, telling us he hadn't seen a real toothbrush in years.

We settled down for a friendly chat that included Maxie, who knew a little German and was over his shyness. The priest was pleased when Maxie told him his father was a preacher and seemed interested when I told him about being first in Italy and described our living conditions at Stalag VIIA. He said he'd served the Church in Australia when he was a young priest and become fluent in English but unfortunately had since forgotten much of it.

A nun came in with the priest's lunch, a bottle of beer, tomato soup, pan-fried potatoes and onions (Kennedy's speciality), boiled mashed turnips, lettuce and for dessert crêpes dusted with powdered sugar. Maxie and I salivated, unable to hide our longing. He asked if we were hungry. We told him we'd like to go to the kitchen and trade for meals just like his. He said he was sorry but that wasn't possible, the convent had little enough food for the nuns and the patients they tended in their hospital.

Keeping only a little of his lunch for himself, he put the rest on a plate and set it before us, apologizing because he didn't have another dish. Maxie and I said we couldn't take his lunch but not very convincingly. He sat at his table and we sat at ours, Maxie and I taking alternate spoonful from the dish like children sharing. It was precious little food for two hungry men but we wouldn't have traded that lunch for the most extravagant Red Cross parcel bash. We kept looking at each other as we ate, grinning. *Isn't this incredible?* Maxie was distracted by the beer. When the priest drank, Maxie swallowed with him, licking his lower lip. After we'd eaten he asked if he could trade for a bottle of beer. The priest said unfortunately not, it was too scarce, even the nonalcoholic kind he'd just had, and apologized for not having thought to share it with us.

He was puzzled by the intensity of our gratitude until we explained it was the first truly civilized meal we'd had as prisoners of war. And the first time in weeks we'd sat at a table or eaten from anything except a tin can. We asked for his name and address so we could write to him after the war. He wouldn't give it to us. Aiding prisoners was a serious offense. Even when we assured him we wouldn't reveal it, he still refused. I've wondered since if it was really because he wanted to be selfless in his kindness.

It was long after twelve, when the detail was supposed to have returned to camp. Maxie started worrying about what might be awaiting us when we got back late. I'd forgotten all about that and got as uneasy as he. The priest walked us to the gate. We shook hands and thanked him again for everything. Maxie trotted to the bridge with me laboring behind him. Crossing the bridge, we passed an Indian foraging party going the other way. One of them looked at me sharply when I said hello to them. He continued on a few feet and then hurried to catch up with me. He had a lean, intelligent face and lustrous, gleaming black eyes. He asked me how the trading had gone, staring at me in a disconcerting but friendly way, as if we were old, close friends. He said, "I live on the road in the first tent. I have many potatoes. I will give you all you can carry. When you come, ask for Ismail." He pressed my hand before he left. I wondered if he were around the bend, or possibly homosexual, but later was told Indian soldiers sometimes inexplicably accepted a total stranger as a close friend on first meeting. I promised him I'd visit him, and intended to, but never got the chance.

Maxie had walked on a few feet and was waiting impatiently and burning with curiosity. He was as puzzled as I was about this bizarre turn and thought I'd be a fool not to go for the potatoes. An MP posted near the other side of the bridge stopped us. "You are prisoners of war?" he demanded. Oh, oh, we thought. He's going to confiscate everything. We acknowledged that we were. "You are looking for bread?" We admitted we were. He said, "Come tomorrow at the same time and I will have a big military loaf to trade with you." Greatly relieved, we promised we would and asked him the shortest way back to Stalag VIIA. He pointed out a lane cutting across a nearby field.

We were really late now. We'd be in deep brown if someone reported us to the new SAO. In the middle of the field we ran into Sergeant Glemnitz, the top noncom from South Compound. He recognized us both and asked with a grin what we were doing outside the camp. We told him looking for wood. He laughed. We'd never been able to put anything over on him. Despite our haste, we lingered to talk with him. It was refreshing to chat with an off-duty Sergeant Glemnitz. I offered him a pack of cigarettes. He took only one. "You remember back at Sagan I would never take more than one cigarette?" he said. I said the circumstances had changed. He wasn't under orders now. "No," he said. "I want you to remember me just as I was when things were different. I want you to remember me as the kind of German who wouldn't take your cigarettes. One as a friend, yes, but more, no. I am not that kind of a man."

He told us he hadn't heard from his family in weeks. They'd been cut off in Breslau by the Russian advance. He was worried about them but not frantic. "You will be free soon, I think," he said. I asked him what he was going to do. "I am a soldier, still," he said with a shrug and a wry smile. "I will go where I am sent, and I will fight until I am ordered to stop." When we parted he turned and shouted, "I hope you got a lot of eggs."

He was an honest, gallant soldier. I never thought I'd see him again. (But I did. In 1985 the Stalag Luft III Former POW Association brought him to our fortieth anniversary reunion. His family had also survived the war. He was quite old then but still as erect as ever. I went up to him and said, "Sergeant Glemnitz, you won't remember me, but once at Moosburg you wouldn't take my cigarettes. Will you take my cigar now?" He did, with a smile and a warm handshake. The only German soldier I ever hugged.)

We hurried toward the camp, our anxiety mounting with every step. We crossed the railroad tracks and hesitated on the road some yards from the entrance debating what to do. I saw a Russian work detail approaching the entrance pushing a wagon. Gesturing for Maxie to join me, I fell in with them. Their guards did nothing. The Russians grinned at us and we grinned back as we kept pace with the wagon. At the first two gates, while the Russians were being counted through, we just stood aside as if we belonged with them and the guards didn't give us a second glance. The third gate was unguarded. One more gate to go, the one to our lager. Maxie and I had worked out a story that we'd gotten separated from our wood-party and been lost for hours. Before we finished telling it the guard had let us in.

Next day a kriegie came to my bunk and told me a goon was looking for me. It was the Catholic corporal I'd met at the convent. He had some onions his friends wanted to exchange for tea or soap. I gave him a couple of cigarettes for himself and tea for his friends. He stayed to talk with me for a while. In previous weeks I'd have walked him outside but there was no longer any reason to worry about a goon in the block. He seemed to feel uncomfortable in a soldier's uniform and was pathetically friendly. He said he'd been a professor of English literature at the University of Vienna and lost his post because he was Catholic. He was starving to discuss books and his familiarity with English classics made me think he'd told the truth. He visited me regularly after that. The kriegies in my bay called him "Westheimer's Goon."

With what I'd brought back, Kennedy and I figured we had enough food in our larder to ride out the last days of the war. But Maxie, like a deflowered virgin, was so entranced by the experience he wanted to go out with me on the next wood-walk and every one thereafter. He was terribly disappointed when I said I wasn't going out again. The area had been picked too clean.

Kennedy fell ill with diarrhea and vomiting. We thought it might be from the quantities of fresh potatoes we were eating. He got too weak to leave his bunk. I went to the dispensary for medicine, but the doctor said regretfully he'd have to come for diagnosis personally. Doc Cox slipped me a little paregoric with strict instructions that Kennedy use it sparingly—there'd be no more when it was gone—and stop eating until the symptoms abated. Kennedy was hungry all the time. He'd eat when he felt better and be sick all over again. It was only after he starved himself for two full days that he recovered.

Unaccountably, I developed a bottomless appetite and capacity for food, astonishing Kennedy. Even during my ravenous periods, and they had been frequent, I'd never needed as much to satisfy my appetite as the others in our combine. Now I was never completely full. Wanting to "stall out," eat until I couldn't eat any more, I cooked us a deep bowl of potatoes and half a can of Spam each, with half a Klim tin of Klim and jam custard for dessert. Kennedy barely made it but, though I was uncomfortably full, I could have eaten more. I never again knew such unappeasable hunger.

A kriegie in our barracks came back from a wood-detail with an Allied propaganda leaflet signed by Truman, Churchill and Stalin advising all Germans, military and civilian, to give aid and comfort to foreign workers and prisoners of war who needed it and warning them of severe reprisals when Allied troops arrived, which they would shortly, if any of us were harmed. It helped explain why kriegies were being treated so solicitously inside and outside the camp.

Knowing we might be parted soon, Radovanovic and I exchanged gifts. He gave me a beautiful Easter box made by a Russian prisoner of painted wood and woven straw, and I gave him my navigator's wings. (The box is still in my family; a daughter-in-law says it's an heirloom.)

Our appel were now American, not German, formations. We were no longer counted in ranks. We assembled in platoon formation and each platoon commander—Kennedy was ours—reported his platoon's strength and the number of absentees. It was like being back in our own army again.

Despite the wood-walks, because so many kriegies had gone trading instead of gathering wood fulltime, we ran short of fuel. One night a band of kriegies began tearing down the wooden partitions of our abort. A Hundführer came with his dog to investigate. They weren't afraid of the Hundführer but didn't think his dog knew the Allies had declared closed season on kriegies. They desisted. After the Hundführer left they started in again. He returned and shouted for them to stop. He had his dog on a short leash now so they didn't. A kriegie who knew a little German explained they'd run out of wood and the abort was the only place left to get any. The Hundführer said, "Oh, I don't care if they tear it up but why must they do it when I'm on duty and get me in trouble? Tell them to wait until I go off and my relief comes and they can do all the tearing down they want to."

We were restless in our barracks, edgy with waiting. Kennedy and I went out one night after dark to visit his army friend, Lowe. It was a nice evening and a lot of kriegies were walking around. A plane roared over so low we instinctively hit the ground. Almost simultaneously there was a sharp explosion from the direction of the cookhouse. We scrambled into the nearest slit trench. It was already full and rimmed with kriegies trying to make up their minds whether to join us or not. There was a small fire at the front of the cookhouse. The explosion hadn't been powerful enough for a bomb. It must have been a flare or an incendiary. The plane was strafing outside the camp now. We feared it might return to strafe the cookhouse area. Shocking. Everybody was supposed to have been briefed this was a prisoner of war camp. The plane never came back. Kriegies poured out of barracks. We climbed out of the slit trench and joined them. The fire wasn't in the cookhouse at all but in an incinerator near it. It might not have been caused by the plane at all, just from something exploding in the incinerator in a rare coincidence.

We began hearing distant, spaced explosions. The artillery men among us said it was fieldpieces and only forty or fifty miles away. My German friend came to see me. He said, "I have heard this sort of thing before. On the Russian Front. Your friends are very near. I think they will be here within twenty-four hours. Then you will be free, and I will be the prisoner."

I lay awake that night wondering if he were only telling me what I wanted to hear, as I suspected Germans did a lot, or had information we weren't privy to.

At ten o'clock the next morning, April 29, 1945, two P-51 fighters roared in and began beating up the camp. For fifteen minutes they made passes rocking their wings or tumbling in aerobatics. Kriegies massed outside, waving and cheering. The fighters slow-rolled and streaked southwest. We heard long, crackling bursts as they strafed ground targets. Why had they taken time off from a strafing mission to entertain us?

I was rounding the edge of a barracks when a burst of fire from a machine gun set up in the cheese factory across the road rattled overhead. I hit the dirt, angry I'd been fired on. Didn't they know kriegies were a protected species? And anyway, I hadn't done anything wrong. There were bursts of fire all around the camp now. A firefight. There obviously were German troops who didn't know Stalag VIIA was an open area.

With no more fire coming inside, I crawled to a spot behind our barracks to join friends. All the ground officers were on the deck or peering from the slit trench. Kriegies who'd never been shot at personally were still on their feet trying to see what was going on. Fighters flew over low on strafing runs, not pausing to entertain us. Firing increased on every side. We knew friendly forces were close. A burst from the cheese factory tower tore through the front end of our barracks. I learned later the only casualty was Doc Cox. A bullet had grazed his stomach. Barely a Purple Heart wound.

We were all on the deck now, apprehensive but exuberant. A colonel came out of the back of our barracks and ordered everyone inside. When I reached our tier I found Kennedy sitting on a lower bunk, a tight, nervous grin on his face. We sat side by side, listening to the battle and talking quietly. What was it going to be like to be free again? Would our troops have food for us, hearty army rations? How long before we'd be home? We were nervous but happy, though not as deliriously as we'd anticipated. Our only concern was that we might be caught in an artillery duel.

Kriegies huddled in lower bunks all around us, out of the line of fire of stray bursts that might whistle through the compound. Schoonmaker was trembling with excitement, smiling. Machine guns opened up from the direction of Moosburg, from the sound of them within the town. Kennedy and I were too nervous to sit still. We went to the washroom to brew up. He split wood while I got out the Nescafe, Klim and sugar, for once not stinting. We crouched near the window while the water heated, peeking out from time to time, seeing only eerie emptiness. There was not a soul, German or kriegie, out of doors.

We talked restlessly, too numbed by what was happening to fully appreciate it. A distant, loud explosion rattled the washroom windows. We thought it must be a mined Isar bridge going up. The battle would be over soon. We were consumed with impatience. Now that freedom was at hand all we could think of was how quickly they'd get us out. We tried making specific plans for our first days at home, but there were so many possibilities we gave up and whispered only of how soon, how soon?

We went back to our bunks to sip our rich brew from tin cans, speaking in tense whispers as all around us were doing, straining for any new sound. We heard one. A heavy rumble. "Tanks," said a ground officer. Kriegies shouted on the main road.

350   A kriegie rushed in the back door, screaming, "A Sherman tank just came in the front gate! We're out!" All firing had ceased but an occasional burst from Moosburg. "Well, Jesus Christ, Westheimer," Kennedy cried, "let's go out and have a look!"

We went out to the main street. Just as we reached the mob there, the cheering began. An American flag was flying from the steeple of the village church. It was over.

It had been two years, four months and eighteen days since we swam out of the *Natchez to Mobile, Memphis to St. Jo*—869 days.

FATHER STANLEY BRACH DIED in San Antonio in January 1990 after a long illness. He was mourned by a far-flung "parish" of Catholic, Protestant and Jewish former prisoners of war at P.G. 21 and Oflag 64.

Larry Kennedy joined his parents in Phoenix and met Beth—a nurse with whom he couldn't help falling in love. Being the sort of man he was, he didn't break the news to his wartime fiancée by phone or letter. He flew to Florida to tell her. (Many years later I had a phone call from a woman in Florida. She said her mother had passed away, and in her effects she'd found World War II letters from a prisoner of war in Europe. She'd always sensed her mother had been in love with someone before her father. I'd been mentioned in some of the letters and had been easy for her to locate. Could I tell her anything about the man who wrote the letters? I could and did.) Kennedy took a job teaching in an elementary school while waiting for the right time to start a business of his own. He did so well and was so highly regarded, he made teaching his career and became principal of a new school. He died suddenly of a heart attack in March 1980. Beth came home one afternoon and found him lifeless on the kitchen floor, a letter to me on the kitchen table ready for mailing. I spoke at his funeral and cried a little. He left three married children and many grandchildren. I'd attended his two daughters' weddings in Phoenix, and in May 1991 my wife and I saw one of them awarded her long-pursued Ph.D. in psychology at Arizona State University. One set of his grandchildren call me "Uncle Grandpa." The school where he was principal took his name and I have a sweatshirt from it that says, "Larry C. Kennedy Trojans."

Zeak Buckner retired from the faculty at Louisiana State University, Shreveport, and died of cancer in January 1981. I phoned Alexander Alvarado in San Antonio to see if he'd been informed. His wife answered, and when I asked for him she said, "Didn't you know?" Little Alvie had died of cancer, too, the previous year.

Al Barnes and Ted Schoonmaker have continued to flourish. We are still close. After operating a business in Michigan, Barnes retired to a Florida beach town. Schoonmaker retired in Miami after long service as editor of a prestigious trade journal. Both have families.

I correspond with Charles Jennette but haven't seen him since our POW days.

My friendships with Dapper Dan Story, his bombardier Ed Griffin, and big Joe Frelinghuysen, the physical fitness buff, have endured, and I continue to see others from P.G. 21 at Oflag 64 reunions and friends from Stalag Luft III at similar reunions.

For some years after the war Chuck Williams would visit me in Houston on business trips, and I visited him in Los Angeles and, after he moved, New York, but in recent years we've kept in touch chiefly by mail and telephone. His sister Rachael was married to Jackie Robinson. Williams told his brother-in-law to look me up if ever he was in Houston. And Robinson did, a couple of years after the war. He came to our house for lunch, bringing Roy Campanella with him. Williams had relatives in Houston. His aunt, Dr. Thelma Patton Laws, was an eminent obstetrician in the black community, and her husband was head of athletics for black high schools of the Houston Independent School District (this was before desegregation). We played bridge with them often—they were much better players than their nephew—and watched Arthur Godfrey on TV at their home. We didn't have a TV set yet.

George Radovanovic wrote me from Yugoslavia soon after the war, and I was able to repay some of his many kindnesses with Care and clothing parcels until his country's economy was back on its feet. He was a stamp collector and sometimes requested specific U.S. commemorative issues before I even knew they were out. In turn, though I'm not a collector, he sent me new issues of Yugoslav stamps more beautiful than those I'd sent him. He had two sons. One became a doctor, the other an army officer. When his wife of many years died, he sent me a snapshot of her in her coffin. I learned that was customary. One day more than forty years after we parted, I received a letter from one of his sons, in German, that George Radovanovic was dead.

Radomir Vidakovich and Ivan Andrejevich, strongly anticommunist, refused repatriation and chose instead to be interned in a Displaced Persons camp. We corresponded and when they had an opportunity to enter the U.S. if vouched for and assured of work, through my job at the *Houston Post,* I located a local Yugoslav who agreed to employ them at his motor court and convenience store. They arrived in Houston in 1950 at the tail end of one of the city's worst floods. They remained in Houston only a short time, leaving for more suitable jobs and to join friends in Detroit. We continued to correspond for a while but eventually lost contact.

I still wish I'd answered the letter from the Luftwaffe corporal I'd met at the convent.